T0362079

Fringe Benefits, Labour Costs and Social Security

Originally published in 1965, this book is concerned with an important yet neglected part of economic life 'fringe benefits' which employers provide for and on behalf of their employees apart from wages and salaries. The book sets out results of an inquiry into the costs of supplementary labour costs for manual workers, with an account of the various influences which help to explain differences in expenditure by different firms. The book then gives comparative figures for Western European countries and considers some of the economic effects of the European levels of supplementary labour costs. The situation in the USA is discussed, as is the relationship of employer-financed welfare schemes and State social security programmes. Chapters on pensions, sick pay and redundancy payments are included as well as those dealing with the history of paid holidays and subsidized welfare facilities such as canteens.

Fringe Benefits, Labour Costs and Social Security

G.L. Reid and D.J. Robertson

Routledge
Taylor & Francis Group

First published in 1965
by George Allen & Unwin Ltd

This edition first published in 2021 by Routledge
2 Park Square, Milton Park, Abingdon, Oxon, OX14 4RN
and by Routledge
605 Third Avenue, New York, NY 10158

Routledge is an imprint of the Taylor & Francis Group, an informa business

© 1965 George Allen & Unwin Ltd

Publisher's Note
The publisher has gone to great lengths to ensure the quality of this reprint but points out that some imperfections in the original copies may be apparent.

Disclaimer
The publisher has made every effort to trace copyright holders and welcomes correspondence from those they have been unable to contact.
A Library of Congress record exists at LCCN: 65002203

ISBN 13: 978-1-032-02680-0 (hbk)
ISBN 13: 978-1-003-18470-6 (ebk)
ISBN 13: 978-1-032-02718-0 (pbk)

DOI: 10.4324/9781003184706

FRINGE BENEFITS
LABOUR COSTS AND
SOCIAL SECURITY

Edited by

G. L. REID AND D. J. ROBERTSON
University of Glasgow

London
GEORGE ALLEN & UNWIN LTD
RUSKIN HOUSE MUSEUM STREET

PRINTED IN GREAT BRITAIN
in 10 point Times Roman type
BY SIMSON SHAND LTD
LONDON, HERTFORD AND HARLOW

PREFACE

Since the introduction of this volume outlines its scope and purpose, we can here limit ourselves to acknowledging the many debts which we, as editors, have incurred in the preparation of this study.

First, of course, our gratitude must go to the Nuffield Foundation whose financial assistance made possible the statistical enquiry into fringe benefits and indeed the volume as a whole. Then our sincere thanks are due to the contributing authors who have worked so diligently in preparing the individual Chapters: they would join with us in thanking colleagues in the University of Glasgow and other institutions who have read and commented upon drafts of individual Chapters. Among those who have aided us are officials of the Ministry of Labour and the Ministry of Pensions and National Insurance in the provision of statistical material in several of the Chapters. We are under a considerable obligation to the companies which participated in the statistical enquiry, and to all those in industry and trade unions who supplied information and who gave their time to discuss the subject with our contributors; we hope that they will find the volume interesting and useful. Finally, the work of the secretarial and technical staff of this Department in preparation of successive drafts of the manuscript should not go unrecognized.

Our last word concerns the relevance to late 1964 of the information and opinions contained therein. By the time this appears in print, parts of the statistical material may be out of date; similarly events may have moved in such a way as to make some of the conclusions unlikely and untenable. This hazard is inherent in the production of a volume which aims both at being topical and at making policy suggestions. We may hope, however, that the book will provide a useful starting-point for current discussions, and that the Chapters which are of wider application will prove of continuing interest.

March 1964

G.L.R.
D.J.R.

CONTENTS

LIST OF CONTRIBUTORS

JAMES BATES   Lecturer in Economics, University of Bristol

G. C. CAMERON   Lecturer in Applied Economics, University of Glasgow

A. G. P. ELLIOT   Personnel Director, Standard Telephones & Cables Ltd.

A. E. HOLMANS   Lecturer in Political Economy, University of Glasgow

G. L. REID   Lecturer in Applied Economics, University of Glasgow

D. J. ROBERTSON   Professor of Applied Economics, University of Glasgow

J. WISEMAN   Professor of Applied Economics, University of York

INDEX OF TABLES

CHAPTER 1

INTRODUCTION

G. L. REID AND D. J. ROBERTSON

I

The term 'fringe benefits' has a somewhat puzzling and fanciful aspect to the uninitiated, and even to those who use it frequently it is elusive and diverse in its meanings. This volume has therefore faced many problems of interpretation, and it is inevitable that the studies presented here are less than comprehensive in their coverage. On the whole the emphasis is on the economic aspects of fringe benefits and especially on labour costs, but it is impossible to restrict the discussion to a narrow economic interpretation. It is self-evident that people expect more from their work than wages: one can cite many possible additional benefits such as companionship, a sense of purpose, and so on—and possibly find an equal number of disadvantages to weigh in the balance. If we were to include as fringe benefits any advantage of work, then all sorts of things could be listed as fringe benefits: even an attempt to be selective leaves a large number of issues open to discussion.

The contents of the book are explained in Section II of this Introduction. Thereafter Section III attempts to describe a little more adequately the concept of fringe benefits as we would like to use it. It is unfortunately the case, however, that there are many points at which we break away from our own conventions and this discussion in Section III is more an illustration of one way to clarify the concept than an attempt to produce a rigid definition. Section IV discusses the increased public attention which has recently been accorded to this subject and the reasons for it.

II. THE SCOPE OF THIS VOLUME

This book originated in a study which began in the University of Glasgow in 1960 with the aid of finance from the Nuffield Founda-

DOI: 10.4324/9781003184706-1

tion. We initially set out to investigate the cost to employers of fringe benefits for manual workers, and hence to say something about the relative importance of different types of benefit as indicated by their cost. Chapter 3 discusses the results of our enquiry which has, we believe, provided a substantial extension to the amount of knowledge previously available: this description of our enquiry is preceded by a discussion in Chapter 2 of other British studies on the cost of fringe benefits which were the limit of knowledge until our data were published. Chapter 4 gives comparative material for European countries, analyses specifically some of the economic effects of fringe benefits in the European situation, and compares their effect on labour costs in Britain as against Europe.

The subsequent chapters (Chapters 5 to 11) are each concerned with a different aspect of fringe benefits and are contributed by several different authors. We have not attempted to justify the precise range of topics which are given a place and know that many potential subjects have been excluded: these chapters do, however, discuss the characteristics and important features of the major types of fringe benefit. Holidays with pay are dealt with in detail in Chapter 10, because little is known of the growth of paid holidays in Britain or of the social and economic problems attaching to them, and because holiday pay is the most costly single item of fringe benefits. Of equal importance to the employee are the three fringe benefits which seek to provide security by giving cash payments during old age, sickness and redundancy, and these are discussed in Chapters 7, 8 and 9 respectively. Of the 'security benefits' occupational pensions are perhaps most important since they are the biggest 'voluntary' item in the fringe benefit budget of most firms (apart from holiday pay), and because they bring most clearly into focus the possible conflict of interest between the individual's part in providing his own welfare, the obligations of the employer to look after his employees, and the obligations which have been assumed by, or thrust upon, the State. The inclusion of Chapters on these security benefits emphasizes the need to discuss in general terms the problems of public or private provision of welfare and the criteria on which the choice between public and private provision should be decided: this contribution, Chapter 6, has been closely related to Chapter 5, which illustrates the situation in the United States where opinions and practice in the pursuit of welfare differ markedly from those in Britain. Chapter 11 deals with a number of company welfare facilities which though economists often think them to be of doubtful value are nevertheless widespread in their use and attempts to explain why companies should introduce or perpetuate them.

Except where otherwise stated the statistics and discussion in this book are concerned with fringe benefits for wage-earners. There is, of course, much to be said on the fringe benefits of administrative staff, particularly expense accounts, company cars and houses, pension schemes and other benefits which executives enjoy, but this has already become a popular and controversial issue despite the almost complete lack of reliable statistics, and there seems to be little to add to the speculations of others. At the same time, we must recognize that staff fringe benefits may be very important in affecting mobility and immobility of labour and the Chapters dealing with individual benefits cannot avoid some comparison between staff provisions and those covering wage earners.

This volume cannot in any sense be regarded as a final authoritative statement of the issues that arise in considering fringe benefits. Discussion is at far too early a point for such a definitive statement to be written and we have certainly not attempted it. It will be clear from a reading of Chapters 5 to 11 that the political and social views of our contributors vary considerably, as do opinions on the value of the particular benefits and their future. To have directed the course of these Chapters so that they all followed some consistent 'line' (even supposing one could have been found and agreed to) or to have edited them into conformity would have had a repressive effect on the discussion and a deterrent effect on our contributors: as it stands, with the author of each Chapter drawing his own conclusions from his own argument, several versions of the story are presented, albeit at the risk of repetition. We have provided a concluding Chapter but have not felt it to be our duty as editors to attempt to use that Chapter to unify or draw together the discussion. Instead, the concluding Chapter restates the main economic issues to which the book is devoted. We hope that the volume will be a useful contribution to a debate which is likely to grow rather than diminish in importance.

III. THE CONCEPT OF FRINGE BENEFITS[1]

So far the term 'fringe benefits' has been used in an *ad hoc* way; we have described what this volume covers and assumed that everyone accepts these as fringe benefits. However, if this particular aspect of labour economics is worth studying separately from other factors influencing the material well-being of the employee, we must take pains to discuss how fringe benefits differ from other types of employee remuneration and labour costs. What difficulties have we found, in common with previous investigators, in marking off the field of study?

[1] This section draws extensively on an article by G. L. Reid, 'The Concept of Fringe Benefits', *Scottish Journal of Political Economy*, IX; pp. 208–18.

B

The problem of stating precisely what is meant by 'fringe benefits'[1] is simply that no generally accepted definition exists. Moreover, confusion often arises because the term, which is usually applied to welfare schemes themselves, is also used to describe the payments which an employee gets from welfare schemes and their cost to the employer. But the payments and cost of welfare schemes must be considered separately, since employer expenditure in money terms is not necessarily equal to employee benefit in a given period. The relationship between them may be indirect and the benefit deferred, as in an occupational pension scheme where contributions are paid over a long period before benefit is received. In addition many welfare schemes are selective in coverage so that not all employees are qualified or eligible to take part. The scope of the term 'fringe benefits' therefore depends in part on whether cost to employer or payments to employee is used as the criterion of selection. The economist can look at fringe benefits from both sides, for both are important; in so far as these benefits provide additional remuneration to employees, existing wage and salary data understate the rise in money incomes, but fringe benefits are probably more important as costs and this is how we will mainly be concerned with them in the discussion which follows. Fringe benefit costs may be provisionally taken to include holiday pay, sick pay, the cost of occupational pensions, and employer contributions to various types of welfare plan. These extra costs of employing labour are frequently ignored today by economists as well as in popular discussion, since weekly or hourly rates of earnings are taken as the basic unit in the study of labour costs. This concentration on short-period wage costs obscures the importance of fringe benefit items, because many of them, even when they represent cash payments to employees, are difficult or impossible to express as a weekly or hourly amount. To get a true measure of labour costs, the economist must take fringe benefit costs into account, especially since recent international studies suggest that such costs can be a considerable proportion of total labour costs.

The difficulty is to decide which items are 'fringe benefits' and which are not. A number of methods have been used to define the term in fringe benefit enquiries. Suggested definitions have varied widely in the range of items included, from the very comprehensive, which would include all expenditure by the employer on labour other than the basic wage,[2] to the restrictive, taking in only those benefits

---

[1] The term 'fringe benefit' did not come into use until the 1950s. It has been traced to 'a gifted regional chairman of the National War Labor Board' in the United States. See J. C. Hill, 'Stabilization of Fringe Benefits', *Industrial and Labor Relations Review*, 7, 2; p. 221.

[2] Quoted by H. H. Macaulay, *Fringe Benefits and their Federal Tax Treatment*, Columbia University Press; New York, 1959; p. 5.

which the employee can convert into cash. In the search for a suitable definition, certain characteristics of fringe benefits have been described. For example:

(1) they all cost the employer money;
(2) they all either add to the employee's pay or are of some service to him;
(3) they are available to all or most of the employees;
(4) their cost rises or falls as the size of the work-force changes.[1]

We can agree generally with the first three of these characteristics, though recognizing that selective and deferred benefits need not necessarily be available even to most of the employees. The cost of benefits may vary with the size of the work-force, but again the existence of selective and deferred benefits means that their cost can depend on part only of the work-force and need not be affected by changes in the number of non-participants. To list characteristics of fringe benefits in this way is useful as a descriptive measure, provided that a suitable list can be agreed, but there may be just as much disagreement over characteristics as there is over definition, and it is desirable to justify a choice of items by a less empirical and more consistent method.

Most work on fringe benefits has been concerned with their quantitative importance, and the definitional problem has been dealt with in various ways. Some enquiries have provided quite arbitrary definitions, others have merely listed the items with which they proposed to deal. The enquiries have something in common, however, in that they have chosen to measure cost rather than value. Quite apart from the claim of cost to be the more useful in economic discussion, there are practical reasons why the enquiries proceeded in this way. Measurement of cost is reasonably objective, but serious problems can arise when estimation of income to the employees is attempted. With immediate fringe benefit payments or benefits which are easily convertible into cash there is little difficulty, but with certain types of welfare scheme which are non-convertible, how does one assess their value to the employee? The assumption that this value is represented by the cost to the employer is invalid, as we have already seen, but even if we accept the assumption and suppose that the overall value to all employees is equal to the cost of the service, the calculation of benefit to the individual employee is still difficult.[2] The cost can be allocated amongst those using the service, but it may be more realistic to consider the number of employees to whom the service was avail-

[1] H. Stieglitz, *Computing the Cost of Fringe Benefits* (Studies in Personnel Policy, No. 128). New York: National Industrial Conference Board, 1952.
[2] This has some practical importance if one wishes to consider tax treatment of benefits, or relative effects on economic welfare of payment wholly in cash and payment partly in benefits of this kind.

able, instead of simply the number using it. The most direct and precise way of estimating the value of a service is to find out the cash value which each employee places on the service and to aggregate these sums.[1] Apart from the obvious practical difficulties, this type of data is of limited validity and is a most uncertain basis for any large-scale quantitative study, and though the subjective approach may in some circumstances be useful where welfare effects of payment methods are concerned, it seems logical to prefer a more objective assessment of fringe benefits and one which is of more economic significance by studying their cost to the employer.

In applying the criterion of cost to the employer, one is side-stepping a general definition of fringe benefits and attempting to define the field of study more strictly and to justify a particular method of classification. We may accept that there are two characteristics common to the items which are to be examined; they should cost the employer money, and they should be of benefit to his employees. This double standard, cost and remuneration (in the widest sense), is applicable to almost all items which make up total labour costs. The first important problem is to establish those items which comprise the narrower group of payments which are employee remuneration in the normal sense of wages or earnings, and so to arrive at an approximation to fringe benefit costs (or supplementary labour costs, as they are sometimes called) by subtracting normal pay from total labour costs. The basic wage (i.e. payment for time worked or work done, exclusive of overtime pay or bonuses) is invariably regarded as part of normal pay, and this may be accepted as an initial assumption. We shall now examine other items of labour costs to see which of them should be included in normal earnings and which are not in this category.

Labour costs can be divided into two main categories:

(A) Payments by the employer *to* his employees including the basic wage, overtime and bonus payments, holiday pay and other items of cash payment. The non-earnings components of this group, which we have yet to define, may be called 'supplementary remuneration'.

(B) Expenditure by an employer *on behalf* of his employees, including contributions to pension and welfare funds, and subsidies for various types of services. This is welfare expenditure.

(A) Payments *to* employees contain some important items of non-wage labour cost and also present the main problem of distinguishing normal earnings and supplementary remuneration. One possible

---

[1] A recent study to which further reference is made in the concluding Chapter shows that those schemes which employees valued most highly were not necessarily those with the highest cost to the employer, and that employee valuations varied greatly.

method of doing this, to distinguish payments for time worked, as earnings, from payments for time not worked, is suitable only in a very broad sense, and cannot easily deal with all items of labour costs: in particular, overtime premium pay and minor interruptions in production create considerable problems.[1] A better method of grouping payments to employees is needed, one which concentrates more on their meaning to the employer and on their relationship to production.

On this basis, payments by an employer to his employees can be divided into two categories according to the effect which they have on the effort of employees, and hence on production. These categories may be called 'current' and 'overhead' payments. By current payments are meant those payments which directly affect effort and production, and which in turn may depend to some extent on them. The most important component of this class is the basic wage. In theory, this is the sum which will induce an employee to offer his services to one firm rather than to go somewhere else or to withhold his labour from the market altogether. In practice, because of the need to induce extra effort in a given time period or extra hours of work from the employee, there are other current payments which make up the gap between wages and earnings. Overtime pay is a most important example of such a payment; assuming that the supply curve of labour is positively sloped over the relevant range, which seems realistic, overtime pay is a powerful inducement to employees to increase the supply of effort at the margin. When overtime pay is treated in this way, *total* overtime pay can be considered as a current payment, and the exact status of the overtime premium is unimportant.

'Overhead' payments are simply those which do not directly, or over a short period, affect effort and production. These are 'supplementary remuneration' or what we have previously called fringe benefit payments. Which items can be included in this category? Holiday pay and sick pay are both clearly overhead payments. Though paid holidays and a sick pay scheme may react favourably on production, this relationship is very indirect and cannot be compared with that which exists between current payments and production. Other examples of overhead payments are gifts, long service awards, redundancy compensation and seasonal bonuses.[2] This type

---

[1] This point is developed at length in the *Scottish Journal of Political Economy* article, op. cit.

[2] Some seasonal bonuses form a large portion of yearly earnings, and these would be classed as current payments. It is difficult to classify payments for minor periods of time off work, such as tea breaks, rest periods, etc. Such payments have no separate existence other than as part of earnings. Any changes in their amount comes about indirectly as a result of a change either in the length of time off work or in the rate of pay. For two reasons they may be treated as current

of classification of payments, however, only applies in the short period when considering the supply of effort of a given labour force. In the long run all payments must to some extent influence an employee's estimation of the advantages of a particular job, and so must affect the supply of labour to that job.

(B) In the past twenty or thirty years, there has been a great increase in the variety of payments which an employer makes *on behalf of* his employees. One of the most important is the occupational pension scheme of which the employer pays most or all of the cost, and there are also many private schemes financed by the employer to provide benefits during sickness or unemployment. Within the firm, a company may provide medical services and welfare schemes, such as social, recreational or canteen facilities. In many cases, employees have opportunities for free education and training either through company schemes or external programmes. There are other items, too, but these are of less social and industrial importance.

Discussion of these items is again concerned less with definition than with justification of a particular way of looking at them. If, for example, we were to apply the distinction between current and overhead payments, we would conclude that all the items listed were overhead payments, since none of them has any direct relationship with effort and production in the short term. But here it is necessary to look at the longer-term indirect relationship which expenditure by employers has with production and the advantages which accrue to the employer. In other words, there is a difference between the two broad categories of labour costs. No one would deny that wages, holiday pay, etc., are payments *to* employees, but to what extent is expenditure on welfare services 'on behalf of' employees? In several of the items given the employer may seem to benefit as much or more than the workers. If we can measure the benefit of each, is it then by looking at the relative gains to employer and employees that we determine the status of particular labour cost items? Simply to apply the two characteristics, of benefit to employee and cost to employer, seems insufficient, since if this is the only criterion, one could describe as 'welfare' *all* expenditure by an employer which in any way benefitted his employees. This might even include non-labour-cost items, such as redecoration of factory premises, and even on the widest definition of welfare expenditure this conclusion seems unacceptable.

This problem is greatly simplified if we recognize employer expen-

---

payments and not included with holiday pay as overhead; firstly, the time off work has some effect on production, and secondly, the payments are part of earnings, itself a current payment, and so cannot be altered without affecting effort and production.

diture on welfare benefits for what it is, an investment in the labour force. An employer makes this outlay *intending* that there should be some return to the company, most usually in the form of an improvement in the quality and efficiency of his labour force. Some items of labour costs are designed principally to attract labour, others principally to retain labour already employed.[1] Current payments are of the first type, but welfare expenditure is mainly retentive in purpose, especially nowadays when most companies provide welfare services and the advantage of any one company in the labour market is likely to be small. The employee can build up a vested interest in the company, both because many schemes provide higher benefits with longer service and because welfare schemes may seem to betoken the company's interest in his well-being. However, to regard welfare expenditure simply as a type of investment is useful only in justifying the existence of some benefit to the employer, it does not help in classifying all expenditure which benefits both employees and employer, often in widely differing proportions. To do this we must introduce openly the idea that there should be a definite scheme or service, one of the principal aims of which is to benefit employees. The conditions then are that some sort of scheme should exist, it should be at least partly financed by the employer, and be so designed that the employees receive specific benefit in cash or kind; if these are fulfilled we may designate the cost 'welfare expenditure'.

The return to 'investment' in the form of fringe benefits may accrue not only to the employee or the company, but to the community as a whole, so that investment in the labour force can be thought of as either private investment or social investment, the former denoting expenditure providing a return to the company as an employer of labour, the latter being expenditure undertaken by an employer from which the community as a whole also benefits: schemes of this type are in effect a type of social security. Clearly, no single item of expenditure by a company can be called *wholly* private or social investment, but it is possible to illustrate their relative importance, as well as the difficulty of making an absolute judgment, by looking at two types of company expenditure and trying to assess returns to the employer and to the community.

(a) *Occupational Pensions*
When an employer makes contributions of this kind, does the investment thus built up have the characteristics mainly of private or of

---

[1] Of course to some extent all items of labour costs have both attractive and retentive elements, since they are all taken into account in an employee's assessment of the relative economic advantages of his present job and alternative employment. The mechanism by which this process may work will be outlined in Section V of the Conclusion.

social investment? The usual arguments for the existence of an occupational pension plan are well known; it induces a sense of security in the employees, tends to decrease labour mobility, while allowing old and inefficient workers to retire, facilitates the retention of key workers, and generally improves morale and hence productivity, as well as giving a company the name of a 'good employer'. These factors suggest that expenditure on a pension plan is private investment, but an occupational pension scheme has a wider meaning than this since one may argue that this particular type of scheme, by providing for employees in their years of retirement, fulfils a social purpose more important than the industrial side-effects to which it gives rise. This does not mean that pension plans will be voluntarily introduced for this reason; naturally the employer is likely to be primarily interested in the effects on his own labour force, but by enabling employees to make provision for retirement which they otherwise would have found difficult or impossible, occupational pension schemes fulfil a social purpose. In addition, employer attitudes to such schemes are to a large extent shaped by Governmental encouragement and legislation.

Although the private pension is normally wage-related and hence emphasizes personal obligation in providing for old age, present British practice may be regarded as essentially an extension of the social security system. The provision of occupational pensions is encouraged in the recognition that they are giving a service which it might otherwise have been necessary for the State to provide. Governmental financial support for these schemes is given in the form of tax reliefs: the White Paper on *Provision for Old Age* stated that:

'the growth of occupational pension provision has no doubt been encouraged by the tax reliefs which have long been accorded to contributions made both by employers and by employees. It has sometimes been suggested that the relief so given to contributions made by employers in some way represents a "subsidy" from the public but this relief is in fact no more than an allowance for tax purposes of a business expense. . . .'[1]

Expenditure on pension schemes, as investment in the labour force, is, however, much more than merely a business expense, and the tax relief does seem to have the nature of a subsidy. Another quite explicit acceptance that occupational pension plans are regarded as a substitute for State action is the first condition laid down in the National Insurance Act of 1959 which must be satisfied by an occupational pension plan contracted-out of the graduated portion of the State scheme provided that:

---

[1] *Provision for Old Age*. Cmnd. 538, HMSO 1958, para. 17.

'the occupational scheme made provision for pension benefit right equivalent to the maximum additional pension rights which would be foregone under the state scheme as a result of contracting out'.[1]

If we admit the primary social purpose of these occupational schemes, expenditure by an employer on them would appear to be primarily social investment rather than private: the extent to which one believes this to be true depends largely on the economic effects of pension plans on the supply and quality of labour.[2]

(b) *Medical and Educational Services*

Expenditure on pensions, then, conditioned by Governmental encouragement and incentive or by law, can be characterized as social rather than private investment in the labour force. Medical and educational services have an element of social advantage, but they give a direct improvement in the actual or potential quality of the labour force as well, so that the classification of expenditure on these items is more difficult.

Company medical services are to some extent controlled by legislation since every company must by law provide certain services. Most companies go beyond this legal minimum, and in doing so they are looking after their own interests, since it is obviously advantageous to be able to give prompt medical attention to sick or injured employees, even if only because a more speedy resumption of work results in fewer lost man-hours. The size of a company and the type of work are also important. One might expect a large company to find it more economic to provide extensive medical facilities rather than rely on the legal minimum and this is particularly true in heavy industries where a high accident rate is likely. From this viewpoint medical expenses are primarily private investment. There is, however, a considerable benefit to the community from this expenditure by employers: first, it is clearly in the national interest that loss of work through sickness should be as small as possible, and secondly, the use of industrial medical services may lessen the burden on the National Health Service. But Governmental influence is of a different type from that exercised over pensions and insurance. The State is acting as an intermediary between employee and employer to influence their relationship with a narrow social purpose in mind, the regulation of conditions of employment for the individual labour force.

Education and training is one of the most difficult types of fringe benefits to justify. It is often said that such expenditure, as a direct

[1] Ibid., para. 41(a).

[2] Chapter 7 deals at length with occupational pensions and their relationship with State social security provisions. The argument of this Section is extended to sickness benefit in Chapter 8.

attempt by the employer to improve the quality of his work-force, is not 'on behalf' of the employees. However, even if one acknowledges that the employer does expect a return from this investment in his labour force, one may also accept that both employer and worker may benefit from expenditure of this kind. It is more difficult to assess the relative gain of each. The immediate gain to the employer may be considerable and clearly represents an item of private investment. But benefit from the investment is more widespread; outlay by employers on education and training, by increasing the quality and efficiency of the working population, can lead to an increase in productivity and hence in national income. Expenditure on education by employers may be private investment yielding a private return to the employer, but it also yields a considerable additional social return, since the employers' initial gain also brings the community benefit.

Summary
In many ways this discussion of the concept of fringe benefits introduces new problems much more than it provides any definition. A first approximation to the cost of fringe benefits can be derived by deducting normal remuneration from total labour costs. Normal remuneration is usually 'current' cash remuneration while 'overhead' cash remuneration is a fringe benefit cost. The allocation of other items of total labour costs as fringe benefit costs raises further difficulties, since payments on behalf of employees, to be regarded as creating fringe benefits, must be associated with a scheme from which employees will benefit, while some labour costs, such as the costs of personnel departments or recruitment, hardly warrant classification as fringe benefit costs since any benefit to the employee is not at all specific. Even if expenditure is of a welfare type and on behalf of employees, the amount of benefit to employees can often be assessed only subjectively and any estimation of its value to the worker is unlikely to coincide with cost to the employer. As well as providing benefits to the worker, all types of fringe benefit expenditure can confer benefits on the employer and perhaps the community as well, and the ways in which, and proportions in which, such benefits accrue to the worker, the employer, or the community, differ from item to item, and from firm to firm. There is no definitive solution of these difficulties: this Section has attempted to state them clearly.

IV. THE GROWING IMPORTANCE OF FRINGE BENEFITS

Ever since this study began a few years ago, there has been a noticeably rising tide of public interest in fringe benefits as additions to income, and more official notice is now being taken of their possible importance as labour costs.[1] There are two intriguing questions: first, why was it unfashionable to talk of fringe benefits before; and second, why should the subject be of such importance just at the moment?

It would of course be a misconception to think of fringe benefits as entirely a twentieth century development. Various items of non-wage remuneration were important before the Industrial Revolution. Where farmworkers had something like an employee status, the contract of employment was a long-term one including many matters which would now be thought of as fringe benefits. Tied cottages and the supply of foodstuffs and other facilities all extended well beyond a simple money-wage relationship. The factory situation created by the Industrial Revolution frequently produced a mixture of wages and payment-in-kind, sometimes accompanied by obligations and duties which do not appear in our contemporary situation. Fringe benefits were, therefore, certainly available to industrial employees in the nineteenth century but they were of a rather different type and provided for a different purpose. Indeed, much social legislation, notably the Truck Acts, attempted to reduce the importance of what we could call fringe benefit schemes of a somewhat unfortunate type. These were designed to tie employees to a single employer or otherwise to reduce his real wage. They were paternalistic in character and were not negotiated, and they could not be claimed as a right but were rather a left-over from the situation in which the master regarded his men as an extension of his household to be 'looked after' both in respect of their physical well-being and in the sense of discipline and control. Naturally such 'benefits' were bitterly resisted by employees and the trade unions of the time and the Truck Acts plus a changing social climate went some way towards securing a more equal relationship in bargaining between worker and employer.

During the twentieth century two significant trends have emerged which have had some effect on the development of fringe benefits. First, collective bargaining has been accepted as the method by which wages and all conditions of employment should be settled. Fringe benefits, as non-wage remuneration of various kinds, were thus provided within a different framework. This is not to say that collective bargaining had a great influence on the growth of fringe benefits; in Britain most types of fringe benefit seem to have spread from causes other than collective bargaining or union efforts.[2] The second trend, of more recent date, is the increase in the number of salaried workers resulting from the growth and professionalism of management and

[1] The culmination of official interest is the current Ministry of Labour enquiry into labour costs; see Ministry of Labour *Gazette*, November 1963, p. 438 and the first footnote on p. 35.

[2] See Section IV of the Conclusion for further discussion of this point.

other 'white-collar' occupations, from the creation of large-scale
units of organization, and from the increasing complexity of production techniques. It is an indisputable fact that salaried workers have
always been given somewhat better treatment in the matter of additional benefits from work, and apart from the obvious conclusion
that the greater the numbers of salaried workers the more important
fringe benefits will be, there are repercussions on benefits for wage-
earners. It has frequently been the case that what salaried staff have
today wage earners will have—or feel they should have—tomorrow.
This emulation effect has been of considerable significance in increasing the *cost* of fringe benefits as well as the range of items since it has
been important in influencing holidays with pay[1] and, to a lesser
extent and much more recently, certain of the security benefits. The
future spread of fringe benefits to manual workers may therefore rely
very considerably on the example of what staff workers already have.[2]

This does not answer either of the two questions at the beginning
of this section, but it adds emphasis to the first of them: if fringe
benefits have existed for so long, and in their modern form have been
growing since the beginning of this century, why has so little attention
been paid to them? If we look from the viewpoint of the attitudes and
interests of British economists the answer is obvious. It is only in the
post-war years that British economists have produced any notable
degree of specialization in the economics of labour. It is natural that
the first efforts should have been directed towards amplifying and
correcting the previously over-simplified position of the economist on
wages, and only recently has much thought been given to other
aspects of employers' labour cost. But this view also reflects the
priorities of our society and the prevailing fashion of the time; had
fringe benefits been more in the public eye, had they cost more or
provided a greater degree of security for employees, they would undoubtedly have been studied by economists and others. Our second
question can be similarly answered; fringe benefits are now attracting
very much more attention simply because recent events and their
recent growth have led to the realization that, in terms of cost to the
employer and advantages for employees, these benefits could be
important. Of course, this answer is incomplete, for we wish to know
what has led to the growth and development of fringe benefits?

The simplest explanation is that in a developing society with a
collective bargaining system, the main concern of employees is to
secure adequate wages, and it is only when this need has been met
that the relationship between employer and worker can develop to

---

[1] See Chapter 10.
[2] This is particularly true if more employers offer 'staff status' to highly-paid
manual workers and this offer is taken to mean comparable fringe benefit provisions to those of clerical or administrative workers.

include other items which previously were considered less important than wage increases.[1] This notion of a 'threshold' level of earnings goes some way to explain the increase of interest in fringe benefits in the past few years, but it is not adequate in itself and there are other social and political factors of some importance. The rise in living standards in Europe and America was accompanied by a changing employer-employee relationship. Enlightened companies no longer looked upon employees as items of equipment, but as individuals for whom the company had a social responsibility albeit a legally undefined and economically uncertain one. The result was somewhat similar to the paternalism of earlier days though the underlying philosophy was in most cases different.

Another expression of this sense of collective responsibility is the appearance in most advanced countries of State-organized social security systems. In Britain the principle has long been that the social insurance network should cover the whole population against the three major risks—old age, unemployment and ill-health—but that cash benefits should be kept to a comparatively low level with the individual making his own provision for any extra benefit which he feels he wants. This has had two main effects. First, there has been scope for employers to introduce company schemes to augment the social security benefits, though this has not necessarily been the reason for the introduction of such schemes; and secondly, the State has intervened in the employer-worker relationship by forcing or encouraging companies to provide a certain level of services for their employees.[2] The most obvious example of the latter is the State's compulsion on every employer to contribute to the National Insurance scheme on behalf of his workers; this is the only item of fringe benefits legally required of an employer. Holidays with pay have not in Britain been established by law (except in Wages Council industries) but the spread from industry to industry of the one-week holiday, and then the two-week holiday, was marked by official encouragement in various ways, for example, through the Fair Wages resolution and recently by the Terms and Conditions of Employment Act. It seems likely that but for the Second World War and the social progress in the years immediately following, Britain would today resemble most other countries in having general legislation laying down minimum standards of holidays with pay.[3] Since 1960 Governmental encouragement of employers to introduce supple-

[1] One must postulate a collective bargaining system here, or make some other assumption that employees have some choice about the types of remuneration which they receive. In the eighteenth and nineteenth centuries, fringe benefits coexisted with sub-standard wages, both being imposed by the employer.

[2] We are here leaving aside legislation on minimum wages or physical conditions of work.

[3] See Chapter 10.

mentary pension schemes has been overt and persistent. The graduated pension scheme compelled those companies not participating in the Government scheme to arrange coverage of their employees by an approved industrial scheme, and this was reinforced by tax concessions on contributions paid by a company on behalf of the employee. Relying on exhortation alone, the Government has repeatedly stressed the desirability of private schemes providing redundancy payments and sickness benefit, but at the time of writing these appeals do not seem to have very much effect.

These influences, then, partly explain why fringe benefits have become more important in the recent past, but there are others. On the evidence of successful trade union pressure for wage increases, one might suppose that the development of collective bargaining would long since have given unions an important role in pressing for fringe benefits of various types, but it is only in the very recent past that manual workers' unions have begun to bargain seriously on fringe benefits. Claims for additional holidays with pay were sometimes included in bargaining during the 'fifties and early 'sixties, but as often as not the demand for longer holidays was tacked on to a wage claim and was the first item to be dropped when the hard bargaining began. Trade unions almost completely ignored sick pay, redundancy payments and pensions, and those schemes which did appear were introduced by employers either unilaterally or with the passive consent of the unions.

There seem to be several reasons for the absence until recently of union pressure. First, the majority of the rank and file of manual workers undoubtedly preferred wage increases to the introduction of supplementary benefits, and union leaders realized that the threshold level of wages had not yet been reached. Though earnings may have been high, basic rates were often very low and there was an incentive to press for wage increases in order to improve this fall-back rate. Moreover these claims for wage increases were fully in tune with the steadily rising prices of the 'fifties and with the pressures of the acquisitive social climate. A second important reason can be seen in the methods of social progress apparently favoured by British trade unions. The unions do not accept the present role of State social security: they believe that National Insurance benefits should be sufficient to maintain standards of living without supplementation from private or industrial schemes, and union attempts to achieve income-security for their members were therefore directed mainly towards political lobbying for increased social security benefits rather than towards bargaining for industrial schemes. Indeed, the introduction of company welfare schemes would have weakened the union case for increased national benefits, and while several sickness benefit schemes have recently been negotiated at a national level the unions have stressed that this does not indicate satisfaction with the National Insurance scheme as it stands.[1] Another possible reason for the unions' failure to negotiate security benefits may rest in the structure of collective bargaining. These benefits are best negotiated at a plant level, but it may be difficult for the individual unions in any plant to agree on the priorities of bargaining. Thus a skilled workers' union might prefer a sick pay scheme while a general union wishes to claim a wage increase on behalf of its lower-paid members. This difficulty has been avoided by the negotiation of union-wide schemes in some industries, but this seems less satisfactory than a company scheme which can be tailored to the special circumstances (and profitability) of an individual firm. The basic reason for the apparent paradox of the post-war period of employers introducing welfare schemes despite lack of pressure by the unions, sometimes even over their disapproval, has been the continued existence of full employment. On the one hand, this strengthened the position of the worker's side in bargaining and made unions more ready to advance, and employers less inclined to resist claims for increases in wages. The very low level of unemployment and the steady increase of money earnings obscured, if it did not entirely remove, the pre-war fear of insecurity of employment and the concomitant disruption of standards of living. There was therefore no reason for the unions in general to place a high priority on achieving security of employment or income, though this was considered to be of vital importance in a good number of local disputes.

On the other hand, the employer had a considerable incentive to introduce welfare schemes of many kinds. For one thing, there was the official encouragement which we noted earlier backed by tax advantages in the case of industrial pension schemes. Then the demand for labour was very high and in many parts of the country it was difficult to attract labour by the direct and obvious wage increase: this would have been matched by competitors in the labour market, and many companies were in any case committed to local wage agreements which it would have been dangerous to breach. The alternative may therefore have been an attempt to influence the supply of labour by providing superior conditions of employment, for example by offering longer holidays to employees or by providing a general sickness benefit scheme or subsidized welfare facilities of other kinds.[2] It is doubtful whether this kind of policy can be successful for long in controlling the labour market for one particular firm unless as a defensive measure to stop employees leaving,[3] but it could account for much of the increase in importance of fringe

---

[1] Trades Union Congress *Report* 1962; para. 447–8.
[2] The habit of offering regular overtime has a similar origin.
[3] This point will be analysed in detail in Section V of the Conclusion.

benefits during the 1950s. And, of course, there is a certain advantage in public relations for a company which is known as a 'good employer'; this was evident to some extent in the 1930s with the garden factories, and today progressive companies are not slow to improve their image by advertising their welfare facilities, whatever the economic justification for them may be.[1]

Fringe benefits, then, are not new but have changed in character over the last fifty years or so. They have become specially important in the post-war period for two main reasons; first, because of the development of our attitudes to social security, and in the past two or three years, the acceptance of the belief that employees are influenced as much by considerations of income-security as by the size of their earnings; and secondly, because of the existence of full employment, with all the detailed issues which this involves. It is likely that fringe benefits will become more important in industry and in the life of the community, and hence will be of growing interest to academics.

[1] These reasons for the introduction of fringe benefits do not explain why one particular company spends more than another, and Chapter 3 will investigate this further by trying to isolate the factors which determined company expenditure in a sample of 350 companies.

CHAPTER 2

SUPPLEMENTARY LABOUR COSTS IN BRITAIN BEFORE 1960

G. L. REID

I

The quantitative importance of supplementary labour costs may be assessed by looking at the total amount spent by all employers on all their various labour costs, comparing this with the total wage and salary bill. As a comparative measure between countries this is useful, and social security expenditures are usually expressed in this way,[1] but the expression on this basis of 'voluntary' expenditure by employers is rather difficult because of statistical inadequacies. In most countries it would require a very much more detailed breakdown of national income and of wage and salary statistics than presently exists. There are exceptions; in the United States, the total of employers' contributions to welfare schemes is easily available,[2] but in Britain there is little information on the importance of supplementary labour costs measured in this way. It is known that in 1958 total payment for annual and public holidays amounted to 6·4 per cent of total wages and salaries,[3] and that employers' contributions to pension schemes in 1961 were estimated to be 2·7 per cent of total wages and salaries.[4] The amount of employers' contributions to National Insurance and Health—in 1962 3·6 per cent of wages and salaries[5]— is also freely available. But even if information on these items were made more complete, by the inclusion of expenditure by employers on the other items of supplementary labour costs, it would be valuable only in so far as it provided a guide to whether expenditure by employers was rising, and to a lesser extent, and subject to a number of difficulties, how Britain compared with other countries. Moreover,

[1] See, for example, *Total Wages and Social Costs*, Council of Europe, Strasbourg, 1961.
[2] See Chapter 5 for full details.
[3] Total Wages and Social Costs, op. cit. Table 2.
[4] Estimates from information supplied by CSO. See also Chapter 5, p. 143.
[5] National Income and Expenditure 1963; HMSO; Table 2.

C

DOI: 10.4324/9781003184706-2

in common with all types of aggregative data these figures could conceal important changes in their constituent elements. For example, expenditure by employers on behalf of staff could increase relative to that on behalf of wage-earners; there could be changes in the importance of supplementary labour cost items within various industries; there could be shifts in the proportion of total expenditure incurred by each industrial sector, or the proportions spent by firms of different sizes might alter. Data on total expenditure conceal changes in the distribution of that expenditure, and, more important, do not give sufficient information to explain the relationship between expenditure on supplementary labour costs and other economic variables, such as industry, wage levels, size of firm, and so on.

To do this, one must use another method of presenting supplementary labour cost data, which involves obtaining expenditure figures from a number of individual firms. Expenditure is usually again expressed in relation to wages or earnings, and the only essential difference between the two methods is the level of aggregation at which the enquiry proceeds. In the 'national income' case, one is seeking the amount spent by all employers in the country on each item of supplementary labour costs, while in the 'company' case, the object is to discover the expenditure incurred by a sample of companies considered in some way to be representative. This latter approach clearly also has its limitations. Usually the sample of companies is far from ideal so that the results can hardly be generalized, and even if some kind of stratified sampling procedure is used, it is difficult to include all the relevant variables. The importance of this method is that it gives a measure of the level of supplementary labour costs in various sectors of industry, with a possibility of accounting for the differences in terms of the economic and social conditions present in each industry. It is also of great value if the results of a company enquiry on supplementary labour costs can be combined with existing wage and salary data on a compatible basis to give some indication of total labour costs in each industry. As well as giving a more realistic measure of labour costs, a company study may incidentally throw some light on how much workers' income is increased by the existence of supplementary labour costs, since some items which are paid in cash, such as holiday pay and sick pay, represent a true addition to employee earnings. But the measurement of employee benefit can only be a by-product of a study based on cost statistics, and it is not possible to secure a reliable or complete estimate of the workers' real income from this type of data.

II. SOME PREVIOUS ENQUIRIES

This section describes some attempts prior to the enquiry conducted by the University of Glasgow and described in the next Chapter to estimate supplementary labour costs. Official statistics in Britain allow only an imperfect estimation of the importance of supplementary labour costs, while company enquiries are also far from satisfactory.[1] As a result we have to rely on incomplete data. Where this results from private enquiries there are the additional drawbacks of voluntary participation, but there have been several investigations which at least give some indication of supplementary labour costs.

1. Ministry of Labour/I.L.O., 1955

The first was carried out in 1955 by the Ministry of Labour on behalf of the International Labour Office, which was undertaking a study of wages and related labour costs in ten European countries, with a view to comparing labour cost components on an international level.[2] Eight industries were selected as reflecting a variety of economic and cost conditions.[3] Considerable efforts were made to achieve comparability between countries, both in the coverage of employees and the information required, and a standard questionnaire was used. This dealt with the calendar year 1955, and details were requested of the following items:

> Basic wages paid for time worked;
> premium pay for overtime, holiday work, etc.;
> bonuses and gratuities;
> payments in kind;
> payment for time not worked;
> obligatory social security contributions;
> non-obligatory social security contributions;
> direct benefits paid to workers;
> subsidies to services for the benefit of workers;
> other payments related to labour costs.[4]

[1] The Ministry of Labour are now undertaking a survey of labour costs similar to that of 1955 and not unlike the University of Glasgow enquiry described in Chapter 3. Advance warning has been given to employers that the survey, covering the year 1964, is to be undertaken, and the much more extensive and detailed information which will result should allow total labour costs in Britain to be estimated accurately almost for the first time. See Ministry of Labour *Gazette*, November 1963, p. 438.

[2] This enquiry was reported in the Ministry of Labour *Gazette*, August 1957, pp. 277–80; and for all countries in I.L.O., *Labour Costs in European Industry*, Geneva, 1960.

[3] These industries were: blast furnaces and iron and steel smelting and rolling; manufacture of machine tools; cotton spinning, doubling and weaving; shipbuilding and ship repairing; radio-electronics (excluded from the British return); boots and shoes; coal mining; and railways.

[4] A precise description of what these classes contained can be found in I.L.O., op. cit., pp. 25–26.

For all except the last two items, subsidies and other payments, separate data were collected for wage earners and salaried staff. Employment information on the average numbers employed, the number of hours worked and the number of hours paid for but not worked were also requested.

In Britain returns from the nationalized coalmining and railway industries covered all employees. In the five private and manufacturing industries, questionnaires were sent to all establishments of more than 500 employees and to a sample of those employing between 25 and 500 employees. Those employing less than 25 were excluded entirely, and this resulted in a considerable bias in favour of large companies. Questionnaires were sent to 500 establishments in the five industries, and 211 usable replies were received. These covered 200,000 employees, about 20 per cent of the total employed in those industries.

TABLE 1. *Coverage of the Enquiry*

INDUSTRY	IN INDUSTRY	NO. OF ESTABLISHMENTS QUESTION-NAIRES SENT TO	REPLIES	NO. OF EMPLOYEES IN INDUSTRY	IN REPORTING FIRMS	% COVERED
Blast furnaces	412	119	42	249,100	92,488	37
Shipbuilding	644	99	29	210,000	28,998	14
Machine Tools	924	59	29	114,100	19,546	17
Cotton	1,409	165	86	260,300	39,041	15
Boot and Shoe	805	58	25	115,800	11,752	10
Total	4,194	500	211	949,300	191,825	20

Source: Ministry of Labour *Gazette*, op. cit.

Table 1 refers to all employees, wage-earners and salaried, but 85 per cent of those covered were operatives, so that between 15 and 20 per cent of the operatives employed in the five industries were covered by the enquiry. The predominance of large companies in the returns of all countries, not only Britain, was assumed to 'result in some upwards bias in the indicated level of wages and of other labour costs',[1] but not in a serious distortion of the data. To check this, the average hourly earnings of the companies in the sample were compared with the official statistics compiled from returns by all companies. For the U.K. the two sets of figures were so similar, with differences of only two or three pence between average hourly earnings of the sample companies and of the whole industrial group, that there would appear to be scarcely any upward bias of earnings.

[1] I.L.O., op. cit., p. 15.

TABLE 2. *Expenditure on Supplementary Labour Costs in seven British Industries, 1955*

EMPLOYERS' EXPENDITURE (AS A PERCENTAGE OF CASH REMUNERATION) FOR ALL EMPLOYEES ON:

INDUSTRY	NATIONAL INSURANCE CONTRIBUTIONS 1	PENSION SCHEMES 2	INDUSTRIAL ACCIDENTS 3	OTHER SOCIAL SECURITY 4	SUBSIDIES TO EMPLOYEES 5	OTHER PAYMENTS 6	Total 7	ESTIMATED TOTAL EMPLOYER EXPENDITURE 8	AVERAGE CASH EXPENDITURE PER EMPLOYEE PER YEAR 9	% OF TOTAL MAN HOURS PAID FOR BUT NOT WORKED 10
Blast furnaces, etc. ..	2·3 (2·3)	1·6 (0·5)	0·4 (0·5)	0·1 (0·0)	0·9	1·1	6·4	13·0	£39 6s 11d	6·4 (5·7)
Shipbuilding, etc. ..	2·5 (2·6)	1·4 (0·2)	0·4 (0·5)	0·2 (0·1)	0·4	0·4	5·3	11·4	£30 18s 11d	6·0 (5·7)
Machine tools	2·2 (2·4)	1·2 (0·3)	0·2 (0·2)	0·0 (0·0)	0·8	0·9	5·3	12·4	£31 2s 1d	7·0 (7·1)
Cotton spinning, etc. ..	3·3 (3·5)	1·9 (0·6)	0·1 (0·1)	0·0 (0·0)	1·5	0·5	7·3	13·4	£27 9s 8d	6·8 (6·8)
Boots and shoes ..	3·0 (3·2)	2·5 (1·8)	0·0 (0·0)	0·0 (0·0)	0·5	0·1	6·1	12·9	£24 10s 8d	6·8 (6·7)
Coalmining	2·3 (2·2)	2·9 (2·1)	0·8 (0·9)	1·0 (1·1)	1·7	1·1	9·8	20·5	£63 2s 6d	6·6 (6·4)
Railways	2·7 (2·8)	1·9 (1·0)	0·0 (0·0)	0·1 (0·2)	0·3		5·0	12·1	£26 18s 6d	7·1 (6·1)

Notes: In cols. 1–4 & 10, the figures in parentheses are for operatives only.

Col. 5 includes 'medical health services; housing; vacation homes, educational and recreational services'.

Col. 6 includes 'recruitment and vocational training; welfare scheme payments; amenity buildings; ablution centres; employee transport; travelling and lodging allowances; safety instructions; work study, etc'.

Col. 8 is an estimate, and includes where possible the value of payments in kind. It also includes an estimate of the cost of holidays.

Source: Ministry of Labour *Gazette*, op. cit.

Table 2 gives the results obtained by the Ministry of Labour enquiry. To move from Table 2, containing figures for all employees, to Table 3, which deals only with operatives, involves two sets of estimation. First, the expenditure on subsidies and other payments must be allocated between wage-earners and salaried workers, and the I.L.O. report adopted the simplest method, of dividing the amount spent between the two classes according to the numbers employed in each. This will possibly lead to an overestimate of expenditure on wage-earners, since medical and health services, canteens, and other services and subsidies may cost more per head for administrative and clerical personnel than for operatives. Secondly, the cost of hours paid for but not worked was not available directly. The I.L.O. estimated this cost by multiplying the total number of hours paid for but not worked by hourly basic wages, but for the U.K. statistics of basic wages were not available and average hourly earnings were used instead. The cost of holiday pay was therefore overstated, since the assumption that all holidays were paid at the rate of average earnings was obviously incorrect. Even now, most employees receive holiday pay at the basic wage rate or a modification of it, and in 1955 this would have been true of the great majority. This estimate of holiday pay is, however, the best which can be made.[1] Table 3 shows the expenditure on supplementary labour cost items for operatives. Coalmining had a much higher total than any other industry, even without the figure of 5·1 per cent which represented the value of free and concessionary coal. Expenditure on pension schemes, other insurance and social payments, recruitment and other subsidies were all higher in coalmining. The cotton industry was second to coalmining in terms of total employer expenditure, mostly because of an unusually large amount spent on canteen services and a high percentage figure for National Insurance expenditure which reflected the lower than average wages in that industry. In other industries too, the National Insurance percentage tended to bear an inverse relationship to the average wage level; thus in the boot and shoe industry the employer's contribution was high in percentage terms, while in steel, coalmining and machine tools it was low. The total of all items for the railways, 10·1 per cent was surprisingly low, due partly to the exclusion of the value of payments in kind. British Railways were unable to estimate reliably the cost of free and concessionary travel to their employees; it must have been considerable though probably not as costly to them as concessionary coal was to the Coal Board.[2] The Transport Commission made an estimate of

[1] Another way of expressing this is simply to say that payment for time not worked represents the same proportion of total remuneration as hours paid for but not worked do of total hours.

[2] The Guillebaud Committee were unable to get estimates of the cost of free travel though concessionary travel cost £2·5m.

TABLE 3. *Expenditure on Supplementary Labour Costs: Operatives only*
PERCENTAGE OF TOTAL CASH REMUNERATION: OPERATIVES ONLY

INDUSTRY	TOTAL CASH REMUNER-ATION £000's	HOLIDAY PAY	OTHER TIME OFF WORK	PAYMENTS IN KIND	NATIONAL INSURANCE CONS.	PENSION SCHEMES	INDUSTRIAL ACCIDENTS	OTHER SOCIAL SECURITY CONS.	MEDICAL AND HEALTH SERVICES	CANTEEN SERVICES	RECRUITMENT AND TRAINING	OTHER SUBSIDIES ETC.	Total
		1	2	3	4	5	6	7	8	9	10	11	
Blast furnaces, etc.	46,734	5·4	0·0	0·1	2·3	0·5	0·5	0·0	0·4	0·5	0·4	0·7	10·8
Ship-building, etc.	14,703	5·3	0·1	0·0	2·6	0·2	0·5	0·1	0·1	0·3	0·3	0·2	9·7
Machine tools	8,804	6·4	0·1	0·1	2·4	0·3	0·2	0·0	0·2	0·7	0·7	0·2	11·3
Cotton spinning, etc.	12,565	6·2	0·1	0·0	3·5	0·6	0·1	0·0	0·3	1·1	0·3	0·5	12·7
Boots and shoes	3,955	6·2	0·1	0·0	3·2	1·8	0·0	0·0	0·2	0·3	0·1	0·0	11·9
Coal-mining	408,802	5·6	0·3	5·1	2·2	2·1	0·9	1·1	0·3	0·0	1·0	1·4	20·0
Railways	237,778	5·8	—	*	2·8	1·0	0·0	0·2	⎱ 0·3 (cols 8–11 combined) ⎰				10·1

Notes: Col. 6 covers contributions to insurance companies or funds.
Col. 7 includes sick pay schemes; payments on birth, marriage or death; severance pay; accident compensation, ex gratia payments.
Cols. 8–11 are estimated: figures were given for staff and employees combined and have been reduced proportionately.
Col. 11 includes housing, educational and recreational services; amenity buildings; transport; lodging allowances; work study, etc.
Cols. 1 and 2 are estimated. It has been assumed that holiday pay is the same percentage of total cash remuneration as holiday hours are of total man-hours.
* Reliable estimates of the value of free travel are not available.

Sources: Ministry of Labour *Gazette*, op. cit., and calculated.

the overall cost of subsidies and welfare services, as no exact figures were available, and the very low inclusive figure given—0·3 per cent —was only half as much as the next lowest industry, boots and shoes, and very much less than any other industry. For these two reasons, the railways' figure certainly seemed to be an understatement of their true position.

2. *Industrial Welfare Society*, 1958

Another enquiry was carried out in 1958 among members of the Industrial Welfare Society.[1] It sought to estimate how much firms spent on 'certain ancillary labour costs', many of them welfare benefits. A questionnaire was sent to 135 member companies of whom 55 replied, and these almost entirely large firms; only two had less than 500 employees, 44 employed over one thousand, and the total employment in the sample was 294,000. The engineering and food industries were heavily represented with twenty and sixteen firms respectively, the other companies being in chemicals, textiles, printing and leather. The sample was therefore not characteristic of manufacturing industry as a whole, but the enquiry did not claim the figures to be representative. It noted also that 'some of the firms . . . have for many years been leaders in the field of welfare', and that 'most of them (were) probably ahead of the average British firm'.[2] The questionnaire covered the financial year ending during 1957, and requested details of the cost to the employer of the following items: medical services, canteen subsidies, sick pay schemes, employer contributions to sick and benevolent funds, convalescent homes, pen-

TABLE 4. *Expenditure on Supplementary Labour Costs for all Employees: per cent of total remuneration*

	NO. OF FIRMS REPORTING EXPENDITURE	RANGE	MEDIAN	AVERAGE EXPENDITURE OF ALL FIRMS	OF FIRMS REPORTING COST
Medical Services	47	0·03–0·74	0·27	0·25	0·30
Canteen	54	0·11–4·03	0·98	1·23	1·25
Sports/Social Club	54	0·01–1·90	0·17	0·28	0·29
Sick Pay	52	0·10–3·35	0·88	1·01	1·07
Pension Scheme ..	55	0·35–20·0	4·00	4·60	4·60
Protective Clothing	51	0·02–2·40	0·44	0·49	0·53
Works Magazine ..	36	0·01–0·54	0·10	0·10	0·15
Housing	17	0·01–3·60	0·18	0·16	0·52
Holidays	54	2·27–8·40	5·20	5·01	5·10
National Insurance	55	1·31–3·50	2·40	2·40	2·40
Other Insurance ..	52	0·03–1·61	0·20	0·28	0·30
Total				**15·81**	**16·51**

Source: From Durham, op. cit., pp. 8–17, Tables 20–22.

[1] W. Durham, *The £.S.D. of Welfare in Industry*, I.W.S., London, 1958.
[2] Ibid., p. 2.

sions, holidays, protective clothing, works magazines, housing, National Insurance and other insurance contributions. Separate data for salaried workers and wage-earners were not obtained.

The cost of each item was expressed as a percentage of total cash remuneration or 'payroll' (i.e. all payments to employees including holiday pay, overtime and shift premiums) and the results presented mainly in terms of a range of payments and a median, but it was also possible to calculate the arithmetic mean, which is useful for comparative purposes. Table 4 shows the results for all companies.

The range of expenditure on these eleven items was generally rather wide. The total of average expenditure on each item, 15·81 per cent of payroll, is considerably higher than the figures for private industry obtained from the Ministry of Labour enquiry (Table 2, col. 10), but it is difficult to make a direct comparison because of differences in the composition of the sample and the circumstances of the enquiries. It is interesting, though, that the I.W.S. companies spent very much more on pension schemes than did those in the 1955 survey, an average of 4·60 per cent against 1·5—2·5 per cent, and this may reflect the 'welfare-minded' sample covered by the I.W.S.

There was a sufficient number of companies in the food and engineering industries to allow comparison between them.

TABLE 5. *Comparison between Food and Engineering Industries: per cent of total remuneration*

	AVERAGE OF ALL FIRMS IN	
	FOOD INDUSTRY	ENGINEERING INDUSTRY
Medical Services	0·35	0·21
Canteen	1·98	0·74
Sports/Social Club	0·39	0·17
Sick Pay	1·54	0·76
Pensions	5·97	2·91
Housing	0·34	0·05
Holidays	5·39	4·35
Protective Clothing	0·97	0·27
Works Magazine	0·15	0·06
National Insurance	2·51	2·29
Other Insurance	0·22	0·36
Total	**19·81**	**12·17**

Source: Durham, op. cit., calculated from Tables 20 and 21.

In these industries, there was a positive correlation between wages and supplementary labour costs; the higher was the wage level, the more did a company spend on these eleven items both in money terms and as a percentage of total remuneration. These figures refer to all employees and they exclude the costs of education, recruitment and training which in many cases were difficult to analyse. For several of the items, it was possible to estimate separately the cost for wage-earners and salaried workers, and this breakdown is shown in Table 6.

TABLE 6. *Supplementary Labour Costs for Works and Staff Employees: per cent of remuneration*

	WORKS: % OF WORKS REMUNERATION	STAFF: % OF STAFF REMUNERATION	ALL: % OF TOTAL REMUNERATION
Canteen	1·11	0·83	0·98
Sports/Social Club	0·19	0·14	0·17
Sick Pay	0·50	2·00	0·88
Pensions	1·45	7·04	4·00
Holidays..	5·20	6·00	5·20
Protective Clothing	0·53	—	0·40
Works Magazine	0·11	0·07	0·10
National Insurance	2·73	2·04	2·40
Total	11·82	18·12	14·13

Source: Durham, op. cit., Table 9.

The works employees' figure was much the same as those for operatives in the Ministry of Labour enquiry (see Table 3), but Table 6 excludes a number of items—medical services, training and education, and other insurance—which might have raised the figures by about two percentage points.

The Industrial Welfare Society survey gave a little more information than did the Ministry of Labour enquiry on the extent of supplementary labour costs and, despite the admittedly unrepresentative nature of the sample, it was revealing to see what a selection of large companies particularly interested in welfare spent on the range of supplementary cost items.

3. *Institute of Economic Affairs, 1959*
Another study dealing only with large companies was published by the Institute of Economic Affairs in 1959, and part of it dealt with the cost of welfare benefits.[1] A questionnaire was sent to 512 companies with net assets of over £2·5 million, and one section requested data on the cost of the following items; canteen; sports and recreational facilities; education and training; long service concessions; charity contributions; pensions; ex gratia payments; and other welfare services. One hundred and seventeen companies with a total employment of 975,000 supplied this cost information, and the total cost of the welfare benefits listed above is shown in Table 7.

[1] R. Harris and M. Solly, *A Survey of Large Companies*, Institute of Economic Affairs, 1959.

TABLE 7. *Welfare Costs for all Employees: per cent of payroll*

INDUSTRY	PER CENT OF PAYROLL					AVERAGE EXPENDITURE, %
	LESS THAN 2	2–5	5–10	OVER 10	Total	
Iron, steel, shipbuilding ..	3	4	3	2	12	5·4
Vehicles, engineering ..	3	13	12	2	30	5·6
Textiles, clothing ..	1	6	4	1	12	5·7
Chemicals, rubber, paper	–	7	11	2	20	4·7
Food	–	2	10	4	16	8·1
Building	–	3	1	1	5	6·0
Distribution ..	–	5	5	3	13	7·2
Transport services ..	–	4	4	1	9	7·0
All	7	44	50	16	117	6·2

Source: Harris and Solly, op. cit., Table X.

This table excludes several important supplementary labour costs, notably holidays and National Insurance contributions, and an estimate was made putting the total cost of these at 8 to 10 per cent of payroll. This would raise the average cost figures in Table 7 to a minimum of about 13 per cent of payroll for chemicals and a maximum of 18 per cent in the food industry.

Table 8 gives the proportions of total expenditure allocated to the main items for salaried and wage-earning employees. The third column estimates the cost of these items as a percentage of payroll, on the assumption that their total cost is 6·2 per cent of payroll as shown in Table 7.

TABLE 8. *Expenditure on Welfare Benefits 1958*

	NO. OF COMPANIES	PER CENT OF TOTAL EXPENDITURE	PER CENT OF PAYROLL
Canteen	135	13·1	0·81
Sports facilities	125	2·9	0·18
Education	120	8·6	0·53
Long service concessions ..	102	—	—
Pensions	138	53·2	3·30
Ex gratia payments	117	6·4	0·40
Other benefits	131	15·8	0·98
Total No. of companies ..	138	—	—
Total per cent	—	100	6·2
Companies giving all benefits	99	—	—

Source: Harris and Solly, op. cit., Table XIX.

Pensions were by far the most important welfare benefit, provided by all the 138 companies, but with all employees covered by a pension plan in only 36 companies, the inequality of treatment of staff and works appeared again; most of the cost of pensions, 3·3 per cent of payroll, was probably due to staff schemes. Another interesting finding was that companies which paid high wages also had high welfare expenditure, but in the sample as a whole there was a very wide range of payment which made generalization difficult, with expenditure ranging from under £10 to well over £100 per employee.

4. *Etudes et Conjoncture*, 1960

This study by the French Institut National de la Statistiques et des Etudes Economiques,[1] which attempted to measure relative levels of labour costs in European countries, is more recent than the others, though the time period it discusses is similar. The results were based on the 1955 International Labour Office enquiry with the statistics brought up to 1958, and to facilitate calculation of the total labour costs, supplementary labour costs were expressed in terms of a percentage addition to average hourly earnings. Table 9 shows the estimated figures for 1957 and 1958 for various industries, and average expenditure on each item.

TABLE 9. *Estimated Supplementary Labour Costs: percentage of hourly earnings*

	OCTOBER 1957	OCTOBER 1958
National Insurance	2·7	3·2
Other insurance, pensions	1·0	1·0
Work accidents	0·3	0·3
Payment for time not worked	6·5	7·0
Other payments	0·5	0·5
Welfare services	2·0	2·0
TOTAL (in all industries)	13·0	14·0
Metal manufacture	12·0	12·5
Engineering	11·5	12·0
Textiles	14·0	14·5
Wool	14·0	14·5
Food*	13·5	14·0
Chemicals*	12·0	12·5
Printing*	10·5	11·0

* The estimates for these industries were rather less precise than those for the others.
Source: Etudes et Conjoncture, op. cit., Table 6; and p. 228.

The method of estimation was not always clear. The amount of holiday pay and National Insurance contributions was calculated after reference to official sources, but even now there are few sources of data on the cost of voluntary welfare services, pensions, and so on. The industry totals in Table 9 seem to be based on a combination of

[1] 'Les Couts de Main d'Oeuvre dans L'Industrie Manufacturiére des Pays Européens et des Etats-Unis', *Etudes et Conjoncture*, May 1960, I.N.S.E.E, Paris.

the I.L.O. and Industrial Welfare Society enquiries summarized above,[1] and so must be considered rather suspect. If they are recalculated on the same basis as the original Ministry of Labour figure, i.e., as a percentage of total cash remuneration, the total for October 1958 becomes 13 per cent of payroll, lower than most of the industries in the 1955 enquiry. This figure of 13 per cent may well be fairly accurate; it is itself founded on the I.L.O. enquiry and it is possible that supplementary labour costs as a percentage of payroll decreased slightly between 1955 and 1958, a period during which weekly earnings, which are roughly equivalent to payroll, rose by about 16 per cent.

III

All these attempts to measure supplementary labour costs in Britain yielded data subject to various sources of error. All the samples were biased in some respect; the characteristics of the samples were not normally described in sufficient detail to allow adjustment of the results so that they might be applied more widely to the whole of industry, and the inclusion in most cases of staff employees as well as wage-earners makes this even more difficult. Although generalization on the basis of these studies is dangerous, the following broad conclusions could be reached as to the extent of supplementary labour costs in Britain before 1960:

1. For operatives supplementary labour costs were between 10 and 15 per cent of total remuneration, probably nearer the former figure in view of the likely upward bias noted by most of the reports.

2. Metal manufacturing and metal working industries tended to have a lower level of expenditure than textiles, food or coalmining.

3. There was some evidence that large firms tended to spend more than small, and that firms which paid high wages also tended to spend more on supplementary labour costs.

4. Supplementary labour costs for salaried workers were considerably higher than those of wage-earners.

These, then, were the main points to be drawn from the available information on supplementary labour costs when the Glasgow enquiry into fringe benefits commenced at the beginning of 1961.

---

[1] An account of the derivation of the figures in Table 9 appears in *Etudes et Conjonctures*, op. cit., p. 209 and pp. 227–8.

CHAPTER 3

THE COST OF FRINGE BENEFITS
IN BRITISH INDUSTRY

G. L. REID AND JAMES BATES

I. SCOPE AND METHOD OF THE ENQUIRY

This Chapter deals with the statistical enquiry into fringe benefits for manual workers which was undertaken by the Department of Social and Economic Research, University of Glasgow. This Section describes the scope and method of the enquiry, Section II gives a full account of the characteristics of the sample, Sections III and IV detail the results and Sections V and VI discuss their significance.

In an enquiry of this type it is sometimes difficult to determine which employees should be covered and in which industries, but in this case the limits of the survey were determined by practical considerations. It was decided at the outset that staff employees of the executive grades should be excluded from the enquiry. For one thing, information on their fringe benefits would have been very difficult to obtain, since few companies would have been willing to provide details of the cost of expense accounts, executive pension schemes, company cars and similar benefits. In addition, though fringe benefits may be a large proportion of executive income, the comparatively small number of employees and the likelihood of considerable variations in practice between companies would have made it difficult to draw any valuable general conclusions. The exclusion of the executive class left a large number of salaried and wage-earning employees who could have been coverered by the enquiry, but since there is no generally accepted classification of 'wage-earning', there was a difficult problem in defining the workers to whom the questionnaire applied. An employee who in one company would be on the salaried staff might be a wage-earner in another. The most convenient and clear procedure was therefore to include in the enquiry only those employees covered by the definition of a manual worker used in the Ministry of

DOI: 10.4324/9781003184706-3

Labour earnings enquiries.[1] Administrative, technical and clerical employees were excluded; more specifically, the enquiry did not cover office staffs, shop assistants, outworkers, managers, commercial travellers, clerks and typists, and salaried persons generally.

A comprehensive survey of all companies was obviously beyond the scope of a voluntary enquiry such as this. The next best solution, a sample stratified by size and industry drawn from the total number of companies operating in Britain, was not practicable, since it was impossible at the time to obtain the necessary comprehensive list of all British companies. The only list of companies reliable and complete within its own definitions was the Stock Exchange register of public companies and this was used in the enquiry. The Stock Exchange list unfortunately has several defects which made it less than ideal for our purposes. First, it meant that private companies were excluded, and though the final sample did contain a large number of private companies which were subsidiaries of public companies, there was no suitable way of contacting independent private companies. Secondly, the list includes a very large number of non-industrial public companies, firms whose business is overseas, and financial institutions; since these firms do not employ manual workers, the questionnaire did not apply to them. Thirdly, the list contains many holding companies whose form is a legal device and who again have no manual workers, though their subsidiaries may employ a very large number. Previous postal surveys have shown that the response rate to this kind of enquiry is usually relatively poor, and so questionnaires were sent to all public companies rather than only to a sample. In addition, a sample of American-controlled companies operating in Britain was selected from Dun and Bradstreet's 'Guide to Key British Enterprises 1961'.

Copies of the questionnaire were sent to all companies to whom it was considered applicable. That is, those employing no manual workers were as far as possible excluded, as were companies whose operations were wholly outside the U.K. In fact questionnaires were sent to many companies who for one reason or another had no manual workers, and a number immediately replied to this effect. A proportion of the total number of those circulated did not reply to the original request for co-operation, nor to a second follow-up letter. It is not possible to say accurately to how many non-respondents the questionnaire was applicable, and this makes calculation of a realistic response rate very difficult. A crude response rate, i.e. questionnaires returned as a proportion of those sent out, would be almost meaningless, and the true response rate, using as a base only companies to which the questionnaire did refer can only be roughly estimated, but

[1] This definition is given in the reports on the earnings enquiries, Ministry of Labour *Gazette*, February and August each year.

it appears to have been between 10 and 20 per cent, probably nearer
the former figure.

The questionnaire[1] required information on various items of
labour costs; though several of the costs listed might not be classified
directly as labour costs (for example, the costs of discounts on products sold or given to employees), they all represented a cost to the
employer and gave some benefit to the worker. There were three
main sections in the questionnaire. The first was concerned with
wages and the important item here was payroll—'total amount paid
to all employees during the year including overtime pay, shift supplements, pay for annual and public holidays, sick pay and all other payments for time off work'.[2] This sum was the base for the percentage
calculations of the other costs. Holiday pay and sick pay, two of the
most important cash benefits paid to employees, were given separately
in this section. The second section, 'Other Company Expenditure',
requested details of the cost of pensions, National Insurance payments, education and redundancy payments. The third was concerned with 'Other Welfare Expenditure', including expenditure on
canteen and social facilities, subsidies for travel and housing and
profit sharing schemes.

During testing of a pilot questionnaire, it was suggested that a
more 'open ended' design of question would give a higher rate of
response. Then Question 8(b) might have read 'Medical Services'
and each firm would have been free to interpret this according to its
own experience, reporting the cost of medical services as it defined
the term. However the gain in response rate would not have been
worth the loss of precision, and the difficulty of reliable analysis pre-
cluded this type of approach. The definition of expenditure covered
under each item was quite strict, so that the questionnaire would be
answered in a consistent fashion, but it was clear that whatever the
form of the questionnaire, it would be difficult for some firms to
answer because of variations in accounting procedure.[3]

As well as the cost questions, the questionnaire was concerned
with certain company information—i.e. the form of the company,
the establishments covered by the return and whether the company
was a subsidiary—and with details of employment. There were two
ways in which to obtain an employment figure. One was by taking an
average of employment figures throughout the year, most conveni-

[1] See Appendix, page 86.

[2] The word 'employees' was restricted to mean 'manual workers'; this is the
meaning which it will bear in the subsequent discussion.

[3] Some companies who were unable to answer the questionnaire as it stood
suggested that with notice of the questions they could have so arranged their
accounting systems as to allow easy response. Such notice was impossible for this
enquiry, but has been given by the Ministry of Labour for their survey covering
1964.

ently of monthly statistics, the other was to take employment at one particular date in the year. The latter method was chosen as being more convenient for respondents, especially as the date chosen was the second pay-week of October 1960, in respect of which a return had already been made to the Ministry of Labour of all employees at work. Another question asked for a breakdown of employment by sex, age and full-time/part-time; it was easier for respondents to effect this breakdown for the single October figure than for a monthly average. To see how representative the October figure was of employment during the year, the maximum and minimum numbers employed at any one time during the year were also requested. A question was included on employment in 1955 to get some idea of the growth in employment terms of the companies in the sample over the years 1955–60, though it did not yield any usable information.

II. THE SAMPLE

The final samples (using this term to mean the establishments which returned the questionnaire) consisted of 350 returns: this excludes a few, less than 10, which were found to be unsuitable for tabulation. This does not mean that 350 companies replied. Some firms submitted several returns in respect of various recording units within the one company. On the other hand, some parent companies included their own operations and those of their subsidiaries in one questionnaire, while many companies replied on behalf of only part of their organizations, such as one plant. In the 350 replies the diversity of responding practice means that the employment figures in the questionnaires do not necessarily refer to an individial company, though for simplicity the following discussion will use the word 'company' to refer to a completed questionnaire.

Table 10 shows the sample classified by size and industry. The industry classifications by Standard Industrial Classification Order were obtained from the Ministry of Labour, the size classification from the questionnaire data. Where a company had units in more than one Order, it was included in the Order where the bulk of its operations lay.

The average size of companies in the chemical and textile industries was significantly smaller than average with $t=1 \cdot 83$ and $38 \cdot 3$ respectively, where $t_5\%=1 \cdot 65$, and that in vehicles and aircraft and metal manufacture significantly larger than average ($t=25 \cdot 5$ and $18 \cdot 0$ respectively).[1] By far the largest number of questionnaires returned

[1] In all the tests involving the whole sample the number of degrees of freedom is over 300, so that $t_5\%$ is $1 \cdot 65$.

D

TABLE 10. *Distribution by Industry and Employment of 350 Responding Companies*

INDUSTRY	LESS THAN 100	100 – 250	250 – 500	500 – 750	750 – 1,000	1,000 – 2,000	2,000 – 3,000	3,000 – 4,000	4,000 – 5,000	5,000 – 10,000	10,000 AND OVER	COMPANIES NO.	%
3. Food, drink, tobacco	1	4	5	4	4	5		1	1	2		27	7·7
4. Chemicals and allied	7	8	13	5	1	6	6	1	1		1	49	14·0
5. Metal manufacture	1	2	5	2	1	4	2	2		6	2	27	7·7
6. Engineering and electrical	3	15	14	16	12	17	9	4	2	2	3	97	27·7
7. Shipbuilding			2	2	1	3	2	2	2			14	4·0
8. Vehicles and aircraft		1	3		1	1	1	2	1	8	3	21	6·0
9. Other metal goods	2		6	3	1							12	3·4
10. Textiles¹	5	8	12	7	6	6	3	1		1		49	14·0
13. Bricks, pottery, glass, etc.		3	2	2		5	1				1	14	4·0
15. Paper, printing and publishing			2	2	3	3	3	1				14	4·0
16. Other manufacturing industries³	1	1	2	2		3		1	3	1		14	4·0
17. Construction			1		2	2						5	1·4
Other³	1	2	2			2						7	2·0
No. of companies	21	44	69	45	32	57	27	15	10	20	10	350	100
Per cent of companies	6·0	12·6	19·7	12·9	9·1	16·3	7·7	4·3	2·9	5·7	2·9		100

Notes: ¹ Includes one company from 'Clothing' and one from 'Leather'.
² Includes two companies from 'Timber, etc.'
³ Includes one company from 'Mining (other than coal)'.

came from the engineering industry, followed by chemicals and textiles.[1]

It had been hoped to compare the distribution by size and industry of the establishments in the sample with that of the whole of manufacturing industry, but it was impossible to identify exactly how reporting establishments were classified in Ministry of Labour statistics. Table 11 therefore can only compare employment in the sample with estimated employment of manual workers in manufacturing industry at October 1960.

TABLE 11. *Industrial Coverage of the Sample*

INDUSTRY	NO. OF MANUAL WORKERS IN SAMPLE COMPANIES	ESTIMATED TOTAL OF MANUAL WORKERS IN INDUSTRY (OCTOBER 1960)	% COVERAGE
3. Food, drink, tobacco ..	43,259	670,000	6·5
4. Chemicals and allied ..	115,687	360,000	32·1
5. Metal manufacture ..	123,920	509,500	24·3
6. Engineering	144,832	1,495,200	9·7
7. Shipbuilding ..	28,171	206,000	13·7
8. Vehicles and aircraft ..	155,259	684,200	22·7
9. Other metal goods	8,647	461,400	1·9
10. Textiles	43,170	739,700	5·9
11. Leather, etc.	*	54,300	Negligible
12. Clothing	*	504,400	Negligible
13. Bricks, etc.	22,324	285,800	7·8
14. Timber, etc...	*	243,200	Negligible
15. Paper, printing, etc. ..	15,563	469,000	3·3
16. Other manufacturing ..	18,636	242,600	7·7
TOTAL MANUFACTURING INDUSTRY	**724,240**	**6,925,400**	**10·5**
17. Construction	13,225	N.A.	—
Other	3,282	N.A.	—

* Because of the small number of participating firms in these industries, the employment figures are not given.
N.A.=not available.

The survey covered about 10 per cent of manual workers in manufacturing industry, though the percentage coverage of the S.I.C. Orders showed considerable variation, ranging from about 32 per cent in chemicals to less than one per cent in leather, clothing and timber.

[1] It should be emphasized again that, in Tables 10 and 11, reporting units are not necessarily companies, so that it is not possible to identify a unit by its employment classification.

TABLE 12. Annual Average Wages per Employee (excluding holiday pay)

INDUSTRY	200–300	300–400	400–500	500–600	£ 600–700	700–800	800–900	900–1,000	NOT AVAILABLE	Total	AVERAGE WAGE
3. Food etc. .. : :		6	6	10	2	3	1	1	2	27	516
4. Chemicals .. : :		3	6	6	19	11	4	1	1	49	618
5. Metal manufacture :			1	1	13	6	1		4	27	706
6. Engineering, etc. :		1	14	35	30	12	1			97	589
7. Shipbuilding .. :			1	5	5	2	1			14	643
8. Vehicles and aircraft :		1			9	4	5	2		21	732
9. Other metal goods :		1	3	2	3	2		1		12	592
10. Textiles .. : :	3	14	24	4	1				3	49	417
13. Bricks .. : :			1	6	5	1	1			14	650
15. Paper, printing, etc. :			2	7	2	2	1			14	611
16. Other manufacturing :	2	2	2	3	2	1	2			14	529
17. Construction .. :					2		2	1		5	768
Other .. : :			2	3	1		1			7	608
No. of companies .. : :	5	28	62	82	94	44	19	6	10	350	
Per cent of companies .. : :	1·4	8·0	17·7	23·4	26·9	12·6	5·4	1·7	2·9	100	

Table 12 gives some indication of the average yearly wage levels in the various industries. The average wages in the vehicles and metal manufacturing industries were significantly higher than that in the rest of the sample ($t=4\cdot85$ and $6\cdot01$ respectively, where $t_5\%=1\cdot65$) while the average wage in the textile industry was significantly lower ($t=14\cdot4$). These average wage figures are only approximate and must be interpreted with caution. For one thing, the method of calculation is crude; the total amount paid to all employees (excluding holiday pay) has been divided by the number of employees at October 1960. The figure for total payroll is in some cases only an estimate and so a potential source of error, but most of the likelihood of inaccuracy comes from the employment figures used. The October figure may be an imperfect representation of the average yearly employment. In fact, the labour forces of some companies fluctuated widely and the average wage figure of Table 12 will be biased upwards or downwards if the October employment was lower or higher than average. To check whether Table 12 was a true representation of average wages, the distribution of average wages was drawn up of only those companies whose employment in 1960 was never less than 90 per cent of the October labour force and never more than 110 per cent of it. One might expect the average wages of these companies (203 in number) to be more accurate than those of the sample as a whole, if the use of the October employment figure was introducing bias.[1] In fact, the distributions of average wages of these 203 'reliable' companies, of the 'unreliable' companies and of the sample as a whole were almost identical. In most industries, too, these distributions are very similar except in food, drink and tobacco and chemicals, where 'unreliable' companies had, on average, lower average wages than 'reliable'. The distributions in Table 12, then, are probably not made substantially more inaccurate by the inclusion of those companies whose labour forces fluctuated considerably during the year.

The sample is biased in several respects. Table 11 shows the overweighting of some industries and the poor representation of others, and there is a predominance of large companies. Very few companies in the sample have less than 50 employees and if the sample could be compared with the whole of manufacturing industry, this bias would become apparent. Since the enquiry covered only public companies and ignored the private company sector which includes a large number of very small firms, a bias of this kind was inevitable.[2]

[1] That there was considerable variation in the labour force throughout the year does not, of course, mean that the October figure is necessarily a bad indicator, but it is more likely that the October labour force is near the average for companies with a smaller variation.

[2] For reasons noted earlier the sample did contain many private companies, almost all of them large.

TABLE 13. *Industrial Coverage of Male and Female Employees in the Sample and in Manufacturing Industry*

INDUSTRY		EMPLOYEES IN SAMPLE AS A PERCENTAGE OF TOTAL EMPLOYMENT		PERCENTAGE OF MALE EMPLOYEES IN	
		MALE	FEMALE	SAMPLE	ALL MANU-FACTURING
3. Food, drink, tobacco	..	6·5	6·4	55·1	54·5
4. Chemical and allied ..	..	35·1	22·5	83·4	76·3
5. Metal manufacture ..	..	25·2	14·8	95·2	92·1
6. Engineering and electrical	..	10·2	8·1	89·3	75·3
7. Shipbuilding	..	13·6	20·1	98·1	98·7
8. Vehicles and aircraft ..	..	23·4	15·8	93·5	90·6
9. Other metal goods ..	..	N.A.	N.A.	N.A.	N.A.
10. Textiles	..	6·0	5·6	44·3	42·7
13. Bricks, pottery, glass, etc.	..	8·2	6·6	81·8	78·3
15. Paper, printing, etc. ..	..	3·7	2·7	71·6	65·6
16. Other manufacturing	..	9·1	5·6	69·7	58·7
Total	..	13·4	6·0	83·7	71·5

N.A.=Not Available.

Table 13 shows the industrial coverage of male and female employees in the sample and in the whole of manufacturing industry. In most industries for which a breakdown was available, the percentage coverage of male employees was higher, notably in the three industrial sectors most adequately covered by the sample. The only exception is in shipbuilding, where a higher percentage of female employees was covered; female employees account for only 1½ per cent of the manual labour force in shipbuilding and in the sample less than 2 per cent of shipbuilding employees were female. The sample contained a higher proportion of male employees than manufacturing industry as a whole, 84 per cent as against 72 per cent, and most of the individual industries followed this pattern.

Forty companies in the sample were subsidiaries of U.S. parent companies. The industrial distribution of U.S. and U.K. companies is given in Table 14.

U.S. companies were on average smaller than British companies in the same industry, but not significantly so. Table 14 also shows, for U.S. and British the average yearly wage per employee in each industrial sector. This average wage was calculated by adding up the total amount paid to employees in all companies and dividing by the aggregate October 1960 employed: it is subject to the qualifications noted earlier on the limitations of such average wage figures. The average wage of employees in U.S. companies was significantly higher than the average for all U.K. companies, but this is because the American firms were mostly in high-wage sectors, e.g. chemicals

TABLE 14. *Size and Average Yearly Wages of U.S. and British Companies*

INDUSTRY		NO. OF EMPLOYEES							Total	AVERAGE WAGE £
		UNDER 100	100–250	250–500	500–750	750–1,000	1,000–2,000	OVER 2,000		
Food, etc.	US ..	..		1	2	1	2	1	7	621
	UK ..	1	4	4	2	3	3	3	20	518
Chemicals	US ..	2	2	5				1	10	749
	UK ..	5	6	8	5	1	6	8	39	677
Engineering	US ..	2	4	1	4	2	1	4	18	649
	UK ..	1	11	13	12	10	16	16	79	616
Vehicles	US ..				1	1		3	4	982
	UK ..		1	3	1		1	11	17	756
Whole Sample	US ..	4	6	7	7*	4	3	9	40	859
	UK ..	17	38	62	38	28	54	63	310	661**

Notes: * Includes one U.S. company not given by industry.
** U.K. Average wage figures is for four listed industries.

and vehicles, with none at all in the lowest wage industry, textiles. Including only those industries containing U.S. companies the U.S. companies' average wage was not significantly higher than that of the British.

Table 15 shows the distribution of sample companies according to the standard geographical regions, with the last column containing companies which had establishments in more than one region. Since this enquiry was undertaken by a Scottish university, it is perhaps understandable that Scottish firms should be well represented, and this region contained 21 per cent of sample companies, more than any other region. The last two rows of the Table show that the multi-regional companies tended to be very large; 16 per cent of companies had 37 per cent of sample employment. Companies in the North Midlands and South-West were also large, while those in Scotland, the South and Wales tended to be small; for example, the sample contained 2·3 per cent Welsh companies, but only 0·6 per cent of sample employment was in Welsh firms.

There are regional differences in average yearly wages, but these are probably influenced as much by structural factors as by the geographical. In Scotland, for example, where low average wages would be expected, almost one-third of companies are in the low-wage textile industry, while the North region average wage is very much higher because of the number of companies in relatively high-wage sectors such as metal manufacture, shipbuilding and chemicals.

III. THE RESULTS

238 companies, or just over two-thirds of those covered, had an expenditure on fringe benefits of between $7\frac{1}{2}$ and 15 per cent of payroll. Fringe benefit expenditure amounted to more than 20 per cent of payroll in only 44 of the 350 companies. As might be expected, there were considerable differences in the industrial distribution of total fringe benefit costs. The food industry had a higher average expenditure than the rest of the sample, with $t=4·79$ $(t_5\%=1·65)$, and the food and chemical industries were the only ones in which any company spent more than 30 per cent of payroll. On the other hand, the two heavy industrial sectors, metal manufacture and shipbuilding had an average expenditure significantly lower than average, with $t=7·45$ and $10·34$ respectively. (See Table 16.)

The measure of employment size used in Table 17 does not allow any definite conclusions to be reached on the relationship between the cost of fringe benefits and the numbers employed, since in some cases whole firms are represented, in others only establishments. An

TABLE 15. *Regional Distribution of Company Sample*

INDUSTRY	NORTH	E. AND W. RIDINGS	NORTH MIDLAND	EAST	LONDON AND S.E.	SOUTH	SOUTH WEST	WALES	MIDLAND	NORTH WEST	SCOTLAND	VARIOUS	Total
Food ..	1	1		3		2		1	3	5	8	3	27
Chemicals ..	4	5	2	3	6	2	2	1	1	8	6	9	49
Metal manufacture	8	3	1		3			1	2	1	4	4	27
Engineering ..	3	7	4	4	12	5	2	2	11	16	15	16	97
Shipbuilding ..	6							1			7		14
Vehicles ..		1	1	1	3		3		4	2	1	5	21
Other metal ..	1	1			3			1	4		1	2	12
Textiles ..	1	7	3		1	2	2		2	8	22	3	49
Bricks, etc. ..				2				1	1	2	3	4	14
Paper, etc. ..				2	1	1			1	1	4	4	14
Other manufacturing		1			3		2		1	4	2	2	14
Construction ..										1		4	5
Other ..	2				3	1							7
No. of companies	26	26	11	15	35	11	11	8	30	48	73	56	350
Per cent of sample companies ..	7·4	7·4	3·1	4·3	10·0	3·1	3·1	2·3	8·6	13·7	20·9	16·0	100
Per cent of sample employment ..	5·6	5·9	2·5	4·8	9·4	1·3	3·2	0·6	6·7	11·3	11·4	37·3	100

TABLE 16. Distribution by Industry of Total Fringe Benefit Expenditure: per cent of total payroll

INDUSTRIAL GROUP	0–5	5–7½	7½–10	10–12½	12½–15	15–17½	17½–20	20–25	25–30	30–35	35–40	40+	N.A.	COMPANIES NO.	COMPANIES %
3. Food, drink, tobacco			1	1	3	4	6	5	3	2		2		27	7·7
4. Chemicals			3	7	12	3	7	5	6	3	1	2		49	14·0
5. Metal manufacture		2	13	10	1									27	7·7
6. Engineering & electrical		2	21	34	18	10	6	1	2				3	97	27·7
7. Shipbuilding			10	4										14	4·0
8. Vehicles & aircraft		2	5	8	2	3	1	2						21	6·0
9. Other metal goods			4	5	2		1	1						12	3·4
10. Textiles			5	18	17	3	2	2	1				1	49	14·0
13. Bricks, pottery, glass, etc.			2	7	3		2							14	4·0
15. Paper, etc.		1	1	4	3	2	1	2	1					14	4·0
16. Other manufacturing			5	4	2	1		2						14	4·0
17. Construction		2		2		1								5	1·4
Other¹			1	3			2	1						7	2·0
No. of companies	—	8	71	107	61	27	28	21	13	5	1	4	4	350	
Per cent of companies	—	2·3	20·3	30·6	17·4	7·7	8·0	6·0	3·7	1·4	0·3	1·1	1·1		100

¹ Includes one company from 'Mining (other than coal)'.

TABLE 17. Total Fringe Benefit Expenditure and Size of Company

FRINGE BENEFIT EXPENDITURE: % OF TOTAL PAYROLL	NO. OF EMPLOYEES											Total
	LESS THAN 100	100–250	250–500	500–750	750–1,000	1,000–2,000	2,000–3,000	3,000–4,000	4,000–5,000	5,000–10,000	10,000 AND OVER	
0 – 5												—
5 – 7½	1	1	1		2	1				1	1	8
7½–10	4	8	13	10	5	12	5	6	1	4	7	71
10 –12½	5	12	25	11	12	17	10	1	3	7		107
12½–15	3	10	11	11	5	11	2	5	3			61
15 –17½	3	4	6	5	1	1	1	3		3		27
17½–20	1	3	3	4	3	6	4			3	1	28
20 –25	2	3	4	1	3	3	2		1	2		21
25 –30		2	3			5	2		1			13
30 –35	2		1	1			1					5
35 –40						1						1
40 –50			1		1				1		1	4
Not Available		1	1	2								4
TOTAL	21	44	69	45	32	57	27	15	10	20	10	350

establishment shown in the sample as employing only a few hundred employees could be part of a company employing many thousands, so that any relationship between size of firm and the cost of fringe benefits might be concealed or distorted. Table 17 must therefore be interpreted with caution, but the sample information can hardly support the conclusion reached by other enquiries both in Britain and overseas that large firms spend more on fringe benefits than small firms,[1] since the correlation coefficient (which was not significant) was $r=0\cdot06$ $(r^2=\cdot004)$. However this sample included very few companies with under fifty employees and almost all the sample were 'large' companies compared with the average size of British undertakings. It is difficult to estimate what the level of fringe benefits might be in these very small companies. On the one hand, they might be paternalistic and so tend to spend a relatively large amount on employee welfare, while on the other hand they might be so small as to find it unecomonic to introduce all the voluntary welfare facilities which larger companies have. If this latter view is correct and if the very small companies unrepresented in the sample are below the limit at which most fringe benefits are desirable or even necessary, there might be a significant correlation between employment size and expenditure on fringe benefits.

Table 18 shows the distribution of sample companies classified by average wages and total fringe benefits as a percentage of payroll. Here the correlation coefficient was $r=-0\cdot11$ $(r^2=0\cdot01)$ significant at the 5 per cent level; there was therefore hardly any tendency for high-wage companies to spend less as a percentage of payroll on fringe benefits than did low-wage companies. It would be surprising for such an inverse relationship to exist for the level of wages must have a considerable effect on the percentage of payroll expenditure on fringe benefits. If average earnings are high, fixed charges such as National Insurance will be proportionately lower, and this also applies to other costs not directly related to earnings. Holiday pay based on the wage-rate rather than earnings will form a lower percentage of payroll the more overtime and bonuses are paid, and to the extent that average earnings are high because of considerable overtime working, the level of fringe benefits will be understated.[2] The textile industry, for example, had a much lower wage level, and this was the major factor in raising the percentage of payroll figures of most

[1] See, for example, W. Durham, *The £.S.D. of Welfare in Industry*, I.W.S., 1959; and 'Supplementary Remuneration for Factory Worker, 1959', *Monthly Labor Review*, January 1962; and U.S. Dept. of Labor, Bureau of Labor Statistics, Bulletin No. 1308, 1962.

[2] In the sample, there was no trace of such an inverse relationship between holiday pay and overtime premium pay, but the statistics of the latter were most uncertain.

TABLE 18. Average Wages and Expenditure on Fringe Benefits as Percentage of Payroll

FRINGE BENEFITS % OF PAYROLL	AVERAGE WAGE £									Total
	200–300	300–400	400–500	500–600	600–700	700–800	800–900	900–1,000	NOT AVAILABLE	
5 – 7½				1	2		2	2	1	8
7½ 10			8	16	24	11	8	2	2	71
10 –12½	2	6	21	26	38	8	4	1	1	107
12½ –15	1	7	16	15	16	3	2	1		61
15 –17½		6	3	7	5	5	1			27
17½ –20		3	5	8	4	5	2		1	28
20 –25	2	3	5	4	3	4				21
25 –30		1	3	4	1	3			1	13
30 –35		2		1	1	1				5
35 –40						1				1
40 –50			1			3				4
Not Available									4	4
TOTAL	5	28	62	82	94	44	19	6	10	350

TABLE 19. *Distribution by Industry of Total Fringe Benefit Expenditure: £ per employee*

INDUSTRY	25-50	50-75	75-100	100-125	125-150	150-175	175-200	200-225	225-250	250 AND OVER	N.A.	COMPANIES NO.	%
3. Food, drink, etc.		6	4	8	4	2				3		27	7·7
4. Chemicals		8	12	12	1	5	4	1	1	3	2	49	14·0
5. Metal manufacture	1	13	9	2	1						1	27	7·7
6. Engineering	8	45	22	11	4	2	1		1		3	97	27·7
7. Shipbuilding	2	8	4									14	4·0
8. Vehicles & aircraft	1	7	9	3		1	1					21	6·0
9. Other metal goods	2	6	3		1	1						12	3·4
10. Textiles	17	20	7		1						4	49	14·0
13. Bricks, etc.	1	6	5			2						14	4·0
15. Paper, printing, etc.		2	6	3			1					14	4·0
16. Other manufacturing	2	8	4	1								14	4·0
17. Construction	1	1	2	1	1							5	1·4
Others		3	1								1	7	2·0
No. of Co's.	35	133	88	41	13	13	7	1	2	6	11	350	
% of Co's.	10·0	38·0	25·1	11·7	3·7	3·7	2·1	0·3	0·6	1·8	3·2		100

establishments. This can be seen from Table 19 which shows the industrial distribution of fringe benefits expenditure in terms of pounds spent per employee.

The textile industry spent less money per employee on fringe benefits than any other industry and its average expenditure of £58 per employee was significantly less than that of the rest of the sample ($t=7\cdot99$, where $t_5\%=1\cdot65$). However differences in industry average wage do not explain the low level of fringe benefit expenditure as a percentage of payroll in shipbuilding and metal manufacture. Though both paid high average wages, they spent on average a significantly smaller than average amount per employee on fringe benefits: in shipbuilding $t=4\cdot31$ and in metal manufacture $t=2\cdot27$, where $t_5\%=1\cdot65$. Similarly, the two industries previously noted as having high expenditure as a percentage of payroll, food and chemicals, had a significantly higher average expenditure per employee than the rest of the sample, with $t=2\cdot96$ and $4\cdot62$ respectively.

Given these differences between industries, it is interesting to speculate on the reasons for variations within each industry. One hypothesis is that 'in a single industry pay and fringe benefits would tend to compensate for each other so that a job carrying more pay would carry fewer or less valuable fringe benefits'.[1] But to prove this hypothesis by using employer cost statistics we would need to assume that the employee benefit is equal or proportional to employer cost, and for most types of benefit this assumption is unjustified. Another hypothesis would suggest that companies which pay high wages can also afford to spend a relatively larger amount on fringe benefits. Table 20 shows the relationship between average wages and fringe benefits per employee. Here the correlation coefficient $r=0.37$ ($r^2=0\cdot14$) and is significant at the one per cent level. High-wage companies therefore tend to spend *more* on fringe benefits in pounds per employee than low-wage companies.

Related to this 'ability to pay' argument is the idea that the proportion of total costs formed by labour costs plays a large part in determining differences in fringe benefits expenditure: the less important are labour costs, the more likely is a firm to pay high wages and to spend more on fringe benefits. If this relationship applied throughout the whole sample, firms in capital-intensive industries would tend to spend more on fringe benefits than those in labour-intensive industries. Table 20 shows that this is not the case as far as this sample is concerned.

[1] *A Survey of Large Companies*, Institute of Economic Affairs, 1959, p. 25.

TABLE 20. *Average Wages and Fringe Benefits per Employee: Manufacturing Industry*

FRINGE BENEFITS £	AVERAGE WAGE £								NOT AVAILABLE	Total
	200–300	300–400	400–500	500–600	600–700	700–800	800–900	900–1,000		
0–25										—
25– 50	3	11	12	6	3					35
50– 75	2	8	34	35	34	10	5	1		129
75–100		5	3	19	38	10	7	2		84
100–125		4	7	10	9	6	1	1		38
125–150			2	3	3	2	1	1		12
150–175				4	2	7				13
175–200			2	1	1	1	2			7
200–225					1					1
225–250						2				2
Over 250						6				6
Not Available			2	3		2	1		3	11
TOTAL	5	28	62	81	91	46	17	5	3	336

TABLE 21. *Inter-industry comparison of Average Wages, Supplementary Labour Costs, and the Importance of Labour Costs in Production*

INDUSTRY	A WAGES AND SALARIES % OF GROSS OUTPUT	1 RANKS ACCORDING TO COL. A LOWEST=1	2 RANKS ACCORDING TO AVERAGE WAGE	3 RANKS ACCORDING TO SUPP. LABOUR COSTS £ PER EMPLOYEE	4 RANKS ACCORDING TO TOTAL LABOUR COSTS COLS. 2+3
3. Food, drink, tobacco	8·61	1	10	2	9
4. Chemicals and allied	12·59	2	4	1	3
5. Metal manufacture	16·49	3	2	7	2
6. Engineering & electrical	30·48	10	7	6	7
7. Shipbuilding	35·02	11	3	9	5
8. Vehicles and aircraft	23·87	6	1	4	1
9. Other metal goods	21·52	5	8	8	8
10. Textiles	20·01	4	11	11	11
13. Bricks, pottery, glass, etc.	29·56	9	5	5	6
15. Paper, printing, etc.	26·84	8	6	3	4
16. Other manufacturing	24·56	7	9	10	10

Source: Col. A and 1 from *Census of Production* for 1958 (Summary tables).

E

In Table 21, each industrial sector is ranked with respect to the following:

1. wages/salaries as a proportion of total costs:
2. average yearly fringe benefits expenditure, pounds per employee:
3. average yearly wage per employee:
4. average yearly amount spent per employee, wages plus fringe benefits expenditure.

If the hypothesis were correct, we would expect the rank difference correlation coefficient between 1 and 2 to be high. In fact it is $0 \cdot 31$, though the two industries which are least labour intensive, food and chemicals, did have the highest level of fringe benefits expenditure. But if the importance of wage costs relative to total costs were the determining factor, it would also help to explain inter-industry differences both in wages and in the total amount spent on labour, which companies would attempt to minimize. That is, there should also be a high correlation between 1 and 3 and between 1 and 4; in fact these rank difference correlation coefficients are very small, with $r = -0 \cdot 21$ and $-0 \cdot 01$ respectively. It might be argued that certain fringe benefits are more easily adjusted by the individual employer than wages which may be subject to collective bargaining, and the greater degree of control over this sector of labour costs might lead to a high correlation between the labour-cost/total-cost ratio and fringe benefit expenditure with a simultaneous low correlation between this ratio and wages. But at the industry level, the effect should be minimized, and in any case the important and costly items of fringe benefits, National Insurance and holiday pay, are partly outside the employer's control.

While inter-industry differences in fringe benefits expenditure are apparently not explained by differences in the labour-cost/total-cost ratio, this might be important at a less aggregative level, in smaller industry groups.[1] Equally, differences between firms in the same industry might depend to some extent on the relative importance of labour costs or of a related measure, the capital employed per man. Unfortunately it was not possible to obtain figures of capital employed for most of the sample companies because of the existence of private companies and the large number of returns referring only to a part of a public company. It is certainly likely that the impact of labour costs on total costs will affect a company's willingness to give expensive concessions on either fringe benefits or wages, but the sample information offers no proof.

A full explanation of what determines company fringe benefits would therefore have to consider the combined importance of the following variables: size of company, industry, average wage, capital

---

[1] At this level, we would expect a greater degree of homogeneity, and fewer of the structural differences which complicate inter-industry comparisons.

per employee. The tests already described suggest that if a regression equation could be derived, it would show that the industry in which a company operated was the most important determinant while within industries average wage would have a higher coefficient than size. It is almost certainly true that there would be a sizeable constant term, and that the variables listed above would have only limited success in explaining fringe benefits expenditure, since they do not take into account the variations in the institutional framework and in company outlook which may lead firms in apparently identical situations to follow completely different welfare policies.

This is what a regression equation might have shown but for several reasons it was decided not to attempt estimation of the co-efficients attaching to these variables. First, the effect of industry was already evident from the t tests, and the correlation of fringe benefits expenditure individually with size and average wage suggested that a multiple correlation would result in low coefficients. Secondly, it was not possible to obtain figures of capital per employee for firms within each industry and this would be an important variable. Thirdly, the estimation of the coefficients would be complicated by the interdependence of the variables. We have already noted the effect of industry on average wage, and there was in this sample a positive correlation between size and average wage ($r=0\cdot53$, $r^2=0\cdot29$). The intercorrelation between the variables could mean that the coefficients were subject to considerable error; though we could correct for these intercorrelations, it is questionable whether the quality of the data warrants this. For these reasons, then, the multiple correlation using three variables was not computed.

Table 22 shows the distribution of sample companies by industry and according to their annual total labour costs per employee, i.e. average wage plus fringe benefits expenditure.[1]

The highest level of total labour costs was in the vehicles industry, significantly higher than the average for the remainder of the sample ($t=4\cdot5$, where $t_5\%=1\cdot65$). In the steel industry, the high wages were enough to make up for the low figure of fringe benefits per employee, and total labour costs per employee were significantly higher than the rest of the sample ($t=5\cdot73$). The textile industry figure was once again significantly lower ($t=14\cdot78$). It is interesting to see that, at this very broad aggregative level, the addition of supplementary labour costs or fringe benefits to average wages has comparatively little effect on the inter-industry cost structure: the rank difference correlation coefficient between industry ranks for average wages and

---

[1] This definition of total labour costs may exclude certain items which some companies might consider to be labour costs. See Introduction, Section III.

TABLE 22. *Annual Total Labour Costs per Employee*

INDUSTRY	TOTAL LABOUR COSTS £											AVERAGE TOTAL LABOUR COST	WAGE
	300–400	400–500	500–600	600–700	700–800	800–900	900–1,000	1,000–1,100	1,100–1,200	NOT AVAILABLE	Total		
3. Food, etc. ..		7	5	7	5		6	1	2	2	27	645	516
4. Chemicals ..		4	4	8	15	5	1	2	1	1	49	749	618
5. Metal manuf.		1		4	13	7	3	2			27	788	706
6. Engineering	1	5	20	32	23	7	1			6	97	658	589
7. Shipbuilding			1	6	4	2					14	718	643
8. Vehicles ..		1		3	6	5	4	2			21	818	732
9. Other metal goods ..		3	1	3	3	1		1			12	667	592
10. Textiles ..	8	22	13	3						3	49	477	417
13. Bricks, etc. ..			4	5	2	2	1				14	693	614
15. Paper, etc. ..			2	7	1	3		1			14	721	610
16. Other manfg.	3	3	1	3	1	3					14	593	529
17. Construction				1	1	1	1				5	768	850
Other ..			1	4			1	1		1	7	608	699
No. of Co's.	12	46	52	86	74	36	18	10	3	13	350		
% of Co's. ..	3·4	13·1	14·9	24·6	21·1	10·3	5·1	2·9	0·9	3·7	100		

total labour costs is $0·95$.[1] There is one noticeable difference though. The very high level of fringe benefit expenditure in the chemical industry meant that average total labour cost per employee was significantly higher than the sample average ($t=1·73$ where $t_5\%=1·65$), though the average wage in that industry was not.

To summarize our conclusions so far on what determined the amount of expenditure on fringe benefits in our sample companies:

(1) There were considerable differences between industries which were not explained by variations in the labour-cost/total-cost ratio, though this may be important in intra-industry comparisons.

(2) Companies which paid high wages tended to spend more on fringe benefits.

(3) There was no significant relationship between size of company and expenditure on fringe benefits, though the absence of very small companies makes this an incomplete conclusion.

There are two other factors on which the questionnaire yielded information:

(4) There were wide variations in regional fringe benefit expenditure per employee. The Southern region was highest (at £135 per employee, almost twice as high as the figure for Wales), with companies in the Eastern region and those in more than one region also having an average expenditure of over £100 per employee. Once again, however, this seems mainly to have been due to the different industrial composition of the regions; the East and South each had a relatively large proportion of companies in the chemical and food industries, which both had high fringe benefits, and no companies in the low sectors, metal manufacture and shipbuilding.

(5) Table 23 shows the expenditure on fringe benefits of U.S. and British companies in the food, chemicals, engineering, and vehicles and aircraft industries.

The average expenditure on fringe benefits by the U.S. companies was significantly higher than the British average for those industries ($t=1·70$ where $t_5\%=1·65$), and the same was true within the food, chemical and engineering industries.

A separate part of the enquiry covered certain nationalized industries. This showed that their expenditure on fringe benefits, as a percentage of payroll, was considerably higher than the company sample average. In fact, the three industries covered had a higher expenditure than 75 per cent of the companies. As might be expected from the generous provisions of the public service schemes, pensions and sick pay cost considerably more than the private industry averages.

---

[1] In this respect British and European statistics reach the same conclusion. See Chapter IV, Section III, Part I.

TABLE 23. *Average Expenditure on Fringe Benefits of U.S. and British Companies*

INDUSTRY		25–50	50–75	75–100	100–125	125–150	150–175	175–200	200–225	225–250	OVER 250	NOT AVAILABLE	Total
Food, etc.	US		1		3		2				1		7
	UK		5	4	5	4						2		20
Chemicals	US			2	2		3	1			1	1	9
	UK		8	10	10	1	2	3	1	1	2		38
Eng'ng	US		9	1	4	2	1					1	17
	UK	8	36	21	7	2	1	1		1		2	77
Vehicles	US	1		2				1					4
	UK		7	7	3								17
Total	US	1	10	5	9	3	6	2			1	2	40
	UK1	8	56	42	25	7	3	4	1	2	4	2	154
	UK2	34	123	83	32	10	7	5	1	2	4	9	310

U.K.1 = UK companies in food, chemicals, engineering and vehicles.
U.K.2 = All U.K. companies.

IV

It is, of course, important to analyse not only aggregate cost data, but also the distribution of expenditure between items. The data were collected in six broad groups:[1]

B—Holiday Pay
C—Pension Plan
D—National Insurance
E—Education
F—Other Payments:
     i Sick pay
     ii Long service payments
     iii Redundancy payments
     iv Ex gratia pensions
     v Insurance schemes
     vi Medical services
     vii Seasonal bonus
G—Other Welfare Benefits:
     i Housing
     ii Travel
     iii Clothing
     iv Canteen facilities
     v Sports or social facilities
     vi Discounts on products
     vii Profit sharing
     viii Other expenditure

Table 24 shows the distribution of expenditure on these six groups incurred by the sample companies, together with the modal ranges. For holiday pay and National Insurance the range of payment was, as expected, rather narrower than that of discretionary payments. The table shows that of the 222 firms reporting expenditure on pension schemes, 50 spent more than 3 per cent of payroll. Contrasting with this was the low average expenditure on education with over two-thirds of companies spending less than one per cent of payroll. This may be partly explained by the definition of education which left more to the discretion of the individual respondent on what should be included than did most other questions. But even with this qualification, expenditure still seems low. For the categories 'Other Payments' and 'Other Welfare Benefits' there was much variation since these each contain a number of different items, but more than half of the respondents spent less than 1 per cent of payroll on the labour cost items in these two categories. In terms of modal ranges, for each of the main cost items, at least two-thirds of the companies fell within a range of not more than 2 per cent.

[1] There were originally seven groups, but overtime premium pay statistics were not suitable for tabulation.

TABLE 24. *Major Elements of Supplementary Labour Cost as Percentage of Payroll, with Modal Ranges*

	% OF PAYROLL												N.A.	RANGE % OF PAYROLL	NO. OF FIRMS	% OF TOTAL
	0	0·01–0·99	1·00–1·99	2·00–2·99	3·00–3·99	4·00–4·99	5·00–5·99	6·00–6·99	7·00–7·99	8·00–8·99	9·00–9·99	10 AND OVER				
Holiday pay	—	—	1	12	51	136	100	38	5	1	—	—	6	4–5·99	236	67·3
Pension plan	125	76	60	36	17	9	11	2	4	1	—	6	3	0–1·99	261	74·5
National Ins.	—	—	4	122	152	44	10	3	3	—	—	—	12	2–3·99	274	78·3
Education	65	202	40	13	8	2	1	2	1	—	—	—	16	0–0·99	267	76·3
Other payments	7	173	71	32	22	9	13	2	3	2	1	8	—	0–1·99	244	69·7
Other welfare benefits	12	159	63	45	20	19	6	10	6	5	1	7	2	0–1·99	234	66·9

TABLE 25. Companies incurring Expenditure on Each Benefit: Percentage of Total Number of Companies in Each Industry

	FOOD, DRINK, ETC.	CHEM.	METAL MANFG.	ENG.	SHIP-BUIL'NG	VEHICLES	OTHER METAL GOODS	TEXTILES	BRICKS, ETC.	PAPER	OTHER MANFG.	CON.	ALL INDUS-TRIES	ARITHMETIC MEAN AS % OF PAYROLL OF ALL COMPANIES	ARITHMETIC MEAN AS % OF PAYROLL OF ALL COMPANIES REPORTING EXPEN'TURE
2. Holiday pay	100	100	100	100	100	100	100	100	100	100	100	100	100	4·80	4·80
3. Sick pay	93	84	11	40	—	38	8	31	36	64	50	60	45	0·32	0·78
4. Pension plan	85	84	56	65	14	67	58	32	71	100	78	60	64	1·50	2·42
5. Ex gratia pensions	74	49	41	53	43	52	67	47	86	78	78	40	55	0·35	0·64
6. Long service	56	51	56	55	57	62	50	51	64	50	57	60	52	0·10	0·19
7. National Insurance	100	100	100	100	100	100	100	100	100	100	100	100	100	3·39	3·39
8 i. Insurance	30	39	15	37	14	62	8	8	36	64	57	20	32	0·08	0·29
8ii. Medical services	81	98	89	97	100	100	83	84	78	100	100	100	93	0·36	0·39
9. Education	70	76	85	89	100	100	75	78	78	100	64	80	85	0·62	0·77
10. Redundancy	19	24	11	20	14	52	9	8	21	21	14	20	19	0·03	0·15
11. Seasonal bonus	63	31	15	21	21	14	33	27	36	64	21	20	27	0·62	2·31
12. Housing	15	16	11	21	7	19	8	24	43	29	14	20	19	0·11	0·63
13. Travel	26	31	11	23	14	48	25	32	29	21	43	60	27	0·16	0·63
14. Clothing	93	100	70	67	43	90	58	41	78	78	78	100	72	0·35	0·50
15. Canteen	85	94	89	93	93	100	83	92	86	100	93	80	92	0·96	1·06
16. Sports/social facilities	70	57	67	70	93	86	50	27	64	78	64	40	62	0·15	0·25
17. Discounts	22	29	—	18	—	14	8	8	14	—	21	—	15	0·04	0·48
18. Profit sharing	7	27	—	8	—	10	8	4	14	21	7	—	10	0·30	1·95
19. Other	26	49	15	21	21	19	33	14	21	50	14	—	25	0·11	0·49

Table 25 shows the proportion of companies in each industry group reporting expenditure on each cost item, together with the average expenditure on each.[1] It is interesting to note that in 1960 almost two-thirds of the companies operated pension schemes for their manual workers, at an average cost of $1 \cdot 50$ per cent of payroll; this survey was carried out before the institution of the Government graduated pension scheme, and several respondents who had no schemes in 1960 mentioned that they would begin to operate a pension plan in 1961.[2] 55 per cent of companies paid ex gratia pensions to their former employees. In many cases this expenditure was additional to that of a pension plan, but the amount of the payments was much smaller, the average for companies reporting this expenditure being $0 \cdot 64$ per cent of payroll. Just over half the companies made some award or payment to long service employees during 1960.

Of the 'classical' fringe benefits, subsidized housing was least popular with less than 20 per cent of companies incurring such expenditure in 1960. At the other extreme, more than 90 per cent spent something on a works canteen, with the surprisingly high average expenditure of $1 \cdot 06$ per cent of payroll. About 60 per cent spent a much smaller amount, on average ($0 \cdot 25$ per cent) on sports and for social facilities for employees. The item least often reported was the cost of discounts on products sold to employees. Profit-sharing schemes were present in 34 companies, which seems a larger proportion than might be expected in a sample of 350 companies.[3] The average expenditure of firms operating a profit-sharing scheme was $1 \cdot 95$ per cent.

The 'security benefits' other than pensions, i.e. sick pay and redundancy payments, are among the most important from the point of view of the employee. About 45 per cent of companies made some payment as a continuation of wages to employees who were off sick, the average payment being 0.78 per cent of payroll, while about a fifth incurred expenditure on redundancy payments. The form of the questions cannot reveal how many of the latter payments were made under a definite scheme. In most cases the average payment per redundant employee was less than £20, as the low average expenditure of $0 \cdot 15$ per cent of payroll might suggest. In a few cases, the redundancy seemed to involve some permanent contraction in the labour force, with an average payment of £85 or more indicating that

---

[1] In Tables 25 and 26, companies reporting expenditure as 'Not Available' were considered as having undertaken expenditure.

[2] It may of course also be true that some schemes were abandoned if companies decided to contract in.

[3] A Ministry of Labour survey in 1954 (reported in the Ministry of Labour *Gazette*, May 1956) showed that profit-sharing schemes were in operation in 408 undertakings.

longer-service employees were being paid off, though in almost all cases the number of employees receiving redundancy payments was less than 2 per cent of the labour force at October 1960.

The proportion of companies incurring expenditure on individual items differed noticeably from industry to industry. The food and chemical industries were outstanding in that for almost every benefit the proportion of companies incurring expenditure was higher than that for the sample as a whole. For example, sick pay and pensions were provided by over 80 per cent of companies in those industries, compared with 45 per cent and 64 per cent for the whole sample. Printing was also well above the sample average, again notably for sick pay and pensions and also for social and welfare facilities. The vehicle and other manufacturing industries were generally above average in the extent of fringe benefits, with certain exceptions such as sick pay in vehicles (38 per cent against the sample average of 45 per cent) and education in other manufacturing (64 per cent against 85 per cent). At the other end of the scale were metal manufacture and textiles both below average in the proportion of companies reporting expenditure. Shipbuilding and other metal goods were also in this category, the former industry containing no companies with sick pay schemes and only two (out of fourteen) with a pension plan.

For sick pay and pensions, it is of more interest to know the numbers employed in the firms providing the schemes rather than merely the number of firms themselves. Table 26 shows the employment in the firms with such schemes, as a percentage of the total sample employment. In most cases, the proportion of employees covered was higher than the proportion of companies incurring expenditure, indicating that the companies reporting expenditure tended to be large. The outstanding exception was sick pay in metal manufacture, which was obviously given only by small companies. However, the figures in Columns 2 and 4 of Table 26 do not indicate the proportion of employees who would actually receive benefit, since some would not. be eligible or qualified or might choose not to take part. Column 5 of Table 26 shows the proportion of employees actually covered in those companies with pension schemes; there was considerable variation between industries, with the figure for all manufacturing industry being almost 70 per cent. If we include those companies without pension schemes, the percentage of employees covered is of course lower, and in the whole of the manufacturing sample, an estimated 54 per cent of employees were members of pension schemes (Column 6).

Although no well-defined relationship was found between fringe benefit expenditure and size, it may be that it was the probability of expenditure rather than expenditure itself which increased with size.

TABLE 26. *Employment in Companies with Sick Pay and Pension Schemes*

INDUSTRY	SICK PAY		PENSIONS			
	1 COMPANIES WITH SCHEMES AS % OF TOTAL COMPANIES	2 EMPLOYMENT IN THESE COMPANIES AS % OF TOTAL EMPLOYMENT	3 COMPANIES WITH SCHEMES AS % OF TOTAL COMPANIES	4 EMPLOYMENT IN THESE COMPANIES AS % OF TOTAL EMPLOYMENT	5 % OF EMPLOYMENT COVERED BY PENSION SCHEMES IN COMPANIES WITH SCHEMES	6 % OF EMPLOYMENT COVERED BY PENSION SCHEMES IN ALL COMPANIES (ESTIMATED)
3. Food, drink, tobacco	93	97·3	85	96·8	59·0	57·1
4. Chemicals	84	96·7	84	99·0	82·9	96·9
5. Metal manufacture	11	1·0	56	86·1	69·1	59·5
6. Engineering	40	38·9	65	66·3	53·6	35·5
7. Shipbuilding	—	—	14	11·2	58·1	6·5
8. Vehicles	38	58·8	67	81·3	81·5	66·3
9. Other metal goods	8	3·5	58	80·1	54·6	43·7
10. Textiles	31	34·0	32	40·0	40·6	16·2
13. Bricks, etc.	36	69·2	71	86·6	67·9	58·8
15. Printing, etc.	64	71·5	100	100	45·3	45·3
16. Other manufacturing	50	34·1	78	98·7	51·6	50·9
TOTAL MANUFACTURING	44	48·5	63	78·1	69·7	54·5
17. Construction	60	86·7	60	86·7	19·6	17·0

TABLE 27. *Companies incurring Expenditure on Each Benefit, as a Percentage of Total Number of Companies in each Size Group*

| | | | | | | NO. OF EMPLOYEES | | | | | | |
| | | | | | | 000 | | | | | | |
	LESS THAN 100	100–250	250–500	500–750	750–1,000	1–2	2–3	3–4	4–5	5–10	10+	ALL SIZES
2. Holiday pay	100	100	100	100	100	100	100	100	100	100	100	100
3. Sick pay	62	41	49	42	31	47	63	40	50	25	50	45
4. Pension plan	43	41	62	58	72	77	74	73	50	70	90	64
5. Ex gratia pensions	33	38	62	51	53	67	59	73	60	50	80	55
6. Long service	19	28	46	51	50	60	63	80	70	70	100	52
7. National Insurance	100	100	100	100	100	100	100	100	100	100	100	100
8 i. Insurance	14	18	34	27	25	28	22	60	50	55	80	32
8 ii. Medical services	67	77	90	98	97	100	100	93	100	100	100	93
9. Education	24	70	75	87	91	88	96	93	100	100	100	85
10. Redundancy	14	5	17	24	16	17	19	33	40	30	60	19
11. Seasonal bonus	43	41	33	27	28	23	19	20	10	20	—	27
12. Housing	14	14	16	16	25	16	22	26	30	25	60	19
13. Travel	19	20	30	24	28	17	33	33	50	50	30	27
14. Clothing	18	52	67	78	66	81	81	80	60	95	60	72
15. Canteen	62	75	90	91	93	98	100	100	100	95	100	92
16. Sports/social facilities	10	29	55	58	62	72	85	93	80	100	100	62
17. Discounts	19	20	17	9	9	17	4	6	10	10	30	15
18. Profit sharing	15	4	14	4	—	12	15	—	10	10	30	10
19. Other	48	25	30	11	13	26	26	20	20	20	60	25

Table 27 shows that within limits this was true. For most items, a lower proportion of very small companies reported expenditure; in the higher size groups (sometimes over 250 employees, sometimes over 500) the proportion of companies incurring expenditure was consistently higher than in the lowest size group. The relationship did not progress with size; that is, very large companies were not more likely to spend money on each individual item than large companies, perhaps indicating that there tended to be economies of scale in the provision of many welfare benefits. For some items, the relationship did not appear to hold, e.g. sick pay. This may be partly explained by the very high proportion of food and chemical industry companies giving sick pay, many of them small companies, and the relative infrequency of sick pay in the large-company industries, metal manufacture and shipbuilding. Table 27, however, suggests that even in the food and chemical industries, very small companies were less likely to give sick pay. In the food industry, the 7 per cent of companies not giving sick pay employed only 2·7 per cent of the workers, while the 16 per cent not incurring expenditure in the chemical industry had only 3·3 per cent of the employees. There were certain differences between the numbers of U.S. and British companies giving each benefit. The U.S. companies were better as far as sick pay and pension plan were concerned, but comparatively few U.S. companies paid ex gratia pensions or made long service payments, presumably a reflection of the relatively recent origin of most of these companies.

V. DISCUSSION

The most important single fact which emerges from the enquiry is the surprisingly low level of fringe benefit expenditure in British industry. The fact that two-thirds of the companies spent between 7½ and 15 per cent of payroll is slightly misleading, since there is a lower limit below which supplementary labour costs are most unlikely to fall. All companies must pay a National Insurance contribution on behalf of each employee, and this will normally amount to 2–4 per cent of payroll.[1] (See Table 21.) Also every firm makes payment to its employees for annual and public holidays amounting generally to three weeks' pay for full-time employees. Table 24 shows that in the sample, holiday pay usually fell between 4 and 6 per cent of payroll, so that every company was more or less obliged to undertake expenditure amounting to 6–10 per cent of payroll. The level of *purely discretionary* payment was therefore low, and this is all the more

---

[1] It may be less if a company employs a large number of married women who do not pay a full contribution.

remarkable, since pensions (a most important discretionary payment) were paid by 225 companies, 172 of these spending up to 3 per cent of payroll on them (the average was 2·42 per cent). This might reduce the range of cost of other discretionary payments in most companies to a very small proportion of payroll.

Before comparing these results with those obtained by earlier surveys of supplementary labour costs, we must estimate the likely bias of the results. The main source is the under-representation of independent private companies and, particularly, small companies. The difficulty of generalizing on the experience of very small companies has already been mentioned. Table 27 suggested that the probability of expenditure on a benefit was lower for small companies (that is, small by sample standards), and it seems likely that the very small companies with less than fifty employees will spend less on fringe benefits than those in the sample. In addition, internal evidence suggests that a fairly large number of the sample companies are leaders in welfare whose expenditure on discretionary payments is likely to be high. These influences all suggest that the average expenditure on fringe benefits of this sample is higher than the average expenditure in the whole of British industry.

For comparative purposes, the bias due to large companies is not serious since the two other enquiries also had few small companies, but there were other differences which make comparison difficult. The Ministry of Labour study for 1955[1] covered only five manufacturing industries, all but one of which were only sectors of an S.I.C. Order. Comparison is therefore possible only for shipbuilding which is included in both enquiries, with a slightly larger number of employees covered in the present study than in the Ministry survey. The total expenditure on supplementary labour costs was very similar, the relevant figures being (Ministry of Labour figures first) 10 per cent of payroll and 2·5 per cent of payroll. There is less similarity in amounts spent on the individual items: the Ministry of Labour figure for National Insurance is 2·6 per cent against 3·2 per cent, that for time paid for but not worked 6·0 per cent against 4·9 per cent.[2] The expenditure for pension schemes was much the same, 0·2 per cent in 1955 and 0·1 per cent in 1960. No conclusions can be drawn from the similarity of the general results, but a later survey of supplementary labour costs carried out by the Industrial Welfare Society and covering fifty-five firms is more revealing.[3] Table 28 shows the estimated cost of various items of

[1] Ministry of Labour *Gazette*, August 1957, pp. 277–80. See Chapter 2.
[2] Time paid for but not worked included holidays, sick leave, and other temporary stoppages.
[3] W. Durham, *The £SD of Welfare in Industry*, I.W.S., 1959. See Chapter 2.

supplementary costs for operatives compared with the average of the sample in the present enquiry.

Considering the differences between the samples and methods of enquiry, the agreement is surprisingly good. It is interesting to note that the I.W.S. enquiry also showed that the level of fringe benefits was

TABLE 28. *Comparison of I.W.S. Survey and Present Enquiry*

| | | % OF TOTAL PAYROLL |
| | I.W.S. CONJECTURAL FIGURE | PRESENT ENQUIRY |
		AVERAGE OF ALL COMPANIES	AVERAGE OF COMPANIES REPORTING EXPENDITURE
Canteens	1·11	0·96	1·06
Sports/Social facilities · ..	0·19	0·15	0·25
Sick pay	0·50	0·32	0·78
Pensions	1·45	1·50	2·42
Holidays	5·20	4·80	4·80
Clothing	0·53	0·35	0·50
National Insurance	2·73	3·39	3·39
TOTAL	11·82[1]	11·47[2]	13·20[2]

[1] Includes Works Magazine costing 0·21%.
[2] Total of listed averages.

highest in the food industry, followed by chemicals, with engineering about average. Heavy engineering was below average, and textiles lowest of all. These rankings compare well with those obtained by the present enquiry.

If one accepts as valid a comparison of the present results with those of the Ministry of Labour in 1955 and I.W.S. in 1958, the conclusion is that fringe benefit expenditure as a percentage of payroll was more or less static: that is, in money terms, it rose at the same pace as earnings. However, it would be dangerous to state this discussion dogmatically; the great differences in the structure of the samples and the obvious bias of each could lead to error. Yet there seems no reason why fringe benefit expenditure should not have increased at this rate. In absolute terms, expenditure undoubtedly increased for several reasons. Between 1955 and 1960 the employers' National Insurance contributions rose, some additional holidays with pay were granted, and the period of high profits and excess demand for labour probably led to the introduction of other welfare facilities, including pension and sick pay schemes. Then, of course, all the goods and services which employers provided for employees must have been more costly in 1960 than in 1955. Average earnings (roughly equal to 'payroll') rose by about 28 per cent between these two dates, and it is not improbable that fringe benefits expenditure also increased at this rate.

There are two issues which should finally be raised, namely the possible effect of supplementary labour costs on total costs, and the cost of fringe benefits for salaried employees. First, what was the impact of supplementary labour costs for manual workers on industrial costs in 1960? Clearly there were considerable differences between firms and industries, but using the data of the enquiry a very rough estimate can be made of the effect on each industrial sector.

Table 29 shows for each Industrial Order gross output less gross profit, which is an approximation to total cost; the share of wages and salaries in total cost; and the share of wages in total cost. The industry averages of fringe benefit expenditure have then been applied to this figure to give the approximate share of supplementary labour costs in total costs. Many assumptions have been made in Table 29 (notably that the 1958 Census of Production data can be used in conjunction with the 1960 fringe benefits data), and the cautions which were stressed in the foregoing discussion have been disregarded, but since the impression is that the enquiry figures were biased upwards, Column 9 of Table 29 may well be a conjectural upper limit on the importance of fringe benefits in terms of total costs.

Table 29 shows that supplementary labour costs were least important in metal manufacturing, food, drink and tobacco and chemicals, despite the high levels of cash expenditure in the latter two industries. Supplementary labour costs were largest as a proportion of total costs in bricks, pottery and glass, paper and printing, and shipbuilding. In no industry did fringe benefits cost more than $3\frac{1}{4}$ per cent of total cost and in most industries the cost is substantially less. The last line of Table 29 gives the average figures for those manufacturing industries covered, and the estimated cost of fringe benefits here was $2 \cdot 15$ per cent of total cost. Column 10 of Table 29 shows the effect of an increase in fringe benefits expenditure of 2 percentage points, the kind of increase which might have resulted from a third week's holiday with pay being granted. The maximum increase in any industry was in shipbuilding, where a 2 per cent increase in supplementary labour costs would have led to an increase of $0 \cdot 6$ per cent in the proportion of total costs formed by supplementary labour costs. In most industries this increase was substantially less, and the average of all industries would have been $0 \cdot 31$ per cent.

These are average figures and in most industries the company spending most on fringe benefits spent about twice the industry average. (See Table 16.) Assuming that these companies had the same wages/total cost ratio as the industry average, their expenditure would be about twice the industry average figures in Column 9. However this assumption on the wages/total cost ratio is hardly justified since it is possible that expenditure on fringe benefits in the 'best' companies is high simply because wage costs (or wages and

F

TABLE 29. *Estimated Importance of Supplementary Labour Costs as a Proportion of Total Costs: Manufacturing Industry*

	1	2	3	4	5	6	7	8	9	10
INDUSTRY	GROSS OUTPUT £M.	GROSS PROFIT £M.	TOTAL COST (1–2) £M.	WAGES AND SALARIES £M.	W. AND S. AS % OF TOTAL COST (4 AS % OF 3)	WAGES AS % OF W. AND S.	WAGES AS % OF TOTAL COST (5×6)/100	SUPPLEMENTARY LABOUR COSTS % OF PAYROLL	% OF TOTAL COST (7×8)/100	S.L.C. AS % OF TOTAL COST AFTER 2% INCREASE
3. Food, drink, tobacco	4263·6	345	3918·6	367·0	9·37	70·81	6·63	21·7	1·44	1·57
4. Chemicals	2309·7	256	2053·7	290·8	14·16	57·73	8·17	19·4	1·59	1·75
5. Metal manufacture	2318·6	213	2105·6	382·3	18·16	78·74	14·30	10·0	1·43	1·72
6. Engineering	3470·3	445	3025·3	1057·6	34·96	64·85	22·67	12·2	2·77	3·22
7. Shipbuilding	496·0	31	465·0	173·7	37·35	82·76	30·91	9·5	2·94	3·55
8. Vehicles and aircraft	2233·0	175	2058·0	533·0	25·90	72·25	18·71	12·3	2·30	2·67
9. Other metal goods	1183·6	112	1071·6	254·7	23·77	72·20	19·40	11·8	2·29	2·68
10. Textiles	1882·6	126	1756·6	376·8	21·45	81·62	16·45	13·3	2·19	2·51
13. Bricks, etc.	591·7	73	518·7	174·9	33·72	76·70	25·86	12·5	3·23	3·75
15. Paper, printing, etc.	1255·7	138	1117·7	337·0	30·15	68·04	20·51	15·6	3·20	3·61
16. Other manufactures	543·1	46	497·1	133·4	26·84	70·37	18·89	12·7	2·40	2·78
all above industries	20547·9	1960	18587·9	4081·2	21·96	70·43	15·47	13·9	2·15	2·46

Sources: Cols. 1, 4 from Census of Production for 1958, Summary Tables.
Col. 2, 6 from National Income and Expenditure, 1959.
Col. 8 from enquiry data.

salaries) are less important than the industry average. Table 29 therefore shows that while supplementary labour costs may form an important proportion of wage costs for manual workers in some industries and some firms, on average their effect on total costs is comparatively slight.[1]

This discussion has referred throughout to fringe benefits for manual workers. Fringe benefits for staff employees are probably more costly as a proportion of the salary bill, but their importance for total costs is problematical. It is possible to make some estimates of the cost of staff fringe benefits relative to those of wage-earners. For example, if salaried workers benefits were just as important in terms of total cost as those of wage-earners—that is, if they cost 1·44 per cent of total cost in the food industry, 1·59 per cent in chemicals and so on, as shown in Column 9 of Table 29—then their cost for the whole of manufacturing industry would be 33 per cent *of the salary bill*. There are two industries in particular in which this method seems to lead to an underestimate of the cost of staff benefits. In the chemical and engineering industries if salaried workers' fringe benefits represented 1·59 per cent and 2·77 per cent of total cost, they would only be 27 and 23 per cent of the salary bill respectively. Almost certainly staff benefits do in fact cost more than this, and so are a higher proportion of total cost in these two industries than are manual workers' fringe benefits.[2]

VI

Finally, we must make some estimate of the increase in supplementary labour costs since 1960, not in money terms, since they will obviously have increased, but relative to payroll. Between 1960 and 1963, the average weekly earnings of male manual workers increased by about 17 per cent; we may accept this figure as an indication of the average increase in payroll, so that to have remained a constant percentage of payroll fringe benefit expenditure in the average firm must also have risen at this rate. For some of the major items it is possible to assess the likely trend between 1960 and 1963. First, National Insurance contributions. Since the beginning of 1961 there have been two major increases in the employer contribution, and in October 1963 the minimum contribution was about 15 per cent higher than in 1961. The contribution for a man earning £16 per week

---

[1] Chapter 4, Section IV attempts to make an international comparison of the effect of supplementary labour costs on unit labour costs in Britain and Europe.

[2] Important staff fringe benefits are holidays which will cost at least 8 per cent of the salary bill (assuming four weeks' holiday), pensions, which should cost at least 5 per cent, and sick pay. There are other costly benefits, of course, particularly for executives.

—roughly the average level of earnings—was also 15 per cent higher, while the contribution for men earning £18 or above had risen by 27 per cent. These figures are for men participating in the graduated pension scheme; for those contracted out of the scheme—just over 4½ million in March 1963, though this includes all employees, not only manual workers[1]—contributions had risen by 25 per cent.[2] The cost of these to the average firm is difficult to calculate, but it certainly seems that most employers' expenditure would have increased by more than 17 per cent, and that the cost of National Insurance contributions was a higher percentage of payroll than the figure given in Section III.

It is rather more difficult to deal with holiday pay. The absolute cash amount of holiday pay might be greater either because more people are getting longer holidays, or because those on holiday are being paid more. The basic holiday is still two weeks, and only about four per cent of manual workers are entitled to basic holidays of more than this period; this proportion has apparently changed little since 1961.[3] It is probable, too, that most of this four per cent are employed either in the public sector or in service industries. Of the 96 per cent of employees who are entitled to two weeks holiday, about 15 per cent are 'in industries or services in which there is provision for additional days of holiday dependent on the length of the individual worker's service with the same employer':[4] once again, this situation is more or less unchanged since 1961, though the number of cases in which this practice exists is said to be increasing. It seems unlikely, then, that the cost of paid holidays has risen very much due to longer holidays, and certainly the increase could not be as much as 17 per cent. The question of higher pay for holidays is again not easy to answer. If all holiday pay were given at the full rate of average earnings, the cost of paid holidays would obviously have increased by 17 per cent, but the great majority of workers still receive holiday pay based on the wage rate rather than on earnings.[5] If all payment for holidays was given at the basic wage rate, the average increase from 1960 to April 1963 would have been about 10 per cent, the amount by which wage rates in manufacturing industry rose over this period. In the absence of changes in the length of holidays, then, paid holidays would cost on average between 10 and 17 per cent more in 1963 than they did in 1960. Taking into account the possibility of longer

[1] *Report of Ministry of Pensions and National Insurance* 1962, Cmnd. 2069. HMSO. Table 3, p. 30.

[2] Ibid., Tables 30 and 31.

[3] *Statistics on Incomes, Prices, Employment and Production*, No. 8., HMSO, March 1964; Section D.8.

[4] Ibid.

[5] In the enquiry, 81 per cent of employees were given holiday pay based on the wage rate. See also Chapter 10.

holidays for some employees and the fact that a proportion of workers are given holiday pay based on earnings, a reasonable estimate of the increase in expenditure on holidays with pay might be 14 or 15 per cent; in other words, they were slightly less important as a percentage of payroll than in 1960.

There are a few other types of expenditure for which a very approximate figure can be derived. First, there is cost of contributions to occupational pension plans. This is sometimes simply a certain percentage of earnings, and in these cases the increase will be the same as that of earnings. But if employer pension contributions are a flat-rate sum for each employed or a yearly payment calculated by an insurance company, there may be a lag which ensures that any rise in earnings is not instantaneously followed by an increasing contribution cost, with the consequent impossibility of predicting the rate of increase of costs. The former type of scheme is probably more common, but the cost of pensions should not have risen any faster than have earnings. Secondly, for the other security benefits, sick pay and redundancy compensation, there are so many unknown elements—the number of new schemes introduced, the provisions of these schemes, the incidence of sickness and redundancy, the type of workers able to take advantage of them, and so on—that it is impossible to say how costs have moved; on a purely impressionistic level, it seems unlikely that the increase could have been as much as 17 per cent, but there is little evidence to confirm or reject this view. Thirdly, the enquiry showed that in 1960 subsidies on a works canteen was the most important welfare cost, and this subsidy will largely consist of the wages of staff, and expenses for food and fuel and light. The average wage rates of full-time industrial canteen staff increased by between 9 and 10 per cent from 1960 to 1963,[1] while the food and fuel and light sectors of the retail price index rose by 10 and 19 per cent respectively. The relative importance of these will vary in different firms according to the method and extent of subsidy, but in most companies the total increase in the cost of canteen subsidy would not have been as much as 17 per cent.

The conclusion we reach, then, is that one item, National Insurance contributions, has probably increased as a percentage of payroll, while others of importance—holidays with pay, pensions, sick pay and canteen subsidies—are relatively smaller at the end of 1963 than in 1960. In aggregate, the cost of fringe benefits seems likely to be less, as a percentage of payroll, in 1963 than it was in 1960. It is certainly difficult to see many items which would so affect the money cost of benefits as to make them relatively more expensive than three years ago.

[1] Ministry of Labour, *Time Rates of Wages and Hours of Work*, 1961, p. 228; 1963, p. 232.

APPENDIX

THE QUESTIONNAIRE FORM USED IN THE ENQUIRY

GENERAL NOTES

1. Completed questionnaires will be treated as strictly confidential, and no company will be individually identifiable in the publication of results.

2. An estimate (qualified if necessary) is greatly preferable to no entry at all. Estimates should be identified by the letter 'E' in brackets after the appropriate figure. If it is impossible even to make an estimate, please enter the letters 'N.A.' in the appropriate space. If there is no expenditure, please draw a line through the appropriate space.

3. Total figures are more important than the constituent items in the totals. For this reason, where individual items of expenditure cannot be given, several of them may be bracketed together and included under one total.

4. Information as to expenditure should relate, if possible, to the calendar year 1960. Where expenditure figures are available only for a financial year, information should be given for the financial year in which the greater part of the year 1960 fell.

5. If the company has more than one establishment, then data may be given for the principal one or for all establishments, depending on how records are kept. It is essential, however, that all data refer to the same establishment(s).

6. The questionnaire refers only to 'operatives'; that is, those employees covered by the Ministry of Labour's definition of 'manual workers' as it is used in, for example, the half-yearly earnings enquiry.

COMPANY INFORMATION

(a) Name of Company...

(b) Form of Company
    Public Limited Company....
    Private Limited Company....
    Partnership....
    Sole Owner....

(c) Are you a subsidiary company?....................................

(d) To which establishments do the following data refer?
Continue on a separate sheet if necessary

....

....

....

....

A. EMPLOYMENT

1. (a) What was the total number of employees in the company during the second pay week of October 1960? (See NOTE 1 below)

    ....

   (b) What was the corresponding figure in October 1955?...............

2. (a) Please complete the following table with respect to October 1960 (second pay week) showing the number of employees in each category.

	Male		Female		
	21 and over	Under 21	18 and over	Under 18	TOTAL
Full-time					
Part-time					
TOTAL					

   (b) What was the maximum and minimum number of employees during the year and what numbers of these were full-time and part-time?

	Date	Total	Full-time	Part-time
Maximum				
Minimum				

NOTE 1: In this question, the term 'employee' includes only those workers covered by the Ministry of Labour half-yearly earnings enquiry. Thus office staff, clerks and typists, managerial and supervisory staff and all salaried persons are excluded. However since many of the subsequent questions cover the year 1960, it is necessary that those workers be included who were temporarily off work (e.g., absent, off sick, on lay-off or annual holidays) during the second pay week of October but who were on the payroll of the company. Thus the figure in 1. (a) will not necessarily be identical with that given to the Ministry of Labour, though the definition is the same. All subsequent questions refer only to employees as thus defined.

B. WAGES

Cost £

3. (a) Total amount paid to all employees during the year, including overtime pay, shift supplement, pay for annual and public holidays, sick pay, and all other payments for time off work. (See NOTE 2.) ....

Cost for:		Full-time	Part-time
	Male		
	Female		

(b) Total cost of premium pay for overtime and of shift supplements. (See NOTE 3.) ....

(c) Total cost of pay for annual and public holidays for employees. Payments for work on holidays should be excluded. ....

What is the formula by which holiday pay is determined? (e.g. percentage of yearly earnings, basic rate, etc.)
....
....
....

(d) Total payments made to employees during sickness, excluding benefits from National Insurance or any other insurance scheme. (See NOTE 4.) ....

NOTE 2: Only direct payment to the employees in the form of wages should be included here, and not expenditure by the company on behalf of the employees. Such items as contributions to welfare plans and National Insurance are excluded.

NOTE 3: Here only the payment above the regular rate should be included. Thus if overtime is paid at time and a half, only the half should be reported. If only total overtime pay is available, an estimate of premium pay should be made and identified as such. Shift supplements here include premium pay for night work, shift work or work on holidays. However if shifts are worked in such a way that all employees are given a uniform bonus for shift work, this should be taken as part of the regular rate for the job and no shift supplement premium pay should be reported.

NOTE 4: Disbursements from an insurance fund should not be included here since these are not paid by the company. Company expenditure in building up such a fund is included in a later question.

C. OTHER COMPANY EXPENDITURE

Cost £

4. Total net cost to the company during the year of pension plan, excluding administrative costs. (See NOTE 5.)

....

How much of this figure is payment for
(a) back service liability: £..........
(b) current service liability: £..........
Is the plan contributory: ....
    non-contributory?.....................
How many employees are
i. eligible for membership: ....
ii. covered by the plan?   ....

5. Cost to the company during the year of ex gratia pensions (See NOTE 5.)

....

Number of recipients...................

TOTAL COST TO THE COMPANY DURING THE YEAR OF THE FOLLOWING PAYMENTS TO OR ON BEHALF OF EMPLOYEES (for definition, see NOTE 1).

	Cost £	Number of employees covered or receiving benefits (See NOTE 6.)
6. Monetary payments made on account of long service, including ex gratia payments and those made under a definite scheme (see NOTE 7), and cost of long service awards made to employees.	....	R ....

NOTE 5: If the company plan is managed by an insurance company or if the company administers its own plan, total employer contributions should be reported, less, in the latter case, any dividend income from investment of the fund. If the company runs its plan on 'pay-as-you-go' lines and pays pensions from current revenue as they become due, please report expenditure for the year on pensions followed by the letter 'P'; as £2,438 (P).

It is possible that some former employees, who did not qualify for the company pension plan, are given pensions on an ex gratia basis. The cost and extent of such pensions during 1960 should be entered in Question 5.

NOTE 6: When an insurance or welfare scheme is in operation, it is sometimes of more interest to know how many employees are covered by the scheme (and are thus potential beneficiaries) rather than the number receiving benefits. For this reason where the letter 'C' has been inserted in this column the number of employees covered should be given. Where the letter 'R' appears, the number of employees actually benefiting during the year is required.

NOTE 7: The monetary payments here referred to do not include ex gratia pensions or promotion with increased pay given to long service employees. They include once-and-for-all cash payments. For example, it may be company practice to give 25 year employees an honorarium of £25, 30 years employee £30, and so on; the company may have no such scheme, but may make ex gratia payments of this nature to individual employees.

	Cost £	Number of employees covered or receiving benefits (see NOTE 6.)
7. Employer's contribution to National Insurance	....	C ....
8. (a) Employer's contributions to any insurance scheme additional to State schemes and pension plan, e.g. sickness, injury, redundancy	....	C ....
(b) All medical services provided partly or wholly by the company including first-aid facilities, plant medical personnel, cost of medical examinations, and other current costs, and annual provision for depreciation of any capital equipment provided by the company, e.g. surgery	....	C ....
9. Education or training of employees partly or wholly at the company's expense, including payment made for time off work.	....	....
If possible, please state how much of this was:		
(a) expenditure by the firm on behalf of the employees, e.g. apprentice training scheme, fees for day release workers, expense of other educational schemes inside or outside the firm. £.........		
(b) direct payment to employees, e.g. wages of day release workers for time off work, payments to full time student employees. £.........		
10. Payments to redundant employees, including both ex gratia payments and those made by the company (not from an insured fund) under a definite scheme. Payment to employees in lieu of notice should also be included.	....	R ....
11. Seasonal bonuses	....	R ....

D. OTHER WELFARE BENEFITS

	Cost £	Number of employees covered or receiving benefits (see NOTE 6.)
12. Financial or other assistance in housing and accommodation for employees: e.g. employee hostels, houses for which company subsidies are given on rent, rates, etc.	....	R ....
13. Free or subsidized travel for employees (e.g. travel to and from work in company vehicles) excluding necessary travel during working hours	....	R ....
14. Provision and maintenance of clothing and uniforms partly or wholly at the company's expense	....	R ....
15. Canteen facilities or subsidized meals (see NOTE 8), including subsidies on running costs of canteen, etc., and annual depreciation provision on any capital equipment provided by the company	....	C ....
16. Sports facilities or clubrooms for employees (see NOTE 8) including subsidies on annual running cost, etc., and annual depreciation provision on any capital equipment provided by the company	....	C ....
17. Discounts on company products sold to employees (excluding cost of distribution), where the products are provided below cost	....	C ....
18. Any plan for profit sharing or purchase of company shares where there is a cost to the company. Dividends, etc., on shares not bought during the year should be excluded	....	R ....
19. Other goods and services provided for employees partly or wholly at the company's expense, e.g. gifts. (Specify below)		
....	....	....
....	....	....
....	....	....
TOTAL COMPANY EXPENDITURE ON ITEMS IN Q. 4–19, SECTIONS C & D. £		

NOTE 8: It is possible that some companies may have one canteen used by both staff and works employees, or a single canteen account, so that the cost for employees as defined in this questionnaire is not known. In this case, the cost should be allocated between staff and works employees according to the numbers covered by the service (or the numbers employed). The resulting figure for 'employees' should be entered and identified as an estimate. The same procedure may be followed, if necessary, in Question 16.

CHAPTER 4

SUPPLEMENTARY LABOUR COSTS
IN EUROPE AND BRITAIN

G. L. REID

I

The enquiry described in the previous Chapter enables some estimate to be made of the extent of supplementary labour costs in
Britain, but the restricted coverage of the original survey and the
sources of bias in the final sample mean that the results are of very
much less value than if a more reliable sample of British industry had
participated.[1] This was perhaps to be expected from a purely voluntary enquiry with no official backing, but in many other countries
there is a great deal of interest in supplementary labour costs and,
consequently, much more quantitative information on them. This is
particularly true of the countries of Western Europe, and those of
North America.

There appear to be two related reasons why statistics of supplementary labour costs have been more readily available in these
countries. First, these costs are a good deal more important there
than in Britain, and this makes it necessary for Government and
industry to have up-to-date and comprehensive information on which
to base policy. Second, the progress of European unity through
E.C.S.C. and Benelux to the European Economic Community has
meant a sophisticated approach to the collection and publication of
economic and social statistics. It is considered essential that the
existing situation should be documented as fully as possible and
international comparisons constantly made, so that it may be clear
how quickly integration is going and where it is proceeding more
slowly than desirable. In the United States, too, the Government
assiduously collects and distributes all kinds of statistical material,

[1] The Ministry of Labour enquiry into labour costs should do much to remedy
this and other criticisms of lack of British data.

DOI: 10.4324/9781003184706-4

beside which the information so far provided by the British Government seems rather meagre. The result of these European and American attitudes has been a number of official enquiries into supplementary labour costs, with those in Europe being of a comparative nature and based on definitions and methods common to all countries.[1] While the enquiries may not be exactly comparable with one another, they generally provide more satisfactory data than any of the British studies.

A summary of the numerous enquiries which have been made would be tedious, and it might do more to confuse the issues involved than to highlight them if all the inter-industry and inter-country comparisons over time were to be made. Indeed, with the comparatively rich sources of data, it is unnecessary to give an exhaustive account of European supplementary labour costs, and instead several key enquiries have been selected to show their development in various countries. This Chapter contain three further Sections; Section II summarizes a selection of the foreign studies, uses the data from these enquiries to compare the levels of supplementary labour costs in these countries, and explains briefly what determines the differences between them; Section III examines the economic effects of different levels of supplementary labour costs, with special reference to the European situation; and Section IV attempts a direct comparison of labour costs in Britain and Europe.

II. ENQUIRIES INTO SUPPLEMENTARY LABOUR COSTS IN EUROPE

Since we are concerned here mainly with comparative data covering as large a part of industry as possible, there were several qualifying conditions used in selecting the enquiries to be summarized. First, the studies themselves should, where possible, cover several countries and use definitions common to all, so that any error through making invalid comparisons is minimized; secondly, the studies should cover a large number of employees and a fairly large cross-section of industry; and thirdly, the data should be in aggregative cost terms relating to all labour cost items rather than only one or two specific items. This Section will therefore exclude the numerous enquiries into particular fringe benefits or individual industries (including the many conducted by the European Coal and Steel Community), as well as limited surveys which may be of particular interest but which contribute relatively little to the general picture.[2]

[1] Another result is a greater willingness of companies to participate in semi-official or private enquiries, such as that conducted by the Chamber of Commerce of the U.S. every two years.

[2] For example, the series of studies *Comparison of Wages and the Cost of Labour in Europe*, Associazione Industriale Lombarda; Milan, 1959, 1960.

Even so, sources of data are so numerous that it has been possible to select some and omit others. One criterion has been reliability, the other chronology—obviously the further back in time is the enquiry, the less relevant is it to the present day. It so happens that the first large-scale comparative study which was reasonably reliable referred to the year 1955, and this enquiry has therefore been selected as the 'base', and all those occurring before 1955 have been left aside.[1] This first enquiry was that of the International Labour Office[2], which was also the source of the British data for 1955 summarised in Chapter 2. In continental Europe, it covered nine countries, of which only the five in western Europe, France, Belgium, West Germany, Italy and Denmark will be considered here.[3] The aim of the enquiry was to provide 'an objective statistical measure of differences in labour costs per man hour', and to do this, eight industries were selected which were common to most countries and 'illustrative of different types of industrial activity'.[4] These were cotton textiles, leather footwear, radio electronics, machine tools, shipbuilding, steel, coalmining and railways. Within the manufacturing sector there tended to be an unduly high proportion of large companies, and some individual cost items were estimated, either because separate figures were not otherwise available for salaried and wage-earning employees, or because the form of the questionnaire did not allow direct cost data to be obtained. These approximations cause some inaccuracy, but are not seriously disturbing when comparisons between countries are being made. Generally, the data from this enquiry are most comprehensive and in terms of sample and method this I.L.O. enquiry is largely successful in overcoming the complexities involved in international comparisons of labour costs. However its usefulness is limited by the restricted industrial coverage, and though the industries represent a variety of cost conditions, cost information from this enquiry is not truly representative of all industries in the countries concerned.

Another study which also considered international comparability to be of prime importance was carried out for the year 1959 by the Statistical Office of the European Economic Community.[5] This set out to present a comprehensive analysis of labour costs in certain

---

[1] This means excluding some of the earlier E.C.S.C enquiries,as well as a study by the French National Institute of Statistical and Economic Studies, 'Comparaison des salaires français et etrangers', *Etudes et Conjoncture*, May 1955. This enquiry will however be used in Section IV of this chapter.

[2] *Labour Costs in European Industry*, I.L.O; Geneva, 1956. Hereafter cited as Labour Costs, op. cit.

[3] Omitted are Greece, Yugoslavia, Austria, Turkey.

[4] Labour Costs, op. cit., p. 13.

[5] 'Couts de la Main d'Oeuvre 1959', *Statistiques Sociales*, 1961, 3: Statistical Office of E.E.C; Brussels, 1961. Hereafter cited as *Statistiques Sociales*, 1961, 3, op. cit.

industries in the E.E.C. countries for 1959, from the starting point that 'any international comparison of labour costs must be based not on wages alone, but on wages and social charges taken together'.[1] This 1959 enquiry was the first stage in a long-term study of labour costs and labour income which should eventually provide a relatively complete and homogeneous record of wages and salaries in the E.E.C. countries. In time, national statistics will be harmonized under common methods and definitions, but meanwhile a series of enquiries such as this gives the best available comparison of wages and labour costs to show where the greatest differences lie. Also by highlighting deficiencies in national statistical techniques, they help towards their ultimate integration.

The quoted sources contain further information on the structure of the E.E.C. enquiry and the characteristics of the sample used in each country. It may suffice here to note that the items of supplementary labour costs were the same as those covered by the I.L.O. 1955 enquiry, with one exception to be noted later, and that the industrial coverage was wider, with fourteen manufacturing sectors included. In the report of the enquiry, the presentation of data was accompanied by a warning on their limitations. First, the statistical information was drawn only from establishments with more than fifty workers, and could not be applied to all firms regardless of size. Secondly, since the survey covered only fourteen sectors of manufacturing industry in 1959, its results could not be extended in time nor could they be generalized to refer to all manufacturing industry. Finally, in some cases the definitions were not strictly adhered to and the methods of calculation altered slightly to take account of particular difficulties, with some slight lack of precision in the data.[2]

The second difficulty is perhaps less important than might seem at first sight. The 1959 enquiry included the most important sectors of manufacturing industry including chemicals, cement, machine tools, electrical engineering, shipbuilding and automobiles, and altogether more than 2,800,000 wage-earners were covered by the enquiry. A second stage of the E.E.C. survey of labour costs covered eight additional manufacturing sectors; these were chocolate and confectionery; fruit and vegetable processing; spaghetti and macaroni; footwear; plywood; furniture; flat and hollow glass; optical and precision instruments.[3] The output of these sectors is not so important either quantitatively or qualitatively as that of the industries covered by the 1959 enquiry, nor do they employ so many workers.

[1] *Social Aspects of European Economic Co-operation*, International Labour Office; Geneva, 1956; p. 34.

[2] *Statistiques Sociales*, 1961, 3, op. cit., pp. 52–3.

[3] A full description of coverage and results of this second enquiry is in 'Salaires C.E.E.', *Statistiques Sociales*, 1961, 3; Statistical Office of E.E.C.; Brussels, 1963.

In 1960 the number of wage-earners in these eight sectors was about 780,000, less than one-third of the number included in the 1959 enquiry. A preliminary report on the third survey has recently been issued.[1] This covers thirteen branches of industry, including meat and fish processing; clothing and millinery; paper and printing; plastics; refining of non-ferrous metal; metal goods; agricultural machinery; and aircraft. The total employment in these industries in 1961 was 1,660,000.

In the remainder of this Section, only the 1959 enquiry will be discussed in detail. The coverage of the 1960 survey is much less important, and in fact the results are broadly similar to those quoted in Table 30. The third enquiry is sufficiently comprehensive to warrant treatment, but the preliminary report included details only of total labour costs, and did not enable supplementary labour costs to be calculated on a comparable basis to the figures in Table 30. Despite the difficulties noted above, the 1959 survey by the Statistical Office of E.E.C. is by far the most satisfactory comparison of labour costs which has appeared, because of the precise definitions and methods consistently applied, the comparatively wide and important range of industry to which the survey applied, the high response rate, and the detail in which the results were published.

In the Tables which follow, two other sources of data on European supplementary labour costs are used, both issued by the French Institut National de la Statistique et des Etudes Economiques. The first, published in 1960,[2] was based on the I.L.O. survey of 1955, and attempted to use later data in revising the data up to 1957 and 1958. The second appeared in 1962[3], and sought similarly to estimate how labour costs had risen from 1959 to 1961, using the 1959 E.E.C. enquiry as a starting point. These revaluations used estimates of the rise in average hourly earnings and estimates of changes in the cost of the various supplementary labour cost items, to see whether the latter had become relatively larger since the base dates.

As the I.N.S.E.E. reports made clear, there were many difficulties in this estimation procedure. For one thing, official statistics of earnings did not always use the same industrial groupings as in the basic enquiries,[4] or they were collected at such infrequent intervals—

[1] 'Couts de la Main d'Oeuvre, 1961, C.E.E.', *Statistiques Sociales*. Supplement 1963; Statistical Office of E.E.C.; Brussels, 1963. A full report will appear in due course.

[2] *Etudes et Conjoncture*, March 1960; I.N.S.E.E.; Paris 1960.

[3] *Etudes et Conjoncture*, August 1962; I.N.S.E.E.; Paris 1962.

[4] The second I.N.S.E.E survey noted this difficulty, with hourly earnings figures easily available for industrial groups, e.g. paper, chemicals, but less reliably so for smaller sectors such as sugar and brewing. See *Etudes et Conjoncture*, August 1962, p. 662.

that the figures were out of date.[1] Also, in any enquiry of this type it is often extremely difficult to find out what changes have taken place in the cost of the various fringe benefits: increases in the cost of legal social charges are easily established, but the extent or cost of contractual and voluntary payments is seldom recorded nationally, and changes in company practice are extremely difficult to generalize. Then even when it is known what changes have taken place, the effect on supplementary labour costs per hour can only be roughly estimated. For example, if longer holidays with pay have been granted to some employees, the consequent increase in overall supplementary labour costs per hour can only be calculated on the basis of assumptions about method of holiday payment, the number and type of employees receiving the extra payment, average earnings of those employees, and so on. One comment on this procedure of separate estimation of earnings and supplementary labour costs is that 'the I.N.S.E.E. has attempted to bring up to date the statistics of the E.E.C. survey by adopting those same national statistics the difficulty of finding comparisons for which in the international field led the E.E.C. to undertake its own survey'.[2]

Despite all these difficulties, data from the I.N.S.E.E. enquiries have been used in the comparison of supplementary labour costs. They are not intended to be anything more than estimates of the movement of labour costs, and since the original enquiries of 1955 and 1959 were reliable in method if not in coverage, the I.N.S.E.E. figures are useful as an interim measure which can be checked against the future more accurate surveys carried out by international statistical agencies. The question still remains, of course, whether an international comparison based on these different sources is worthwhile. All of the enquiries into supplementary labour costs have stressed that their conclusions were applicable only to the sample and to the time period which they have covered, but in the absence of fully consistent data, it is interesting and useful to examine the results of the various surveys as if they were comparable with one another and in some way representative of the general level of labour costs in the countries concerned. Table 30 is a compendium of information from various enquiries, showing the course of supplementary labour costs in manufacturing industry from 1955 to 1961. Since this comparison is, strictly speaking, invalid, the sources of the enquiry have been listed in some detail; the main ones have been discussed above, but two enquiries have not been mentioned. One is

---

[1] In some cases changes in wage rates were used, adjusted to take account of probable differences between wages and earnings. *Etudes et Conjoncture*, August 1962, op. cit., pp. 661–2.

[2] C. Vanutelli, 'Labour Cost in Italy', *Banca Nazionale del Lavovo*, December 1962; p. 361n.

G

the survey of labour costs in Swedish industry[1] which achieved a good coverage—93 per cent of employees in all companies with more than 100 employees—and should therefore be representative of large companies in Swedish manufacturing industry. The other is the series of enquiries by the U.S. Chamber of Commerce which cover a sample of some 1,100 companies; this is a valuable continuing series, though comparison of the Chamber of Commerce results for 1959 with those of a U.S. Department of Labor survey of a statistically reliable sample suggests that the former were subject to considerable upward bias.[2]

The main source of inaccuracy in Table 30 is thus likely to be differences in coverage of the enquiries listed as sources. All appear to have, by accident or design, an over-representation of large companies, but in most cases the generalization of the results from the sectors of industry covered to the whole of manufacturing industry cannot be taken as completely valid. A further difficulty is that the items of supplementary labour costs may be defined differently in different countries, and an item which is included by some investigations may be excluded by others; for example, the cost of recruitment was excluded from the Swedish, American and British enquiries but included in the two European ones. Usually, however, the cost of these disputable items is small and does little to upset the general impression of Table 30, since the difference between the five E.E.C. countries and the others is too large to be entirely explained by such slight differences in coverage. Finally, there is one item in the European enquiries which has been omitted from the Table, namely bonuses and gratuities. In the earlier study by the I.L.O. this description covered only payments which were not a function of work performed, but the later E.E.C. definition in some cases included productivity bonuses and certain types of payment by results which in all other enquiries were considered to be part of normal earnings rather than supplementary labour costs. To achieve consistency, therefore, bonuses and gratuities have been excluded from all the figures quoted for the European countries. This leaves them rather lower than they would have been had 'non-wage' bonuses been included, and this especially affects Italy, where year-end and Christmas bonuses are important, and to a lesser extent, Germany.[3]

---

[1] *Labour Costs in Swedish Industry*, 1958, Swedish Employers Confederation, Stockholm, 1960.

[2] *Fringe Benefits*, Chamber of Commerce of the U.S., Washington, D.C. Comparison of the 1959 enquiry with Bulletin 1308, Bureau of Labor Statistics which used a larger and more valid sample, suggests that the Chamber of Commerce figures are two or three percentage points too high. This comparison and a full discussion of the two enquiries can be found in Chapter 5, Section V.

[3] See Labour Costs, op. cit., Table 13.

TABLE 30. *Supplementary Labour Costs for Wage-Earners in British, European and U.S. Manufacturing Industry: 1955–61*

| | | | PERCENTAGE OF PAYROLL | | | |
	1955	1957	1958	1959	1960	1961
Belgium	25·47	27·96	27·96	30·06	—	32·92
France	36·79	42·65	43·50	48·42	—	50·22
West Germany	28·96	33·45	35·66	34·74	—	35·09
Holland	—	—	—	32·85	—	33·09
Italy	51·31	51·46	53·53	56·43	—	56·93
U.K.	11·3	11·67	12·56	—	13·9	—
Sweden	—	—	13·6	—	—	—
U.S.	—	20·3	—	21·6	—	23·6

Sources: Belgium, France, West Germany, Holland and Italy:
  1955—I.L.O., *Labour Costs in European Industry.*
  1957–8—I.N.S.E.E., *Etudes et Conjoncture,* March 1960.
  1959—'Couts de la Main d'Oeuvre' C.E.E. 1959; *Statistiques Sociales* 1961, 3; E.E.C. Statistical Office.
  1961—I.N.S.E.E., *Etudes et Conjoncture,* August 1962.

  U.K.
  1955, 1957, 1958—as above.
  1960—Enquiry data.

  Sweden
  1958—*Labour Costs in Swedish Industry* 1958, Swedish Employers Confederation.

  U.S.
  1957–9–61—*Fringe Benefits,* Chamber of Commerce of the U.S.

Table 30 gives an indication of the progress of supplementary labour costs between 1955 and 1961, though the benchmarks for the E.E.C. countries are 1955 and 1959 when the most satisfactory surveys were conducted. It is important to note that this measure of supplementary labour costs is relative to payroll (or, roughly, relative to earnings), and comparison of 1955 and 1961 figures in the Table shows how much faster supplementary labour costs rose than did payroll.

There are in Table 30 striking differences between countries in the level of supplementary labour costs in any one year. The average level of Belgium, France, Germany and Italy is about three times that of Sweden or Britain, while the United States occupies an intermediate position, higher than Britain but considerably lower than the E.E.C. average. It is interesting too to compare the rate at which supplementary labour costs increased in the various countries. France experienced the fastest rise between 1955 and 1961, about 40 per cent, while the slowest was in Italy, about 10 per cent. In Britain supplementary labour costs as a percentage of payroll rose by about one-fifth between 1955 and 1961. These increases are relative to increases in earnings, and are considerably greater in absolute terms; in France, for example, supplementary labour costs expressed in francs per hour rose by just under 70 per cent. But these international differences in rates of increase have done little to reduce the gap between the E.E.C. countries in general and Britain, and the main task is to explain why this gap should exist at all.

TABLE 31. *Main Items of Supplementary Labour Costs in Britain and Europe: 1955 and 1959*

		BELGIUM	FRANCE	GERMANY	ITALY	AVERAGE	U.K.[1]
			PERCENTAGE OF PAYROLL				
Hours paid for	1955	8·18	6·85	8·54	10·24	8·45	6·40
but not worked	1959	9·52	8·59	9·35	12·84	10·08	4·8
Obligatory social	1955	18·16	29·91	13·08	40·00	25·29	3·03
security payments	1959	17·32	29·87*	14·61	35·34	24·29	3·4
Non-obligatory social security	1955	0·13	0·60	6·01	0·16	1·73	0·90
payments	1959	0·80	2·22	3·95	1·02	2·00	2·3
Payments in	1955	0·13	1·64	0·40	2·05	1·06	0·11
kind	1959	0·33	1·83	1·13	0·96	1·06	N.A.
Other[2]	1955	1·17	9·83	5·48	5·03	5·38	1·8
	1959	2·09	4·49	5·70	5·94	4·56	2·3

[1] U.K. figures for 1955 and 1960.
[2] Includes direct payments, subsidies, welfare benefits, other social contributions.
    * Includes some social taxes.
Sources: Statistiques Sociales, 1961, 3; op. cit.
        Labour Costs, op. cit., Table 13.

Table 31 shows the main items of supplementary labour costs in four of the E.E.C. countries for 1955 and 1959, and in Britain for 1955 and 1960. For most of the items, European costs are at a higher level than British. The European average for the cost of hours paid for but not worked was more than twice the British figure in 1959, reflecting the more generous provision of annual and public holidays enjoyed by the worker in the E.E.C. countries, especially in Italy. By contrast the British employer spends more as a percentage of payroll on non-obligatory social security payments such as contributions to an industrial pension plan or the cost of a sick pay scheme. But the difference between total supplementary labour costs in Britain and Europe is largely due to the very high levels of obligatory social security contributions in Europe, especially in France and Italy where they are about ten times the British figure.

These high social charges in Europe are a result of the financial structure of national social security schemes which is rather similar for all E.E.C. countries, but considerably different from the system ruling in Britain. In Europe, the cost of national social security schemes—including insurance against old age, sickness, industrial injury and unemployment, as well as family allowances and other schemes—is borne very largely by the employer. In only a few cases does the employer pay less than half the cost, and in all the E.E.C. countries the industrial injury and family allowance schemes are financed entirely by social charges on the employer. The British employer on the other hand makes only one explicit payment to the finance of social security in his contribution to National Insurance. The result of the different methods of finance is shown in Table 32, which gives the sources of social security revenue in Britain and Europe.

TABLE 32. *Sources of Social Security Revenue in Britain and Europe:* 1960

| | PERCENTAGE OF TOTAL REVENUE | | | |
	INSURED PERSONS	EMPLOYER	STATE	OTHER
Belgium	23·3	42·5	26·4	7·8
West Germany	37·3	40·9	17·9	3·9
France	19·2	68·9	7·1	4·8
Italy	15·2	72·4	7·1	5·3
Luxembourg	26·9	42·0	20·7	10·4
Netherlands	44·9	38·4	7·0	9·7
United Kingdom	27·0	21·0	51·5	0·5

Source: E.E.C. Statistical Office, *Statistiques Sociales*, 1962, 4: U.K. National Income and Expenditure, 1962.

It appears, then, that in Europe the employer contributes about one-half of social security revenue and the State about one-fifth, whereas in Britain these proportions are reversed, but this is basically a mis-leading impression. For one thing, the Table refers only to payments by the employer *specifically* for social security finance. In fact, finance of social security from general taxation revenue as in Britain means that other taxes are higher than they would have been had the continental method of finance been chosen, so that British companies are making some contribution—how much it is impossible to allocate—to the cost of pensions, National Insurance and the welfare state in general by their payments of profits and income tax. Second-ly, allocation of the origin of social security revenue to employer and State as in Table 32 seems implicitly to assume that the employer somehow has to find the whole of his contribution out of profits, and as the next Section will show, this assumption is incorrect. It is difficult to say exactly how social charges are financed—that is, who really pays the social charges—but it is certainly wrong to consider them entirely as a charge on profits.

It is the different content of this category, legally required pay-ments, which has determined the relative amount of supplementary labour costs in Britain and Europe, but this itself is a reflection of the different aims and structure of social security in Europe with its emphasis on the provision of an adequate minimum income, and of the orthodox financial objective of financing expenditure entirely from contribution revenue, with the consequent taxation on employers via social charges as a fruitful source of this revenue. What we must now do is to consider some of the effects of this method of finance.

III. THE ECONOMIC EFFECT OF SUPPLEMENTARY LABOUR COSTS

The cost of these fringe benefit items, including both social charges and voluntary payments, is to the employer part of labour costs just as normal wages are, but changes in their amount or their structure have a much less predictable effect on production costs, and their influence on the labour market is more subtle and indirect. For one thing, they are determined by many factors other than collective bargaining agreements and since they do not directly represent income to the employee, their effect on mobility of labour and labour force structure is difficult to forecast.

1. *The Effect of Supplementary Labour Costs on the Wage Structure*
In Britain, it is usually assumed that the wages structure as it is revealed by Ministry of Labour enquiries corresponds more or less exactly to the structure of labour costs. Thus the vehicle industry, which has very high average earnings, is thought to have a high level of hourly labour costs, and textiles and other low-wage industries to be low in terms of labour costs. This assumption implies either that the level of supplementary labour costs is generally fairly low, so that they do not make much difference to the wage structure, or that any inter-industry differences in supplementary labour costs do not cause the labour cost structure to be very different from the structure of wages, because the industries which have low wages generally have low supplementary labour costs and vice versa, so that there is an exact correspondence between the wage structure and the labour cost structure. Now it may be permissible to reach these conclusions as far as Britain is concerned, since in this country the level of supplementary labour costs is not very high and differences between industries not sufficient to make up for the very much more important differences in wages; Chapter 3 shows that there were few differences between the wage structure and labour cost structure in Britain in 1960.

However the same is not necessarily true of Europe, where in 1959 supplementary labour costs ranged from 30 per cent of payroll in Belgium to 56 per cent of payroll in Italy. Clearly there could be considerable differences between the wage structure and the pattern of labour costs in European industry, and the E.E.C. enquiry of 1959 contained detailed studies of individual industries which make possible an examination of the effect of supplementary labour costs on the structure of wages and labour costs both between industries and among countries.

In the inter-industry comparison, the most precise way of showing this is to ask whether total hourly labour costs show a greater degree of variation because of the addition of supplementary labour costs than do hourly earnings. There are two opposing hypotheses here One is that supplementary labour costs are 'on the whole more uniform in different industries in the same country than are wages',[1] and that they will therefore tend to reduce the inter-industry variation in labour costs. This seems possible on *a priori* grounds because of the structure of certain of the social charges. For example, holiday pay is closely related to wages, and certain of the legal social charges are either a fixed sum irrespective of wages or vary with wages only up to a ceiling contribution.[2] This would tend to damp down the degree of fluctuation relative to that of wages. The other hypothesis is that supplementary labour costs are liable to vary more than earnings, for several reasons. First, the range of voluntary or contractual payments can obviously be very wide depending on a company's welfare policy, the attitude of its employees and their representatives, the industry in which it finds itself, and so on. Secondly, the methods of assessment can vary between industries so that different levels of social charges are payable on behalf of employees earning the same amounts; for example, employers' contributions to the industrial injury insurance schemes in Europe usually vary with the risk involved.[3] Thirdly, when the social charges are fixed by collective bargaining contract there may be regional variations, as in Italy where employers in some urban areas pay a higher level of social charges. Then of course if social charges are levied only up to a certain level of wages, 'the industry that uses large numbers of relatively low-paid workers will have to pay relatively more than the industry which uses small numbers of highly skilled workers'.[4] All these factors would tend to make supplementary labour costs more variable than wages.

Table 33 contains statistics of hourly wage costs, supplementary labour costs and total labour costs for the fourteen industries in five European countries covered by the 1959 enquiry. The first part of the Table shows, for each country, the average of these three types

[1] I.L.O., Social Aspects, op. cit., p. 44. This was written at a time when there was no reliable statistical information on which to base conclusions.

[2] *Tableaux Comparatifs des Regimes de Securité Sociale*, E.E.C. Commission, Brussels, 1962.

[3] Ibid., Tableau VII, 3.

[4] M. W. Hald, 'Social Changes in the E.E.C. Countries: some Economic Aspects,' *Economia Internazionale*, November 1959; p. 689.

TABLE 33. *Average Wages, Supplementary Labour Costs and Total Labour Costs in Europe 1959*

1. AVERAGES WITHIN COUNTRIES

| | WEST GERMANY | | | BELGIUM | | | FRANCE | | | ITALY | | | HOLLAND | | |
	HOURLY WAGES	HOURLY S.L.C.	HOURLY T.L.C.	HOURLY WAGES	HOURLY S.L.C.	HOURLY T.L.C.	HOURLY WAGES	HOURLY S.L.C.	HOURLY T.L.C.	HOURLY WAGES	HOURLY S.L.C.	HOURLY T.L.C.	HOURLY WAGES	HOURLY S.L.C.	HOURLY T.L.C.
Mean (Belgian Francs)	30·1	11·3	41·4	31·2	10·2	41·4	26·6	14·3	40·9	20·6	13·2	33·8	24·8	8·1	33·0
Average deviation from mean	3·1	1·8	4·8	4·2	1·5	5·5	3·3	2·2	5·4	2·9	1·9	4·8	1·6	1·1	2·4
Deviation as % of mean	10·3	16·0	11·6	13·4	14·8	12·3	12·3	15·2	13·2	14·0	14·7	14·3	6·6	13·4	7·3

2. AVERAGES WITHIN INDUSTRIES

| INDUSTRY | MEAN (BELGIAN FRANCS) | | | AVERAGE DEVIATION FROM MEAN (BELGIAN FRANCS) | | | AVERAGE DEVIATION AS % OF MEAN | | |
	HOURLY WAGES	HOURLY S.L.C.	HOURLY T.L.C.	HOURLY WAGES	HOURLY S.L.C.	HOURLY T.L.C.	HOURLY WAGES	HOURLY S.L.C.	HOURLY T.L.C.
Sugar	26·1	10·7	36·7	3·1	1·9	3·2	11·9	17·8	8·8
Brewing	26·1	10·6	37·7	3·9	1·6	4·3	14·8	15·1	11·4
Wool	21·7	8·9	30·6	2·2	2·0	2·3	10·0	22·4	7·4
Cotton	21·5	8·9	30·4	3·3	1·3	2·3	15·5	14·6	7·5
Synthetic fibres*	27·2	14·4	41·6	5·3	2·5	6·6	19·5	17·3	15·9
Paper	26·7	11·0	37·6	3·6	1·6	4·0	13·4	14·5	10·6
Chemicals	28·0	13·2	41·2	3·4	2·3	4·1	12·0	17·4	10·1
Rubber	27·7	11·8	39·5	2·4	2·5	2·6	8·5	21·2	6·5
Pottery	21·6	8·8	30·5	2·4	1·6	2·4	11·2	18·2	7·9
Cement**	30·5	13·7	44·2	5·8	1·2	6·0	19·0	8·8	13·6
Machine tools	30·4	13·2	43·6	4·2	1·4	3·7	13·8	10·6	8·5
Electrical engineering	25·8	11·3	37·1	3·0	1·6	3·7	11·6	14·2	8·5
Shipbuilding	30·8	13·7	44·5	5·2	2·3	4·5	16·9	16·8	10·2
Vehicles*	33·7	17·0	50·7	2·0	2·1	2·0	5·9	12·4	3·9

* Three countries only.
** Four countries only.
Sources: Statistiques Sociales, 1961, 3; op. cit.

of cost together with the average deviation of the industries from the mean expressed in both Belgian francs and as a percentage of the mean itself. This measure of variability shows clearly that our second hypothesis is true, and that supplementary labour costs were considerably more variable than wages. This was especially so in Germany where the average deviation from the mean was about 10 per cent for wages as against 16 per cent for supplementary costs, and in the Netherlands where the respective deviations were 6½ per cent and 13½ per cent. Social charges then were more variable than wages, but the more interesting fact is that total labour costs—wages plus social charges—also showed a greater degree of variation than wages themselves, though in all of the countries the difference between the percentage deviations was small, being most substantial in Germany at 10·3 per cent and 11½ per cent for wages and total labour costs respectively. Of course, these findings can refer only to the time period and the industries covered, and the fact that total labour costs are largely made up of wages makes the comparison imprecise. An earlier study using the data of the I.L.O. 1955 enquiry also found that 'social charges widened inter-industry disparities in hourly wages', though it too noted that' it cannot be conclusively established that the disparities are in fact *caused* by the existence of social charges'.[1] Another more direct way of showing that social charges do not tend to bring about an equalization of labour costs is to compare the absolute levels of hourly wages and supplementary labour costs. A full listing of the industries covered by Table 33 would make it apparent that industries in which hourly wages were high also spent a large amount on supplementary labour costs, and in the three main countries (Germany, France and Italy) the rank difference correlation coefficient between industry ranks for hourly wages and hourly supplementary labour costs was +0·9 or greater. However, despite the greater variability of total labour costs, there was very little difference between the ranking of industries according to hourly wages and that for total labour costs; this would be apparent if full industry figures were given for each country, and in fact the rank difference correlation coefficient between wages and total labour costs was at least +0·95 in all countries. This means that the industries with high wage-costs also had high labour costs, and suggests that the effect of supplementary labour costs on relative hourly cost levels in industry was fairly small.

Part 2 of Table 33 provides information on international differences in wage and labour costs in each industry. A full comparison would show a good deal of consistency in the industrial wage structure with hourly earnings tending to be relatively high in the same industries in different countries. For example, the vehicle industry had the

[1] Hald, op cit., p. 689.

highest hourly wage costs in the three countries with such an industry, while wage costs in shipbuilding, machine tools, and chemicals were relatively high in all countries. Similarly, wool, cotton and pottery generally had low wage costs. There were some differences naturally, because of different levels of productivity between countries, and because the industries were obviously not identical in structure nor were they at the same stage of development in all countries. Once again, social charges were generally more variable than wages, except in three industries which were not represented in every country and marginally in shipbuilding. The effect of social charges, however, was here to reduce international variability in labour costs. In every industry hourly wage costs showed more variation than total labour costs; for example, in cotton the average deviations from the mean are 15·5 per cent and 7·5 per cent respectively, and in shipbuilding 16·9 per cent and 10·2 per cent. Comparing Parts 1 and 2 of the Table, it is clear that hourly labour costs of the same industry in different countries generally show more similarity than the hourly labour costs of all industries within each country; that is, the structural factor is more important than the geographical.[1] The two industries of which this is manifestly untrue are, again, not present in all countries. As the process of economic integration advances, tariff barriers fall and labour becomes geographically more mobile, the international variations of hourly labour costs within each industry may become even smaller, especially if increases in productivity are much the same for each country; it is important, too, that the existing similarity of labour costs will itself facilitate this integration.

2. *The Extent and Incidence of Social Charges*

There are other economic consequences of the European level of supplementary labour costs. A comparison of the structure of labour costs in Britain and Europe reveals not only that supplementary labour costs are much less important here, but that the British employer is in a much stronger position to influence and perhaps control the amount of supplementary labour costs which he pays. For in Britain almost every labour cost item, wages and fringe benefits, is negotiated.[2] While it is true that holidays with pay are more or less statutory, each company or industry is free to negotiate or refuse increases in holiday pay or longer periods of vacation, and apart from this, only the National Insurance contribution is imposed on the employer by the Government, and this normally amounts

---

[1] *Exposé sur l'Evolution de la Situation Sociale dans la Communauté en* 1961, E.E.C. Commission, Brussels 1962, p. xxxiii.

[2] Except, of course, in Wages Council industries where wages are fixed by law and only some fringe benefits open to negotiation.

only to four or five per cent of hourly earnings. The position in Europe is quite different; since the power of State regulations has made considerable inroads into the collective bargaining process, the employer has very much less control over the total amount of his labour costs. For example, minimum holidays with pay are legally established in most European countries. In Belgium and Germany the *minimum* annual vacation is 12 days per year, and in France 18 days, with longer periods for long service employees.[1] In addition, legally established public holidays are much more numerous than in this country, though again some public holidays are established by convention or collective agreement. The cost of days paid for but not worked in Europe in 1959 ranged from just over 10 per cent of direct wages in France to almost 17½ per cent in Italy; not all of this would be attributable to legally required holidays, but most of it would be. In addition the Christmas bonus which Italian wage-earners receive is established by law. This bonus was equivalent in 1960 to 200 hours paid at average earnings, about one month's pay,[2] and this must account for most of the figure of 9·42 per cent appearing under the heading 'Bonuses and Gratuities' in the 1959 E.E.C. enquiry.

Much more important than the cost of holidays or bonuses are the social security contributions which all employees are legally required to pay on behalf of their workers. Table 34 illustrates the level which these contributions reached under the general schemes covering most wage-earners.

For these particular schemes, therefore, the average firm would in 1962 have been liable to contributions totalling about 40 per cent

TABLE 34. *Rates of Employer Contribution to*
Social Security Schemes in Europe, 1962:
% of earnings

	GERMANY	ITALY	FRANCE
Sickness Insurance	4·55	7·2	
Illness Insurance	} 14 .	10·5	} 14·25
Old Age Insurance			
Family allowances	1	17·5	13·5
Work accidents*	1·7	3·7	3

* The actual rate varies with occupational risk; these figures are 1961 averages quoted in *Social Security Programs throughout the World* 1961, U.S. Dept. of Health, Education and Welfare, 1961.
Source: Tableaux Comparatifs des Regimes de Securité Sociale, op. cit.

[1] Office Statistiques des Communautés Européennes, *Statistical Information,* 1963, 1; p. 167.
[2] *Comparison of Wages and the Cost of Labour in Europe,* Associazione Industriale Lombarda, 1960, p. 42.

of earnings in Italy and 32 per cent in France.[1] In Germany and the
Benelux countries, contribution rates tend to be somewhat lower, but
even in the country with the lowest level of contributions, the
Netherlands, the total cost to the average firm would probably have
been about 15 per cent of earnings. Such a structure of labour costs
means that these social charges amount to about one-third of total
labour costs in Italy, over one-quarter in France, and about one-fifth
in Germany and Belgium. This part of labour costs is thus removed
from the arena of collective bargaining; employers can influence the
level of social charges very indirectly by political pressure, and here
they are opposed not only by considerations of national economic
policy and public finance, but also by the countervailing force of the
trade unions. For the structure of the Common Market is such as to
allow representative powers to trade unions, and with their collective
bargaining strength limited by organizational schisms and comparatively low degrees of unionization,[2] progress has often been
more easily made by concentrating on the achievements of legislative minimum benefits through national social security schemes.
Some of the effects of this method of bargaining through its repercussions on employee income will be discussed later. Here the point
of interest is the extent to which part of labour costs is determined by
an outside agency, and so becomes compulsory and unavoidable.

This, at any rate, is the contention of European employers, that
these social charges are unavoidable and their effect in increasing
labour costs places European companies in a weaker competitive
position *vis a vis* British and Northern American rivals who do not
have to pay these high social charges. This argument contains several
fallacies. While it is true that in the E.E.C. countries legal social
charges are much lower, taxation in Britain to finance State schemes
and expenditure on negotiated social security schemes in America are
higher and so are wage costs, though it is impossible to say whether
these are sufficient to offset the lower levels of social charges. Then,
of course, in so far as labour costs do affect competitiveness in international trade, it is only through their relationship with labour
productivity, and it is the level of labour cost *per unit* which is important and not labour costs per hour. But the important implica-
tion of the European argument is that the employer himself somehow is forced to find the amount of the social charges from profits,

---

[1] The total level of employer social security contributions in Italy in 1961 was
between 45 and 50 per cent of hourly earnings; *Etudes et Conjonctures*, August
1962, Table 24.

[2] See R. Colin Beever, *Trade Unions in the Common Market*, P.E.P.; London
1962. Very recently, European trade unionists have urged that trade unions
should have a much greater voice in decisions affecting the future progress of the
E.E.C. See *European Community*, April 1964.

that they 'unavoidably' add to labour costs. The truth is that the incidence of social charges can be shifted by the employer to the consumer by increasing prices, or to the employee, by reducing wages. These two types of shifting are very similar, since employees are consumers, and in either case a relative reduction of real wages is involved. However it is simpler to separate them for descriptive purposes.

First, the shifting of social charges to the consumer. An increase in social charges is to the employer exactly the same as an increase in any other cost, and his natural reaction faced by such an increase is to raise prices so as to cover it and leave profits unchanged. But rigidities in pricing arrangements impose a structural limitation on his speed of action, and for this reason, and perhaps also to maintain a degree of consumer goodwill, there is likely to be a time-lag between the imposition of the social charge and the attempt to increase prices. During this time, the social charge will be a direct increase in costs and profits will be reduced accordingly, so that in the short-run the incidence of the social charge stays on the employer. In this situation and with this particular time period, part of the hypothetical European employers' argument is correct; social charges do add directly to costs. But in the longer-run, a rise in prices can take place. A company's ability to do this and so to shift this incidence to the consumer is limited by the characteristics of the product market, notably by the price-elasticity of demand for his product and the possible existence of price agreements, but these constraints will tend to be less important when a rise in costs uniformly applies to all firms in the industry, as in the case of an all-round increase in social charges. Then the labour costs of every domestic competitor are increased by the same percentage amount (though the increases in total costs will differ between firms), and the effect of the higher level of prices will be minimized. Indeed, if the price increases are simultaneous and immediate, the competitive structure of an industry might be relatively little disturbed by an increase of social charges, and production would continue at a higher level of prices with consumers bearing the burden of the social charges, which would have no effect on the relative costs of production.

However this process of shifting is not instantaneous, as there will be considerable differences in the ability of firms to raise prices at all and the speed with which they can do so. Variations in elasticities of demand and supply. and in the structure of production costs as well as different degrees of institutional flexibility or rigidity (for example, in the collective bargaining framework) will all affect the rate of change of prices and, more indirectly, of profits and wages. Though it would be impossible to separate out these influences from those of other more important economic variables, the shifting of the incidence of social charges to the consumer will mean that at a given time the composition of demand and production, the demand for and supply of labour and the process of exchange generally will all be different from those ruling either before the imposition of the social charges, or afterwards when all the changes have worked themselves through.

Still in the short-run, another effect of any attempt by raising prices to cover the cost of social charges is likely to be countered by a claim from employees for an increase in wages to compensate for the fall in the real wages. If the employer is forced to agree to such a wage claim the incidence of the social charges is transferred back to profits, and unless one side or the other capitulates, the process has all the makings of a cost-induced inflationary situation in which the incidence of the social charges may shuttle backwards and forwards until lost in the rounds of price and wage increases. If the employer is to shift the incidence onto consumers without beginning a wage-price spiral, either the employees must not be sufficiently strongly organized to secure the compensatory wage increases, or productivity must be rising rapidly enough to allow these increases without much (or any) increase in labour costs per unit. But it is in a situation where these two conditions are fulfilled that the employer may be able to shift the incidence of social charges to the employee directly, instead of indirectly by increases in price. Once again, the process is by no means instantaneous; the employer could not, for example, force employees to bear the social charges by cutting money wages, and in the short-run, an increased social charge must still come out of profits. But as productivity rises it may be possible for the employer to retard wage increases, so that wages rise by less than the full amount of productivity increase. The difference between the two would be equal to the amount of the social charge, then borne by the wage-earner, and profits would recover to their former level without an increase in prices.

This kind of shifting directly to the employee is rather easier to investigate statistically than the other, though again it is impossible to show cause and effect. However, Table 35 suggests that European social charges may have been shifted to the wage-earner.

Table 35 shows that the countries with the lowest level of wages tended to have the highest level of legal social charges, which could indicate that employers have generally been able to retard wage increases to make up for the higher level of social charges. The exception to this general impression is the Netherlands where wages and social charges were both relatively low. But in the Netherlands the insured person (i.e. the employee) is already liable for a much higher social security contribution than in the other countries; 45 per cent of total social security revenue in the Netherlands came from

TABLE 35. *Wages and Supplementary Labour Costs in Manufacturing Industry* 1961

| | WAGE INDEX | % OF HOURLY EARNINGS | |
		LEGALLY REQUIRED PAYMENTS	TOTAL SUPPLEMENTARY LABOUR COSTS
West Germany	=100	18	47
Netherlands	82	16	49
Belgium	82	22	47
France	80	34	69
Italy	53	48	91
U.K.	120	4	14

Source: Etudes et Conjoncture, August 1962.

contributions from the insured, compared with 37 per cent in Germany and less than 30 per cent in the other countries.[1] The position of the Netherlands in Table 35 may mean that the employees, already bearing a fairly large social charge, have not been able to shift the burden of their contributions to the employer; that is, they have not been able to negotiate higher wages to compensate for their high social security contribution. The relation between social charges and wages shown in Table 35 is suggestive, but it is impossible to prove that the incidence has been shifted, and the uncertainty of the speed of the process means that a longer comparison over time between increases in social charges and wages would not be valid. However there is other evidence at an aggregative level indicating that employers have probably shifted the incidence of social charges to the consumer and employee. A United Nations bulletin, discussing the relationship between wages and social benefits, noted that the depressing of wages in France, Italy and Belgium 'is not necessarily due to the existence of high family allowances, but rather to the particular methods of financing them' (i.e. by social charges on the employer), and it pointed out that 'the percentage share of wages in the National income of France decreased between 1938 and 1950 by an amount corresponding to the increase in taxes on wages paid by employers'.[2] Another authority showed that 'the real income of French wage-earners and their share in the national income were about the same in 1952 as in 1938 and cited the opinion of the French Ministry of Finance that since wage income had remained stable it must be presumed that the increased social payments were met by offsetting contractions in direct wages'.[3]

[1] *Exposé sur l'évolution de la situation sociale dans la Communauté en* 1961, Commission of E.E.C., July 1962; Annexe V, Table 3.

[2] United Nations; *Economic Bulletin for Europe,* Vol. 4, 2; 1952, p. 46.

[3] Quoted in Hald, op. cit., p. 686n.

These statistics cover a long period, and illustrate the position after all the possible short-run changes have occurred. But even in the short-run it is impossible to isolate the effect of social charges and attempts by employers to shift their incidence to consumers and employees. Probably this effect is not very large, even though social charges themselves may be a comparatively large part of the cost of production, since there are many more important economic factors determining the process of production and distribution. In the long-run, though, it is generally agreed that the effect of social charges on the cost of production is negligible, as the statistics seem to show. The I.L.O. report was of the opinion that, 'social security payments which are roughly proportional to wages and salaries will not in the long-run increase labour costs . . . and the total amount of labour costs which business enterprises are able to sustain will not be much affected by such taxes'.[1] They will eventually be shifted entirely on to employees either through a rise in prices causing a reduction in real wages, or by the depression of wage increases which would otherwise have taken place.

3. Some Effects of the European System of Social Charges

In the long run, then, the argument that social charges put European employers at a competitive disadvantage appears to be untrue: instead they react to the disadvantage of the European wage-earner whose wage income is lower than it might have been had there been no social charges. This effect of social charges and social security generally on wage-income and work incentives is of some interest. It was noted earlier that employers' contributions were usually a percentage of wages up to a certain level of wages, the 'ceiling'.[2] Above this level, the contribution did not vary with wages, but was a fixed sum calculated by applying the percentage contribution to the ceiling, the maximum wage taken for contribution purposes. In France in 1961, the ceiling level of earnings was 700 francs per month. This was considerably above the level of average earnings in manufacturing industry—about 500 francs per month—but less than the average earnings of some industries, e.g. printing and chemicals, and considerably lower than the earnings of skilled employees. In this range where the tax ceases to vary with earnings, there was obviously an incentive for the employer to employ skilled labour at relatively high wages, since the social charge then becomes a lower percentage of earnings. The degree of discrimination against unskilled or semi-skilled labour becomes greater the lower is the ceiling on which contributions are based.

[1] Social Aspects, I.L.O., op. cit., p. 156–7.
[2] In Italy and Luxembourg contributions are generally based on the whole of earnings.

Since 1961 both France and Italy announced their intention to amend their family allowance schemes by doing away with the ceiling wage on which contributions are based. In France, this process of *deplafonnement* was to have been effected in one swift operation, whereupon employers would pay contributions of 12 per cent of the total of each employee's earnings instead of 14¼ per cent on the first 700 NF per month.[1] However, the French government decided not to proceed with the abolition of the ceiling, and instead the ceiling was raised from 700 NF to 800 NF per month and the rate of contribution lowered to 13½ per cent.[2] In Italy the removal of the ceiling is proceeding in stages, but the employer contribution in manufacturing industry will eventually be 17½ per cent of earnings instead of 33 per cent of the first 1000 lira.[3] The reason for these changes was simply to increase the revenue accruing to the schemes, but it is important to note that the labour-force discrimination is reversed. If all social charges were to be levied on this basis, employers would have no incentive to hire high-wage or skilled labour, rather would they tend to hire low-wage workers and there would certainly be an incentive to keep wages down; for this reason, the proposed change in France was bitterly attacked by employee organizations. It is difficult to say what the effect of social charges on labour force structure now is in those countries which still have contributions based on a ceiling (France, Germany, Belgium and the Netherlands) as this depends on the relationship between the level of earnings and the height of the ceiling, but the existence of social charges which do not vary with wages will tend to make employers reluctant to employ additional workers if they can possibly avoid it. For the employer will have to pay social charges on behalf of each new employee, and it is obviously much more economic for him to try to reduce, relative to wages, the burden of social charges which he already pays. This can be done by extensive overtime working; production and wages will both increase and the amount of social charges payable will be spread over a higher wage bill and greater output.

Though the changes in French and Italian family allowance schemes may reduce the tendency of employers to treat social charges as a kind of capital charge on the employment of each man, there is no doubt that in the 1950s the extent of social charges was a powerful incentive towards a very long working week. This was notably true even in Italy; at a time of considerable unemployment, weekly hours were among the highest in Europe. In that country in 1955, it was

---

[1] Details of the proposed changes appeared in *La Vie Francaise*, September 22, 1961.

[2] *Exposé sur l'évolution de la situation sociale dans la Communauté en* 1961, Commission of E.E.C.; Brussels, 1962; p. 184.

[3] I.L.O., *International Labour Review*, LXXXV, 4; April 1962; p. 403.

H

stated that 'long weekly hours are used by non-agricultural employers to avoid taking on new hands ... because of associated heavy fixed labour costs and obstacles to subsequent lay-offs'.[1] Since 1955, the proportion of employees in manufacturing industry working more than 40 hours per week has increased steadily. In 1961, 96 per cent did so, while 76 per cent worked 45 hours or over, and with unemployment still relatively high this suggests that employers were continuing to accept the possible disadvantages of overtime working in order to lessen the impact of the social charges. This course of action was particularly attractive in Italy because the ceiling wage on which contributions are based was low, so that most skilled employees and those working overtime would have been earning amounts well above the ceiling.[2] Thus hourly overtime labour costs might well have been lower than straight-time labour costs, with the overtime premium being less important than the full level of social charges levied on a wage below the ceiling.

Some observers in the United States have suggested that fringe benefits may constitute a barrier to reducing the present unemployment in that country, since employers can more cheaply work overtime with the existing labour force. Garbarino has recently shown that this argument is unlikely to be true, and that additional overtime is a very much more expensive way of increasing production than hiring new employees.[3] He points out, however, that the 'fringe barrier' thesis can be partly rehabilitated. First, one must take into account turnover costs other than those already contained in wages and fringe benefits: if these are added, the relative advantage of overtime is diminished, especially when seniority regulations demand complex labour force adjustments. Secondly, the higher the proportion of fringe benefits which are not proportional to wages but simply depend on the employment of a worker, the more incentive will managements have to hold down employment. It is this second case which so affected the Italian employment situation.

One effect of the European system of social charges, then, has been to encourage the working of longer hours—so creating unemployment to some extent—and provide some incentive to the employer to hire skilled labour where at all possible.[4] However, a paradox of this system of social charges is that it can have an in-

[1] G. H. Hildebrand, 'The Italian Parliamentary Survey of Unemployment', *American Economic Review*, December 1955, p. 887.

[2] The gradual raising and abolition of the ceiling on family allowance contributions will reduce the incentive of employers to engage high-wage labour.

[3] J. W. Garbarino, 'Fringe Benefits and Overtime as Barriers to Expanding Employment', *Industrial and Labor Relations Review*, April 1964, p. 426.

[4] Hildebrand notes that another effect in parts of Italy was 'the proliferation of small family enterprises ... as a means of escaping society security levies and union wage scales'. Hildebrand, op. cit., p. 895n.

herent tendency to diminish the supply of skilled labour. There are two reasons for this. First, the discrimination against low-wage workers which prevailed in the 1950s (and may still be of some importance) applies equally to the employment of apprentices, since employers may be unwilling to pay the large social charges which they would incur on behalf of these young workers. This evidently had a considerable influence in Italy, where high social security charges are cited as one of the main reasons for the restriction of the traditional apprenticeship system in the northern regions.[1] Thus although there were shortages of skilled labour, the supply of apprenticeships (or potentially skilled labour) which firms were willing to provide was small. But the demand for apprenticeship may also tend to be lower under the European system of social security. If we leave for the moment social charges and their effect as costs to look at the disbursements from social security schemes and what they mean as income to employees, it is clear that the financial inducement to employees to become skilled may be comparatively small. For the main aim of the social security programmes in Europe is to provide a minimum income by a redistribution of income not so much between rich and poor as between the high-wage employee or salaried worker and the low-wage worker, and in some countries, notably France and Italy, minimum living standards are protected by increases in social benefits rather than wages. The most important form of this non-wage income has been the family allowance. Table 36 shows the amounts of family allowances in Europe in 1961 compared with the average earnings in three industries.

TABLE 36. *Average Monthly Earnings and Monthly Family Allowances* 1961

BELGIAN FRANCS

	AVERAGE EARNINGS			FAMILY ALLOWANCES			
	PRINTING	BASIC METAL	TEXTILES	ONE CHILD	TWO CHILDREN	FOUR CHILDREN	SIX CHILDREN
Belgium	6,653	7,092	5,258	446	1,051	2,840	4,908
France a:	7,135	6,101	4,066	—	642	2,577	4,847
France b:				395	1,432	3,565	5,845
West Germany	7,623	8,554	6,521	—	*	999	1,999
Italy	3,744	4,457	2,551	395	799	1,580	2,369
Netherlands	6,101	6,140	5,704	271	566	1,262	2,113

Notes: France: a=general level of family allowances
  b=family allowances where there is only one breadwinner.
  Germany: *=If family income is less than 600 DM (7,500 FB) an allowance of 25 DM (321 FB) is paid for the second child.

Sources: Average earnings: calculated from I.L.O. Yearbook of Labour Statistics, 1962.
  Family allowances: Statistical Office of E.E.C., *Statistical Information* 1963, *No.* 1. Tableau 17, p. 178.

[1] Hildebrand, op. cit.

It is very difficult to estimate comparable monthly average earnings for the whole of industry, but two of the manufacturing industries chosen, printing and basic metal, were among the highest in terms of average earnings, while the other, textiles, was rather low. The relationship between these levels of earnings and family allowances is most interesting. In Italy and Belgium, the amount of allowances going to a large family was only slightly below average earnings in the textile industry, while in France the family allowance for six children was very considerably above average earnings in the textile industry, and for a family with a single income it approached average earnings in the relatively high-wage basic metal industry. Clearly the existence of this source of non-wage income must lessen an employee's incentive to increase his potential work-income by undertaking a course of training and so becoming skilled. It seems unlikely, however, that this disincentive effect will be important in the long-run, in the light of rapidly changing technology and the consequent increase in the demand for skilled workers, leading to increases in the skill differentials which will make the acquisition of a skill much more important financially. It is this, together with the desire for increased earnings opportunities as the aspiration level of the unskilled worker rises, which will tend to limit the disincentive effect of high social benefits, rather than reductions in the levels of benefits themselves.

These results of a high level of social charges indicate that they might be important as one aspect of broad economic policy. Their employment effects appear to be quite definite; a high flat-rate charge will tend to discriminate in favour of high-wage workers within comparable occupational groups and make employers more eager to hire skilled labour. This tendency may be offset by the incentive not to take on new workers but to work long hours with a smaller labour force so as to spread the amount of social charge over a large output. The strength of these conflicting influences will depend on the relative levels of wages and social charges, but a policy which for some reason includes a high flat-rate social charge seems certain to have a deleterious effect on employment. The same is true to a lesser extent of social charges levied on an *ad valorem* basis, as a percentage of earnings, except that the effect appears through the employer's attempt to minimize his wage bill. He will be therefore anxious to hire low-wage labour where possible, and also to keep wages as low as possible. A policy embodying an *ad valorem* social charge is likely to be bitterly attacked by trade unions as discriminating against employment and making it more difficult for them to raise wages.[1] This employment effect of high social charges is one reason for the

[1] The Labour Party's social security plans appear to involve exactly this type of social charge in, the form of a large increase in employer contribution.

current discussion of a payroll tax, which would bring home to employers the 'true cost' of employing labour. The corollary is that the relative prices of capital and labour should change so as to increase investment, though it is impossible to say whether this will happen in the general case without making specific assumptions.

High social charges, then, may have different economic results, but this should not be allowed to obscure our previous important conclusion that in the long-run proportional social charges will have little effect on production costs. The imposition of a social charge will have an immediate effect on the numbers and types of worker whom employers wish to hire, but gradually the incidence of the social charge will be shifted on to workers and consumers. We cannot say how far this process will go, as it depends on structural factors, but an *ad valorem* social charge imposed on all firms is likely to be least easily shifted when there is first, a strong trade union movement which prevents employers paying wages lower than the increase in productivity merits; and second, a high degree of domestic and international price competition to make compensatory price increases more difficult, though price control would be a more positive means of doing this. The employer, then, will gradually cease to bear the burden of the social charges, so long as the two factors mentioned above are partially or totally absent, but this does not necessarily reverse the employment and discrimination effects of social charges. Even when the shifting process has entirely worked itself through, there will still be a tendency for the employer to minimize the effects of social charges on his labour costs by changing the structure of the labour force. It is obviously important when social charges are used to influence employment to know that the policy implications are not seriously affected by shifts in the incidence of the charge.

IV. LABOUR COSTS IN BRITAIN AND EUROPE

After comparing the amount of supplementary labour costs in Britain and Europe and examining some economic aspects, it remains only to combine the data surveyed in Section II with earnings statistics to show the relative levels of wage costs and labour costs per hour in different countries.

In Table 37, the figures for European wages and supplementary labour costs have been taken from the 1961 revaluation by the French National Institute of Statistical and Economic Studies of the E.E.C. 1959 enquiry.[1] The British figures are altogether more conjectural. Average hourly earnings for all employees were calculated from the Ministry of Labour earnings and hours survey for April

[1] *Etudes et Conjoncture*, August 1962, op. cit.

1961.[1] From the Glasgow enquiry, a more detailed industrial classification was used to identify firms in industries broadly similar to those contained in the E.E.C. survey. Thus, while all firms in shipbuilding, metal manufacture, and chemicals industry groups could be used, from the vehicle and aircraft group, only the firms actually producing vehicles were extracted, and from engineering those firms in electrical engineering were obtained separately. For these firms, an industry average of supplementary labour costs, or fringe benefits expenditure, was calculated as a percentage of earnings on the same basis as in the I.N.S.E.E. study, and this was applied to the figure of average hourly earnings to give total labour costs per hour. Finally the European figures were converted from national currencies to shillings, to allow an easier basis of comparison; this conversion was made at the official exchange rates ruling at April 1961.

There are several limitations to the use of the data.

1. Though the Glasgow enquiry referred to the year 1960, its results have been applied to the earnings statistics of April 1961 without qualification. It has therefore been assumed that there was no change relative to earnings in supplementary labour costs during this period. In fact, there must have been an increase in April 1961 with the raising of the employer's National Insurance contribution, but this has not been taken into account.

2. There is bound to be inaccuracy in the combination of the enquiry data with official earnings figures, though this may be less serious than might appear. For the estimates of supplementary labour costs are probably those of progressive companies, while it is also likely that the average hourly earnings of employees in the sample companies would have been higher than the national averages. To some extent, then, the two sources of bias will tend to cancel out, but in so far as any bias still exists, the figures of total labour costs per hour in Britain are probably higher than if all companies in each industry had been included. Also, the predominance of large companies in the Glasgow enquiry is rather less important for comparative purposes, since the European figures also exclude very small enterprises.

3. The comparison between Britain and Europe will be more reliable for some sectors than others. It is most trustworthy where a reasonably homogeneous industrial group exists and the coverage in the Glasgow enquiry was fairly high. On this criterion, the most valid sections of Table 37 are those dealing with chemicals, shipbuilding, vehicles and metal manufacturing, while electrical engineering is less satisfactory for one reason or another. All in all, though, the figures should be taken to indicate only orders of magnitude.

[1] Ministry of Labour *Gazette*, August 1961, pp. 321–5.

TABLE 37. Hourly Earnings and Labour Costs in Britain and Europe, April 1961

	CHEMICALS			SHIPBUILDING			VEHICLES		
	HOURLY EARNINGS (SHILLINGS)	SUPPLEMENTARY LABOUR COSTS (% EARNINGS)	HOURLY TOTAL LABOUR COSTS (SHILLINGS)	HOURLY EARNINGS (SHILLINGS)	SUPPLEMENTARY LABOUR COSTS (% EARNINGS)	HOURLY TOTAL LABOUR COSTS (SHILLINGS)	HOURLY EARNINGS (SHILLINGS)	SUPPLEMENTARY LABOUR COSTS (% EARNINGS)	HOURLY TOTAL LABOUR COSTS (SHILLINGS)
Belgium	4·25	48·8	6·32	5·19	63·2	8·47	—	—	—
France	4·26	80·0	7·67	4·33	72·3	7·46	5·16	79·5	9·26
West Germany	5·57	61·8	9·01	5·55	41·8	7·87	6·05	46·6	8·92
Italy	2·76	99·3	5·50	3·26	96·6	6·40	3·57	113·3	7·60
Netherlands	4·41	50·7	6·66	4·57	49·4	6·84	—	—	—
U.K.	5·87	30·0	7·63	6·01	9·6	6·59	7·83	12·5	8·81

	STEEL			ELECTRICAL ENGINEERING		
	HOURLY EARNINGS (SHILLINGS)	SUPPLEMENTARY LABOUR COSTS (% EARNINGS)	HOURLY TOTAL LABOUR COSTS (SHILLINGS)	HOURLY EARNINGS (SHILLINGS)	SUPPLEMENTARY LABOUR COSTS (% EARNINGS)	HOURLY TOTAL LABOUR COSTS (SHILLINGS)
Luxembourg	7·31	40·1	10·23	—	—	6·27
Belgium	6·24	38·1	8·72	4·26	47·4	6·81
France	4·39	70·9	7·62	4·18	62·7	6·95
West Germany	6·63	45·7	9·69	4·80	45·0	5·28
Italy	4·39	72·0	7·62	2·71	94·4	5·80
Netherlands	5·09	64·8	8·39	3·80	52·6	6·00
U.K.	6·68	11·5	7·45	5·24	13·8	

Sources: See text.

It is now generally recognized that at the time of the abortive Common Market negotiations British wages were still higher than in Europe, and some 'anti-marketeers', ignoring the importance of supplementary labour costs, assumed that the same was true of hourly labour costs and that unfair competition therefore existed. Table 37 is an estimate of the situation in April 1961. In every industry British *wage-costs* were higher than any in the E.E.C. countries, except in the steel industry, where the notoriously high-cost Luxembourg steel industry paid higher hourly earnings. West Germany's hourly wage-costs were closest to Britain's, and in most industries were only slightly lower, by some threepence or sixpence per hour. Hourly earnings in France, Belgium and the Netherlands were fairly similar, at least one shilling per hour lower than in the U.K., with France tending to be rather lower than the other two. In all industries, hourly wage-costs were lowest in Italy by a wide margin, being generally about half the figure for the U.K.

But the pattern of hourly *labour costs*, taking into account the effect of social charges, welfare expenditure, paid holidays and other payments, is very different. In no industry did Britain rank higher than third in terms of total labour costs per hour. Western Germany had the highest overall level of labour costs, though Belgium and France had the highest costs in shipbuilding and vehicles respectively, and once again Italy was lowest, though the variation in labour cost between countries was less than variations in hourly earnings.[1] British labour costs per hour were lower than those in France and Germany in almost every industry: indeed, in steel, British labour costs were lower than in any Common Market country, and in shipbuilding only Italy had (slightly) lower labour costs.

The effect of this on international competitiveness is uncertain, for it depends on the cost structures of each industry—the importance of labour costs differs considerably between industries—and the relationship between labour costs per hour and output per man-hour. For example, in the U.S., labour costs per hour are very much higher than in any European country, but because of the high level of labour productivity, these high hourly labour costs have been spread over a large output, and prices have remained so competitive that the U.S. has consistently run a large surplus in her balance of trade. If therefore the importance of supplementary labour costs as a factor affecting unit labour costs is to be estimated and the relative experience of Britain and Europe compared, we must introduce some measure of labour productivity.

Table 38 shows the relationship between indices of labour costs per hour, output per man-hour or productivity, and unit labour costs in manufacturing industry in Britain and four European countries.

[1] See Section II, Part 1 of this Chapter, where this is set out in detail.

The official statistics of hourly earnings have been combined with estimates of supplementary labour costs in 1953 and April 1961, to give hourly labour costs. The index of output in manufacturing industry has been divided by an index of employment in manufacturing (adjusted by changes in average weekly hours worked) to give an index of output per man-hour, except in the Netherlands where no official statistics of hours worked were available; in that country, the index is of output per man-year. The combination of these two indices gives an index of labour costs per unit. In addition, the table shows indices of unit *wage* costs, to show how the inclusion of supplementary labour costs alters the international comparison.

TABLE 38. *Unit Wage and Labour Costs in Manufacturing Industries, April* 1961

1953=100

	WAGE COSTS PER HOUR	LABOUR COSTS PER HOUR	OUTPUT PER MAN-HOUR	UNIT WAGE COSTS	UNIT LABOUR COSTS
France	186	218	176	106	124
West Germany	175	188	150	117	125
Italy	144	171	139	104	123
Netherlands	180	206	137	131	150
U.K.	160	169	128	125	132

Sources: General Statistics; O.E.C.D.
       Yearbook of Labour Statistics, 1955, 1962; I.L.O.
       Etudes et Conjoncture, May 1955 and August 1962; I.N.S.E.E., Paris.

Like all tables which attempt to reconcile national data whose scope and coverage are not the same, Table 38 bears a spurious air of accuracy, yet it is probable that the relative positions of the countries in question are correct, and the discussion will proceed on that assumption.[1]

Take first the index of unit wage-costs per hour. This shows that British wage-costs rose faster than in the three main E.E.C. countries, by some 20 index points in the case of Italy and France, but slightly slower than in the Netherlands. These results are not unlike those obtained by Lamfalussy in his comparative study of Britain and

[1] It is important to note that, in order to allow comparison of these data with those obtained by A. Lamfalussy, *The United Kingdom and the Six:* an *Essay on Economic Growth in Western Europe,* Macmillan; London 1962, some figures in Table 38 have been extracted from an enquiry not so far discussed, 'Comparaison des Salaires Francais et Etrangers', *Etudes et Conjoncture,* May 1955, Institut National de Statistiques et des Etudes Economique, Paris, 1955, which contains a detailed description of the problems involved in estimating supplementary labour costs. Comparison of the 1953 figures with those for later years suggests that the European estimates are rather too high, but if Table 38 were reconstructed with 1955 as base using the I.L.O. supplementary labour cost data, the picture would be substantially similar, except that the German index of unit wage and labour costs would be slightly *higher* than that of Britain in 1961, instead of slightly lower.

Europe, though he used a different earnings series[1], and the use of a slightly longer time period in Table 38 means that unit wage-costs in France increased by less than Lamfalussy's figure—because of a large increase in industrial production in early 1961—and unit wage-costs in the Netherlands by considerably more, because of a much higher level of wages in 1961 than in 1960.[2] But Lamfalussy then asserts that these figures 'show quite convincingly that labour costs rose faster in Britain between 1953 and 1960 than in any of the E.E.C. countries'.[3] This is manifestly true of wage costs, except perhaps in the Netherlands, but Table 38 shows that, when supplementary labour costs are taken into account (as they must be to get a true picture of cost differences), international variations in labour costs per unit are very much smaller. British labour costs per unit rose much less than in the Netherlands, and only very slightly more than in Italy, France or Germany. It is also interesting to see that, except in Italy, hourly earnings in Europe rose more quickly between 1953 and 1961 than in Britain, and that all European countries experienced a steeper increase in hourly labour costs than did Britain. Therefore, as Lamfalussy says, 'the deterioration in the competitive position of British manufacturing cannot be ascribed to any faster rise in British wages' or, indeed, British labour costs, and 'the decisive difference is to be found in the rate of increase of productivity'.[4]

V. CONCLUSION

It is not the purpose of this study to investigate the reasons for the relative levels of productivity in Britain and Europe. What this chapter has attempted to do is to show what fringe benefit items cost the employer in Britain and Europe, and explain that the differences exist largely because of legal social charges which themselves result from differences in methods of social security finance. Some of the economic aspects of these supplementary labour costs and social charges have been explored, including their effect on the inter-

[1] Lamfalussy used the O.E.D.C. earnings index, while the present study used the statistics of hourly earnings contained in the Statistical Appendix to the *International Labour Review*.

[2] Lamfalussy's figures for unit labour costs per hour in 1960, which may be compared with those in the last two columns of Table 38, are (1953=100)— France—117; West Germany—109; Italy—101; Netherlands—121; United Kingdom—127. Cf. Lamfalussy, op. cit., Table 13.

[3] Lamfalussy, op. cit., p. 59.

[4] Ibid., p. 60. In Appendix 1 to his book, Lamfalussy acknowledges that his wage cost statistics are in fact wage earnings, and cites *Etudes et Conjoncture* as evidence that the results of Table 13 are broadly confirmed by wage-cost statistics. This is true as we have seen, but the addition of supplementary labour costs does considerably narrow the gap between Britain and Europe.

industry and inter-country wages structures, their influence in limit-ing the scope of collective bargaining and possible importance in affecting work incentives and labour-force structure. Finally, a comparison of labour costs in Britain and Europe has been made. It was shown that in 1960 hourly labour costs in certain important industries were lower in Britain than in France, Germany and Italy. An index of productivity was introduced, and it was estimated that, from 1953–61, unit wage-costs increased faster in Britain than in the main European countries, though the disadvantage was fairly small in the case of West Germany. Finally, a more important conclusion was that, taking into account supplementary labour costs, unit labour costs in France, Germany and Italy rose almost as much between 1953 and 1961 as they did in Britain.[1]

[1] Recent data suggest that hourly wage-costs (and probably supplementary labour costs) have been increasing faster in Europe than in Britain, and that the rapid increases in productivity of the late 1950s have now moderated. Conse-quently the index of unit labour costs in Table 38 might well in 1963 have been lower for Britain than for Germany, France or Italy.

CHAPTER 5

FRINGE BENEFITS IN THE UNITED STATES[1]

A. E. HOLMANS

I

'Fringe benefits' have in recent years played a much more prominent role in bargaining between employers and unions in the U.S. than in Britain, and much more information has been collected about them by the Department of Labor in the U.S. than by the Ministry of Labour in Britain. This chapter will outline the development of fringe benefits in the U.S. and their present scope and coverage. As was pointed out in the Introduction, varying views are held about what constitutes a fringe benefit. Attention here will be concentrated on schemes under which the employer pays all or part of the cost of protection for his employees against the main sources of insecurity of income, namely the cost of medical treatment, and loss of income as a result of old age, illness, or unemployment, together with holidays with pay. The last is not a protection against insecurity, but is the main item of expenditure on time paid for but not worked. Other types of expenditure by employers confer benefits on employees, such as the provision of sports facilities and subsidized canteens, but there is less information about their extent, and what there is indicates that they are small relative to the other items.[2] Provision for the costs of medical treatment and protection against loss of income through old

[1] The author is indebted to Mrs Dorothy Wilson for valuable comments and criticisms on Chapters 5 and 6.
[2] A survey conducted by the U.S. Chamber of Commerce in 1961 found that expenditure on meals for employees equalled 0·4 per cent of payroll, and that miscellaneous payments, described as 'compensation payments in excess of legal requirements, payments to needy employees, etc.' amounted to 0·3 per cent of payroll, and discounts on goods and services purchased by the employee from the company 0·1 per cent of payroll. U.S. Chamber of Commerce, *Fringe Benefits* 1961, Table 4.

DOI: 10.4324/9781003184706-5

age, injury, illness, or unemployment can, of course, be arranged through State schemes of social security instead of through private schemes financed in whole or in part by employers; but discussion of the advantages and disadvantages of State schemes and private provision, both in general and in the U.S. specifically, will be postponed to the next chapter.

II. THE GROWTH OF PUBLIC WELFARE IN THE UNITED STATES[1]

In a survey of the growth in the U.S. of private schemes for providing protection to employees against insecurity of income, we must first consider briefly the main reasons why the growth of public schemes of social security was slower in the U.S. than in Britain and most European countries, for the way in which State schemes develop cannot but have a strong effect on the scope for private initiative.

The federal system itself has served to delay the introduction and extension of schemes of social security in the U.S. by imposing limits on what can be done by national legislation. These limits can be altered by means short of amending the Constitution, for the Constitution has been adapted to changing circumstances by successive small unwritten changes, but the speed of such changes has been kept down by the tradition of States' Rights, a force still to be reckoned with in the nineteen-sixties. The legal forms together with the States' Rights tradition create a reluctance to accept changes which would increase the power of the Federal Government. If opposition to the assumption of new economic responsibilities by the Federal Government results in the matter being left to the States, the prospects of inaction are much greater than if the Federal Government were to assume the responsibility. For this there are two main reasons. The first is that the apportionment of seats in State legislatures has tended to favour the rural areas against the cities and suburbs, giving disproportionate power to the agricultural community and especially to small-town businessmen and lawyers, an extremely conservative group in American politics; the second reason lies in competition between States to attract new industry, which exerts strong pressure to keep down the burden of taxation on business, so that the extent to which States can set up social insurance schemes financed by compulsory employers' contributions is limited by this inter-State competition.

The slower growth of social welfare services in the U.S. is, however, only partially explicable in terms of federalism; indeed, as well as

[1] An account of the income-maintenance public welfare programmes in the U.S. and some of the economic issues to which they give rise can be found in Margaret S. Gordon, *The Economics of Welfare Policies*, Columbia University Press; New York, 1963.

being a principle in its own right, 'States' Rights' has been a battle-cry of groups resisting change, from defenders of slavery in the nineteenth century to opponents of Roosevelt's 'New Deal' and its successors. The reasons for the strength and persistence of *laissez-faire* ideas in the U.S. can only be touched on here. The success of the economic development of the U.S., leading to an average standard of living higher than that in any other part of the world, redounded to the credit of what had by the early twentieth century come to be known as 'The American System' or 'The American Way'. Notwithstanding the reform legislation enacted as a result of the 'Progressive' movement in the decade before 1914, the American economy before 1929 was very much a private enterprise economy, and the ideology of *laissez-faire* had become invested with overtones of national patriotism. Among the achievements of the 'Progressive' decade was the enactment of Workmen's Compensation legislation in the main industrial States, but nowhere in the U.S. was there established a system of sickness benefits and health insurance comparable to that set up in Britain by the National Insurance Act of 1911. Some States provided for old age pensions that were payable on proof of need, but apart from this only general poor relief and private charity were available to deal with poverty caused by old age, illness, or unemployment.

The shock that was necessary to overcome the resistance to an expansion of the social welfare responsibilities of the Government was provided by the Great Depression. With State and local governments impoverished by a fall in their tax revenues, only the Federal government could meet the need, since in the last resort it could finance its expenditure through using its power to create money. At first the Federal measures were simply schemes of emergency relief, but in 1935 the Social Security Act was passed, to provide permanently against destitution from specified causes. Its provisions were comprehensive, going a long way towards bringing American provisions for social security into line with those of other industrial countries. The Act set up a system of contributory old age and survivors' pensions, with the size of the pensions related to earnings when at work. Grants-in-aid to the States were provided for assistance to old people in need and dependent children.[1] In addition the States were compelled to establish unemployment insurance schemes by the imposition of a Federal tax, against which contributions to approved State unemployment insurance schemes could be credited. The Act was challenged as going beyond the powers conferred on the Federal Government by the Constitution, but the courts sustained it.[2]

---

[1] i.e. children whose parents or guardians have insufficient resources to maintain them without assistance.

[2] The Supreme Court held that both the pension scheme and the unemployment insurance tax were valid exercises of the power of the Congress to 'lay and

The Social Security Act is still in 1964 the main landmark in the development of official schemes of social security in the U.S. Subsequent legislation has raised the levels of benefit and extended coverage to most groups who were excluded under the original Act, but the scope of compulsory social security schemes is still that of the Act of 1935, except for insurance against permanent and total disability, which was added to old age and survivors insurance in 1956. Insurance against loss of income through illness or injury not covered by Workmen's Compensation legislation and against the costs of medical treatment has not yet become general in the U.S.,[1] and their enactment would probably require a shift to the Left in dominant political opinion similar to that which took place in the 1930s. Since 1938 the informal coalition of Republicans and conservative Southern Democrats has held sufficient power in Congress to veto further moves to expand the economic functions of the Federal government, and from 1953 to 1961 the Administration was also unsympathetic to large measures of social reform. The conservative coalition's veto has not extended to minor measures of social reform, but, as President Truman found in 1949 and President Kennedy in 1962, it can prevent drastic new Federal legislation on welfare. The American Medical Association's skilfully conducted campaign against compulsory health insurance doubtless strengthened opposition to it, but the campaign could not have succeeded had there been a solid majority of opinion in the country in favour of national health insurance and a liberal majority in Congress as in the 1930s. In 1960 and again in 1962 there was considerable support for the inclusion of hospital treatment among the benefits provided for retired people under O.A.S.D.I.[2] This proposal failed of enactment in both years, despite President Kennedy's support in 1962. It appears probable, as of 1964, that something on these lines will eventually be enacted, but general compulsory health insurance seems far away, and there is little interest in extending compulsory sickness insurance to those employees not covered by it.

---

collect taxes . . . to provide for . . . the general welfare of the United States'. (*Helvering v. Davis* (301 U.S. 619) and *Steward Machine Co v. Davis* (301 U.S. 548)). Both cases were decided in 1937, the former by a 7–2 majority, the latter by 5–4.

[1] Insurance against loss of income arising from illness or injury not arising out of employment (termed 'nonoccupational disability' in the U.S.) is provided compulsorily for railway employees by Federal law; and for employees in industry and commerce in California, New Jersey, New York, and Rhode Island by State Law. For a summary of the provisions of the four State schemes and the Federal scheme for railway employees, see Margaret M. Dahm, 'Temporary Disability Insurance in the United States', *International Labour Review*, Vol. 78 (1958), pp. 552–74.

[2] Old Age, Survivors, and Disability Insurance. Prior to the inclusion in 1956 of insurance against disability, the scheme was known as O.A.S.I.

III. THE GROWTH IN PRIVATE PROVISION

Tables 39 and 40 give some details of the growth of private schemes providing protection to employees against insecurity of income. For the period before World War II, details of the increase in the number of employees covered are available for pension schemes only; for other benefits the only indicator available is the rise in the amount paid in contributions. Since private schemes covered only a small proportion of employees in the 1930s, the slow growth of public social security schemes cannot be attributed to private schemes having already met most of the need. As late as 1940 private pension schemes covered only 15 per cent of all employees outside agriculture and government service.[1]

TABLE 39. *Numbers Covered by Private Pension Plans*

1930	4,000,000
1935	3,800,000
1940	4,100,000
1945	6,400,000
1950	9,800,000
1955	15,400,000
1960	21,600,000
1961	22,600,000

Note: The 1930 and 1935 totals include 1,300,000 and 1,100,000 respectively who were covered by railway pension plans.

Source: Historical Statistics of the United States, Series X-483; *Statistical Abstract of the United States*, Table 385; and *Social Security Bulletin*, April 1963, p. 12.

The growth of private schemes in the U.S. accelerated during World War II. The trade unions, which in the 1930s had been engaged in vigorous and often violent struggles for recognition and hence had little opportunity to concern themselves with the more complex problems of pensions and health insurance, turned to fringe benefits as a way in which the war-induced shortage of labour could be turned to their members' advantage within the limits set by the wage stabilization policies to which they had agreed. Most employers were anxious to find means of attracting and retaining labour, and hence had little inducement to offer vigorous resistance to the unions' demands. In the first three years after the end of the war collective bargaining centred mainly on straightforward wage increases, but in 1949 there was a shift of emphasis towards the negotiation of pension rights and health insurance benefits, caused partly by the cessation in mid-1948 of the

[1] The number of employees covered by pension schemes was taken from Table 39, and the total number of employees (excluding agriculture and government service) from *Historical Statistics of the United States*, Series D.48 and D.56.

TABLE 40. *Private Employers' Contributions to Pension and Welfare Funds*

			TOTAL PRIVATE WAGES AND SALARIES	EMPLOYERS' CONTRIBUTIONS		TOTAL EMPLOYERS' CONTRIBUTIONS AS PERCENTAGE OF WAGES AND SALARIES
				PENSIONS	OTHER	
1930	..	..	41,033	130	30	0·4
1935	..	..	36,690	140	40	0·5
1940	..	..	41,395	180	102	0·7
1945	..	..	82,664	830	302	1·4
1950	..	..	124,121	1,750	993	2·2
1955	..	..	174,927	3,190	1,333	3·2
1960	..	..	222,942	4,490	4,139	3·9
1961	..	..	226,991	4,550	4,396	3·9

Notes: Amounts are in $ million.

The amounts in the column headed 'other' were obtained by subtraction of the estimate of employers' contributions to pension funds from the estimate of all employers' contributions. Paid sick leave is excluded, whereas payments for sickness insurance for employees are included.

Source: Wages and salaries and total employers' contributions from *U.S. Income and Output*, Table 1–8, and *Survey of Current Business*, July 1963, Table 2; contributions to pension funds from *Historical Statistics of the United States*, Series X-486; and *Social Security Bulletin*, April 1963, p. 12.

rise in prices, which made wage increases less urgent. The 1949 settlement in the steel industry, providing for both pensions and health insurance, was especially important in setting a pattern, or rather a target, for union negotiators in other industries to match. In subsequent years there was a steady tendency for larger benefits and more extensive coverage to be negotiated as agreements came up for renewal. The most notable innovation in benefits negotiated on behalf of employees in the 1950s was supplementary unemployment benefit (sometimes referred to as the 'Guaranteed Annual Wage'), but after rapid initial growth in a few industries in 1955–7 there had been little further expansion by 1964.

The success of the trade unions' efforts to secure the inclusion of pension rights and health insurance in agreements negotiated with employers is shown in Table 41. The Table gives the number of employees covered by negotiated schemes, both in absolute terms and as a proportion of all employees covered by collective bargaining agreements.

The trade unions in the U.S. did not choose negotiated health insurance benefits in preference to more extensive provision of social security benefits through the public sector. In 1949 and 1950 they were very prominent among the groups supporting President Truman's national health insurance plan, and in 1960 and 1962 gave strong support to the proposal to extend the benefits under O.A.S.D.I. to include hospital treatment for retired people. There seems little doubt,

I

TABLE 41. *Coverage of Union-Negotiated Pension and Health Insurance Schemes*

			PENSIONS		HEALTH INSURANCE	
				PROPORTION OF ALL COVERED BY		PROPORTION OF ALL COVERED BY
			NUMBER (MILLION)	EMPLOYER-UNION AGREEMENTS	NUMBER (MILLION)	EMPLOYER-UNION AGREEMENTS
1948	..	..	1·7	11%	2·7	18%
1950	..	..	5·1	34%	7·1	47%
1960	..	..	11·1	60%	14·5	78%

Source: Department of Labor, *Monthly Labor Review*, March 1962, p. 275.

though, that the failure of efforts to enact a system of national health insurance induced the unions to place more emphasis on health insurance in collective bargaining.

IV. THE PRESENT COVERAGE OF FRINGE BENEFITS

Table 42 summarizes information on the coverage of three major fringe benefits—retirement pensions, health insurance, and sickness benefits. The data refer to the year 1961, the latest for which the statistics collected by the Department of Health, Education and Welfare are available.

TABLE 42. *Coverage of Private Pension, Sickness, and Health Insurance Schemes in 1961*

	NUMBER OF WAGE AND SALARY EARNERS COVERED (MILLION)	PERCENT OF TOTAL WAGE AND SALARY EARNERS	NUMBER OF DEPENDENTS COVERED (MILLION)	TOTAL NUMBER OF PERSONS COVERED (MILLION)
Private and Public Employees				
Life insurance and death benefits	45·9	78·2	3·6	49·5
Accidental death and dismemberment	21·3	36·2	—	21·3
Hospital treatment (a)	41·3	70·2	64·7	106·0
Surgical (a)	39·4	67·1	61·4	100·8
Regular medical (a)	31·2	53·1	46·9	78·1
Major medical expense ..	11·6	19·7	19·9	31·5
Private Employees Only				
Temporary disability (b) ..	25·8	51·7	—	25·8
Supplemental unemployment benefit..	1·8	3·6	—	1·8
Retirement pension	22·6	45·3	—	22·6

Notes: (a) 'Hospital treatment' comprises room and board, nursing, and ancillary services, but does *not* include the fees of surgeons and physicians for attention in hospital. These are covered by 'surgical' and 'regular medical' respectively.

(b) Illness and injury not arising out of employment. Includes both sickness insurance and formal sick pay schemes.

Source: 'Growth of Employee-Benefit Plans, 1954–61', Tables 1 and 2, *Social Security Bulletin*, April 1963.

The data in Table 42 refer to all wage and salary earners. From a survey carried out by the Bureau of Labor Statistics in 1961–62 of fringe benefits in the metropolitan areas of the U.S., it is evident that the proportion covered by pension schemes is higher among office workers than among plant workers. The proportion covered by sickness insurance or sick leave was the same (four-fifths) for both office and plant workers, though for plant workers the cover was provided predominantly through sickness and accident insurance and for office workers through paid sick leave. The proportion covered by hospital treatment and surgical insurance was very slightly lower among office workers than among plant workers, and the proportion covered by medical insurance slightly higher.[1]

1. *Pensions*

The pension rights provided through private schemes are in most instances supplements to the benefits provided through O.A.S.D.I. Successive amendments to the Social Security Act have broadened its coverage to include practically all wage and salary earners other than Federal Government employees and many State and local government employees (who have separate pension schemes) and part-time and casual workers. Practically all new entrants to private pension schemes will therefore be covered by O.A.S.D.I. as well. The broadening of coverage has taken place fairly recently (through the Social Security Amendments of 1950, 1954, and 1956), so that there are still considerable numbers of people receiving private pensions but no O.A.S.D.I. pension; but their numbers will dwindle as more and more of those who retire from private employment have been covered by O.A.S.D.I. for long enough to acquire title to a pension.

Private pension plans in the U.S. are so diverse in their provisions that it is difficult to describe them briefly. This is especially true of the amounts payable. These are related to length of service, wages or salaries earned while covered by the scheme, or sometimes to both; but the formulas used are many and varied and are subject to change as a result of negotiation. The only way of expressing the benefits in terms of a common measure that permits comparison and averaging is to compute the annual or monthly benefit ultimately payable (assuming there to be no changes in the scheme in the meantime) to a new entrant on specified assumptions about length of service, average earnings, and age of retirement. This method was used by the Bureau of Labor Statistics in analysing the benefits payable under the 300 collectively-negotiated pension plans in its sample, which covered 4,672,700 employees. It was assumed for purposes of com-

[1] 'Supplementary Benefits in Metropolitan Areas, 1961–2', Table 4, *Monthly Labor Review*, March 1963, p. 297.

putation that the employee would retire at the age of 65 after 30 years' service, with average earnings of $4,000 or $5,600 a year. The Table shows the number of employees in the sample covered by plans which would ultimately yield to new entrants benefits in the given ranges of monthly amounts, on the assumptions specified about retirement age, length of service, and average earnings.

TABLE 43. *Monthly Pension (Including O.A.S.D.I.)*
Ultimately Payable to New Entrants, 1959

PENSION				AVERAGE EARNINGS $4,000 A YEAR		AVERAGE EARNINGS $5,600 A YEAR	
				NUMBER COVERED 000	PER CENT OF TOTAL	NUMBER COVERED 000	PER CENT OF TOTAL
Under $160	..	..	..	395·9	8·5	62·7	1·3
$160–$179 ..	..	..	..	1,332·2	28·5	851·5	18·2
$180–$199	..	..	..	1,935·8	41·4	425·8	9·1
$200–$219 ..	..	..	..	539·2	11·5	2,040·1	43·7
$220–$239 ..	..	..	..	176·4	3·8	440·0	9·4
$240–$274 ..	..	..	..	282·0	6·0	403·7	8·6
$275 or over	..	..	..	21·2	0·5	448·9	9·6
				4,672·7	100·0	4,672·7	100·0

Source: Bureau of Labor Statistics, *Pension Plans Under Collective Bargaining*, Bulletin No. 1284, Tables 21 and 22.

At 1959 levels of income, $4,000 a year was fairly representative of earnings (before tax) of unskilled workers in manufacturing industry, and $5,600 was representative of skilled workers' earnings. Almost 80 per cent of the former earnings group would receive a monthly pension of less than $200, while 71 per cent of the latter would get a monthly pension of more than $200. However, when the amount of pension is related to normal earnings, the position of the lower income group becomes more favourable. Table 44 shows the average pensions that would ultimately be payable to new entrants who earned average incomes in employment covered by the pension schemes of $4,000 or $5,600 a year over their whole working lives: the pension of a man earning $4,000 would be 56 per cent of his average monthly pay, compared with 46 per cent of one earning $5,600.

Nearly all the occupational pension schemes included in the sample studied by the Bureau of Labor Statistics provided for a minimum period to be worked in covered employment in order to qualify for a pension at all. For about 80 per cent of employees covered by the plans studied, the minimum period of service was ten years or more,[1]

[1] Bureau of Labor Statistics, Bulletin No. 1284, Table 7.

TABLE 44. *Average Monthly Pensions Payable under O.A.S.D.I. and Negotiated Private Pension Plans*

	AVERAGE EARNINGS $4,000 A YEAR	AVERAGE EARNINGS $5,600 A YEAR
O.A.S.D.I. Pension	$112·00	$127·00
Pension from private scheme	$75·50	$86·83
Total	$187·50	$213·83
Total as percentage of average monthly pay (before tax)	56%	46%

Source: Bureau of Labor Statistics, *Pension Plans Under Collective Bargaining,* Bulletin No. 1284, Table 18.

and such minimum service periods can exclude significant numbers of people from entitlement to pensions on account of mobility of labour,[1] especially since multi-employer plans are the exception among pension schemes in the U.S.[2] Outside a few industries where multi-employer pension schemes exist, loss of employment normally means loss of expectation of a pension, except where rights previously acquired are protected by vesting. 'Vesting' provides to the employee a right in a pension fund based on all or part of the employer's contribution, in the event of his leaving employment covered by the pension plan before retiring age. On leaving covered employment the employee is always entitled to have refunded to him contributions he himself has made, usually with accrued interest, but since employers' contributions are usually much larger than employees' contributions,[3] the loss of expectation of benefit based on employers' contributions is a serious matter. In its study of 300 collectively-negotiated pension plans the Bureau of Labor Statistics found that in 1958 (the latest year for which data are available) plans providing for vesting covered 57 per cent of all employees covered by plans included in the sample.[4] In nearly all such plans vested rights were provided only after a minimum period of service, commonly 10 or 15 years, Vesting thus protects the pension rights of the long-service employee who is laid off before reaching the normal retiring age, but rarely does anything for

[1] For some data on the extent of mobility of labour, see Chapter 6, Section II. The number of people who lose their expectation of a pension for this reason is, however, not known.

[2] Just over one-third of all employees covered by plans included in the sample studied were covered by multi-employer plans. Bureau of Labor Statistics, Bulletin No. 1284, Table 8.

[3] Estimates by the Social Security Administration put total employers' contributions in 1961 at $4,550 million and employees' contributions at $780 million. *Social Security Bulletin,* April 1963, p. 12.

[4] Bureau of Labor Statistics, *Pension Plans Under Collective Bargaining— Vesting Provisions and Requirements for Early Retirement,* Bulletin No. 1259, Table 3.

the employee who stays with any one employer (or group of employers who are parties to a multi-employer pension scheme) for less than 10 years. But the number of employees who for this reason are unable to acquire pension rights is not known.

2. *Health Insurance*

As indicated in Table 42, insurance against medical costs is of four types: hospital treatment (or 'hospitalization'); surgical; regular medical (including physicians' services rendered in hospital); and major medical expense; it is fairly common, though, for cover under the first three to be provided under a single scheme of benefits arranged on behalf of employees. The inclusion in hospital insurance plans of limits on the number of days in hospital or on the payment per day in hospital, and reimbursement only for specified services instead of for all services,[1] led to the inclusion of 'major medical expense' insurance among the supplementary benefits provided for many employees. Introduced in the early 1950s by commercial insurance companies, this type of insurance covers the cost of medical services of all kinds, whether received in hospital or elsewhere. The benefits payable are subject to an upper limit, but it is much higher than under ordinary hospital insurance, hence the advantages in cases of prolonged illness. The reimbursement is not, however, complete; typically the beneficiary has to pay the first $100 or so himself, and 20 per cent or so of the remainder.[2]

There is considerable variation among the occupational health insurance schemes in the scope and extent of the benefits provided, but in general the costs of hospital treatment are covered, leaving the costs of medical attention outside hospital, medicines, and dental treatment to be financed individually. More details of the benefits provided under health insurance schemes, together with discussion of the extent of the coverage and the proportion of private expenditure on medical care that is financed through insurance, may be found in the next chapter.

3. *Sickness Insurance and Sick Pay*

The coverage of public insurance schemes which provide cash payments to people temporarily unable to work as a result of illness or injury not arising out of their employment is much less extensive in the U.S. than in most countries of Western Europe and the Commonwealth. Under Federal legislation railway employees are covered by sickness insurance; and under State legislation employees in industry

[1] For details, see Chapter 6, Section II.
[2] For further details, see Bureau of Labor Statistics, *Health and Insurance Plans Under Collective Bargaining—Major Medical Expense Benefits*, Bulletin No. 1293.

and commerce in California, New Jersey, New York, and Rhode Island. In Rhode Island the benefits are provided out of a State fund, financed by a payroll tax levied on covered employees; in the other three States the benefits are financed by the employer, who can either insure through the State fund or, as most do, insure privately, subject to minimum standards of benefit being met.[1] Most government employees are covered by formal sick pay schemes; in 1960 practically all full-time employees of the Federal Government were covered, as were 82 per cent of full-time employees of State and local governments.[2]

In Table 42 it was shown that just over one-half of all private employees were covered by sickness insurance or formal sick leave schemes. Included in this figure, however, were employees in California, New Jersey, and New York covered by schemes drawn up in compliance with laws requiring such coverage; if they are excluded, just over 44 per cent of employees in the remaining States were covered. In addition, it is known that some employees not covered by formal sick pay schemes receive sick pay informally, but no estimates are available of the number of employees concerned or the amounts paid.[3]

Table 45 shows estimates by the Social Security Administration for the year 1960 of the benefits received from sickness insurance and formal sick pay schemes by employees covered by temporary disability insurance laws; other private employees; and Government employees. These estimates are set against corresponding estimates of income lost as a result of sickness. It is not possible to deduce how effective the various private schemes were in maintaining the incomes of all employees covered by them, for the estimate of income-loss applies to all employees, not just to those covered by sickness insurance or paid sick leave; but it is clear that the protection afforded to Government employees compared very favourably with what was available to private employees.

4. Supplemental Unemployment Benefit

When the first agreements providing for supplemental unemployment benefits were being negotiated, the term 'guaranteed annual

[1] For details of the State schemes and of the Federal scheme for railway employees as of 1958, see Margaret M. Dahm, 'Temporary Disability Insurance in the United States', *International Labour Review*, Vol. 78 (1958), pp. 552–74. It is estimated that in 1961 these schemes covered about 12 million employees. *Monthly Labor Review*, June 1963, p. 626.

[2] 'Income-Loss Protection Against Short-Term Sickness', Table 4, notes 4 and 5, *Social Security Bulletin*, January 1962.

[3] Moreover, the security provided for a given expenditure is less than under a formal scheme, since the employee cannot be sure of what payments he will receive and how long they will continue.

TABLE 45. *Sick Pay and Income-Loss in* 1960

	INCOME-LOSS	BENEFIT	BENEFIT AS PERCENTAGE OF INCOME-LOSS
	($ MILLION)		
Employees covered by temporary disability insurance laws	1,775	435	24·5
Other private employees and self-employed persons	5,687	1,131	19·9
Government employees	1,165	821	70·5
Total	8,627	2,387	27·7

Note: Benefits include $387 million from individual sickness insurance.
Source: 'Income-Loss Protection Against Short-Term Sickness', Tables 1, 2, 3, and 4, *Social Security Bulletin,* January 1962.

wage' was sometimes used. This term is misleading, since it can imply the equivalent of salaried status or that employers who are parties to such agreements have undertaken to pay employees specified amounts of wages throughout the year, irrespective of the proportion of the year for which the employee works. What the schemes provide, however, are benefits related to wages earned when in employment, for a limited period of unemployment. The most usual formula provides that benefits shall be related to straight-time[1] hourly earnings, less any State unemployment benefit received. The number of weeks for which benefit may be drawn is determined by the length of time for which the employee has been with the company,[2] and is subject to a maximum that is different in different agreements the longest being one year.

The benefits provided are thus in no sense a 'guaranteed annual wage'. They are financed out of a trust fund into which the employer makes regular contributions according to an agreed formula, and payment is therefore conditional on the resources of the fund being adequate. In addition, benefit is sometimes not paid to those made unemployed as a result of labour disputes. For example, the 1962 agreement between U.S. Steel and the United Steelworkers provided that no benefits should be paid to employees made unemployed as a result of strikes by other employees of the company, by members of the same union working for other firms, or by transport employees whose strikes interfered with supplies of materials or sales of products. After an initial burst in 1955–7 when supplemental unemployment schemes were negotiated in the motor vehicle and steel

[1] i.e. excluding premium pay for overtime or Sunday work.
[2] The period required to qualify is usually short. In the scheme operated by the U.S. Steel Corporation, for example, an employee receives one-half of a 'credit unit' for each week worked for the company (or absent through industrial injury) and in the event of dismissal is entitled to one week's benefit for each 'credit unit' up to a maximum of fifty-two.

industries, there has been little further expansion in coverage of such schemes. Indeed, employment in the motor vehicle and steel industries has tended to fall, reducing the numbers covered by supplemental unemployment benefits schemes.

5. *Holidays with Pay*

In American terminology there is the same distinction between 'holidays' and 'vacations' as between public and annual holidays in Britain. Paid vacations for plant workers have existed considerably longer in the United States than paid holidays; establishments employing nearly 40 per cent of all production workers in manufacturing provided paid vacations in 1937, whereas paid holidays for production workers were practically unknown before World War II.[1]

In 1961–62 practically all office workers and more than 90 per cent of plant workers in metropolitan areas of the U.S. received five or more paid holidays a year. Two-thirds of all plant workers received at least seven paid holidays a year, and one-quarter received at least eight, while among office workers the respective proportions were just under four-fifths and one-half.[2]

The length of paid vacations, both for office workers and for plant workers, is usually related to length of service, but the relationships vary, and are not easy to summarize. For plant workers the commonest arrangement is for one week's paid vacation after completion of one year of service, two weeks after two to five years of service, and three weeks after ten to fifteen years. Practically all plant workers covered by the Bureau of Labor Statistics enquiry were covered by schemes which provided up to two weeks' annual vacation, and three-quarters were covered by schemes providing for a third week's vacation for employees completing the requisite length of service. Just under one-third were covered by schemes which made provision for vacations of four weeks, for which twenty to twenty-five years of service was typically required. Vacations for office workers are similar, except that the length of service required to qualify for two- and three-week vacations is usually shorter than for manual workers.[3]

[1] Bureau of Labor Statistics, *Employer Expenditure for Selected Supplementary Remuneration Practices for Production Workers in Manufacturing Industries, 1959*, Bulletin No. 1308, pp. 12–14.

[2] *Monthly Labor Review*, March 1963, p. 294, Table 1.

[3] *Monthly Labor Review*, March 1963, p. 295, Table 2. These data, which relate to all private establishments in metropolitan areas, may be compared with the provisions of collective agreements relating to vacations, which are analysed in 'Paid Vacation Provisions in Major Union Contracts, 1961', *Monthly Labor Review*, August 1962. Practically all collective agreements in manufacturing industry provided for paid vacations, as did most agreements in the service trades; but in the construction industry three-quarters of all employees covered by collective agreements were covered by agreements which made no provision for paid vacations.

The types of benefit discussed in this Chapter are not the only kinds of fringe benefit in the U.S. Others include paid leave for discharging civil duties (e.g. jury service), severance pay, Christmas bonuses, discounts on goods purchased from the company, and many other items; but in terms of cost their importance is small compared with the types of benefits discussed above. Such facilities as subsidized canteens and sports grounds are not dealt with here because there are no readily available data either on employer's expenditure on such facilities in the U.S., or the number of employees with access to them.

V. THE COST OF SUPPLEMENTARY BENEFITS

There are two sets of data on the cost of supplementary benefits in the U.S. The first consists of estimates of average expenditure (as a percentage of payroll, or per man-hour) on supplementary benefits in a sample of firms or establishments; the second of estimates of total expenditure on pension schemes, health insurance, and employees' life insurance. Unfortunately it is not possible to integrate the two because of differences in coverage, both in the type of supplementary benefit included and the category of employees to whom the data relate.

The main sources of data on the average cost of supplementary benefits per man-hour or as a percentage of payroll are surveys conducted by the Bureau of Labor Statistics and the U.S. Chamber of Commerce. The U.S. Chamber of Commerce undertook surveys every two years from 1947 to 1961 inclusive, and covered manufacturing industry, construction, mining, public utilities, hotels, wholesale and retail trade, and banking, insurance, and finance. Except for the banking, insurance, and finance group, the survey was confined to hourly paid employees. The survey carried out by the Bureau of Labor Statistics related to 1959, and covered production employees in manufacturing industry only. The findings of the Bureau of Labor Statistics's survey and of that part of the results of the U.S. Chamber of Commerce's 1959 survey that related to manufacturing industry are compared in Table 46, together with the U.S. Chamber of Commerce's data for 1961.

The U.S. Chamber of Commerce's 1959 enquiry thus yielded higher estimates of the cost to employers in manufacturing industry of pension schemes, health, accident, and life insurance, and paid holidays and vacations than did the enquiry conducted by the Bureau of Labor Statistics. The definitions used in specifying the employees in manufacturing to be covered were not identical, but they were similar in effect.[1] Differences in methods of selecting the samples are,

[1] For the definitions used see U.S. Chamber of Commerce, *Fringe Benefits* 1959,

TABLE 46. *Cost to Employers of Certain Supplementary Benefits for Production Workers in Manufacturing Industry, 1959 and 1961*

	EXPENDITURE AS PERCENTAGE OF GROSS PAYROLL		
	BUREAU OF LABOR STATISTICS 1959	U.S. CHAMBER OF COMMERCE 1959	1961
1. Legally required payments	4·5	4·5	5·5
2. Pension plans	2·4	3·3	3·4
3. Health, accident, and life insurance ..	2·1	2·4	3·0
4. Supplemental unemployment benefit ..	0·1	0·1	0·1
5. Severance or dismissal pay	*	*	*
6. Christmas and end-of-year bonuses ..	0·5	0·5	0·5
7. Paid sick leave	0·2	0·3	0·4
8. Paid vacations and holidays	5·7	6·3	6·7
9. Paid leave for military duty, jury service, voting, and personal circumstances ..	*	0·1	0·1
Total for benefits specified	15·5	17·5	19·7
Total excluding legally required payments	11·0	13·0	14·2

Note: * denotes less than 0·05 per cent.

Source: Bureau of Labor Statistics, *Employer Expenditures for Selected Supplementary Remuneration Practices for Production Workers in Manufacturing Industries 1959,* Bulletin No. 1308, Table 1; U.S. Chamber of Commerce, *Fringe Benefits 1959,* Table 4, and *Fringe Benefits 1961,* Table 4.

however, probably much more important in accounting for the differences in the findings. The U.S. Chamber of Commerce's sample of manufacturing firms was drawn from *Poor's Register of Directors and Executives,*[1] omitting firms with less than 100 employees. There were 692 manufacturing companies in the sample. The Bureau of Labor Statistics' sample consisted of establishments, not firms, and was drawn from lists of manufacturing establishments kept by State unemployment insurance authorities. Establishments with four employees or more were included in the population sampled; a stratified probability sample was drawn, and the findings calculated from replies from 4,400 establishments.[2] An indication of the significance of the exclusion from the U.S. Chamber of Commerce's sample of firms employing 100 people or less is given in Table 47. The comparison is not exact, because of the difference between an 'establishment' and a 'firm', but the error this introduces is probably small since most small firms have one establishment only.

---

p. 36; and Bureau of Labor Statistics, Bulletin No. 1308, p. 113. Only that part of the U.S. Chamber of Commerce's findings that relates to manufacturing industry is compared here with the study by the Bureau of Labor Statistics.

[1] U.S. Chamber of Commerce, op. cit., p. 35.

[2] Bureau of Labor Statistics, op. cit., p. 112.

TABLE 47. *Expenditure on Supplementary Benefits in Manufacturing Industry in 1959, Analysed by Size of Establishment*

	PERCENTAGE OF GROSS PAYROLL			
	UNDER 100 EMPLOYEES	100–499 EMPLOYEES	OVER 500 EMPLOYEES	ALL ESTABLISH-MENTS
1. Legally required payments ..	5·2	4·8	4·1	4·5
2. Pension plans	0·9	1·8	3·3	2·4
3. Health, accident, and life insurance	1·4	2·0	2·4	2·1
4. Supplemental unemployment benefit	*	0·1	0·2	0·1
5. Severance and dismissal pay ..	*	*	*	*
6. Christmas and end-of-year bonuses	0·7	0·5	0·4	0·5
7. Paid sick leave	0·1	0·1	0·3	0·2
8. Paid vacations and holidays ..	4·1	5·2	6·6	5·7
9. Paid leave for military duty, jury service, voting, and personal circumstances	*	*	0·1	*

Note: * Denotes less than 0·05 per cent.
Source: Bureau of Labor Statistics, Bulletin No. 1308, Tables 1 and 37.

The differences between average expenditures (as percentages of gross payroll) on pension schemes, health insurance, paid sick leave, and paid holidays and vacations in establishments with less than 100 employees and the averages for all establishments were thus large, too large to be attributed solely to sampling variation. It therefore follows that the exclusion of firms employing less than 100 employees from the population sampled by the U.S. Chamber of Commerce's enquiry introduced an upward bias if the findings were applied to manufacturing firms of all sizes.

The picture of expenditure on fringe benefits presented by the U.S. Chamber of Commerce's 1961 survey is similar to that presented by the 1959, except that expenditures were rather higher relative to payroll. Employers' contributions to statutory schemes of social insurance rose, as did payments to private schemes, especially for health insurance, which accounted for the largest part of the increase. An increase in expenditure, relative to gross payroll, for paid holidays and vacations also took place.

The U.S. Chamber of Commerce's biennial enquiries provide data on changes in the cost of fringe benefits over the fourteen years from 1947 to 1961. Fifty-five manufacturing companies were included in the sample in each year, and direct comparison of expenditure on fringe benefits by those companies is therefore possible. The number of companies is small, and caution is therefore required in applying the data derived from it to manufacturing industry as a whole, even bearing in mind the reservation about the exclusion of small firms. Even so, the comparison in Table 48 is of value in showing the tendency of expenditure on fringe benefits to rise relative to payroll.

TABLE 48. *Expenditures on Fringe Benefits by Fifty-Five Manufacturing Companies, 1947–61*

EXPENDITURE AS PERCENT OF GROSS PAYROLL

		LEGALLY REQUIRED PAYMENTS	PENSIONS, HEALTH INSURANCE, SICKNESS INSURANCE	HOLIDAYS, VACATIONS, PAID SICK LEAVE
1947	..	3·1	2·8	4·2
1949	..	2·9	3·8	5·5
1951	..	3·0	4·9	5·8
1953	..	2·8	5·8	6·4
1955	..	3·1	6·3	6·7
1957	..	3·8	7·1	7·9
1959	..	3·9	7·2	8·1
1961		4·7	7·9	8·3

Source: U.S. Chamber of Commerce, *Fringe Benefits* 1961, Table 18.

As mentioned above, the data on the cost of fringe benefits as a proportion of gross payroll cannot be linked directly to available aggregate data on contributions to pension funds and other payments on behalf of employees, for the aggregate data refer to all wage and salary earners, whereas the Bureau of Labor Statistics' survey was restricted to production workers in manufacturing industry and that part of the U.S. Chamber of Commerce's survey that related to manufacturing industry covered hourly paid workers only. The survey and the aggregate data are therefore not directly comparable. Table 49 shows employers' expenditure on pension schemes, health insurance, and sickness insurance schemes in 1950 and 1961.

TABLE 49. *Employers' Contributions in 1950 and 1961*

	AMOUNT IN $ MILLION		PERCENTAGE OF TOTAL PRIVATE WAGES AND SALARIES	
	1950	1961	1950	1961
Employers' contributions to private pension and welfare funds	2,743	8,946	2·2	3·9
Of which:				
Contributions to pension funds ..	1,750	4,550	1·4	2·0
Other	993	4,396	0·8	1·9
Employers' contributions to compulsory social insurance	3,070	9,090	2·5	4·0

Source: U.S. Income and Output, Table III-6; *Survey of Current Business,* July 1963, Tables 2 and 24; *Social Security Bulletin,* April 1963, Table 5, p. 12.

Table 49 shows the rapid rise of employers' contributions, both in absolute amount and relative wages and salaries, to private pension and welfare schemes. The increase was especially rapid in the 'other' group, which consists predominantly of health insurance. At the same time contributions to public schemes of social insurance also rose, mainly to O.A.S.D.I., which accounted for almost three-quarters of the increase in employers' contributions to social insurance. One measure of the importance of employers' contributions to private pension and welfare schemes is that they were almost equal in size in 1961 to compulsory social insurance contributions; only one-half of private employers' contributions to insurance schemes for their employees' benefits were to compulsory schemes.

VI. CONCLUSION

The expansion of schemes which provide health insurance and pension rights for employees as part of their remuneration has taken place fairly recently in the U.S. While the rapid growth of schemes providing insurance against the costs of hospital treatment may well owe something to the failure of President Truman's attempt to secure the enactment of compulsory national health insurance, the slow growth of public schemes of social security in the U.S. (compared with European countries) was not due to the existence already of a well-developed system of private schemes, for, as Tables 39 and 40 make clear, most of the growth of private schemes came *after* the establishment of compulsory schemes by the Social Security Act; private pension schemes have expanded side by side with the Old Age and Survivors Insurance scheme. By 1961 nearly one-half of all private employees were covered by pension schemes, and if peripheral members of the working population (housewives working part-time, students, and schoolboys, for example) are excluded, the proportion of regular full-time private employees who were covered is considerably greater. Over two-thirds of all employees have some cover against the cost of hospital treatment for themselves, and most of these for their dependents. Practically all full-time employees of Federal, State, and local governments are entitled to paid sick leave, and just over one-half of all private employees are covered either by formal sick leave schemes or by sickness insurance. In general, the employees best protected by occupational health insurance, sick pay, and pension schemes are skilled workers in industry, especially those who work for large firms and are covered by collective bargaining agreements.[1] But, as the next Chapter will show, it is clear that in

---

[1] Expenditures on these benefits are larger, relative to pay roll, in large establishments than in small, are larger in establishments where average pay is relatively high than where it is low, and where trade unions are strong. Bureau of Labor Statistics, Bulletin No. 1308, Tables 36, 37 and 38.

many cases it is those who most need protection who are not covered.

Precise comparisons with Britain are not possible on account of differences of definition, but certain rough comparisons are none the less of interest. The findings of the British surveys discussed in Chapters 2 and 3 relate to manual workers in manufacturing industry and construction and are based on data received from a sample of companies; the American data most readily comparable are therefore the findings of the U.S. Chamber of Commerce's survey of fringe benefits in manufacturing industry. As indicated above, comparison with the Bureau of Labor Statistics study suggests that the omission of small firms from the sample imparted an upward bias, but it is likely that a similar bias is present in the findings of the British survey. Taking both the British and the U.S. surveys at face value, and comparing the British data (which relate to 1960) with the U.S. Chamber of Commerce's 1959 survey, it is clear that on the average expenditure on the main fringe benefits was higher, relative to payroll, in the U.S. than in Britain. Expenditure on pension plans in the U.S. amounted to 3·3 per cent of payroll, whereas in Britain it was only 1·50 per cent; inclusion of ex gratia pension payments raises the figure to 1·85 per cent, still well below the American level. Likewise, expenditure on holidays with pay was estimated at 6·3 per cent of payroll in the U.S., compared with 4·80 per cent in Britain. Expenditure on sick pay, on the other hand, was about the same in both countries, 0·3 per cent of payroll in the U.S. and 0·32 per cent in Britain. The most important difference, however, is that American firms incur substantial expenditures for the provision of health insurance, which the existence of the National Health Service makes unnecessary in Britain, at least for most manual workers. In Britain the number of occupational health insurance schemes where the employer pays part of the cost is believed to be small, with nearly all the beneficiaries being highly-paid salaried staff.

A comparison can also be made between employers' expenditure on contributions to pension funds, relative to wages and salaries paid. The aggregate data include contributions to pension schemes for all employees, both manual and non-manual, in all lines of business, and therefore cannot be related directly to the data on expenditure on pensions as a proportion of payroll, which refer only to manual workers in manufacturing industry. A further problem in comparing expenditure in the U.S. and Britain lies in the boundary between sectors. The American data relate to the private sector of the economy, whereas the British data relate to the private sector and the nationalized industries taken together, In this group it is estimated that employers' contributions to pension schemes totalled £342 million,[1] equal to 2·7 per cent of wages and salaries in the same sectors.[2] Comparison with Table 49 shows this to be a considerably higher proportion than that estimated for the U.S. The aggregate data on pension contributions suggest that employers' expenditure is higher, relative to wages and salaries, in Britain than in the U.S.; the data drawn from a sample of firms (mainly in manufacturing) suggest the opposite. Differences in coverage and definition account for a large part of the contrast; the enquiry covered only manual workers, and even then, it excluded those in the nationalized industries who are all members of pension schemes. For most salaried staff, pension contributions would amount to more than the $1\frac{1}{2}$ per cent average of the enquiry, which may itself be much above the average cost of all pension schemes for wage-earners. However, for a comparison of this kind, it is not possible to be more precise without far more extensive and detailed data about the cost of private pension schemes both in the U.S. and Britain.

[1] Taken from an analysis of 'employers' contributions—other' (*National Income and Expenditure*, 1962, Table 2, item 13e) supplied by the Central Statistical Office.

[2] Wages and salaries in the private sector were estimated from income from employment in these sectors (*National Income and Expenditure*, 1962, Table 12) by subtraction of employer's 'other' contributions (£342 million) and employers' contributions to National Insurance, the latter estimated by *pro rata* allocation of total employers' contributions according to the estimates of the distribution of total employment as between sectors published in *Economic Trends*, December 1962.

CHAPTER 6

PUBLIC VERSUS PRIVATE PROTECTION AGAINST INSECURITY

A. E. HOLMANS

I. THE PROBLEM AND THE CRITERIA OF JUDGEMENT

How far should insecurity of income arising from illness, the costs of medical treatment, old age, and unemployment be provided through compulsory State schemes rather than left to private provision? This is a controversial issue in many countries. In Britain the leading parties differ about the roles of private and State superannuation schemes, while in the U.S. the finance of medical care became the subject of fierce political controversy when President Truman proposed a scheme of compulsory health insurance in 1949, and again in 1960 with the introduction of the bill to provide for hospital treatment for retired people as part of the Social Security scheme. In this Chapter the main advantages and disadvantages of compulsory State schemes and private schemes, especially those arranged as part of employees' remuneration, will be examined. Much of the analysis will be based on a comparison of American and British practice, since the U.S. provides the best example of extensive reliance on private provision against insecurity of income. The provision of financial security in old age is not discussed here since it gives rise to economic problems not associated with the provision of security against the financial consequences of illness and unemployment. The very long term of the liabilities means the accumulation of large capital reserves,[1] and this has a direct effect on total saving, its distribution between sectors, the working of the capital market, and the control of industry. Chapter 7 discusses the economics of private and public pension schemes.

The criteria used to assess the relative merits of the different

[1] The only system in which there is no occasion for the accumulation of large reserves is a State scheme financed on the 'assessment' principle.

K

DOI: 10.4324/9781003184706-6

methods of providing security against loss of income through unemployment, illness, or injury, and against the cost of medical treatment, must first be outlined. In any specific case political opinions and political history are important, and at times decisive, as was shown in the outline of the growth of public schemes of social security in the U.S.[1]. Effectiveness in providing the desired benefits and administrative efficiency are important, but so is political acceptability, not only in the obvious sense that a paper scheme which is not politically acceptable will not be put into practice until such time as the balance of political opinion changes, but also since economic and social welfare are but parts of general welfare. Thus a scheme which provides social and economic benefits in a way that does not conflict with people's political or moral views contributes more to the general welfare than a scheme which is technically and economically just as good, but which conflicts with people's susceptibilities.

The first group of criteria are those of social administration, of ensuring that those who need the protection are provided with it in the most economical way.

(a) *The provision of comprehensive cover.* The risks against which public schemes can provide protection are run by everyone who derives his income from employment or is dependent on someone who does so; practically everyone in the community is therefore potentially in need of protection. On this ground there is an advantage in a form of provision which covers everyone rather than one which leaves any member of society without protection, other than those whose resources are sufficiently large for them not to need it. While a State scheme need not cover all those at risk, it can do so, and this is one of the main arguments in favour of the use of compulsory State schemes. Private schemes, on the other hand, provide protection for members of specific groups, and it is highly unlikely that all who are subject to the risk will be members of a group which is protected. A patchwork of separate schemes, whether public or private, will almost certainly leave gaps, so that part of the population liable to the risk will be without protection. In a country which relies on private schemes it is probable that not everyone at risk will be protected, and one of the strongest motives for the introduction of compulsory State schemes is to extend to everyone the protection that some had previously obtained privately.

Some may be outside the coverage of any private scheme for administrative reasons, in that they do not belong to any occupational or social group through which they could have access to protection, or for financial reasons, since their incomes are too low for them to

---

[1] See Section II of the previous Chapter.

purchase protection privately. A third possibility is that some people simply ignore the risk until it is too late; on paternalistic grounds it may then be justifiable for the State to intervene, but in this instance the intervention could take the form of compulsion to insure privately rather than the introduction of a State scheme.

(b) *The provision of adequate benefits.* Protection against the risk is provided only if the benefits are adequate for the purpose. A scheme which provides payments towards the costs of medical treatment will provide security only if the payments are large enough to cover that part of the costs that the individual cannot meet without hardship out of his own resources. What is 'adequate' varies, of course, with time and place. Changes in medical techniques and in the prices of goods and services used in providing medical treatment lead to changes in the level of benefits required to meet the costs of treatment, and as levels of real income change the levels of benefit required to give security of income necessarily change. A level of benefit (in real terms) that was adequate in 1911 is unlikely to be thought adequate in the 1960s; nor would a level of benefit that appeared adequate in Britain give equal protection in the U.S. where average real income per head is about one-half to two-thirds higher.

(c) *Adaptability to circumstances.* Although the risks against which social security schemes can provide protection affect very large sections of the community, not all may be at risk to the same extent. There is thus a case for adapting benefits to meet particular circumstances and for the use of a method of providing the benefits which makes differentiation possible. For example, frictional unemployment will probably be much higher in an industry where labour turnover is high (e.g. the construction industry) than in one where labour turnover is lower, and there may be a case for larger short-term unemployment benefits in an industry where frictional unemployment is high. How much differentiation should be allowed raises political questions about the desirability of cross-subsidization, whether charges should deliberately not represent costs so that those consumers who can afford it pay at a higher level and subsidize those who are worse off and are charged at less than the cost of providing the service for them. For example, a private medical insurance scheme which excludes the poor risks can provide protection on better terms than a scheme whose charges must cover good risks and bad. Since a person who is medically a bad risk usually is so through no fault of his own, there may be a case for restricting the amount of differentiation and thus making the good risks subsidize the poor to some extent. Except in relation to administrative costs, which will be increased by extensive differentiation of benefits, this is a matter for political decision about social policy, rather than for economic calculation.

(d) *Administrative efficiency.* To provide protection against insecurity the benefits must be made available promptly when the risk matures. To do this for a large number of people an extensive organization is required, and minimizing the amount of resources devoted to administration consistent with efficiency in supplying the benefits is an important criterion in deciding the way in which protection should be provided.

(e) *The speed with which results are required.* If it is desired that protection should be extended quickly to large numbers of people, there is an obvious advantage in intervention by the State either to run the service itself or to impose by law minimum standards which firms must observe. If it were desired that schemes to provide compensation for redundancy should be available to all who are likely to need them, reliance on private initiative by firms or by the trade unions with which they bargain might lead to years passing before complete coverage was achieved.

The next group of criteria relate to the economic effects, both at the level of the firm and industry and also on the national economy as a whole.[1]

(f) *Effects on the allocation of labour between firms.* Supplementary benefits such as sick pay are part of the means by which firms bid for labour, and such benefits may have a power to attract labour different from an equal expenditure on higher wages or salaries.

(g) *Effects on mobility of labour.* This differs from (f) in that, if supplementary benefits are available only to employees who have been with the firm for a minimum length of time, then the higher the proportion of total remuneration that consists of supplementary benefits, the greater will be the loss incurred through changing employment.

(h) *Effects on firms' costs of production.* Supplementary benefits provided by firms for members of that part of their labour force that is varied in response to short-run changes in output are part of direct (or variable) cost. When prices are set by means of unit direct costs plus a margin[2] a change in supplementary benefits affects selling prices in the short run in the same way as a wage increase. If the benefits are financed from general taxation the effect will be much less direct and probably weaker; not all the extra taxation will fall on profits, and that part which does fall on profits will affect prices only to the extent that it alters firms' views about the size of the margin over direct costs that they want to achieve. The difference could be significant when cost-inflation exists or is feared, or if the prices

[1] Criteria (f) and (g) are also discussed in the conclusion to this volume.
[2] No specific variant of 'cost-plus' pricing is assumed here; the argument does not depend on any particular method of determining the margin, or the output used for estimating unit direct cost.

quoted for internationally traded goods are getting out of line with the prices quoted by competitors.

(i) *Effect on the size of the budget*. If protection against insecurity is provided through State schemes financed through special contributions from those covered or from general taxation, Government revenue and expenditure are larger, relative to the gross national product, than they otherwise would be. Now although the stabilizing properties of the fiscal system do not depend solely on its size relative to G.N.P., the larger the budget relative to G.N.P. the greater, other things (notably the progressiveness of the tax structure) being equal, will be its automatic stabilizing effect. As the level of output and employment fall, so will tax payments, more than proportionately if the tax structure is progressive. At the same time expenditure will increase, mainly through increases in the numbers drawing unemployment benefit; the budget moves towards a deficit, and personal income after tax falls by less than income before tax, insulating consumers' expenditure to some extent from the fall in income and cutting down the secondary effects on employment and output. Clearly this stabilizing effect will be more powerful if tax payments are fairly large relative to income than if they are small. The same process works in the opposite direction, of course, when incomes are rising.

Likewise the scope for discretionary stabilizing measures is greater when the budget is fairly large relative to G.N.P.; tax reductions to deal with a temporary deflationary situation are more easily made when the desired addition to demand can be achieved by reducing tax rates rather than abolishing particular taxes altogether, since for administrative reasons a tax whose revenue will be needed again later cannot be abandoned completely.

On the other hand, if the inclusion in the budget of social welfare benefits ensures that tax rates are high even in 'normal' (i.e. not notably inflationary or deflationary situations), it will be the more difficult to use tax increases to combat inflation if an excess of demand should emerge, since if tax rates are high already, resistance to further increases will be all the stronger.[1]

The final group of criteria are those of general acceptability. Two separate strands can be distinguished.

(j) *Freedom of choice*. How important is freedom of choice, as against paternalism, in deciding the form of remuneration and of protection against life's hazards? This is mainly a political and ethical question, but it can be a wider one, especially where medical services

[1] See A. T. Peacock and J. Wiseman, *The Growth of Public Expenditure in the United Kingdom* (Oxford University Press, London 1962), Chapter 2, for discussion of the importance of ideas of the 'normal' or 'tolerable' tax burden as a constraint on financial policy.

are concerned. Views about the proportion of income that should be
devoted to medical care will differ, and if private provision is relied
on, those who want a considerable part of their increment of real
income to be devoted to better medical care will find it relatively
easy to make their demand effective. If this could only be done by
securing an expansion of a State scheme, it would be very difficult,
especially if only a minority wanted it in the sense of being willing to
pay for it.

(k) *Acceptability on social grounds*. The value of the benefits
received by the unemployed, the sick, and the aged do not depend
simply on the amount or real value of money, but also on the terms
on which they are provided. Most people have a sense of independence and a dislike of the idea of receiving 'charity', with its im-
plication of rescue by an outside agency because they have failed to
provide for themselves. Benefits that are paid as of right from an
entitlement built up by contractual contributions thus have an
advantage in not only providing security but in doing so in a way
that does not have any disagreeable social or psychological overtones.
A private insurance scheme necessarily provides the benefits in
return for contractual payments, and a State scheme can do so
partially, depending on the way in which it is administered.

From the point of view of comprehensive cover the advantage
clearly lies with the State scheme, which can include the whole
community, though of course it need not do so. This comprehensive-
ness avoids the danger inherent in reliance on private schemes of
reducing mobility of labour by raising the cost of moving in terms of
temporary or even permanent loss of rights to benefits. Moreover,
the British practice of financing medical care mainly through general
taxation raises the size of the budget relative to G.N.P. compared
with what would happen if it were financed privately or through a
separate State trust fund whose finances could not be used for purposes of economic stabilization.

On the other hand, benefits received through private schemes are
less likely to be open to objection as appearing to be charity or
having any overtones of poor relief, an important factor in countries
where a stigma attaches to being in receipt of poor relief. Reliance on
private provision also makes possible extensive differentiation according to circumstances, probably more so than under a State scheme.
How much differentiation is desirable is a matter of political judgement; against the obvious attractions of provisions which take
account of the wishes of groups, instead of requiring everybody to
accept what was designed for the majority, must be set the tendency
of those who are better-than-average risks to obtain protection more
cheaply through private insurance than through a State scheme
which has to cover the poorer risks as well. The poorer risks are then

left without cover except at prohibitive cost, or have to be covered by State provision. How far, for example, should the young be able to obtain protection against medical costs at rates which reflect the lower-than-average incidence of illness in their group rather than contributing towards protection for the old through paying at rates dependent on the incidence of illness in the whole community, including the old? This is a question of social policy which can only be decided on political grounds.

II. PRIVATE PROVISION OF MEDICAL CARE

By far the most important contrast between British and American practice in the provision of social security lies in the way in which medical care is organized and financed. It is therefore appropriate to illustrate and amplify the criteria outlined in the previous section by considering the advantages and disadvantages of public and private schemes for the finance of medical care in the light of American practice. The main reasons for the slow growth of public schemes of social security, and hence for reliance on private provision for the finance of medical care, were outlined in Chapter 5, but it is necessary here to sketch briefly the way in which medical care in the U.S. is financed, for only thus can its merits be compared with a compulsory State scheme such as exists in Britain.[1]

Not all medical care in the U.S. is financed privately. Apart from environmental health services and medical research, some medical services are provided to individuals directly by governmental agencies. Treatment for mental illness is the most important of these services; because of the long periods for which this form of treatment is required, it has to be provided publicly for everyone (except the very small minority who can afford private treatment) if it is to be provided at all. Veterans[2] are entitled to free treatment, as of right, for all disabilities arising out of their service; and they may also receive treatment in Veterans Administration hospitals, if there is room, for other disabilities. This privilege is important on account of the large number of veterans, and considerable use is made of it.[3]

---

[1] A useful source book is J. F. Follman, Jr, *Medical Care and Health Insurance —A Study in Social Progress*, Richard D. Irwin, Inc; Homewood, 1963.

[2] The Veterans Administration estimated that in 1961 there were about 22·4 million veterans (ex-servicemen who served during hostilities) in civil life, or 46 per cent of the male population aged twenty-five or over. Estimated number and age distribution of veterans from *Statistical Abstract of the United States*, 1962, Table 353; age distribution of the male population from Table 20.

[3] The Veterans Administration estimated that in October 1961 (the latest date for which the information is available) just under one-quarter of all V. A. patients were being treated for non-chronic disabilities not arising out of their service. *Statistical Abstract of the United States*, 1963. Table 369.

One or two small groups, such as merchant seamen and Indians living on reservations are also entitled to medical treatment provided by a Federal agency, the U.S. Public Health Service. In addition the Federal Government finances medical care for dependants of members of the Forces, and makes grants-in-aid to the States towards the provision of medical care for recipients of Federally-aided public assistance.[1] Together with the State governments it finances under the Kerr-Mills Act[2] hospital treatment for old people unable to afford it but not otherwise eligible for public assistance.

With the exceptions mentioned above, medical care in the U.S. has to be financed privately, either directly or through insurance. Table 50 shows total private expenditure on the various catefories of medical care and the amount financed through insurance, including group insurance that is provided as part of employees' remuneration. In the Table all insurance benefits paid are allocated to hospital care or physicians' services, but a few insurance plans provide additionally for care in nursing-homes, nursing at home, and drugs. Payments through insurance for these extra services are, however, still small, and inability to estimate them separately does not lead to a serious over-estimate of the proportion of expenditure on hospital care and physicians' services financed through insurance benefits.

TABLE 50. *Private Expenditure for Medical Care and Amounts Met Through Insurance* 1960

	TOTAL (EXCLUDING PAYMENTS FOR INSURANCE SERVICE) ($ MILLION)	INSURANCE BENEFITS ($ MILLION)	INSURANCE BENEFITS AS PER CENT OF TOTAL
Hospital care (a)	5,324	3,357	63·1
Physicians' services (a)	5,090	1,639	32·2
Dentists' services	1,992	–	–
Drugs and drug sundries	3,930	–	–
Eye-glasses and appliances ..	1,219	–	–
Other professional services ..	886	–	–
Nursing-home care	280	–	–.
All medical care	**18,721**	**4,996**	**26·7**

Note: (a) 'Hospital care' does not include physicians' services rendered in hospital. These are charged for separately and included under 'physicians' services'

Source: 'Private Medical Care Expenditures and Voluntary Health Insurance 1948-60', Tables 1 and 2, in *Social Security Bulletin*, December 1961.

[1] Recipients of those categories of public assistance which are financed in part through Federal grants-in-aid, viz, assistance to the old, blind, permanently and totally disabled, and dependent children.

[2] P.L. 86–778, passed in 1960.

The categories of medical care not generally financed through insurance account for a large proportion of total private outlay on medical care, even though a substantial part of the cost of hospital treatment is met through insurance. The whole cost of hospital treatment is sometimes not recovered even by those who are insured.[1] There are three main reasons: maximum limits to the amounts payable per disability or the number of days for which hospital care is provided;[2] maximum limits to the amount payable per day in hospital;[3] and the inclusion in many health insurance plans of specified hospital services only instead of all services that may be required.[4] Such limitations are probably inevitable in private insurance, for only if the maximum liability can be specified is it possible to assess the premium required to provide cover against the risk. Consequently the protection against the costs of long-lasting illness is less than a State scheme can provide, though, of course, a State scheme may also contain limitations on the amount or duration of benefit.[5]

The exclusion of most medical services other than hospital treatment is probably inevitable on account of the administrative costs of dealing with claims for reimbursement for a very large number of items, most of them small.[6] Nevertheless, the categories of expenditure other than hospital care are large, as can be seen from Table 50 and from estimates of average expenditure per family on medical care.[7] Families in urban areas spent an average of $284 in 1958, of which $58 was for prescriptions and other medicines and $41 for dentists' services. These amounts were quite high in comparison with the median family income (excluding farm families) before tax

---

[1] For details see U.S. Public Health Service, *Proportion of Hospital Bill Paid by Insurance* (P.H.S. Publication No. 584–B–30, November 1961).

[2] Among employees covered by plans providing room and board in hospital for a specified number of days, in 1959 practically all were covered by plans which provided a limit of 120 days or less; for one-quarter of employees the maximum was seventy days or less. Bureau of Labor Statistics, *Health Insurance Plans Under Collective Bargaining: Hospital Benefits Early* 1959 (Bulletin No. 1274), Table 11.

[3] In 1959 four-fifths of those employees covered by plans of this type were covered by plans which specified limits from $10 to $17 per day, though other plans included in the sample studied provided limits which ranged from $8 to $21. In 1959 the average daily charge in a men's ward was $18·40 in New York City, $14·50 in Pittsburgh, and $12·00 in Kansas City. *Statistical Abstract of the United States*, 1961, Table 468.

[4] Blood for transfusions and X-rays are sometimes excluded from the list of specified services. Bureau of Labor Statistics, Bulletin No. 1274, p. 21.

[5] The scheme recommended by President Kennedy in 1962 to provide hospital benefits for O.A.S.D.I. pensioners is an example.

[6] For a discussion of administrative costs, see pp. 156–7 *infra*.

[7] Estimates derived from a probability sample comprising 2941 families in a survey conducted by the National Opinion Research Center, University of Chicago. *Statistical Abstract of the United States*, 1961, Table 87.

in the same year of $5,331.[1] Moreover, 24·2 per cent of all families had incomes below $3,000 and 14·4 per cent had incomes below $2,000, so that for significant numbers of American families direct payments for medical services must have been large relative to income; for them payment in regular instalments, either through insurance or through taxation, would probably have been easier than larger payments at irregular intervals when the service was used.

Private health insurance in the U.S., including insurance provided as part of employees' remuneration, was thus far from defraying all the medical expenses even of those covered by it. Substantial numbers of people have no cover at all; Table 42 in Chapter 5 showed that about one-third of all wage and salary earners were not covered by occupational schemes against hospital and surgical costs, and there is no ground for believing that most of those excluded were those least in need of insurance; if anything, the opposite is likely to have been true.[2] Loss of coverage on leaving the firm's employment, together with the ineligibility of newly-hired employees until they have been on the firm's payroll for a minimum period (typically three months) mean that unemployment is liable to carry with it loss of protection not only for the employee but for his dependents.[3] In a country such as the U.S. where the mobility of labour is high[4] this is no negligible hazard. Moreover, the self-employed are not able to take advantage of the group insurance against medical costs that is available to employees. Some of the self-employed are well-to-do businessmen who can easily afford individual insurance or have sufficient liquid resources not to need insurance against medical costs at all, but there are large numbers of self-employed people with

[1] *Statistical Abstract of the United States*, 1960, Table 420. The income data in this paragraph refer to families and exclude unrelated individuals.

[2] In manufacturing industry average expenditure on health, accident, and life insurance for plant workers averaged 1·7 cents per plant man-hour in establishments where hourly earnings were 'low' (under $1·60 per hour); 3·7 where earnings were 'middle' ($1·60 to $2·20) and 6·7 where earnings were 'high' (over $2·40). Bureau of Labor Statistics, *Employer Expenditure for Selected Supplementary Remuneration Practices for Production Workers in Manufacturing Industries*, 1959, Bulletin No. 1308, Table 36. The differences could be caused either by differences in the size of benefits or the inclusion in the averages of establishments where expenditure was zero.

[3] In just under half the plans studied by the Bureau of Labor Statistics the coverage terminated immediately the employee left the employment covered, or on the first of the month following. The other plans provided for continued coverage, typically from one to six months. Bureau of Labor Statistics, Bulletin No. 1274, pp. 23–4.

[4] The number of employees laid off monthly in manufacturing industry averaged 2·2 per hundred in 1961 and 2·4 per hundred in 1960. These monthly figures, which exclude employees who left voluntarily, were equal to 26·4 and 28·8 per hundred in the years as a whole. *Statistical Abstract of the United States*, 1962, Table 316.

lower incomes who need insurance just as much as do wage-earners.[1]

People who do not belong to a group through which they can obtain insurance against medical costs can in principle obtain it through individual insurance policies, but this is very expensive in comparison with group insurance. In Table 51 running costs are compared with income from contributions of certain classes of insurance in 1958–60, the three-year average being taken to minimize the effect of short-term fluctuations. 'Running costs' are defined as income from contributions less benefits paid, and therefore include tax payments and additions to reserves as well as costs of administration proper.

TABLE 51. *Insurance Against the Costs of Medical Treatment Contributions and Running Costs 1958–60*

TYPE OF INSURANCE	CONTRIBUTIONS (A)	$ MILLION RUNNING COSTS (B)	(B)AS PERCENT OF (A)
Blue Cross	1,534	88	5·7
Blue Shield	635	65	10·2
Insurance Companies—Group Policies	1,854	169	9·1
Insurance Companies—Individual Policies	806	395	49·0

Notes: The Blue Cross and Blue Shield plans are non-profitmaking; the Blue Cross schemes are sponsored by the American Hospitals Association and provide hospital service benefits; the Blue Shield plans are sponsored by local medical societies and provide surgeons' and physicians' services.
Source: Calculated from data in Table 6 of 'Private Medical Care Expenditures and Voluntary Health Insurance 1948–60', *Social Security Bulletin*, December 1961.

Judged by the criterion of comprehensive cover, the American system of relying on private action has distinct disadvantages in that the numbers excluded are large, and in many instances those excluded are, if anything, even more in need of cover than those who have it; the poorer self-employed, the unemployed, and retired people[2] are much more likely to be without cover than those in well-

---

[1] The Bureau of the Census estimated that in 1961 there were a monthly average of 2,744,000 self-employed in agriculture, and 6,388,000 in other industries and trades. In 1960 (the latest year for which data are available) the estimated median income of 'spending units' whose heads were self-employed (outside agriculture) was $7·920, compared with $6,140 for skilled manual employees and $5,180 for semi-skilled. *Statistical Abstract of the United States*, 1962, Tables 297 and 455.

[2] In 1959, out of 4,894,000 workers covered by plans included in the Bureau of Labor Statistics's study, 2,077,000 had coverage which extended beyond their retirement. Of these three-quarters were entitled to the same benefits after retirement as before; the rest to reduced benefits. Bureau of Labor Statistics, Bulletin No. 1274, Table 20.

paid regular employment. The high running costs of individual health insurance schemes, relative to benefits provided, go a long way towards preventing those not covered by group schemes from obtaining cover through insuring individually. It is also open to argument whether the benefits under hospital insurance are really adequate, because of limits to daily benefit and the exclusion of some services; in particular, the benefits are likely to be least adequate in cases of prolonged illness. The exclusion of most doctors' services outside hospitals, dental services, and medicines from the scope of insurance schemes also leads to disadvantages. The amounts payable for these services at any one time are less than for hospital treatment, but the payments are intermittent and can be large relative to the liquid assets possessed by most people of average means.

Since the minimum period of employment with a firm which has a health insurance scheme in order to qualify for benefits is usually short, it is probable that such schemes do not have the adverse effect on mobility of labour that non-transferable pension schemes are liable to produce.[1] Not all employment carries with it the benefits of health insurance, however, so that there is probably some reduction in mobility on account of unwillingness to move if it means giving up coverage under a group health insurance scheme.

The use of private insurance schemes as in the U.S. does give scope for variation in a way that a State scheme does not. Unions whose members want an increment of their remuneration to consist of medical services rather than other goods and services can obtain this through bargaining for better insurance coverage instead of a wage increase, gaining the substantial economies of group insurance compared with what could be obtained by receiving a straightforward wage increase and using it to purchase individual medical insurance. Such flexibility can be obtained under a State scheme without paying twice either if contracting-out is allowed, or if it is possible to have supplementary privately arranged benefits in addition to the basic benefits provided through the State scheme. Contracting-out is not usually allowed for medical insurance; if it were, the State scheme would be left with all those who were poorer risks. The extent to which it is possible to use supplementary private schemes to provide benefits over and above those provided through a compulsory State scheme depends on the details of the State scheme.

Administrative costs must also be considered, for the administration of private health insurance absorbs resources in the same way as a compulsory State scheme. The costs of administration of a com-

---

[1] For some evidence on differences in rates of labour turnover between those establishments with pension plans and those without, see 'Effects of Private Pension Plans on Labor Mobility', *Monthly Labor Review*, March 1963, pp. 285–8.

pulsory State scheme are substantial, and it is sometimes concluded that savings in administrative costs are among the advantages of relying on private provision. American experience casts doubt on this view, however. As was shown in Table 51 above, costs of administration even of group insurance schemes are not negligible, and for individual insurance they are very high, amounting to almost half of contribution income. The administrative costs of private health insurance in the U.S. cannot, unfortunately, be compared directly with those of the National Health Service in Britain, since the form of the accounts renders it impossible to extract from the health departments those items corresponding to the costs of administration of the private health insurance schemes in the U.S. Moreover, since most of the cost of the National Health Service is met from general taxation, some part of the cost of tax collection should be debited against it, but there is no way of specifying how much, as taxes are not earmarked for specific services.

In summary, it is considered that although reliance on private provision against the costs of medical care permits flexibility and variation according to the preferences of fairly small groups (and occasionally of individuals), in a way that is probably less easy to achieve under a State scheme, it has important disadvantages. The chief of these is the inability to provide comprehensive cover even against the costs of hospital treatment. Many of those excluded from cover under group schemes are probably just as much in need of cover as those who have it, if not more so. In some instances the benefits also appear less than adequate, particularly in cases of prolonged illness. Since most medical attention outside hospital, medicines, and dental treatment are not included, it is far from evident that reliance on private provision is any cheaper in terms of administrative costs than State provision. Judged purely from the point of view of social administration, therefore, it appears that the balance of advantage favours the finance of medical care through a State scheme rather than through private insurance, but much wider issues of political acceptability are present, both ideological and practical. On the ideological plane, private action may be preferred to public even at some cost in loss of efficiency and harm to some individuals in the community.[1] On the practical level there is the problem, with very serious political and ethical implications, of arranging in a State scheme for a relationship between the medical profession and the State that is acceptable to the former in preserving professional freedom and integrity, yet at the same time safeguarding the taxpayer against misuse of the service or needless expense.

[1] For example, those who do not belong to any group through which they can obtain insurance collectively.

III. PUBLIC AND PRIVATE PROVISION AGAINST
INCOME-LOSS

Under this head are considered the means of spreading income over the earning and non-earning periods within a man's working life. Chapter 7 discusses the means of providing for an income after working life has come to an end; in this Chapter, therefore, attention is confined to the spreading of income within working life. The main risks against which protection is required to ensure continuity of income are illness and injury and unemployment, but it is convenient also to discuss paid holidays under this head, since their purpose is to spread income within the year to cover a foreseen (and desired) non-earning period.

1. *Loss of Income during Sickness*[1]

Protection against loss of income through inability to work on account of illness or injury poses different problems from the finance of medical care. The latter poses problems of making payments which are generally intermittent but often large, too large to be paid out of the liquid assets most people of modest means can accumulate. The problem can beset anyone, whether in employment or not. On the other hand, loss of income through sickness is a problem mainly of wage and salary earners, since an income that is not derived from employment is not affected by illness.[2] Some of the criticisms of reliance on private schemes as a means of financing medical care, e.g. the omission from coverage of large numbers of retired people and the unemployed, therefore do not apply to private sick pay schemes.

The consequences of a temporary cessation of income depend partly on the size of the income. Out of a high income a family is likely to have entered into commitments which cannot be reduced in the short run without hardship. The commitments may be legal—for example payments on a mortgage or hire-puchase transactions—or social, in the sense of a style of life to which the family has become accustomed. Sickness benefits based on a concept of subsistence are therefore likely to be inadequate to support the level of expenditure to which large numbers of people have become formally or informally committed. Higher flat rate benefits do not provide a solution, for a level of benefits high enough to meet the needs of the better-paid wage-earner might well approach the normal wage of the lowest paid, especially those who have large families. The answer appears to be to relate sick pay during short-term illness or injury to pay received

---

[1] Chapter 8 examines various ways of providing sickness benefits in Britain, and many of the points mentioned here are dealt with in detail in that Chapter.

[2] For some people working on their own account the cessation of income if they fell ill would be as abrupt as for a wage-earner; but this is unlikely to be true of all.

when in employment, and the question to be considered is whether this can best be done through private or public provision.

There can be no doubt that the administration of a State scheme which provided benefits related to earnings would be more complex than a scheme which provides flat-rate benefits. Under the latter the only information required by the paying agency is the doctor's certificate and the number of dependents the claimant has. If benefits were related to earnings extensive reference to departmental records would be needed,[1] which could be time-consuming in the case of employees who changed their jobs frequently. On administrative grounds there is thus a strong case for extensive reliance on private sick pay schemes if it is desired that in cases of sickness of short duration benefits should be related to normal pay. Casual workers and those who change their jobs frequently would be difficult to fit into such private arrangements, however, and for those who are ill for long periods State provision would still be necessary.

If it were intended that for short periods of illness sick pay related to earnings, paid by employers, should replace flat-rate benefits paid from the National Insurance Fund, it seems unlikely that reliance could be placed on private initiative alone. In the U.S. little more than one-half of all employees in the private sector are covered by sickness insurance or formal sick pay schemes.[2] Some of the employees not covered are part-time workers and peripheral members of the labour force such as housewives and students, but even if these groups are excluded as not being in need of insurance, it is evident that there remains a substantial group of employees who have no formal protection against loss of income during sickness. Individual insurance by those not covered by group schemes is not the solution, for running costs are as high relative to premiums paid in sickness insurance as in medical insurance.[3] In the U.K. also the coverage of private sick pay schemes is far from universal.[4] If reliance were to be placed on private sick pay schemes for protection of income during short illnesses instead of the National Insurance Scheme, it would therefore probably be necessary to im-

[1] If benefits were related to earnings, contributions would also have to be so related. Records of contributions paid would provide the data required for determination of the amount of benefit payable.

[2] See Chapter 5, Table 42. The figure excludes the informal arrangements for sick pay which are known to exist in some firms, for the extent of such coverage is not known.

[3] It is estimated that in 1958–60 running costs (defined in the same way as for medical insurance) averaged 50·0 per cent of total premiums. Calculated from 'Income-Loss Protection Against Short-Term Sickness 1948–60', Table 2, *Social Security Bulletin*, January 1962.

[4] Just over half of all employees, including the public sector, were members of sick pay schemes. See Chapter 8, Section III, 2.

pose a legal obligation on employers to provide schemes which met minimum standards; to rely on competition in the labour market and bargaining by the trade unions would probably expose many employees to injustice in a long transition period, for American experience suggests that with sickness insurance as with insurance against the costs of medical care, reliance on private provision has the disadvantage of leaving large gaps in the coverage.

In summary, it is suggested that provision of protection against loss of income during short-term illness through sick pay schemes operated by employers has substantial advantages compared with a State scheme if differentiation according to level of income when in employment is desired. The amount of differentiation needed is large, and could probably be provided more economically through private arrangements than through a State scheme. In order to ensure comprehensive coverage, however, such private provision would have to be made legally obligatory, and in order to ensure adequate benefits minimum standards would also have to be set. It is probable, however, that State provision would still be necessary for casual workers, and would clearly be necessary to care for those with long-lasting illness.

2. *Unemployment and Redundancy Pay*

Here it is necessary to distinguish between three sets of circumstances: (i) unemployment caused by seasonal fluctuations in demand or by temporary disturbances such as those caused by strikes in other industries or by bad weather; (ii) cyclical unemployment; and (iii) structural unemployment caused by technical change or long-lasting changes in market conditions which reduce permanently the demand for a firm's products. In case (i) the employer will want his former employees back, or replacements for them, within a short period of time; in (ii) he will want them back eventually; and in (iii) he will not want them back at all.

Whether an employer will lay off men in case (i) depends on whether, if laid off, they will take other jobs, and, if they do, whether they can be replaced. The employer can only lay off men for such reasons if the expected period of unemployment is too short for those laid off to think it worthwhile to try to find new jobs, or if the demand for labour is sufficiently slack for him to be able to find new workers of the kind required when the amount of labour needed is back to normal. In principle, of course, employees could save out of their pay when in work to provide against these temporary interruptions to income. A scheme of supplementary unemployment benefits paid for by the firm takes on the nature of a savings scheme for transferring receipts from the earning to the non-earning periods; there might be also an element of tax saving in transferring income between income tax years if the result of the unemployment would be to make the employee's marginal rate of income tax lower than it would otherwise be. Normally, the averaging of earnings that short-term supplementary unemployment benefits provide is something for which trade unions could bargain if their members were interested in it; compulsion could be justified only on paternalistic grounds. From the employer's point of view, the main disadvantage is that such a scheme drawn up to deal with short-term unemployment would impose on them a liability, at least for a certain length of time, when the unemployment arose from cyclical or structural causes. The liability would therefore fall to be met at a time when the firm's ability to do so was weakest, unless the benefits were financed from a fund built up out of regular contributions of specified amounts. If that practice were followed, however, the size of the benefits would be dependent on the size of the fund, and might well turn out to be considerably less than had been expected. Special problems might also arise in industries where a strike by a small number of men can render a much larger number unemployed within a short time, where employers might not welcome the prospect of having to pay benefits which would reduce the pressure from other employees to end the strike.

Cyclical unemployment is a different problem. Declines in output are generally accompanied by more than proportional declines in profits and if labour costs are made less of a variable cost by supplementary unemployment benefit schemes, there would be an even greater fall in profits and an increased danger of firms being made bankrupt and having to close down. Even if it is assumed that official economic policies will succeed in preventing recessions deeper or longer than those which have occurred in the U.S. since World War II, there seems no reason to disagree with the generally held view that protection against cyclical unemployment must be provided through State schemes. The Government can meet the payments through deficit financing, if appropriate, while private firms clearly cannot; an increase in consumption brought about through extra unemployment benefits paid by firms could well be offset by lower investment as a result of firms' worsened financial position. In the short run there would be little or no gain, and in the long run economic growth would be impaired by the slowing down of the expansion of capacity.

Unemployment caused by structural changes in markets or techniques of production is in principle distinct from cyclical unemployment, but in practice it is often very difficult to distinguish them. The pressure on firms to close obsolete plant is generally greatest in time of recession when profits are harder to earn and high-cost plant is a serious competitive disadvantage, in contrast to conditions of boom

L

when high-cost plant can be kept in service in order to limit delivery delays. Likewise the pressure on profit margins which recessions impose give an added stimulus to efforts to cut costs by increasing efficiency, and such cost cutting may well lead to redundancy if the labour force had been allowed to expand unduly in more prosperous times when the pressure to cut costs was less. Redundancies caused fundamentally by structural changes are therefore likely to be more numerous during recession, when firms' ability to pay compensation is at its lowest. This itself is an argument for financing redundancy payments through a State scheme rather than imposing a legal obligation on firms to be met as best they may.

The case for a scheme to provide compensation to employees made redundant is primarily one of equity, reinforced by the fact that fear of redundancy strengthens employees' resistance to technical changes which would probably be beneficial from the point of view of the national economic interest. The benefits of technical progress may take many forms, including improvements in the quality of goods and services produced without commensurate price increases; price reductions; increases in pay for those employees in the industry who retain their jobs; and a faster rise in exports that permits national economic policies to be more expansive than would otherwise be possible, and so conferring benefits over the whole economy. The benefits of technical change are thus widely, and therefore thinly, spread; the costs, on the other hand, are highly concentrated, being borne by those whose skills lose their market value or whose capital assets become obsolete, often through no fault of their own. In general, it seems reasonable to argue that on grounds of equity the losers should be compensated by the gainers, and the question becomes one of whether the compensation should be financed by the displaced man's employer, or by the tax-paying community as a whole. In some circumstances a case may be made along the following lines for imposing the cost on the employer. The loss inflicted on the man displaced is a social cost of the technical change, and if there is imposed on the employer an obligation to compensate the displaced man, this social cost will influence his decision whether or not to make the technical change. The profitability of the change from the point of view of the firm will be lower, and the price of the product to buyers higher (provided that prices reflect costs, if only approximately) than they would have been had no compensation been paid. The beneficiaries of the change are required to compensate the losers, and the change will take place only if the gains more than offset the losses.[1]

[1] The argument does not rest on the assumption that the same conditions apply in the real world as are required in welfare economics to demonstrate an unequivocal gain from change. All that is maintained is that the procedure outlined

However, the above argument only applies where the compensation would be paid by the same agency or firm that takes the decision whether or not to introduce the technical change. In many cases, perhaps the majority, the displacement of labour is caused by technical changes introduced by other firms, or shifts in demand arising from extraneous causes. In these cases, to impose the obligation on the employer to pay compensation would not lead to the beneficiaries of the change meeting the cost, even indirectly. In extreme cases it would lead to the burden being laid on a firm that was in no position to pay. The simplest way of providing moderate amounts of compensation for the redundant worker would be to impose on firms an obligation to provide severance pay, perhaps related to length of service, to employees dismissed through no fault of their own, but such a procedure would not necessarily impose much of the cost of technical change on the beneficiaries of it, and, since payments would probably be concentrated in periods of declining general demand, the burden would fall on firms at the most inappropriate time.

There is thus a case for a national scheme of redundancy compensation, and if it is intended that the beneficiaries of technical change should bear the cost, there should not be any differentiation of contributions between industries according to how likely redundancies there are thought to be. Such differentiation could only be based on past events,[1] as the future prospects of industries are necessarily uncertain, and there are strong arguments on grounds of equity for financing redundancy payments out of general taxation, primarily as this would ensure that all those who benefit from technical change would contribute something towards the cost. If the argument is accepted that the benefits of technical change are likely to take the form of improvements in quality and falls in prices (compared with what would otherwise happen) and of increases in real national income per head as a result of faster economic growth, then it follows that members of the general public are likely to share in the benefits roughly in proportion to their income or expenditure. The burden of taxation is allocated between individuals roughly according to income and expenditure, with the result that individuals' contributions to meeting the cost of compensation for redundancy would be approximately related to their shares of the benefits. The correspondence between benefits and contributions to meeting the costs would

---

is one method of ensuring, in the circumstances specified, that costs of redundancy are taken into account.

[1] Under the 'merit rating' system, employers' contributions for unemployment insurance in the U.S. are related to the proportion of the firm's erstwhile employees becoming unemployed. For a general application of this principle, see S. Please, 'The Economics of Redundancy Compensation', *District Bank Review*, March 1963.

admittedly be rough and ready, but probably less so than under the other ways of financing compensation, such as a levy on all firms or payment to the dismissed man by his former employer.

To sum up, it would appear that there is no case for departing from the generally accepted view that protection against loss of income arising from cyclical unemployment is best provided through public schemes, both to ensure adequate benefits under conditions when firms' ability to pay is often at its lowest, and also to prevent firms' costs from rising at the most inconvenient time, as they would do if they had to pay out substantial sums in unemployment benefit when their output and receipts were falling. For both compensation for redundancy and short-term unemployment benefit the criteria of adequate benefits and minimum effects on firms' costs point towards the use of State schemes rather than reliance on private schemes; if comprehensive cover is desired, it would be necessary either to make private schemes compulsory, or to use a State scheme. The main argument in favour of the first of the above alternatives is administrative; the employer's wage and salary records would give him all the information necessary for the calculation of redundancy compensation based on pay and length of service, whereas a public Department administering such a scheme would have to obtain this information from the employer. Considerations of equity, as was suggested above, point towards a public scheme, financed out of general taxation.

3. Holidays with Pay

There are probably few who would dissent from the view that holidays with pay are most conveniently financed by the employer. Differentiation of the amount paid per employee is desired, especially according to the amount of normal pay, so that the administrative costs of a State scheme to provide the same degree of differentiation would probably be high. The incidence of holidays with pay can be accurately foreseen, so there is no question of heavy potential liabilities which would make insurance necessary. The sole question of policy is whether minimum standards for paid holidays should be prescribed by law, or whether they should be left to the initiative of employers and the unions with which they bargain. To obtain comprehensive coverage with adequate standards of benefit, legislation is probably necessary. When labour is short, competition among employers for labour will exert pressure on those providing holidays with pay that are below the general standard to bring their conditions into line; but the market for labour services is a notoriously imperfect market, so that an unconscionable time may elapse before competition extends the benefits to everybody. The case for intervention is that it will bring about promptly what will probably happen eventually anyway.

The objection to the imposition by law of minimum standards higher than those which would be met in the absence of compulsion arises mainly from the effect this would have on the costs of those firms which would have offered lower benefits. If their not providing standard benefits resulted in their earning greater than normal profits, the firms would simply be taking advantage of imperfections in the labour market, and there could be no economic objection to requiring them to bring their holidays with pay up to standard; but if the reason for their providing less than standard benefits was that the profitability of employing labour in their particular industry was less than normal, the effect of compelling them to incur increased labour costs through providing longer holidays with pay would be akin to the effects of minimum wage legislation. In the first instance the effect would probably be to force firms to reduce the number of their employees, by an amount dependent on the elasticity of their demand for labour. Whether it is considered desirable to compel firms to release labour from employments where productivity is too low to make possible 'adequate' remuneration (including holidays with pay) depends on what prospects there are of employing the labour in other industries where productivity is higher. In considering how great the displacement of labour would be, it is necessary to distinguish between the effect of an increase in labour costs incurred by one firm only in a competitive industry, and the effect of an equal increase incurred by all competitors, as would happen if minimum standards were imposed by law. In the first case the firm which raised wages, or conceded longer holidays with pay, would be put at a competitive disadvantage; but for the industry as a whole the effect on sales of a price increase caused by increased labour costs would be much less than for a single firm, a point which is well understood in connection with minimum wage laws. But just as inter-industry wage differences play a part in allocating labour between firms, especially in changing the pattern over time, so also could differences in holidays with pay; and to set minimum standards in a way that was intended to eliminate inter-industry, or even inter-firm differences in holidays with pay would suppress one way in which firms can compete for labour.

IV. CONCLUSION

The choice between public and private schemes for the provision of protection against insecurity can be made partly on economic and administrative grounds, but social and political views are probably more important, and an explanation of the main differences between

American and British practice must be sought mainly in political circumstances, both present day and historical. Any discussion which is primarily in economic and administrative terms must necessarily make political and social judgements; but even though widely varying opinions are held, there would probably be broad agreement on certain basic principles; for example, most people would accept that provision must be made to prevent destitution through illness and unemployment, and that people should not be left to suffer because they cannot afford medical treatment. If this is accepted, the criterion of comprehensive cover becomes a very important one, and the gaps in coverage which American experience suggests are liable to result from reliance on private provisions are a very serious criticism of it. Private health insurance, pension schemes, and sick pay schemes in the U.S. are a long way from covering all employees, even excluding the marginal members of the working population such as students and housewives. In Britain also the coverage of private pension and sick pay schemes is far from complete. It therefore appears that if coverage for all those at risk is desired, private schemes must be supplemented by public, or else the coverage of the private schemes made general by the imposition of a legal obligation to provide the benefits. Complete coverage through the second method would be hard to obtain in that it is highly unlikely that everyone in the community will be a member of a group through which he can obtain protection. Complete coverage could be obtained by the first method, under which a State scheme would provide for those not covered by satisfactory private schemes; but it is highly likely that the State scheme would be left with those people who were the poorest risks, while those who were better risks, for example medically, obtained protection fairly cheaply through group schemes confined to themselves. In addition, non-transferable rights in private insurance schemes increase the cost of changing employment; it is pension schemes that are most important here, but in so far as health insurance and sick pay schemes have any effect on mobility of labour, it can only be to impede it.

The advantage of private provision lies mainly in adaptability according to circumstances, of permitting differentiation of benefits according to the needs of the case and the willingness of those concerned to pay. The provisions of a State scheme must be related to the circumstances of the majority, or even, as under a scheme like National Insurance in Britain that provides flat-rate benefits, to the circumstances of the lowest paid who are required to contribute.

The balance of advantage between private and public provision varies according to the risk against which protection is desired. There is a clear distinction between those risks which follow from a man being dependent for his income on his earnings from employment, such as loss of income through illness, injury or unemployment, and those that do not, such as his having to incur heavy expenses for medical treatment. *Prima facie* there is a stronger case for providing protection against the former risks by schemes that form part of employee's remuneration than against the latter. If reliance is placed on occupational schemes to provide protection against income-loss, those who are not employees are excluded automatically, but they have no need for the protection since they are not at risk. But everyone, including the non-employed, risks having to meet heavy charges for medical treatment, so that reliance on private provision through occupational schemes will leave substantial gaps in coverage that cannot be filled by individual insurance on account of its high cost, which places it beyond the reach of the poorer non-employed people and many of the aged. Occupational health insurance is a special case of group health insurance and equally good terms could probably be negotiated on behalf of members of a political party or sports club as for a firm's employees who were the same in number, sex, and age. The employees are, however, privileged in that the employer's contribution is taxable neither as profits to the firm nor as income to the employees, whereas premiums would have to be paid by members of a club out of taxed income, and while it would be very difficult for the contributions of hundreds or even thousands of members of a voluntary organization to be gathered together without expense, the firm has only one premium to pay. The high running cost of individual health insurance make this inappropriate as an alternative for most of those of working age not covered by occupational schemes, and for retired people the higher incidence of illness and hence higher premiums put individual health insurance still further beyond the means of most. Viewed in this way, the balance of advantage appears to lie with public schemes for providing protection against costs of medical care, provided, of course, that it is politically acceptable.

On the other hand, if it is desired that sick pay, at any rate in the short term, should be related to normal pay, there are considerable advantages in private provision, subject to minimum standards prescribed by law if complete coverage is required. A State scheme that provided sick pay related to normal earnings would be practicable—in the U.S. unemployment insurance benefits are related to wages earned by the beneficiary—but payments by employers would seem administratively to be a simpler way of doing it. State provision for those who were ill for extended periods would still be necessary, and so probably would a State scheme for those who changed their employer often; the necessity of keeping records for this group, however, would considerably complicate the State scheme.

The type of unemployment compensation that can most appropriately be provided by the firm is supplementary benefit during periods of seasonally low production and random interruptions to production, a method of averaging income over the year which is possible if the likely extent of the benefits likely to be payable can be foreseen. Cyclical unemployment is not a risk which is insurable privately, for the probabilities of the various insured persons at risk becoming unemployed at a point in time are not independent one of another as, for example, are the probabilities of members of a health insurance scheme being taken ill with appendicitis. Redundancy payments could be provided privately, either as a result of the normal workings of collective bargaining where the unions are interested in such benefits, or as a result of an obligation imposed by law; but we have seen that such a procedure in many instances would not impose the cost of providing the compensation on the beneficiaries of technical change and might impose extra costs on firms at the very times when they were least in position to bear them.

There can thus be no general answer to the question of whether public or private provision against insecurity should be relied on, except on the basis of political views which, as a matter of principle, rule out the one or the other irrespective of any other advantages or disadvantages that it may have. Where the insecurity does not arise out of the fact of employment, the provision of protection as part of employees' remuneration is an unsatisfactory approach, as compared with a State scheme, because of the gaps in coverage left. Where the insecurity arises directly from the fact of being dependent for a living on income from employment, the case for providing protection as part of remuneration is much stronger, though, of course, whether the private provision should be left to the initiative of firms and unions is a matter of political opinion, depending on the balance struck between the desirability of comprehensive cover and the importance attached to private initiative. To discuss the advantages of different methods of financing public schemes, e.g. out of general taxation or through special taxes paid into separate funds; out of employers' contributions only or out of employees' contributions as well, would be outside the scope of this Chapter. A fairly detailed analysis of the fiscal systems and political institutions of the countries being discussed would be needed before even tentative generalizations could be offered, and even then such conclusions would probably have little or no validity if applied to countries other than those on whose experience the generalizations were based.

CHAPTER 7

OCCUPATIONAL PENSION SCHEMES[1]

J. WISEMAN

The nature and present problems of occupational pension schemes in Britain can be understood only in the light of history, and that history concerns not only the development of the schemes themselves but also the collateral evolution of State pensions and other relevant public policies concerned with such matters as taxation and economic stability. Accordingly, this Chapter will first describe the growth of occupational schemes up to 1958, then the policies that have affected that growth: this involves a rather lengthy but unavoidable description of the history of State pensions. In the light of this background, the present situation will be described and some comment offered upon what seemed to be the significant issues for current policy.

I. THE DEVELOPMENT OF OCCUPATIONAL PENSION SCHEMES TO 1958

1. *General Coverage*

Information as to the importance of occupational pension schemes is not easily obtained on a consistent and reliable basis over any period of years. The available statistical information is summarized in Table 52.

In 1958, a survey by the Government Actuary estimated that $8 \cdot 75$ million workers were covered by some kind of formal arrangement providing for retirement benefits. About five million of those covered were members of private schemes, the others being employees of the public services (including the armed forces), or of the nationalized industries.

The great growth in coverage has occurred since the Second World War, but some schemes have been in existence for a very long time,

---

[1] I am indebted to Mr Arthur Seldon for the generous provision of advice and information.

DOI: 10.4324/9781003184706-7

TABLE 52. *Coverage of Occupational Pension Schemes*

YEAR	PRIVATE SCHEMES MILLION	PUBLIC SERVICES AND NATIONALIZED INDUSTRY MILLION	TOTAL MILLION
1936	1·6	—	—
1951	—	—	6·3
1952	3·1	4·0	7·1
1956	4·3	3·8	8·1
1958	5	3·8	8·75
1960	5·5–6	3·8	9·3–9·8
1964	6·5–7	3·8	10·3–10·8

Notes: The figures come from a variety of sources and should be treated as rough estimates only: they differ both in details of coverage and in statistical procedure. (E.g. the 1936 statistics are based upon a fairly complete survey of non-discretionary annuity schemes in the private sector only: figures for 1952–8 come from a not entirely satisfactory sample survey.) The 1936 figure is from a survey covering private schemes only: the public sector was excluded and no total is therefore available.

Details of the composition of the 1951 total are available, but the definitions of public and private sector differ from those used for subsequent years: the figures have therefore been excluded as misleading. For the same reason the 1951 total is an under-estimate and the growth from 1951 to 1952 is consequently overstated.

Sources: 1936   *Ministry of Labour Gazette*, May 1938.
1951   A. Seldon, *Pensions in a Free Society* (Institute of Economic Affairs), and Bacon, Bromfield and Spratling, *Preservation of Pension Rights*, Institute of Actuaries 1957.
1952–58 *Occupational Pension Schemes*, A Survey by the Government Actuary, HMSO, 1958.
Report of the Committee on the Economic and Financial Problems of the Provision for Old Age, Cmnd. 9333.
1960–date: Estimates prepared by Mr A. Seldon on the basis of random samples, and published in a variety of sources. The current coverage is confirmed by the estimate of 10·5 million given by Pilch and Wood, *New Trends in Pensions*, Hutchinson, 1964.

particularly in the public sector.[1] The civil service scheme was initiated as long ago as 1834, and has since been taken as a model for schemes covering other public authority employees. These schemes spread between the wars: teachers in local authority schools have had a scheme since 1918, statutory provision for police was introduced in 1921, and legislation providing for pensions for local government employees was passed in 1922 and 1937, and for firemen in 1925. In the private sector, the joint stock banks were paying 'retiring allowances' (normally ex gratia) around a hundred years

[1] Information will be found in the references given at Table 52, and a useful summary description in 'The History of Retirement Pensions', *Midland Bank Review*, August 1957.

ago, and the railway companies and some few other large enterprises had superannuation schemes before the First World War. The spread of superannuation schemes in private commerce and industry was slow, however, until after the Second World War. Growth has been associated *inter alia* with a change in character of the pension arrangements, and in the attitude of employers and employees thereto: occupational pensions developed as a form of employer-benevolence, a reward for the 'faithful servants', discretionary in character but difficult to dishonour in practice. They have evolved into a part of the contract of employment, a postponed wage- or salary-payment.[1]

In 1918, it is estimated that there were under 400 staff schemes which paid mostly pensions, and approaching another 400 provident funds paying lump sums only.[2] These were almost entirely single-firm schemes, although there were a few group schemes covering more than one firm by means of assurance or deferred annuity contracts: these provided for small benefits and contributions.[3] As late as 1936 only 1·6 million employees in private employment were members of occupational schemes. This figure had almost doubled by 1952 and by 1958 was around six million.

2. *Characteristics*
The statistics of numbers covered conceal a considerable diversity of detail. For example, a pension scheme may be contributory or non-contributory. It may cover all employees, or discriminate between salary and wage-earners and/or men and women. The scheme may or may not provide for outside insurance of benefits, and may have a variety of conditions as to pension ages, cash and pension benefits, death-in-service benefits, and so on. Pensions may be wholly or partly preserved (vested) when an employee changes jobs, or may be preserved for changes within particular sectors, or may be lost. The list is not exhaustive, and what follows should be regarded as a general description rather than a complete statement. Also, the implications of particular differences are by no means obvious. For example, contributions can be 'shifted' (e.g. by way of wage increases),

[1] A survey of 117 large companies in 1958 showed pensions as accounting for more than half of total company expenditure on fringe benefits. (R. Harris and M. Solly, *A Survey of Large Companies*, Institute of Economic Affairs, 1961.) Occupational pensions must have been in the mind of the commentator who said that it was becoming necessary to retire or get sick to discover whether one had had a rise!

[2] *Report of the Committee on the Taxation Treatment of Provisions for Retirement* (Cmd. 9063) (Millard Tucker Committee Report), HMSO, 1954.

[3] The first large scheme insured with a life assurance office was set up in 1930, by the Gramophone Co (now Electrical and Musical Industries), and administered by the Legal and General Assurance Society. See A. Seldon, 'Pensions for Prosperity' in *Radical Reaction* (Institute of Economic Affairs), 1961, p. 203.

so that there can be no certainty that the economic consequences of such schemes will differ in any particular fashion (if at all) from those of non-contributory schemes. Again, the fact that benefits are not externally insured may mean no more than that some large firms have better facilities to carry such risks internally.

Some information can be obtained about schemes for public sector employees where these have resulted from legislation. For the rest, detailed information about occupational schemes has become available only intermittently: in the case of private schemes, for the recent past and for two earlier years in which there were special (public) enquiries.[1]

The public sector schemes are not without diversity. The earliest such scheme, for civil servants, has to some extent served as a model for later schemes, but has itself undergone a good deal of modification. It provides, for men and women alike, a non-contributory pension right based upon the average salary during the last years of service. Service beyond the retiring age of 60 secures an increased proportion of salary as pension. Teachers and employees in the National Health Service, in contrast, pay contributions, but the benefits are again related to average salary in the years before retirement and the scheme is not funded. Police, firemen and prison officers have a contributory scheme, but can obtain maximum pension after only thirty years' service. Commissioned officers of the armed forces qualify for a non-contributory pension determined both as to size and as to necessary length of service by the actual rank attained. Distinct from these unfunded schemes are those affecting local government employees and the salaried employees of nationalized industries: these are funded and contributory, and provide for 'terminal salary' pensions. On the fringe of the public sector, university teachers and some associated employees contribute to the Federated Superannuation Scheme for Universities: this is funded and provides pensions related to average pay over working life.

In 1936, the 1·6 million workers covered by private pension schemes consisted half of administrative and salaried staff and half of manual wage-earners, the latter group being concentrated in a quarter of the total number of schemes. Of the 6,544 firms covered, 60 per cent were members of group schemes, but the rest having their own (direct or assurance company) scheme, accounted for 1½ million of those covered. The group schemes were commonly restricted by grades or classes of employment or by type of establishment, with the result that wage-earners accounted for only a sixth of those covered by such schemes as against more than a half of those in individual-firm schemes.

Sixty-one per cent of the employees were required to pay some form

[1] See references to Table 52.

of contributions, commonly flat-rate or graded by salary group. These contributions varied in amount but were generally higher (often 2–5½ per cent of salary) for salaried staff than for wage-earners. Pension receivable showed a similar variation, the amount being determined by a number of methods of which one of the most common was the payment of a fraction of average salary times length of service: the average might be of all service or of a specified terminal period. Retirement age was commonly 60–65 for men, but earlier for women. Minimum age at entry was generally 18–21 (occasionally higher for females), and the maximum age fixed for new entrants was rarely under 50–55.

There was also a good deal of diversity in the way funds were accumulated to pay pensions. Some operated simply through the purchase of annuities with the total contributions. Others were insurance schemes using deferred annuity policies and these might be associated with endowment assurance policies.[1] Many schemes gave the employee an option to vary the form in which benefits were taken: commonly, for example, a cash option might be taken in preference to the annuity earned by the employee's own contributions. Many 'internal fund' schemes required a minimum length of service as a qualification for pension; and most pension schemes made membership a condition of service for new employees.

Broadly (but not precisely) comparable later information was provided by the results of the sample survey conducted by the Government Actuary. Estimated membership of occupational schemes in 1958 was 8¾ millions, of whom 3¾ millions were in the public service and nationalized industries, the other 5 millions of employees in private industry being divided as to 2⅓ millions in internal schemes and 2⅔ millions in schemes insured with life offices.[2]

Salaried staff were more adequately covered than wage-earners: the sample showed that in 1956 71 per cent of male and 34 per cent of female salaried staff of firms with schemes were members of pension schemes, as against 38 per cent and 23 per cent of wage-earners. These figures also indicate a much more complete coverage of male than of female workers. The proportion of total staff covered for pensions was much lower in insured schemes than in non-insured schemes, and insured schemes were more prevalent among smaller employers (three-quarters of those covered by large-employer schemes[3] were in non-insured schemes, as against one-third in the case of other employers).

[1] Schemes providing for endowment but not for an annuity were excluded from the survey. See Notes to Table 52.

[2] The total number of active schemes at this time was estimated at 35,000–40,000.

[3] These include a small number of schemes open to groups of employers.

About 38 per cent of the members of private pension schemes did not have to pay an employee's contribution. Where a uniform percentage contribution was required, it ranged from 1–11 per cent of salary or wages, but was 5 per cent for more than half those covered. But uniform percentage contributions affected only a quarter of all employees paying contributions, being rather less common than contributions related to salary range.

In respect of their other characteristics, pension schemes had begun to show a good deal of diversity. Thus, schemes covering one-quarter of the employees determined the pension payable as a fraction of pay for each year of service, but the Government Actuary listed five other methods, the last being a catch-all labelled 'other basis': this group included one in five of those covered. Similarly, eight types of policy are listed as being used by insured schemes (including 'other policies'), though almost all employees in such schemes were covered *inter alia* by group deferred annuity policies or by term life assurance.

The usual age for retirement was 65 for men and 60 for women, with some 'spread' above and below these ages. These were (and are) the minimum National Insurance pensionable ages, which perhaps helps to account for the lack of change since 1936. About half the members had the option to convert part of the pension at retirement into a lump sum, and a range of other options existed in various schemes. Most common minimum age of entry was 21, and the most common maximum entry age was still 50–55.

The Report brings out some interesting similarities and differences between the public and private sector schemes, additional to the ones implicit in the earlier descriptions. For example, age of entry tended to be the same in both groups, but salaried staff in the public service were more generally able to retire at 60. Both groups commonly related the size of pensions for salaried staff to terminal salary, that of wage-earners being a fixed sum or related to average pay times length of service. It was more usual for membership to be compulsory in public than in private employment, and less usual for a qualifying period to be imposed.

To conclude this Section, some reference must be made to the preservation (vesting) of pension rights. As we shall later see, this has important implications for public policy. But little information about the historical importance of vested rights is available. The 1938 study does not refer to them. A survey carried out by the National Association of Pension Funds found that in 1950 only one firm in six in the private sector operated a scheme providing for vested rights on job-change, but the members of the Association are predominantly employers with self-administered schemes, so that the figure cannot be taken as representative of private schemes as a whole.[1] Insurance

[1] The unreliability of the data becoming available at this time is illustrated by

schemes at this time mostly provided for employees changing jobs to have a refund of their own contributions.

Adequately comprehensive information is made available for the first time in the 1958 sample survey, after interest in the matter had been stimulated by the Phillips Committee. In these circumstances, further discussion of the facts and problems of vesting is best deferred to Section III which discusses the present position.

II. PUBLIC POLICIES AFFECTING THE EVOLUTION OF OCCUPATIONAL PENSIONS

The evolution of occupational pensions up to 1958 was conditioned by public policies bearing upon provision for retirement. Three sorts of policies are of major interest: they concern the development of State pensions, tax policies affecting saving and particularly saving through occupational schemes, and policies affecting the level of employment and prices. All three are of importance. The first must be considered at some length in order to bring out the relevant characteristics of public policy, but the others can be treated more summarily.

1. The Development of State Retirement Pensions[1]

Some kind of organized public action for the relief of poverty and distress, including poverty in old age, has existed in Britain for at least 360 years, since the Poor Law of 1601 provided for assistance (primarily in kind) out of parish rates. This arrangement persisted broadly until the National Board of Commissioners was established in 1834, when a co-ordinated policy of social assistance was implemented which was intended to reflect changed industrial and urban living conditions. The needy old remained dependent upon the parish, but were now maintained in workhouses. Not surprisingly, this policy stimulated interest in other means of providing for income-security during old age: the development of occupational pension schemes in the public sector, already described, is a piquant commentary on nineteenth century social policy.

the very different results given by a survey of 238 schemes published by the Industrial Welfare Society. Using a very different concept of transferability, this study showed that 115 out of 155 staff schemes and 58 out of 83 works schemes provided for some 'preservation'. (W. Durham, *Industrial Pension Schemes*, 1956.) The sample was biased towards firms interested in staff welfare programmes, and is thus likely to have been unrepresentative of firms as a whole.

[1] Useful general information on the history and characteristics of State pensions will be found in A. T. Peacock, *The Economics of National Insurance*, Hodge, 1952; F. W. Paish and A. T. Peacock, 'Economics of Dependence, 1952–82', *Economica*, November 1954; and R. M. Titmuss, *Problems of Social Policy*, Official War History, HMSO, 1950.

The first State pension scheme dates from 1908. Both this scheme, and later ones, are characterized by some confusion between technical questions and issues of principle. Also, the development of State pensions has been marked by frequent conflict between political expediency, the short-term needs of the Exchequer, and the demands of principle. To bring this out, it is useful to look at the historical process in terms of its implications for three basic characteristics of a State pension programme: these concern the prior obligations imposed by the scheme (e.g. the requirement, if any, to make contributions while working), the attitude to size of pension (e.g. it may be related to other means or independent of them), and the qualifications to receive pension (e.g. the limitation, if any, placed upon the earning of other income). Needless to say, there will be elements in any one pension policy that touch more than one of these categories.

The 1908 scheme imposed no prior obligation for receipt of pension: all men and women reaching the age of 70 were eligible. However, the non-contributory nature of the scheme provides a first illustration of the triumph of convenience over principle; it seems to have been accepted not from a belief in its intrinsic merit but because there was no experience of contributory schemes and it was believed that they would be difficult to operate administratively. The maximum size of the pension was explicitly fixed below subsistence level: it was intended simply as a supplement to the other income of the pensioner and his family. Further, the size of pension was subject to a test of means, payment in full being reserved for those cases which exhibited an appropriate degree of poverty. It follows that qualification to receive pension would be affected by the earning of other income. The scheme quickly resulted in the payment of some pension to more than half of those over 70.

These arrangements continued until 1925, unchanged save for adjustments in the money value of the pension and in the details of the means tests, etc. There was pressure for the removal of the means test, exemplified by the recommendations of a Departmental Committee in 1919, but there was also growing concern about the burden of pensions on the Exchequer, consequent upon the increasing proportion of pensioners to total population and the increase in the size of money pensions. A new scheme introduced in 1925 attempted to deal with these problems. This introduced the contributory principle, the imposition of such a prior obligation now being accepted as feasible in the light of experience with State health and unemployment schemes. The size of the pension was determined actuarially, subject to certain major qualifications to be described. The contribution was set at 9d. for male workers and 4½d. for female workers, the payment being made half by the employee and half by the employer and collected along with the similar contributions to the health and unemployment insurance schemes. Pension entitlement was calculated on the basis that collections should suffice to meet pension payments, on the assumption that beneficiaries had entered the working force at 16 and made contributions thereafter until retirement. Men and women so qualified were entitled to pension at 65 without test of means.

The simplicity of the scheme was reduced by some supplementary provisions. First, pensions on a non-contributory basis were also granted to those reaching the age of 70. Second, for married couples the wife, if not employed, qualified for pension on the basis of the husband's contributions. Third, the size of the pension to be paid under the contributory scheme, although decided generally by an exercise of the kind just described, was common to all pensioners. That is, the qualification to receive the standard pension was simply to have made the requisite contributions between the inception of the scheme and age 65, however long or short that period might be. It was intended to increase contributions three times every ten years until (in 1956!) the scheme became self-supporting. This never happened, for reasons to be explained. Fourth, it was recognized that the pension might in fact prove too small to meet the needs of some, and relief under the Poor Laws continued to be the ultimate resort of this group.

These changes brought most of the working population within the ambit of State pensions (contributions were paid by all earning less than £160 per annum). Contributions helped to meet the cost, but the residual obligations of the Exchequer remained considerable. Pension payments amounted to £57 millions in 1933, only about two-thirds of this being for contributory pensions.

Save for an increase in the annual earned income limit, the 1925 scheme continued unchanged until the Second World War. By this time, the pension of ten shillings (£1 for a married couple) was becoming increasingly inadequate to provide subsistence. In 1940, therefore, the arrangements for outdoor relief were replaced by the payment of supplementary pensions, which were made available at Exchequer expense to all pensioners whose income fell below subsistence as assessed by the Assistance Board. The payment was determined by the difference between subsistence and actual income as determined by a household means test. This latter qualification was quickly replaced by a personal means test. At this time, the retirement age for women was reduced from 65 to 60, despite the fact that women had a longer expectation of life.

The situation so created was not expected to persist; it dealt with the immediate difficulty in so far as supplementary pensions were paid to twice as many pensioners (nearly a million) as had formerly been helped by outdoor relief. But it left the general scheme un-

M

changed and the basic pension at its 1925 level. More radical reform awaited the results of the survey undertaken by Sir William Beveridge, the report of which appeared at the end of 1942.[1] It is worth outlining the recommendations of this Report, both because it is a landmark in the development of British State pension schemes and because the differences between the recommendations and the subsequent legislation are instructive about the evolving characteristics of public pension provision.

The proposal was for a scheme imposing a prior obligation by way of contributions during working life. These contributions would be higher than in the existing scheme, but would continue to be at a flat rate. Pensions (40/- for a married couple, 24/- for a single person) would be available to all as of right and without test of means; the State pension itself was to provide a general guarantee of subsistence. There were, however, to be certain necessary qualifications for receipt of these new pensions. In the first place, the higher rates of pension were to be introduced gradually over a period of twenty years; this was intended to preserve the contributory principle and to avoid the deficits that the Exchequer would have to meet if all pensioners were paid at the new level from the date of inception but contributions were calculated on the basis of the working life of a new entrant to the labour force. Also, an earnings rule was to be imposed: to exercise his 'right' to pension, a man of retirement age must forego other earnings, for apart from a small exempted sum, any such earnings were to be deducted from pension entitlement. But those postponing retirement would qualify for increasingly higher pensions. Finally, supplementary (assistance) pensions would continue to be available without contributory qualification but subject to a test of means.

These proposals led to the 1946 National Insurance Act, but the scheme introduced by that Act differed from the proposals in certain respects. The basic pension (26/- or 42/- for a married couple) was made immediately available to all, including existing pensioners whether they had contributed under the 1925 scheme or had qualified for a non-contributory pension.[2] For the first five years after retirement, pension was payable if the recipient did not earn more than £1 a week by part-time employment; this limit was later raised successively, reaching 50/- in 1956. Extended employment brought a higher pension, and men were in any case treated as having retired when they reached 70 (women when they became 65). These changes, once again, weakened the contributory principle and left the scheme dependent upon Exchequer support at least for the lifetime of the existing members of the labour force at the date of its introduction. The subsidy (known as the Exchequer Supplement) was fixed initially

---

[1] *Social Insurance and Allied Services*, Cmd. 6404, 1942.
[2] New contributors had to wait for ten years to become eligible.

at one-sixth of the size of contributions. In the event, the deficits were very much larger than had been envisaged, primarily because the benefits and contributions were adjusted periodically to take account of inflation and rising living standards, and so to reduce what were argued to be 'undesirable' increases in the proportion of pensioners receiving National Assistance payments. At the same time, persons of retirement age have been forming an increasing part of total population; one person in fifteen was of retirement age in 1911, one in seven in 1959, and, it is estimated, one in five by 1980. Since at each step the 'principle of universality' was broadly maintained, in that contributions continued to be flat-rate while the new level of pension was paid to all (including existing pensioners), deficits were inevitable.[1]

By the late 1950s, there was a widespread feeling that reform was needed; the deficits were producing an increasing burden on the Exchequer, and the pension was nonetheless failing to provide subsistence for many, without supplementation, in the prevalent conditions of inflation. The three political parties all produced proposals incorporating radical changes in the existing scheme, and the Conservative Government passed the National Insurance Act in 1959, introducing the present scheme as from April, 1961.[2] This scheme is described in detail in Section III.

2. *The Tax Treatment of Savings for Retirement*
Tax arrangements have encouraged saving for retirement in Britain for more than a century. Income tax reliefs on life insurance payments were allowed from the beginning of the income tax in 1799, withdrawn later, and from 1853 granted again and extended to deferred annuities. Later developments have extended the concessions particularly in the area of occupational pensions. Some tax relief is allowed on premiums paid by individuals on their own policies and on payment by employers into insurance company occupational schemes. Relief may also be claimed in respect of privately administered pension schemes. Employers may treat their own contributions,

[1] The cumulative effect of the changes described for the importance of the prior obligation to pay contributions can be illustrated by a simple example. A married man who retired in 1958 after paying full contributions since 1926 would have been entitled (if his wife was 60) to a pension with a capitalized value of £2,650. The sum total of contributions by himself and his employers would be less than £200.

[2] The three sets of proposals were contained in *Provision for Old Age*, Cmnd. 538, *National Superannuation* (Labour Party) and *Security for Our Pensioners* (Liberal Party). They are discussed in J. Wiseman, 'Pensions in Britain', *Finanzarchiv*, No. 19/3, 1959. See also A. T. Peacock, 'The Economics of National Superannuation', *Three Banks Review*, September 1957, and J. Wiseman, 'The Government's Pension Plan', *London and Cambridge Economic Service*, March 1959.

or benefits paid from the firm's resources, as a business expense. The
Finance Act of 1956 extended tax privileges to directors and the self-
employed, following the recommendations of the Millard Tucker
Committee. The 1956 Act provided that individuals receiving an
annuity should be liable for tax on the interest portion of the payment rather than the annuity as a whole, and that deferred annuity
contract premiums could be treated generally as an expense for tax
purposes. The precise character of the tax relief available varies with
the particular type of occupational pension scheme chosen: the provisions were laid down in the 1952 Income Tax Act and fall generally
within one or other of Sections 379 and 388 of that Act, as subsequently modified. Table 53 sets out the general nature of the concessions available under the two sections.

TABLE 53. *Tax Treatment of Occupational Pension Schemes*[1]

'379' SCHEMES (USUALLY DESCRIBED AS 'FUNDS')	'388' SCHEMES
1. May not provide tax-free lump sum retirement benefits	A quarter of the retirement benefits may be taken in tax-free lump sums.
2. Pensions in contributory schemes may not exceed £3,000 a year.	No predetermined upper limit to pensions: depends on earnings and length of service.
3. Benefit at death: pension for de-pendant (lump sum in some cir-cumstances).	Benefit at death: dependant may draw lump sums representing full capital value of pension.
4. Investment income not taxed.	Investment income taxed.
5. Employees' contributions wholly tax free.	(About) two-fifths of employees' contributions allowed against tax.
6. Tax deducted from pension as in PAYE.	Tax on pension usually paid at standard rate (with rebate reclaim-able).
7. Tax at quarter standard rate pay-able on contributions withdrawn by employees.	No tax payable on contributions withdrawn.

It is clear that these tax arrangements are (and have been) of prime
importance for the development and detailed structure of occupational pension schemes. The arrangements are discussed further in
subsequent sections.

3. Stabilization Policy

The inability or unwillingness of British governments to control inflation since 1945 has affected the development of occupational pension schemes both directly and through its influence upon other
relevant public policies—and particularly upon the development of
State pension provision.

[1] The Table is taken from an article by Arthur Seldon in *The Times* of December
3, 1960.

Inflation has encouraged the development of occupational schemes, for two reasons. First, the benefits of tax concessions to employers have been enhanced, and the cost of providing pensions reduced accordingly. Secondly, excess demand for labour has encouraged employers to use long-term fringe benefits such as pension entitlements to try to reduce the mobility of labour. Inflation encourages mobility of a kind that employers tend to regard as inimical to satisfactory production planning, on-the-job training, and the exercise of adequate foresight on the part of younger employees in particular. Also, in a 'seller's market' for labour pension schemes tend to spread by emulation. At the same time, these same encouraging influences have inhibited employers from making pension schemes transferable, since the ability of employees to carry pension rights with them from job to job reduces the efficiency of the pension scheme in tying the worker to his employer. Protagonists of State pensions have also pointed out that inflation reduces the real value of retirement income and capital unless these can be adjusted *pari passu* with rising prices: the Government's failure to check rising prices thus becomes a criticism of private pension arrangements. There are indications that the form of occupational schemes may be increasingly influenced by the need to take inflation during retirement into account.

Simultaneously, inflation in the post-war period has destroyed the 'actuarial' aspects of State pension policies. Schemes described in Section II(1), intended initially to provide a subsistence income at retirement, have quickly failed to do so, facing the Government with the recurrent need either to modify the State scheme or to supplement it. The policies actually introduced to deal with this difficulty have come to be of direct relevance for the future of occupational pensions, as we shall see in the next two Sections.

III. RETIREMENT PENSIONS SINCE 1958

The recent development of occupational pension schemes has been greatly influenced by the new departures in State pension provision embodied in the 1959 National Insurance Act. These developments in State pensions will be described first, before turning to the evolution of private provision.

1. *State Pensions*

The distinguishing feature of the scheme embodied in the 1959 Act is the introduction of pensions and contributions graduated with income. This idea had been accepted by both Labour and Conservative parties, though the graduation proposed by the Labour Party was a more integral part of the whole pension programme than is the case in the policy actually implemented. The 1959 scheme retained the prior obligation to pay contributions during working life, but the size of the contribution was now to be the sum of two parts: a flat-rate payment by worker and employer on earnings up to £9, and an additional (graduated) contribution, fixed initially at 8½ per cent of earnings between £9 and £15 per week. The size of the pension at retirement also became the sum of two parts; a general flat-rate pension related to the flat-rate contribution (and fixed in the initial proposals at the national subsistence levels of the existing scheme: £2.10.0 for a single person, £4 for a married couple), and a graduated pension of a size determined by the size of graduated contributions. Effectively, the scheme gave a man 1/– per week of additional pension for each £15 of graduated contributions.

As in previous schemes, a number of qualifications were to affect the actual operation of the pension plan. First, the new pension levels would become available to all at retirement, irrespective of actual contributions. In the case of the basic pension, this is the now customary 'principle of universality', already described. In the case of the graduated contribution, it amounts to treating all contributions as equal irrespective of the time they are made; a shilling contributed in the week before retirement brings the same entitlement of graduated pension as a shilling contributed in the first week at work. Effectively, this scheme abandoned the last pretence of actuarial soundness; no attempt was made to preserve an actuarial relationship between benefits and contributions even for a youth entering the scheme at 16. Instead, income and expenditure were intended to be kept in current balance, so that the fund could 'pay as it goes', with the help of a continuing but defined Exchequer Contribution and periodic increases in contributions.

Secondly, employers could 'contract out' of the graduated part of the scheme, provided that the authorities were satisfied that they operated a private scheme that was financially sound, and that employees were guaranteed pension rights in respect of periods of contracting-out that were no less than the rights that would have been obtained by making maximum differential contributions to the State scheme over the same period.[1]

Thirdly, the 'earnings rule' was retained, though the specific qualifications for receipt of pension were necessarily modified. Those continuing to work would make further flat-rate and graduated contributions and accumulate further pension entitlement. In addition

---

[1] At the initial levels of contribution and benefit, this meant that a departing employee must be provided with an entitlement equivalent to that furnished by the State scheme for a worker paying maximum contributions (25s 6d a week) on earnings of £15 or more. This liability remains unaffected by the facts that the worker might have earned less than this, or that he might be leaving his employer well before pensionable age.

half the graduated pension forgone would be treated as an additional contribution.

Finally, in particular respects the scheme represented a return to the earlier (Beveridge) ideas; it was intended to limit the Exchequer Contribution by a formula; this would allow the Exchequer commitment to rise, but more slowly than the cost of benefits under the scheme.

The 1959 scheme as a whole was more comprehensible as a means of restricting the growth of the Exchequer Contribution and as a short-term political expedient than as a consistent application of any particular set of principles. The income from the differential contributions would become available at once, while differential pensions would only have to be paid on any scale after a longer period than any earlier scheme has gone without fundamental amendment. At the same time, the scheme introduced a new redistributive concept. Comparison of the benefits to be obtained for differential contributions with those obtainable privately at the time of inception of the scheme indicated that the State scheme offered a much poorer return to the young and higher-paid contributor. This was because the differential payments were to be used in part to finance the basic pension scheme; a fact which was recognized by the scheme requiring a higher basic contribution from workers contracted-out than for those contracted-in. Further, the redistributive character of the scheme was also affected by the limitation of differential contributions to incomes up to £15. As a result, the burden of the contribution changed over different income ranges. At £9 a week, the original contribution would have been about 4·6 per cent of earnings. Below this, it would become progressively larger. From £9–£15 per week the proportion would be almost constant. Thereafter, it would fall regularly (no further contributions being payable) to (e.g.) 2·7 per cent of earnings at £25 a week. It is implausible to explain this situation save in terms of a desire to limit the short-term growth of the liability of the Exchequer. In fact, the scheme was amended before it was even introduced, as a consequence of continuing inflation. The basic pension benefits and contributions were raised in November, 1960. Further adjustments in these amounts were made in 1963, and an extension of the upper limit of the graduated part of the scheme from £15 to £18 was introduced at the same time.

2. Occupational Pensions

(a) *Contracting-out*. Occupational pension schemes could not but be affected by these new State pension arrangements, but the results (and particularly the numbers contracted-out) have been different from those officially expected. Membership of occupational pension schemes is estimated to have risen from 8·75 millions in 1958 to

more than 10½ millions now. The growth has been almost entirely
in private schemes, which covered 5 million workers in 1958 and
now embrace perhaps 6·5 million or more.

The Government Actuary was instructed in 1958 to assume for his
technical purposes that 2½ million employees would be contracted-
out. It was argued that the 1960 changes would make no difference to
this estimate or to the decisions firms were then in process of making
about contracting-out, since the differential between employees contracted-in and those contracted-out was left unaffected. The argument was unconvincing: the additional contributions increased both
the pension costs of employers and the compulsory levy deducted
from the worker's pay packet, and both these changes could influence
the attitude of those concerned to their occupational pension scheme.

In the event, 4·3 million workers had been contracted-out by the
time the graduated scheme came into operation by April 1961, and
by January 1963, when the Bill amending the scheme was introduced,
the number had risen to 4½ millions. The global figure conceals a
marked difference between private and public sectors. Although the
numbers contracted-out in private employment have been rising
more rapidly than elsewhere, the total number of employees in such
schemes (1·8–2 million) is still less than a third of all employees
covered: this compares with around 70 per cent of employees in the
public services and two-thirds of those in nationalized industries.

(b) *The character of occupational pension schemes.* The character
of the private schemes has also affected, and been affected by, the
new State pension arrangements. The most recent information available on private occupational pensions is provided by a study *New
Trends in Pensions*[1] which presents the results of a sample survey
conducted in 1963 and giving information for 180 companies. This
brings out an interesting characteristic of contracting-out: 61 per
cent of the companies had contracted some male employees out, but
this proportion is compounded of 68 per cent of firms with insured
schemes and only 37 per cent of firms with private funds.[2] The major
reason for this difference may perhaps lie in the administrative problems of contracting-out, as the authors suggest, although the evidence
is not entirely convincing, and contracting-out may also have placed
private funds at a comparative disadvantage in adjusting the size of
contributions to deal with withdrawals. Another possibility is that
internal schemes cover a higher percentage of lower-paid workers
with a financial advantage in participating.

[1] *New Trends in Pensions*, M. Pilch and V. Wood (Hutchinson), 1964. The
sample survey has a number of deficiencies. The authors draw attention to these,
and to the comparable difficulties of the earlier study by the Government Actuary
(pp. 15–24).

[2] Only 61 of the 103 companies contracting some workers out did so for all
scheme members: the rest commonly contracted female employees in.

The most important administrative problem created by contracting-out concerns the payment of large numbers of small pensions to employees leaving after short periods of service. Companies with insured schemes can pass this problem on to the insurance companies organized to deal with it: some of the latter already undertake such payments subject to a minimum level of £6 per annum, and others would be likely to do so in response to pressure. Of course, such a policy must involve the scheme in costs. Private schemes must use other methods. They can provide a transfer-value for the departing employee only if the employee's new firm can and will accept it. Otherwise, the alternatives are a payment-in-lieu to the National Insurance Fund (which is expensive for lower-paid workers because the necessary payment is determined by the benefits that would accrue if full graduated contributions had been made to the State scheme), or simply keeping track of the growing numbers of small pension payments involved.

More medium-sized schemes (50–500 employers) were contracted-out than small schemes, probably for administrative and cost reasons. The proportion was also smaller for large than for medium-sized schemes, reflecting the large number of private schemes in the former group. The survey also indicated that comparatively few employers distinguish staff and manual workers in deciding whether or not to contract-out, and this remains true even where separate schemes are in existence for the two groups.

The survey gives information about coverage by companies rather than about numbers of employees affected by particular pension policies. This makes precise comparison with the earlier surveys difficult. Nevertheless, some interesting facts about the present characteristics of occupational pension provision emerge: 97 per cent of the companies which gave information had schemes covering staff and senior executives, and as many as 72 per cent also had pension provision for manual workers. No firm with a scheme for senior executives did not have one for other staff: 'top hat' schemes of course existed, but they were additional to general schemes rather than a discriminatory substitute for them. The percentages are to be treated with care: the authors themselves believe them certainly to show too high a coverage, if only because response to the survey questionnaire was likely to be better from those with schemes than from those without them. But the figure for coverage of manual workers remains surprising, in the light of the finding of the 1958 survey that 38 per cent of male and 23 per cent of female employees of firms with schemes were covered. Two possible reasons for the high percentage are suggested. First, it includes all pension schemes with a defined scale of benefits, whether funded or not. This prevents accurate comparison with earlier surveys excluding unfunded schemes, but it may give a more accurate impression of the numbers of workers currently enjoying pension rights. Secondly, whatever the other consequences of the new State scheme, it appears to have encouraged the spread of at least minimal coverage among manual workers, simply because firms with a pension plan covering any part of their labour force have perforce had to take a decision about contracting-out, and have consequently been stimulated to extend their decision and their pension arrangements to cover the rest of their labour force. This is not to suggest, of course, that the State scheme might not inhibit the development of private schemes in the longer term, if the costs of the State scheme increase further and if there is continued political uncertainty about the future of the State's arrangements.

Female as well as male workers were covered by the schemes operated by 85 per cent of the companies, but the female workers were commonly subject to more stringent conditions. The survey found a predominance (84 per cent of the responding companies) of contributory schemes. This is difficult to reconcile with the common impression that non-contributory schemes have been growing in importance since the Second World War. In fact, examination of schemes by date of introduction does suggest that non-contributory schemes have been becoming more popular, although only slowly. Since non-contributory schemes make difficulties for contracting-out, it seems likely that any growth in such schemes since 1958 must reflect a willingness to 'build on top' of the State scheme rather than contract-out of it.

The improvement in the tax treatment of Section 379 schemes after the 1956 Finance Act, described earlier, has had the effect of reducing insurance premium rates and hence of reducing the contribution levels in new schemes in particular. The most common contribution to final salary schemes remained 5 per cent of salary.

Another interesting finding concerns the division between private funds and insurance schemes. With small schemes of up to 350 members, less than 1 in 10 had a private fund. Above this level, private funds accounted for 40 per cent of all funds until we reach schemes with a membership of over 1,000. 61 per cent of these larger schemes were private. The distribution reflects the importance of individual company circumstances and problems: it is clear that over most of the range the possible technical advantages or disadvantages of a private fund in terms of size must frequently be offset by the valuation placed upon other attributes of insurance provision. This difficulty of generalization about the 'right' kind of scheme for particular sizes of coverage extends to current trends. The survey shows that an increasing proportion of new schemes have been insured. This may simply reflect the fact that pension coverage has been spreading from larger to smaller companies: there is some tentative evidence to-support such an interpretation but there is also evidence that insured schemes are being encouraged by a desire to benefit from larger-scale investment: actuaries have begun to attempt to offer the advantages of large-scale investment to medium-sized firms with insurance schemes.

About half the schemes related pension entitlement to average salary: rather fewer used final salary, and only 6 per cent used any other system. (There is, of course, a good deal of detailed diversity within these two broad groups.) In present conditions, the final salary scheme has definite advantages and a trend towards such schemes is discernible. The pension entitlement usually varied with salary grade and time of service in the grade. Retirement ages continued to be determined by the provisions of the National Insurance Scheme. 95 per cent of the companies had a retiring age of 65 for men and 91 per cent had 60 as the comparable age for women. These were not compulsory retirement ages; almost all schemes made provision for early or late retirement with appropriate pension adjustment.

Only 29 per cent of the schemes covered by the survey permitted the option of exchanging retirement benefit for cash. This is a surprisingly low proportion, in view of the 1958 estimate that half of the members of schemes had such a right. The figures are not of course directly comparable, but it is difficult to believe that the small tax disadvantage incurred in providing such an option should be widely considered important enough to inhibit its development. Pilch and Wood (who suggest that the major obstacles to the spread of cash options are paternalistic) also produce some support for the view that 'it seems probable that the percentage of schemes providing cash benefits will tend to rise rather than fall in the absence of any specific adverse legislation or other outside factor' (p. 60).

Twenty-one continued to be the most common age of entry for men, while 25 was most usual for women. With very few exceptions, upper age limits for entry were fixed at or near the pension age.

Finally, the survey gives some information on the development of vesting.[1] This is again not entirely comparable with earlier information given in the 1958 Report of the Government Actuary. This earlier report said that pension transfer arrangements 'are not mentioned' in insured schemes, 'although it is believed that the trans-

[1] Pilch and Wood also provide a useful definition of a vested right: ' . . . any guaranteed right to benefits under the scheme other than those secured by his own contributions (excluding for this purpose the minimum benefits which may have to be preserved under contracted-out schemes)'. (p. 66).

This is a more restrictive definition than has been used in some of the other studies referred to. But it directs attention to the essential matter; the treatment of those contributions and benefits over which the employer has some discretion.

ferring employee almost invariably has the right to take with him the policy representing his own contributions and frequently is entitled also to the contract secured by the employers' contributions on his behalf' (para. 38). Only about a quarter of the members of private non-insured schemes in 1956 benefited from transfer arrangements, and then normally at the employers' discretion. Further, a fifth of these members were entitled only to the refund of their own contributions plus interest, and less than a half could claim the full actuarial reserve. Transfer arrangements were nearly universal, though normally subject to employer's permission, within the public service and nationalized industries. But here also there were restrictions; only 57 per cent of employees were entitled to the full actuarial reserve in the scheme, and there was almost no transferability between public sector employments and the rest of the economy.

The 1963 survey found that about one company in six of the sample gave vested rights. The proportion is not directly comparable with the 1958 information. In addition to the general problems of differences in the sample and of comparing information about schemes with information about membership, there are difficulties concerned with the particular information and definitions used. The later survey covers all types of scheme, and transferability is defined to exclude those benefits which are secured by the employee's own contributions and which normally accrue to the employee under any type of scheme, and also the equivalent pension that is a requirement of the graduated State scheme for those contracted-out. The figure also relates only to benefits accruing on voluntary change of job, so excluding redundancy, etc., payments. Also, only *guaranteed* vested rights are included, and many of the companies so excluded in fact normally gave such benefits 'subject to approval of Company or Trustees', or on some similar condition.

While the proportion may seem small, and in any case may be an over-estimate, Pilch and Wood believe that 'it represents four or five times as many schemes as most people would have expected.'[1] Given the restrictive definition of transferability used, this is probably not an unreasonable assessment. This is an important development; we shall comment further upon it in the next Section.

IV. PROBLEMS OF CURRENT POLICY

1. *The General Issues*

The introduction of graduated State pensions has made the influence of State pension policy upon the evolution of occupational schemes more intimate than at any time in the past. But the future of the State scheme itself is not easy to forecast. The most confident pre-

[1] Op. cit., p. 67.

diction one might make is that the present arrangements are unlikely to persist for long without change. It has already been argued that the State scheme was introduced for reasons of expediency, and it has in fact been modified twice since first announced. There is widespread dissatisfaction with it, and some kind of action will in any case become unavoidable if prices continue to rise and the present rate of contracting-out continues: the Government will be forced either to change the scheme or to accept the increasing dependence on the Exchequer that the 1959 proposals were designed to prevent.[1]

While there is a probability that the scheme will be changed, however, it is less easy to make a confident prediction as to how. There is widespread disagreement about the principles involved, as well as about the technical possibilities of different methods of provision. We can show the spread of opinion by describing briefly two polar views. One of these sees the primary role of the State as the alleviation of poverty and distress, whatever its cause, with other provision for old age primarily to individuals and private institutions. At the opposite extreme there is an attitude to pension provision which sees the State as the universal provider, using its powers to ensure that the old have pensions not only at a level that would ensure a subsistence standard, but of an amount that bears a direct relation to their earnings in working life and to the growth of community output. This essentially paternalistic and extensive view of the role of the state would obviously leave much less scope for occupational pensions.

The first view has been clearly put by Mr A. Seldon. 'In a society which values personal liberty,' he says, 'which increasingly yields incomes high enough to permit saving for retirement, and in which people are capable of apportioning income between working life and retirement, arrangements will as far as possible be left to individuals. . . . This [decision about provision for retirement] is an intimate, elemental, personal decision, and a free society will not lightly tamper with it.'[2]

The opposite view argues that occupational pensions have been and are creating 'two nations' in Britain, and that the distinction between the two groups is socially undesirable and should be removed by the extension of existing State pension arrangements.[3] Thus, the social security plan put forward by the Labour Party in April 1963 made proposals that would have the effect of providing all workers with half-pay at retirement in respect of eligible earnings. This would be done by gearing both the flat-rate and the wage-related pension

---

[1] The Fund loses about £10 a year each time an employee is contracted-out.

[2] *Radical Reaction*, op. cit., p. 202.

[3] See e.g. B. Abel-Smith and P. Townsend: *New Pensions for Old*, Fabian Society, 1955, and official publications of the Labour Party.

to national average earnings and by greatly increasing the present
£18 limit. Contributions would be wholly wage-related, and there
would be traditional arrangements providing back-services rights for
all existing employees. The scheme would accumulate heavy reserves,
which would be invested in securities and would make the pension
scheme a major factor in the capital market and in the control of
industry.[1]

Seldon, in contrast, proposes the repeal of the 1959 Act, and the
implementation of tax and other policies to encourage private provision for retirement. In the longer term, National Insurance would
be wound up by the gradual reduction of benefits towards the
actuarial value of contributions. Old people would be required to
make returns of income and those in need would receive assistance
payments (the name of these being changed to convey the proper
spirit of an honorarium) as of right.

A choice between these alternatives must depend at least in part
upon personal views about the desirability of paternalistic government. But certain technical considerations are also involved:

(1) The Labour Party proposals would perpetuate certain 'principles' from past pension schemes which are not easy to justify. As
we have seen, the evolution of State pensions has been characterized
by short-term expediency, and particularly by a recurrent desire to
minimize the burden of pensions on the Exchequer. Also, the schemes
have attempted to solve within a single programme the problem of
assuring a subsistence standard for the needy aged and the separate
problem of ensuring that individuals exercise prudence in providing
for their own retirement.[2] It is this confusion which explains the recurrent attempts to devise State pension schemes that shall depend upon
contributions but nevertheless ensure subsistence for all by providing
a common standard of benefits. Inevitably, these schemes have run
into difficulties whenever the economic environment or other
circumstances have changed, and the door has been opened to
'pensioneering', concerned primarily with the immediate political
(vote-catching) popularity of particular pension proposals. The
Labour Party proposals are most plausibly seen as such a proposal.

An important result of the confusion is to elevate the provision of
a standard level of pension into a 'principle'. This 'principle of universality', which we have already met, is incompatible with the relation of State pensions to the actuarial value of individual contributions and with the separation of the community's obligation to help
the needy from the individual's obligation to try to take care of him-

[1] Evidence about this is provided by Seldon, *Pensions in a Free Society*, op. cit.,
pp. 14–16, and Peacock, 'The Economics of National Superannuation', op. cit.
[2] For further discussion of this question, see J. Wiseman, 'Pensions in Britain',
op. cit.

self. It has its roots partly in earlier dislike of the Poor Law and in the harsh pre-war administration of the National Assistance scheme, but its continued support rests upon its emotional appeal rather than upon reason. There is no reason why a community should feel ashamed to help the needy because they are needy, or why this should not be done in a fashion that avoids humiliation to the recipients. At the same time, there is no reason to provide a pension at or above subsistence for all in order to help the minority who need it: our attempts to do so in Britain have produced a kind of gigantic confidence trick by which the Government takes money out of one of a man's pockets in order to take credit for putting it back in the other. Further, there is adequate evidence that the 'principle of universality' has operated in the past against the provision of appropriate standards for the needy. It is much less costly for the Exchequer to help those in need directly than to do so by raising the pension level for all in retirement: governments have therefore been slow to increase pension levels when economic conditions have changed: the invoking of the 'principle' in post-war years has not prevented large numbers of the aged becoming dependent upon a National Assistance scheme less than ideally organized for the purpose.

Advocates of the Labour Party approach are not unaware of the inconsistency of a programme that labels the equal treatment of unequals in welfare (pension) provision as a 'badge of citizenship'. But the concept of universality has deep roots, and they are unwilling to abandon it.[1]

On this score then, there is ground for arguing that the Labour proposals would perpetuate a confusion that has bedevilled pension policy in the past, and that we would certainly be better without.

(2) The 'two nations' argument is also uncomfortable. The Labour Party was arguing in 1957 that two-thirds of the labour force would never have an occupational pension, for technical reasons of difficulty of provision. But the statistics given in earlier sections show that this prediction has already been amply falsified. Its proponents appear greatly to have exaggerated the difficulties facing smaller firms in providing occupational pensions. Even in 1956 the Government Actuary estimated that 28,200 of the 37,500 schemes had fewer than fifty members, and the numbers of such schemes has been growing since then. Evidence from other countries (particularly the U.S.A.) suggests that workers in many trades argued to be 'difficult' can be covered, especially if trade unions are interested and co-operative. There is at present interest in the development of 'federal' schemes (in

[1] A good illustration of ambivalence in this regard is to be found in R. M. Titmuss, *The Irresponsible Society*, Fabian Society, 1960.

which industrial or occupational groups could be jointly accommodated) in Britain. Such schemes would have the incidental advantage of facilitating preservation of pension rights.

In any case, the contrast drawn between those covered by occupational schemes and those condemned to survive on the 'pittance' of the State pension is surely exaggerated. If workers really place a high value on pension provision, then one would expect firms without schemes to be driven by competition for labour either to pay relatively higher salaries and wages or to emulate the firms who do have such schemes. No convincing arguments have been advanced to suggest that this cannot happen, and there has been general acceptance of the view that occupational pensions have in fact been widely used as a means of trying to retain labour during the post-World War II inflation.

Further, there is no reason why those who prefer higher current pay to additional pension provision should be required to make more than minimal (subsistence) provision for themselves, or why those who wish to make their own individual arrangements above this level should not be permitted to do so and provided with similar tax privileges to the members of organized schemes.[1]

(3) On the other side, it is pointed out that the Seldon approach ignores the imperfection of the insurance market and the political and social influence of the large insurance companies. This argument emphasizes the lack of 'accountability' of the insurance companies and controllers of pension funds. Father Harbrecht has argued that the ultimate beneficiaries have little control over their pension funds in the U.S.A. and that real power rests with those who manage the investments,[2] and Professor Titmuss has said of the British life assurance companies that they concentrate power in few hands and make it accountable to virtually no one. As occupational pensions grow, it is argued that the influence of such funds over industry must increase, and because of cautious investment policy must be expected to diminish the flow of capital to risky ventures.[3] The divorce of ownership and control, while important, is hardly a matter to be solved by State pension policy: it is a particular manifestation of the quite general difficulties that arise out of delegation. Save for those who would abolish the joint stock company and limited liability, the problem is one of how to make this divorce compatible with the safeguarding of the interests of 'shareholders' (and pension fund contributors). This is a difficult problem for public policy: but it is better

---

[1] The 1956 Finance Act, referred to earlier, is a step in this direction. More still needs to be done to help the casual or irregular employee.

[2] P. P. Harbrecht, *Pension Funds and Economic Power*, Twentieth Century Fund, 1959.

[3] R. M. Titmuss, *The Irresponsible Society*, Fabian Society, March 1960.

handled by general measures than by specific policies directed to the destruction of the private insurance market.

The major question to be asked of that market from the point of view of pension provision is: do those responsible behave in a fashion that is concerned to further the interests of the contributors? Seldon argues that the funds and companies do respond to changes in market conditions, and are generally willing to invest in risk capital, but that there is too much variation in the response for one to believe that all pensioners are being universally served with adequate efficiency. (For example, the percentage of equities in the assets of 15 mutual life offices was found to vary from $36 \cdot 8$ to 12 per cent.) Also, competition between life offices is less than perfect, in that there are more than 80 such offices, but most of the business is done by about a dozen. However, the degree of monopoly inherent in this situation is smaller than might at first appear: the offices are in competition with other methods of providing for occupational pensions, including the setting up of private schemes, and competition of this kind has been invigorated and made more effective recently by the activities of Trustee Companies and American banks.[1] Also, the very growth of occupational schemes has produced an improvement in specialist consultancy services that improve the efficiency of the market from the viewpoint of the pensioner. As investors, the pension funds are in competition *inter alia* with investment trusts, banks, and building societies, as well as with individual investors.

In any case, policy cannot be decided solely by the argument that the insurance market is insufficiently concerned with the interests of future pensioners: we must think in terms of relevant alternatives. Those who castigate the private insurance market do not normally have in mind the need for policies to make competition more effective. Their interest is rather in its replacement by some form of public ownership, or at least control, and an important step towards that replacement would be the investment of the funds of a greatly expanded State pension scheme. But the policies of a State pension fund can never be divorced from politics: Mr Gaitskell himself explained that the Beveridge proposal to relate pensions to contributions in the early years of his pension plan was rejected because the apparent 'discrimination against pensioners' would have been politically un-

---

[1] '... among the most aggressive salesmen in the pension field today are the Trustee Companies, American banks and others, interested in selling their services to employers who are operating, or can be persuaded to operate, private funds. This is by no means an unhealthy development, inasmuch as it helps to make insurance companies more competitive and more receptive to new ideas. It must, therefore, ultimately benefit all employers, whatever type of scheme they have. Those concerned with private funds can scarcely complain that their case is not fully argued in the market-place, however, while they have such vigorous and doughty allies to espouse their cause.' Pilch and Wood, op. cit., p. 36.

N

popular. This political involvement extends to the use of reserves. Professor Peacock has demonstrated that the use of the National Insurance Funds had been determined by the general exigencies of immediate public policy rather than by the interests of State pensioners in the past (and this not only in the Dalton era),[1] and there would be no reason to expect the political influence to be any less if the Labour Party scheme were implemented. Indeed, the proponents see the political power deriving from the pension fund as one of the advantages of their proposals. The resources could be used e.g. for the 'socially effective' (politically determined?) purposes that Professor Titmuss says the insurance companies ignore. Perhaps more important, the reserves building up in the early years could be used to buy ordinary shares, replace the influence of the insurance companies (whose pension business would be diminished if not destroyed), and so extend governmental control over industry. Not everyone will find this prospect appealing. There may perhaps be arguments worth considering for public ownership *per se*, but it is very much less easy to justify the use of a State pension programme to pursue such a goal indirectly.

In sum, I would take the view that, while pension policy involves judgments of value about social ends over which people can plausibly disagree, there is much to be said in present British conditions for restricting the role of the public sector to the alleviation of poverty and distress. While there may have been times (of widespread unemployment, poverty and distress), when it was convenient if not unavoidable to pursue such a goal by way of general pensions provided subject to a principle of universality, those times are no longer with us. We could and should be more generous to our poor, including our aged poor. But there is no good reason to continue subsidizing those who are not in want by means of a State pension plan, or for obliging anyone to participate in a scheme that obliges him to provide for more than a subsistence standard of living in retirement. If the State scheme distinguished between the social obligation to relieve poverty and the individual obligation to exercise prudence in providing for old age, public policies could be more rationally framed and occupational pensions begin to fulfil a more satisfactory role as part of a contract of employment.

2. *Some Immediate Reforms*

To enunciate a policy attitude is not necessarily to believe that it will immediately be shared by government; it has already been suggested that the likeliest short-term developments in the current climate of opinion in Britain are for the present scheme to be adapted marginally or for it to be replaced by the much more comprehensive Labour

[1] *The Economics of National Insurance*, op. cit.

Party programme. In this final section, I propose to treat seriously the present Conservative Government's assurance that it wishes to foster rather than discourage the development of occupational pension schemes, and comment briefly upon some of the detailed changes that might make the existing arrangements function more satisfactorily.

First, even if present State pension arrangements are retained in other respects, there are strong arguments for reconsideration of the present pension ages. The Phillips Committee pointed out that the present ages of 65 for men and 60 for women are biologically implausible (women live longer) and economically and socially damaging whilst associated with an 'earnings rule' of the kind now in operation.[1] The latter rule is of course bound up with the subsidization of State pensions from general taxation, and hence with the confusion of aims already discussed. But some relaxation of the present rules would be justified even if no other reforms were possible. Such a reform would probably also encourage a greater (and desirable) diversity in the retirement ages and conditions of occupational schemes.[2]

Secondly, the tax treatment of saving for retirement is still capable of improvement. In particular, it would be worth considering what more might be done to encourage the development of (private or occupational) pension provision for those in casual or short-term employment. At the administrative level, there is room for change in the interpretation of the tax law as to the size of benefits ranking for tax concessions in occupational schemes: at present, this discriminates against those who work for more than one employer. These reforms, while valuable of themselves, would need to be incorporated in much more sweeping changes if steps were taken to deal with the final problem to be discussed: that of the vesting of occupational pension rights.

The evidence adduced in the last section suggested that transfer-

---

[1] It is of interest that there is no common practice as to retirement ages in other countries, and that State schemes not uncommonly use different ages for different occupations.

[2] J. E. G. Utting and Dorothy Cole have provided evidence in *The Economic Circumstances of Old People*, Occasional Papers in Social Administration, No. 4, 1962, that in present conditions in Britain single women and widows are particularly liable to suffer hardship in old age. This is not a conclusive argument against changing the present inflexible rules, but rather makes a case for wider reform. Utting and Cole see it as an argument for more generous State pension provision, perhaps increasing with age. But in this wider context they advance no convincing arguments against the alternative mentioned earlier, of a separation of social and private responsibilities and a radical re-definition of the nature and (administrative etc.) implications of the former. In any event, it is clear that any such hardship arising from the suggested changes in retirement ages would have to be alleviated.

ability had probably been growing among private schemes. Also, the benefit of providing transfer values for lower paid contracted-out workers (in place of payments-in-lieu to the National Insurance Fund assessed on notional earnings of £18 per week) has stimulated further interest in, and some development of, vesting arrangements for this type of worker.[1] But progress remains slow and there is a long way to go to general transferability. The public sector schemes generally preserve pensions for movements over a wide range of public employment, but this greater generality is to some extent offset by the almost complete absence of transferability when movement is from public to private employment.[2]

Two major arguments are used for more general vesting. These concern taxation and equity on the one hand and labour mobility on the other. Both turn out on examination to be more complex than is generally appreciated.

The simple attitude to the tax issue asserts that both the employee's and the employer's contributions are subsidized by the taxpayer, and hence to return to an employee only his own accumulated contributions when he becomes redundant[3] or changes his job is to withhold what is his by right. This ignores the fact that although the contributions attract tax relief, the pension earned by them is subject to tax.[4] The benefit thus amounts not to the absolute relief but to the difference in tax liability during working life and after earning ceases. During working life both employee and employer can claim relief on their contributions. This relief comes at a time when income (and hence tax rates) is normally higher than it will be when tax is paid on the pension payments.[5]

Though the benefit of tax relief may be smaller than is usually understood, however, it nevertheless exists and a loss is incurred by an employee whose rights are not transferred on job-change. The in-

---

[1] See Section III (2) (b), and Seldon, quoted in Pilch and Wood, op. cit., p. 157.

[2] The classic example is that of Lord Beveridge, who lost ten years of pension rights on moving from the Civil Service to the London School of Economics. An equally piquant case is quoted in the *Sunday Times* of April 10, 1964: a civil servant is reported as giving up eighteen years' rights on resigning to stand for Parliament!

[3] Schemes more usually provide for vesting in cases of redundancy than in cases of job-change. But it is by no means a universal right. Arguments developed here for vesting on job-change apply *a fortiori* to redundancy.

[4] R. W. Abbott points out also that the tax allowances received in respect of payments into a pension fund are of equivalent value to the allowances which would be received if there were no fund and the pensions were paid out of profits. 'Preservation of Pension Rights', *British Tax Review*, Jan.-Feb. 1964, p. 30.

[5] Tax recouped on occupational pensions after retirement is almost invariably less than the value of the earlier relief. In most cases, it is also less than the tax that would have been paid had the employer's contributions ranked as salary. See Pilch and Wood, op. cit., p. 113.

equity of the situation is emphasized if the employers' contributions are thought of as deferred pay. They then constitute essentially a saving on his behalf, an offset to the higher pay he would have demanded in the absence of a pension scheme, and should thus be his by right. On this view, whatever the employer's interest in retaining labour, his *authority* should extend only to *future* pension rights, and not to those which he has already awarded during employment.

The employer, on the other hand, sees occupational pensions as part of the 'package deal', including also pay and other fringe benefits, which he makes with his workers. As was earlier explained, their value to him lies particularly in their influence in reducing labour mobility: this helps to explain both the growth and the diversity of pension provision during the post-war inflation. Vesting might thus reduce the interest of employers in pension schemes, by reducing their expected efficiency from this point of view, and encourage substitution of other types of fringe benefit. The lack of interest of individual employers in vesting is increased by the fact that an employer providing transferability unilaterally can expect an increase in the costs of administering his own pension scheme but no *quid pro quo* from other employers in respect of workers joining his firm.[1]

Information as to the actual effects of pension schemes on mobility, or upon the changes that do or might result from increased transferability, is very meagre. The Phillips Committee discussed the importance of occupational schemes for mobility and flexibility, and more recently NEDC has given non-preservation as a reason for lack of mobility, but neither source provides any concrete evidence.[2] Such other information as exists is random in character: it suggests that pension rights may perhaps be given less weight by the general body of employees than is commonly assumed, and so may not have a major influence on mobility.[3] Mr Basil Taylor, who has recently argued a forceful case against the lack of vesting of pension rights for executives, does not in fact adduce evidence or argument that mobility is greatly reduced thereby, but argues only that it might be if executives appreciated the full extent of their loss.[4]

---

[1] While it is not easy to generalize about the cost to employers of giving vested rights, expert opinion favours the view that they need not be prohibitive for most types of scheme *if vesting becomes more common*. General vesting might indeed be expected to reduce costs per £1 of pension benefit provided, by producing economies in costs of termination and replacement of benefits. See Pilch and Wood, op. cit., p. 158; Bacon, F. W., Bromfield, A. E., and Spratling, F. H., *Preservation of Pension Rights*, Institute of Actuaries, 1957, and references cited therein.

[2] Cmd. 9333, paras. 246–53, and *Conditions Favourable to Faster Growth*, 1963 HMSO.

[3] See R. W. Abbott, op. cit.

[4] Basil Taylor, 'Pension Rights—A Study in Inequality', *Westminster Bank Review*, Nov. 1962. The appended biographical note says that Mr Taylor's interest

In sum, there is a plausible inference that labour mobility is impeded by occupational pension schemes. But there are many other factors affecting mobility. How important pension rights are relative to these, and how the situation would be changed by more general vesting, remain matters of doubt.[1]

It must also be emphasized that mobility is not the sole or even necessarily the most important objective of economic (including pension) policy, particularly in times of inflation. The Phillips Committee pointed to the value of a 'measure of stability' (para 247): other observers have been less cautious.

However, while these arguments suggest caution, they do not destroy the case for more general vesting. Rather, they indicate the need for a pragmatic approach, aimed at ensuring general vesting without destroying the variety and flexibility of private pension arrangements. Public intervention of some kind is called for, not simply because of the equity arguments just discussed (which we have seen to be less strong than they seem), but because policies are needed to overcome the problems that face individual employers in providing for vesting unilaterally,[2] and because it would be appropriate for the public authorities to give a lead by liberalizing their own arrangements to embrace transfers between the public and private sector. Contrary to popular belief, there is no evidence that public employment is at present more generous than private employers: in the nature of the public schemes, people leaving public employment probably carry pension rights less frequently than those changing between private employments.

There are a number of technical and legal problems to be solved if vesting is to be generalized by suitably flexible methods, such as the differential tax treatment of schemes providing for different degrees of flexibility. Specification of the nature of the right to be transferred is not an easy matter: how is it to be defined in respect of final salary schemes so that the arrangement is both just and not discouraging.

---

in the question stems from his having twice forfeited his rights *on changing jobs*. Mr Taylor is clearly not unaware of his loss; he presumably made a good enough deal to make it worth his while to change nonetheless. Indeed, it is arguable that at this level the effects of non-transferability, like those of high marginal tax rates, are more likely to show in a widening of salary differentials as a result of realistic bargaining than in the serious inhibition of senior executive mobility. Of course, it remains open to question whether such a result is in the community interest.

[1] The difficulties of discovering the precise effects of pension plans on labour turnover are discussed in Section II of *Private Pension Plans and Manpower Policy*, by Hugh Folk (U.S. Dept. of Labor).

[2] This problem would be made easier by a growth in the interest of trade unions in occupational schemes, similar to that which has already taken place in the U.S.

to the evolution of such schemes? Nor will it be easy (though it would be useful) to remove the discrimination against private schemes described in Section III (2) (b). There would also be need to reform not only the tax law but also Inland Revenue procedures: these at present can deprive an employee of vested rights, e.g. if he chooses to take the benefit of his own contributions in cash. But though there is room for disagreement about these complex technical and legal issues, there is a considerable body of authoritative opinion that they could be solved, given the will.[1] It is time to make a beginning, if occupational pensions are to be encouraged, and if we are to make the most of their potential contribution to economic and social well-being.

[1] For discussion of these technical issues see *inter alia* Pilch and Wood, Seldon, Abbott, and Bacon, Bromfield and Spratling, op. cit., also W. Phillips, 'Making Pension Scheme Benefits Fully Transferable', *British Tax Review*, Jan.-Feb. 1964.

CHAPTER 8

SICK PAY

G. L. REID

I.

To the individual the economic problems created by sickness or illness are twofold: he may face heavy medical expenses, and he may expect to lose income while off work. In this country, the National Health Service removes any fear of inability to meet the cost of being ill, though Chapter 6 shows that in other countries with other systems this may not be true. The main economic difficulty which anyone incapacitated through sickness faces in Britain is having to maintain his normal standard of living; this is the cost of sickness to the individual. More directly, there is the cost of sickness to the employer, in dislocation and lost production, and the cost of sickness to the community in the sense that if sickness is minimized the national income will be increased, National Insurance benefits lowered, and perhaps medical costs reduced. The problem which this Chapter faces is the effect of various types of sickness benefit—and particularly industrial sick pay schemes—on these costs of sickness.

It is difficult to deal precisely with the costs of sickness, as most of the statistical information is at once incomplete and too detailed, but it is possible to get a fairly clear idea of the magnitude of the problem; Section II does this by examining the amount of recorded sickness from national statistics, the probable effect on industry, and the difficulty of income-maintenance during sickness which faces the individual. Section III summarises presently-available information on company sick pay schemes and estimates their importance, while Sections IV and V outline the future of public policy towards income-maintenance during sickness, and discuss the part which company sick pay schemes may play.

II. THE INCIDENCE AND EFFECT OF SICKNESS

1. The Extent of Sickness Absence
Almost the only reliable information on our health as a nation comes

DOI: 10.4324/9781003184706-8

from the Ministry of Pensions and National Insurance. The recorded extent of sickness absence can be shown in several ways, but by any measure the amount of sickness leading to an interruption of employment is enormous. Yet the fact is that the official figures, in giving only the *recorded* extent of absence, understate the true incidence of sickness. There are two main reasons for the difference between the recorded amount and the actual amount of sickness absence: certain categories of persons are not insured for sickness benefit,[1] and spells of sickness which last for less than four days are not generally reported to the Ministry, since benefit is not payable for these first three 'waiting days' unless the spell lasts for four days or longer. The one or two-day coughs and sneezes therefore escape official recognition, and so does the one-day uncertified absence which a firm may charitably put down to sickness.

The exclusion of part of the population from insurance against sickness and so from the official statistics is shown by the fact that, at June 1958, 19·98 million people were insured against sickness,[2] as against an estimated insured population of about 24½ million.[3] The difference is due largely to the number of married women who have elected not to contribute on their own behalf.

In 1957, 88 per cent of the total male population aged between 15 and 69 were insured against sickness, whereas less than one-third of the total female population (15–64) were so insured,[4] and there is no reason to suppose that the figures will have altered since then. The effect of these excluded categories and of the neglect of short absences will be discussed below.

The various measures of the extent of sickness absence each give a slightly different picture of the situation. Table 54 shows one measure, the number of new claims received during the year. (A

---

[1] These categories are:
'(a) men over age 65 and women over age 60 who are retirement pensioners; and all men over 70 and women over age 65;
(b) members of the armed forces;
(c) mariners while at sea;
(d) most non-industrial civil servants (who do not normally claim sickness benefit until an illness has lasted six months);
(e) married women and certain widows, who have chosen not to be insured for sickness benefit (two-thirds of all married women in employment have chosen not to pay flat-rate contributions).'
Ministry of Pensions and National Insurance *Annual Report* 1961; para 395 (4).
[2] *Digest of Statistics Analysing Certificates of Incapacity* 1957/8, Appendix II; M.P.N.I.; HMSO, 1961.
[3] Annual Abstract of Statistics, 1962; HMSO, 1962.
[4] *Digest of Statistics*, 1957/8, op. cit.; Table H. It is estimated that in 1958, 2·3 million married women elected not to pay contributions under the main scheme.

'new claim' is a claim submitted at the beginning of a spell of incapacity for work.)

TABLE 54. *Number of New Claims for Sickness Benefit* (*Thousands*)

YEAR		YEAR	
1951	7,545	1957	9,609
1952	6,587	1958	7,887
1953	7,376	1959	8,768
1954	7,173	1960	8,319
1955	7,919	1961	9,152
1956	7,762	1962	9,002

Source: Ministry of National Insurance, *Annual Reports* 1950–3.
Ministry of Pensions and National Insurance, *Annual Reports* 1954–62

The yearly number of new claims is considerably affected by outbreaks of illness of epidemic proportions such as the influenza of autumn 1957 and early 1961. Making some allowance for these, there has been a higher level of new claims in the years since 1954 than in any year before 1954, and in 1962 there was a total of nine million new claims out of an insured population of just under twenty million. This does not mean that 45 per cent of the insured population drew benefit, as some claimants had more than one spell of sickness during the year, and Table 55 illustrates this for 1955–6, a year for which a full analysis was made.

TABLE 55. *Distribution of Insured Population according to Number of Spells 1955–6, per cent of each category*

NUMBER OF SPELLS	MEN	SINGLE WOMEN	MARRIED WOMEN
0	72	68	64
1	21	24	26
2	5	6	7
3 or more	2	2	3

Source: National Insurance Acts, 1946 to 1959: *Report by Government Actuary on Second Quinquennial Review*, HMSO, 1960: Appendix 5, Table IX.

Just under 30 per cent of the population at risk drew sickness benefit, and about a quarter of those claiming did so more than once. A higher percentage of women than of men claimed sickness benefit.

Measures of this kind, in terms of the number of new claims submitted, do not tell us much about the economic effect of sickness, the numbers off work or the consequent dislocation of production. Table 56 fills in one of the gaps by showing the number of people incapacitated by sickness on the third Tuesday of each month, and the proportion which this forms of the insured population. Since 1956 the monthly figure of those incapacitated has never dropped below three-quarters of a million and has many times exceeded one million. The cyclical pattern of sickness absence is obvious, with the peak in January and February and the lowest point in June and August.[1]

TABLE 56. *Number of Claimants Incapacitated by Sickness and Average Proportion of Insured Population*

| | THOUSANDS | | AS PER CENT OF |
	1962	YEARLY AVERAGE 1957–62	INSURED POPULATION
January	1,352·4	1,102·6	5·5
February	1,033·7	1,103·0	5·7
March	1,033·8	1,018·6	5·1
April	959·7	908·0	4·5
May	889·0	871·3	4·4
June	859·5	836·4	4·2
July	809·7	803·1	4·0
August	801·8	801·5	4·0
September ..	833·2	851·3	4·3
October	899·1	1,001·3	4·9
November ..	911·1	928·9	4·6
December.. ..	922·5	908·4	4·5
Monthly Average..	**942·1**	**927·8**	**4·6**

Source: Ministry of Pensions and National Insurance, *Annual Reports* 1957–62.

The fact that between 4 and 6 per cent of the insured population is drawing sickness benefit at any one time raises some interesting questions as far as the individual employer is concerned, but an even more direct way of looking at the effect of sickness is to consider the number of days for which sickness benefit was paid—the measure sometimes inaccurately called 'days lost'. Table 57 indicates that in each of the six years up to June 1961 sickness benefit was paid for between 250 and 300 million days. It is interesting to note that the average figure of 278 million days of sickness incapacity is about ninety times the number of days lost through strikes, and in fact would be equivalent to the yearly effort of over a million employees. It is difficult, however, to use this figure as more than a rough indication of the economic effect of sickness on industry. Apart from the defects of the official statistics, it is wrong to equate days of sickness benefit with days lost. To use the concept of 'days lost' as a measure of the industrial cost of sickness implies that the insured person was a potential employee whose sickness interrupted his industrial career. Table 58 shows that in many cases this was not so.

[1] Only once has this cycle been seriously disturbed, when the Asian 'flu epidemic of October 1957 saw almost 1½ million people (7·5 per cent of the insured population) incapacitated: this is the highest monthly figure ever recorded.

TABLE 57. *Number of Days Incapacity for which Sickness Benefit was Paid: 1954–61*

MILLIONS OF DAYS

	JUNE 1954 TO JUNE 1955	TO JUNE 1956	TO JUNE 1957	TO JUNE 1958	TO JUNE 1959	TO JUNE 1960	TO JUNE 1961	YEARLY AVERAGE
Men	186·51	187·69	179·55	202·69	198·76	194·28	199·88	192·76
Women	90·26	87·59	82·87	89·69	83·73	79·95	79·07	84·74
Total	276·77	275·28	262·42	292·38	282·49	274·93	278·95	277·50

Source: Ministry of Pensions and National Insurance. *Annual Reports,* 1955–61

TABLE 58. *Sickness Benefit Claimants on May* 31, 1958, *by Duration of Spell*

	NUMBER OF CLAIMANTS (THOUSANDS)	PER CENT OF TOTAL CLAIMANTS	PER CENT OF CLAIMANTS WITH SPELLS UP TO
All	814·06	100	—
up to 1 month	249·84	30·69	30·69 up to 1 month
1 month–3 months	138·82	17·05	47·74 up to 3 months
3 months–6 months	73·92	9·08	56·82 up to 6 months
6 months–1 year	65·20	8·01	64·83 up to 1 year
1 year–2 years	64·06	7·87	72·70 up to 2 years
2 years–3 years	39·54	4·86	77·56 up to 3 years
3 years–4 years	28·12	3·45	81·01 up to 4 years
4 years–5 years	23·80	2·92	83·93 up to 5 years
5 years–6 years	20·52	2·52	86·45 up to 6 years
6 years–7 years	15·02	1·85	88·30 up to 7 years
7 years–8 years	13·24	1·63	89·93 up to 8 years
8 years–9 years	12·42	1·53	91·46 up to 9 years
over 9 years	70·10	8·61	100·00 all durations

Source: Ministry of Pensions and National Insurance, *Digest of Statistics Analysing Certificates of Incapacity*, 1957/8: Table 17.

At end-May 1958, 35 per cent of those incapacitated had been off work for at least a year, and they accounted for over 86 million days of sickness incapacity, about one-third of the yearly total. It is questionable whether the days of incapacity of these long-term sick should be included in an assessment of the industrial importance of sickness. While they are nominally in the labour force, they have not been gainfully employed for at least a year and in many cases for very much longer, with more than 130,000 claimants having been incapacitated for more than five years. The yearly figures of days of incapacity give a picture of the amount of recorded sickness in the insured population, but they are an imperfect indicator of the effect of sickness on industry and the likely cost of sickness absence.

2. *Sickness and the Individual Firm*[1]

The official national statistics show that the labour force must *always* be below its nominal strength because of sickness, but it is not possible to deduce what the sickness experience of any one firm will be. The consequence of sickness will be more or less unfortunate depending on the characteristics of the labour force and precise way in which it is affected by sickness, but a direct comparison between the M.P.N.I. statistics and the experience of a firm would give misleading results. For one thing, the official figures refer to all insured persons including the long-term sick who would no longer figure in the sickness absence statistics of a company. Then there are a very con-

[1] The effect of a company sick pay scheme will be ignored for the time being, though as we shall see a sick pay scheme may have a considerable influence on the pattern of sickness absence.

siderable number of married women who have elected not to be insured against sickness. All their absences will not appear in M.P.N.I. records, though they might account for a considerable part of a firm's sickness absence, especially in such industries as textiles and food which employ many married women. It does appear too that the relevant characteristics of insured and non-insured women are 'substantially different . . . and the sickness records of the two groups are therefore likely to be different'.[1]

A third important factor is the short absence of less than four days which may contribute to a firm's total of sickness absence but will not appear in official records. The M.P.N.I. statistics of incapacity for work can therefore be used only to suggest influences which may be important in determining the sickness experience of an individual company, but in this they are extremely helpful.

One important factor is the age composition of the work-force. The older an insured person, the more likely is he to be off sick. Of those incapacitated at May 31, 1958, about 2 per cent of men aged between 25 and 29 were incapacitated, compared with 13 per cent of men aged between 60 and 63. If spells of over six months are omitted so as to exclude the long-term sick, the proportions are respectively 1·32 per cent and 4·82 per cent.[2] A more direct way of showing the effect of age on sickness incapacity is seen in Table 59, which gives the average number of weeks of sickness per employed person. This Table excludes self-employed persons, but includes the long-term sick who are insured as employed persons.[3]

TABLE 59. *Average Number of Weeks of Sickness Benefit per Employed Person per Year: Average of 1953/54–1957/58*

AGE	MEN	SINGLE WOMEN	MARRIED WOMEN
15–19	0·84	1·05	2·17
20–24	1·00	1·35	1·89
25–29	1·03	1·84	2·20
30–34	1·19	2·34	2·85
35–39	1·31	2·56	3·43
40–44	1·55	2·91	3·85
45–49	1·90	3·55	4·40
50–54	2·67	4·43	5·13
55–59	4·10	5·92	7·04
60–64	6·45	—	—
Average ..	2·04	2·26	3·44

Source: National Insurance Acts; *Report by Government Actuary on Second Quinquennial Review*, HMSO, 1960; Table II, p. 37.

[1] G. Mary Jones, 'Incapacity for Work among the Insured Population of Great Britain', *British Journal of Preventive and Social Medicine*, 13, 1959, p. 84.
[2] *Digest of Statistics*, op. cit., Table 18.
[3] Self-employed persons had a much more favourable sickness record than did employed persons.

Table 59 is a composite one, and the figures of average weeks of benefit reflect two separate effects, the number of spells of incapacity and the duration of each spell. It is the latter effect which is most important in giving the high average weeks of benefit for older employees. Table 60 gives the spells of sickness beginning in 1957–8 per 100 insured persons in each age group.[1]

TABLE 60. *Spells of Sickness Commencing per* 100 *Insured Persons in Each Age Group:* 1957/58

AGE	EMPLOYED PERSONS MEN	SINGLE WOMEN	MARRIED WOMEN
15–19	57	71	62
20–24	54	63	57
25–29	48	54	49
30–34	46	47	48
35–39	44	46	57
40–44	44	44	58
45–49	45	42	60
50–54	50	41	54
55–59	54	39	50
60–64	59	—	—

Source: Second Quinquennial Review, op. cit., Table VIII, p. 41.

There is no indication that the average number of new spells increases with age. In fact for men, the youngest age groups have almost as bad a sickness record as the oldest, while for women the number of new spells decreases with age. This means that the high sickness rates for older persons in Table 59 must result largely from longer spells being more common in the higher age groups, and this conclusion is confirmed by Table 61.

This Table will exclude many of the long-term sick as it deals only with spells terminating during the year, though a proportion of long-term spells will have been terminated, some of them by retirement on pension at age 65. Clearly higher age groups tend to have longer spells of sickness, and though very few spells last for more than 13 weeks—for employed men less than 3 per cent of all spells— they make a considerable contribution to total sickness. It was noted earlier that spells of over one year's duration account for about one-third of the number of days for which sickness benefit is paid, and the importance of long spells in general can be seen from the fact that the average duration of a spell is about 33 days whereas the median duration in 1958 was 11 days.[2]

[1] Because of the Asian 'flu epidemic of 1957, the figures are higher than in a normal year, but the relative picture is much the same as a normal year.
[2] *Digest of Statistics*, 1957/8, op. cit., Table 9.

TABLE 61. *Spells of Sickness Terminating 1955-6 per 100 Insured Persons in Each Age Group*

	DURATION OF SPELL IN WEEKS							
	NOT OVER 1	OVER 1 LESS THAN 2	OVER 2 LESS THAN 4	OVER 4 LESS THAN 13	OVER 13 LESS THAN 26	OVER 26 LESS THAN 52	OVER 52	ALL DURATIONS
Employed men								
Aged 15–29	12·6	12·2	6·8	3·6	0·5	0·2	0·2	36·1
30–44	10·1	11·4	8·3	4·6	0·7	0·2	0·3	35·6
45–59	7·5	11·1	11·6	8·2	1·6	0·5	0·5	41·0
60–64	6·3	10·8	14·5	12·8	2·8	1·1	1·9	50·2
15-64	**9·7**	**11·5**	**9·4**	**6·0**	**1·0**	**0·4**	**0·4**	**38·4**
Employed single women								
Aged 15–29	13·0	15·1	10·0	4·8	0·5	0·2	0·3	43·9
30–44	6·5	10·2	10·3	6·6	1·2	0·5	0·5	35·8
45–59	4·2	8·0	11·3	8·5	1·8	0·8	0·9	35·5
15–59	**9·9**	**12·6**	**10·3**	**6·0**	**0·9**	**0·4**	**0·5**	**40·6**
Employed married women								
Aged 15–29	8·0	12·4	11·9	9·6	1·5	0·4	0·4	44·2
30–44	6·7	12·0	14·9	11·0	1·7	0·8	0·8	47·9
45-59	4·2	9·6	14·6	11·6	2·2	1·0	1·1	44·3
15–59	**6·4**	**11·4**	**13·5**	**10·6**	**1·8**	**0·7**	**0·7**	**45·1**

Source: Second Quinquennial Review, op. cit., Table X, p. 42.

Tables 59, 60 and 61 can tell us something about the effect on sickness absence of a high proportion of female employees, but it is rather difficult to generalize because of the large numbers of employed married women who are not insured. Table 59 shows that women in general have a less favourable sickness record than men, but the sickness rates of single women may be lower than Table 59 suggests, since a high proportion of single employed women are in the 15–29 age groups. Though single women of this age group have a relatively low sickness rate, Table 60 indicates that the average number of spells was higher than either men or married women of the same age group, and also higher than that of older single women. The pattern of absence for young single women therefore appears to consist of a large number of short spells. It is not possible to deduce anything about the likely sickness absence of married women in industry since those who are insured are a minority of the total labour force of married women,[1] but the insured married women seem to have a less favourable record than either of the other two groups. In general,

[1] About one-third of employed married women were contributors in 1958. See *Second Quinquennial Review*, op. cit., Appendix 6, Table E.

employers of female labour are thus likely to find a higher level of sickness absence, the degree to which this is true depending on other characteristics of the firm or industry.

There is some evidence that the incidence of sickness varies geographically, as Table 62 suggests.

TABLE 62. *Proportion of Men Incapacitated per* 100 *at Risk, at Some Time During* 1955–6, *and on June* 2, 1956

REGION	NUMBERS INCAPACITATED PER 100 AT RISK	
	AT SOME TIME	ON JUNE 2, 1956
London and South East	23	2·9
Southern	24	3·1
South Western	27	3·8
Eastern	26	3·2
North Midland	28	3·4
Midland	25	3·4
Wales	38	6·2
East and West Ridings	31	4·2
North Western	30	4·3
Northern	35	4·9
Scotland	31	4·6
Total	28	3·8

Source: G. M. Jones, op. cit., p. 81.

Scotland, the North of England and Wales were above average both in the number incapacitated at some time during the year, and in the numbers incapacitated at June 2, 1956. This may be partly due to the distribution of industry, since there is no doubt that occupation affects the incidence and duration of sickness. Unfortunately no such breakdown of official sickness statistics is presently available.[1] If the figures in Table 62 were corrected for occupation, the apparent geographical dividing line between above-average and below-average sickness experience might disappear.

These factors which will influence the rate of sickness in industry have been estimated from official statistics so that they all refer only to absences of four days or longer. 'Short absences' have not been considered, but they may be no less important.[2] One writer suggests that in some cases they account for half the total sickness absence and have quite a different pattern of causes.[3] It is rather difficult to

[1] See Ministry of Pensions and National Insurance, *Annual Report* 1961, paras. 381–3, for details of an inquiry which should throw light on this question. Publication of the results is expected during 1964.

[2] The classification generally adopted is that absences of four days or longer are 'long absences', and those of one, two or three days 'short' absences. See Medical Research Council, Report of Industrial Health & Research Board No. 85. 1944.

[3] J. P. W. Hughes, 'Sickness Absence Recording in Industry', *British Journal of Industrial Medicine*, 1952, 9, p. 264.

O

estimate how much this form of sickness absence adds to the 'cost' of sickness as a whole. The official records do not, as we have seen, purport to say how much sickness 'costs' the economy, but we may accept the average figure of 275 million days incapacity as the amount due to long absences. To exclude the long-term sick by arbitrarily removing the days of incapacity of those who have been sick for one year or longer means reducing this figure by about one-third, to 185 million days, but the short absences might more than compensate for this, so that the total number of days lost due to sickness of employed persons may be as much as 300 million.

However, this figure does not tell us very much about the true cost of sickness, since neither a working day nor a day of sickness is a standard measure,[1] and it would be foolish to claim that 300 million days' production is irretrievably lost every year because of sickness. The economic effect of sickness depends to a large extent on the reactions of the employer, and the individual circumstances of each case. For example, short absences may be more disturbing than long. For if an employee is incapacitated for several weeks, his company, with foreknowledge of his absence, can make alternative arrangements; but a spate of unexpected one-day sickness absences though yielding fewer days of incapacity, could cause chaos and disrupt production. The concept of lost production is a hazy one, too. Clerical or administrative workers may find it relatively easy to catch up on the arrears of work after several days of sickness, and absences of white-collar workers may mean only that a number of other similar employees each work a little harder. Of course, a few employees are indispensable especially in very small firms, but a company seldom grinds to a halt because one man is off sick: often the ability to carry on without much trouble comes as a surprise both to the company and to the 'indispensable' employee. In production work, too, there is usually scope for this sort of substitution: assignments can be rearranged so that someone else takes over the absentee's job or sometimes so that his tasks are postponed to wait for him. Where there is a more homogeneous labour force composed of semi-skilled or unskilled workers, the probability of lost production through sickness is even smaller, since again the number of the labour force who are at work will be able to make up the arrears.

This is not to deny that sickness, even 'normal' sickness, can cause considerable disruption and dislocation in industry; the unexpected sickness or sickness of key personnel, such as the absence of a skilled member of a team or of a foreman, will be much more important than the types of sickness absence discussed in the last paragraph.

---

[1] The day of incapacity used in official statistics is of course a standard measure but not a day of sickness as used here.

Then the non-appearance of an executive may paralyse part of a firm. How many companies have had to postpone giving or receiving an order because 'Mr X is the only man who knows about this side of the business and he's off sick'? But sickness, while it may be an unforeseen contingency for the individual, is something which a company must expect, and about which it has certain definite information which should enable it to make some kind of allowance. For example the employer may know from past records that absence ranges from 2 per cent in summer to 5 per cent or more in winter, and that certain definite trends have been established within his own organization. One large-scale study of sickness absence of Government industrial workers found that older workers tended to be off sick more often than younger, and for longer periods, that unskilled workers had a higher absence rate than skilled men, and that absence of workers on incentive payment schemes was lower than that of time-paid men.[1]

Given, then, that there are trends, possibly of a more individual nature but enabling the employer to forecast within reasonably narrow limits the extent of sickness absence, how can an employer try to minimize his losses through sickness? There appear to be two courses which an employer can follow in order to make up for the permanent under-strength of his labour force. First, he may rely on the redeployment process to allow work to carry on at much the same rate as before, and accept the consequent dislocation as a failure of this policy; or second, he may try to ensure that the labour force is permanently slightly above the 'full attendance' minimum, so that, assuming no sickness at all, the company is overmanned. In fact, a combination of these is most likely, since all companies are in a sense overmanned in that the existing labour force could if necessary increase the level of production considerably, though in the process unit production costs are likely to rise, because of increased overtime working or other inefficient use of men or machines. Yet as this section has shown, certain industries are very much better able to rely on redeployment than others, this policy being more likely to succeed where mass-production techniques using semi-skilled employment prevail. Industries which are highly capital-intensive using skilled labour which is difficult to juggle around may be more likely to overman to some extent. Whatever the policy—and it may simply be a *laissez-faire* reliance on 'muddling through'—it is complicated by the cyclical nature of sickness which means that a policy successful in summer may fail in winter, or that one year's policy may be unsuccessful the next.

[1] R. B. Buzzard & W. J. Shaw, 'An Analysis of Absence under a Scheme of Paid Sick Leave', *British Journal of Industrial Medicine*, 1952, 9, pp. 284–5.

TABLE 63. Sickness Benefit, Average Earnings and the Cost of Living: 1952–63 (*Married man with two children*)

	1951	1952	1953	1954	1955	1956	OCTOBER EACH YEAR (1951=100) 1957	1958	1959	1960	1961	1962	1963
Sickness Benefit	100	123	123	123	147	147	147	187	187	187	219	219	259
Average earnings	100	108	114	123	134	143	152	155	163	175	184	191	201
Retail price index	100	107	109	112	118	122	127	130	130	132	138	142	146
Benefit as % of earnings	33	38	35	33	36	34	32	40	38	35	39	37	42

Sources: Annual Abstract of Statistics; Ministry of Labour *Gazette.*

3. *Income Maintenance during Sickness*

There has been little work published on the ease or difficulty with which those incapacitated maintain their standards of living. This is understandable since there are so many variables depending on individual circumstances. There is the question of differing patterns of expenditure out of identical incomes, which may mean that some families find it relatively easy to adjust to a lower income level. On the other hand, it is often impossible to judge exactly how far normal work income is maintained, as the National Insurance sickness benefits vary with family responsibilities and can be supplemented from many sources, both public and private. Indeed in the average case such supplementation was very necessary as Table 63 shows.

Up to early 1963 sickness benefit for a married man had never been more than 40 per cent of average male earnings. The pattern of increases in sickness benefit followed approximately a three year cycle, with the benefit-earnings ratio falling from 38–40 per cent by about five percentage points before the next increase. This regularity was abruptly broken by the increases in March 1963 which came less than two years after the previous rise. The increases in 1952, 1955 and 1958 came after the earnings index had overtaken the index of sickness benefit, but from 1959–63 National Insurance benefits have risen considerably faster than earnings, and over the whole period 1951–63 much more quickly than the cost of living. But even with the most recent increase the standard family still received less than half of average earnings in sickness benefit. This assumes that there is only one member of the family earning: where several members of the household work, the sickness of the main breadwinner will be a much less serious matter. Then, of course, anyone incapacitated through sickness does not pay income tax on the amount of benefit, but this is unlikely to add very greatly to income for most wage-earners, as a married man with two children who earns £780 per annum would ordinarily pay less than 10 shillings a week in income tax. In theory it will be more important that anyone in receipt of National Insurance benefit is relieved of the contribution which he would normally pay, at present 12 to 19 shillings per week, but ordinarily the employee will exclude this sum from his calculations of earnings, so that the rise in income is more apparent than real.

There is some information on the extent to which incapacitated employees manage financially, but it is naturally difficult to generalize from it as so much depends on the individual's present condition and past habits, not to mention the nature and duration of his incapacity. One study was carried out by the Institute of Community Studies which investigated a small sample of incapacitated men.[1]

[1] Phyllis & Peter Willmott, 'Off Work Through Illness', *New Society*, January 10, 1963.

Apart from relying on earnings of other members of the family, those in the sample tended to take one or more of three courses: (i) drawing on savings; (ii) borrowing from friends or relatives; or (iii) reducing the level of expenditure below what might be considered a minimum, including not meeting rent and hire-purchase commitments.[1] This study also found, not surprisingly, that 'the longer an illness lasts, the greater the family's difficulties are likely to be',[2] and certainly short-term sickness of a few days or weeks can in most cases be accommodated by drawing on savings or temporarily defecting on hire-purchase payments. But all three methods of adjusting expenditure and income are essentially short-term, and sickness of more than a couple of months could see their possibilities exhausted. The problem is acute for those who have been sick for several months, whose savings have dwindled, who are already in debt and who have no immediate prospect of being fit for work. There is, of course, National Assistance supplementation, but the I.C.S. study found that a large proportion of their sample thought of this as a last resort to be tried when all else had failed. The report considered that a number of their respondents would have been better off had they taken advantage of N.A.B. supplementation but only 10 per cent of them did so. This is comparable to the official figures of households in receipt of supplementation to sickness benefit. (Table 64).

TABLE 64. *Proportion of Households in Receipt of National Assistance Board Supplementation to Sickness Benefit*

DECEMBER EACH YEAR

YEAR	PER CENT	YEAR	PER CENT
1951	15	1957	10·6
1952	14·5	1958	10·2
1953	16·2	1959	12·4
1954	14·8	1960	13·3
1955	13	1961	12·6
1956	12·1	1962	14·3

Source: Ministry of National Insurance, *Annual Reports* 1950–3.
Ministry of Pensions and National Insurance, *Annual Reports* 1954–62.

Evidently few households do resort to National Assistance. In part this may be due to a psychological unwillingness to do so prompted by the notion that whereas sickness benefit is a 'right', National Assistance is 'charity', but it is just as likely to be caused by lack of eligibility, sufficiency of other means, or by an ignorance of the conditions under which supplementation can be obtained.[3]

[1] This study also found that industrial sick pay schemes were most important. See Section III.
[2] Phyllis & Peter Willmott, op. cit., p. 17.
[3] It is clear from the I.C.S. study that many people had only a very hazy notion of how and when they could apply for supplementation.

Another inquiry which confirms several of the points made above was carried out in Bristol in 1958.[1] It dealt with 226 families in which the earnings of the householder had been interrupted, but the sample was (deliberately) not typical of sickness claimants. In only fourteen cases—about 6 per cent of the sample—was the period of unemployment less than twelve months, and of these fourteen incapacitated men nine were over 50.[2] This inquiry was therefore concerned with the long-term and older sick. As we have seen, this group is numerically less important, but the results of this inquiry emphasize the seriousness of the problems facing the long-term sick. All families were in receipt of National Assistance benefits—though their attitudes to this type of income were much the same as in the I.C.S. study[3]— but only about 20 per cent were actually in debt.

Private insurance is unlikely to be able to fill the gap. Most schemes have only a limited period of benefit (often two years) and fairly severe entrance qualifications. A relatively new type of insurance, permanent sickness insurance, allows an unlimited period of benefit which cannot be cancelled solely because of adverse claims experience. The premiums payable by the insured person may be sizeable, and extra premiums charged according to the employment category, age, sex and general state of health.[4] A leading company in the field of permanent sickness insurance had in 1962 only about 12 per cent of policy-holders outside the employment category of professional or sedentary workers. Clearly this type of sickness insurance is potentially very valuable, but its contribution to income-maintenance for manual workers must be small.

Our conclusion must therefore be that, in the absence of any supplementary income, the standard of living of a manual worker who is off work sick will almost always suffer. One of the important questions of this Chapter is to what extent industrial sick pay schemes can or should provide this extra income as a protection for the standard of living.

III. SICK PAY SCHEMES

The previous section discussed the extent and effect of sickness without taking into account the existence of industrial sick pay schemes which arrange for an employee to be given part or all of his normal earnings during his period of sickness. This section will con-

---

[1] 'A Study of Families in which Earnings are interrupted by Illness, Injury, or Death', Dept. of Economics (Social Studies Section), University of Bristol, 1958.
[2] Ibid., p. 11.
[3] Ibid., pp. 36–7.
[4] See D. J. Bond, 'Permanent Sickness Insurance', *Journal of the Institute of Actuaries Students' Society*, Vol. 17, Part III.

sider first the characteristics of most sick pay schemes for manual
workers in private industry, and then attempt to assess their importance to the problems of income maintenance and their possible
and actual effect on the employer.

1. *The Mechanics of Sick Pay Schemes*

There has been one official survey of sick pay schemes, carried out by
the Ministry of Pensions and National Insurance in 1961–2, and
based on a 5 per cent sample of employed men and a $2\frac{1}{2}$ per cent
sample of employed women insured for sickness benefit.[1] This large-
scale survey and a number of smaller enquiries[2] have demonstrated
that in this particular field of industrial relations (as in many others)
there is nothing approaching general practice. The types of scheme
and way in which they operate can greatly differ from company to
company. Any attempt to list general features runs the risk of
obscuring this diversity, but there are certain basic factors which
appear to be common in most situations.

(i) The majority of non-manual workers are covered by some kind
of sick pay arrangements. It is now generally recognized that sick
leave with full pay is a normal condition of employment for salaried
administrative staff, and lower staff grades are rapidly coming to
secure similar generous schemes. The M.P.N.I. survey found that
more than 85 per cent of professional, clerical and administrative
workers were covered, while the Institute of Office Management in
a survey of about 200,000 office workers found that in all the 753
establishments in the sample, sickness payments were given either
under a definite scheme or as an ex gratia payment.[3] This Chapter
is mainly concerned with manual workers, while the Ministry of
Pensions survey deals with all workers, salaried and wage-earning;
the information which it gives is therefore not fully applicable, but
since it is by far the most complete and detailed summary of sick
pay schemes, it will be quoted here with due allowance made where
necessary.

(ii) In most cases, sick pay schemes require some service qualification by the participating employee though this may not be true for
staff. The period is usually a period of months, say six or twelve, but
in a few cases it may take several years' service to be eligible for a
sick pay scheme. The M.P.N.I. survey found that about 19 per cent

---

[1] Report on an Inquiry into the Incidence of Incapacity for Work: Part I:
Scope and Characteristics of Employers' Sick Pay Schemes: HMSO, 1964.

[2] See, for example, *Sick Pay Schemes and Sick and Benevolent Funds*, Industrial
Welfare Society, 1957; *Company Sick Pay Schemes*, Institute of Personnel
Management, 1959; *Sick Pay Schemes and Sick and Accident Funds for Works
Employees*, Ministry of Labour Information Service, 1961.

[3] *Office Staff Practices*, 1961. Institute of Office Management, 1961; p. 18
and Table 7.

of all men covered had to fulfil a qualifying period of six months (notably in public administration and defence, and the public utilities), while 27 per cent had to work for one year, notably in mining and transport; only about $2\frac{1}{2}$ per cent had to serve for longer than a year. It also found that the requirement to serve a qualifying period was much more common in partly skilled and unskilled occupations, where only about 30 per cent and 26 per cent respectively received sick pay from the first day of illness. General observation suggests that a company may require employees to undergo a medical examination, and most reserve the right to have an incapacitated employee inspected by a company-nominated doctor. It is common, too, for there to be a minimum age limit, e.g. 18 or 21 years, and for the scheme to be confined to full-time employees. Thus even in companies where employees receive payment while off sick, by no means all of the work-force will be covered.

(iii) Sick pay may be either a flat-rate sum, as it was for about one-fifth of men found in the M.P.N.I. enquiry to be covered by sick pay arrangements, or a percentage of wages or earnings, but for manual workers it seems unlikely that complete income protection is given. It is normal for the employer to take into account the amount of National Insurance sickness benefit; flat-rate sick pay is generally a small weekly sum paid in addition to National Insurance (seldom as much as £3, according to the M.P.N.I. survey), while with wage-related sick pay the employer 'makes-up' National Insurance to a stated percentage of the wage or earnings. It seems to be uncommon for the N.I. benefit to be made up to normal earnings of manual workers, but a number of schemes provide for a make-up to the basic wage. About 70 per cent of male employees found in the M.P.N.I. inquiry to be covered by sick pay arrangements received full wages either with or without the deduction of National Insurance benefit, but this included staff as well as manual workers and full wages here meant either basic wages or normal earnings. The smaller inquiries have shown that other less generous schemes provide employee income during sickness amounting to three-quarters or two-thirds of normal basic wage. The level of sick pay can also vary with time—e.g. 13 weeks at basic wage less N.I. benefit, followed by 13 weeks at half of the basic wage less N.I. benefit—and may be related to length of service, with long-service employees getting a higher proportion of their basic wage. In one or two cases where sick pay is a flat-rate sum, the amount may actually increase with the length of absence. The unofficial inquiries also suggest that female employees always receive a smaller flat-rate sum or a lower percentage of wages, but in the Ministry of Pensions sample 90 per cent of women covered for sick pay received full wages with or without deduction of National Insurance. For both male and female manual workers, it appears to be common for many schemes not to give sick pay for short absences of, say, three to six days or less. The M.P.N.I. study found that 72 per cent of all male employees had no 'waiting days' for benefit, but waiting days were more common for the partly skilled and unskilled occupational groups.

(iv) The period for which sick pay is given varies with length of service. Sometimes the period of benefit depends directly on duration of employment, as when an employee receives one week of sickness pay for each year of service. In most companies the stated maximum period is six months or less: a few have a longer maximum, and some allow an extra discretionary period of sick pay. In the Ministry of Pensions and National Insurance sample, about 60 per cent of male employees with sick pay were covered by schemes providing a maximum period of payment of six months or less, while almost a quarter of employees covered were in schemes where the maximum period of payment was at the company's discretion. In partly skilled and unskilled occupations, though, almost three-fifths and three-quarters respectively of male employees with cover were entitled to sick pay for varying periods up to 13 weeks, while less than one in ten had entitlement lasting longer than six months. It is interesting to note, too, that in June 1961 only from 6–10 per cent of men incapacitated for between three and six months were still receiving sick pay, while for those who had been sick for a longer period the proportion was 3–7 per cent.

(v) Many firms also have sickness funds to which the employee contributes a small weekly sum, normally less than one shilling, getting in return a flat-rate sum of sick pay.

2. The Extent and Cost of Sick Pay Schemes

There are two main sources of data on the coverage of sick pay schemes, namely the Ministry of Pensions and National Insurance survey of 1961–2, which is much the more reliable, and the University of Glasgow inquiry of 1960. Table 65 shows the extent of sickness benefit provision in manufacturing industry as revealed by these two inquiries.

The information in Table 65 does not enable us to say how many manual workers were covered by sick pay schemes, since the figures in Column 2 show only the number of employees in firms with schemes, and membership of schemes is likely to be restricted to certain groups of employees. The fact that 'all manufacturing' figures for Column 2 and Column 3 are much the same only underlines the 'welfare biased' nature of the Glasgow inquiry; the M.P.N.I. survey covers all employees, salaried and wage-earning, and the similarity therefore indicates that in the Glasgow inquiry either the proportion of firms with sick pay schemes covering

TABLE 65. *Proportion of Employees covered by Sick Pay Schemes in Manufacturing Industry*

INDUSTRY	1 UNIVERSITY OF GLASGOW* % COMPANIES WITH SCHEMES	2 % OF INDUSTRY SAMPLE EMPLOYMENT	3 M.P.N.I.** % SAMPLE COVERED BY SCHEMES
Food ..	93	97·3	71·7
Chemicals	84	96·7	84·2
Metal manf.	11	1·0	26·7
Engineering	40	38·9	44·3
Shipbuilding	—	—	33·8
Vehicles ..	38	58·8	49·4
Other metal	8	3·5	32·4
Textiles ..	31	34·0	29·8
Clothing ..	N.A.	N.A.	30·5
Leather ..	N.A.	N.A.	26·3
Bricks, etc.	36	69·2	43·4
Timber ..	N.A.	N.A.	29·1
Paper, etc. ..	64	71·5	56·4
Other manfg.	50	34·2	47·8
All Manufacturing	**45**	**48·5**	**49·3**

Notes: * Manual workers only.
** All employees.

manual workers was very high (and Column 1 suggests that this was true), or that the proportion of employees actually covered by these schemes was comparatively low. In the Ministry of Pensions survey 57 per cent of workers in all industry were covered, and in the nationalized industries, professional services and public administration about 90 per cent. A summary by social class showed coverage of male employees to be 88 per cent in professional occupations, 57 per cent in skilled occupations, 52 per cent in partly skilled occupations, and 41 per cent in unskilled occupations. The latter two figures are higher than one would expect to find in manufacturing industry alone, since all eligible wage-earners in the nationalized industries are covered by sick pay schemes and they were included in the M.P.N.I. survey.

To the employer any advantages, tangible or otherwise, which accrue from sick pay schemes are only of importance in so far as they seem to him to outweigh the cost of providing them. The multiplicity of schemes and the differing patterns of absence in different labour forces make it difficult to estimate how much sick pay schemes should cost. It is possible to reach some estimate from the national statistics of sickness absence on the following assumptions:

(i) that all days of incapacity of those who have been sick for one year or longer should be excluded, since those people ought not to be considered as part of the labour force;

(ii) that short absences of less than three days should not be taken into account, since many or most sick pay schemes do not pay for these days;

(iii) that if industrial sick pay schemes were a universal condition of employment, the average number of weeks of incapacity would increase by 50 per cent.[1]

If the official figures of the average number of weeks of benefit[2] are adjusted in accordance with these assumptions, and if an employer was liable to pay his workers the full rate of earnings without deductions when they were off sick, the scheme would cost him about 4½ per cent of earnings for men and single women, and about 6½ per cent of earnings for married women.

In fact, there are several reasons why a sick pay scheme for manual workers would cost much less than this amount:

(i) Manual workers are usually not given sickness benefit at the full rate of earnings. Sometimes they are given the full basic wage, which may be considerably less than normal earnings. This may be offset by the likelihood that manual workers will have a higher sickness rate than staff so that the figures in the previous paragraph, which refer to all employees, may be too low.

(ii) Even where sickness benefit is as large as the full basic wage, the employer normally only makes up the National Insurance benefit, so that the employer's liability reduces with every increase in National Insurance benefit.

(iii) Many wage-related schemes do not provide for sick pay to be made up even to the basic wage and sick pay is often given as a flat-rate sum which will reduce, as a percentage of payroll, with every increase in earnings. In firms where only a proportion of the basic wage is paid or where there is flat-rate benefit the cost would be even lower.[3]

(iv) Women may not be given sick pay on the same basis as men; National Insurance benefit may be made up to a lower percentage of the basic wage or the flat-rate sum set at a lower level.[4] Women may also have less favourable qualifying conditions than men. The higher sickness rates of women are therefore not necessarily reflected in a higher cost as a percentage of female earnings, and since there are normally many fewer women than men in the work-force the impact on the cost of a scheme may not be large.

From these estimates derived from the average number of weeks'

---

[1] The basis of this assumption is explained in Part 3 of this section.

[2] *Second Quinquennial Review*, op. cit., p. 37.

[3] In the M.P.N.I. survey almost 70 per cent of all employees received benefit at the rate of 'full wages'.

[4] The Ministry of Pensions inquiry found that 90 per cent of female employees covered by sick pay arrangements received sick pay at the full rate of wages.

TABLE 66. The Cost of Sick Pay Schemes

1. INDUSTRIAL WELFARE SOCIETY

INDUSTRY	% OF PAYROLL										NOT AVAILABLE	Total
	0·01 0·25	0·26 0·50	0·51 0·75	0·76 1·00	1·01 1·25	1·26 1·50	1·51 1·75	1·76 2·00	2·01 2·25	2·26 2·50		
Food	1	2	1	1		1	1	1			4	12
Chemicals	2	2		1						1	2	8
Metals	1			1							1	3
Engineering	2		2	1	1	1		1		1	4	13
Textiles	1				1						1	3
Bricks, etc.	1											1
Timber					1							1
Other		1					1				2	4
Total	8	5	3	4	3	2	2	2	–	2	14	45

2. UNIVERSITY OF GLASGOW ENQUIRY

INDUSTRY	% OF PAYROLL										OVER 2·50	NOT AVAILABLE	Total
	0·01 0·25	0·26 0·50	0·51 0·75	0·76 1·00	1·01 1·25	1·26 1·50	1·51 1·75	1·76 2·00	2·01 2·25	2·26 2·50			
Food	6	2	2	2	4	4		2			1	2	25
Chemicals	4	7	1	6	3	3	5	3	4		2	3	41
Metal manuf.		1	1									1	3
Engineering	17	5	2	2	3	1			1		1	4	36
Vehicles	3	2										3	8
Other metal	1												1
Textiles	10	2	2				1					3	18
Bricks, etc.	1	1	2	1									5
Paper, etc.	3	2	1	1								2	9
Other manfg.	2	2		1								2	7
Other	3		1			1		1				1	7
Total	50	24	12	13	10	9	6	6	5	–	4	21	160

Source: Sick Pay Schemes and Sick and Benevolent Funds, I.W.S., 1957.

incapacity, it seems as if the cost of a sickness payment scheme need not be large, and in many cases the cost of the scheme is held down by the conditions attaching to benefit. For example, a period of waiting will cut out the costly short absences and employers with a pre-dominantly female labour force can make allowances for the higher sickness rate by more stringent regulations and lower rates of benefit.

There are two main sources of data on the actual cost of sick pay schemes, i.e. the survey by the Industrial Welfare Society and the Glasgow University inquiry into fringe benefits described more fully in Chapter III of this volume. The cost of the schemes is shown in Table 66.

Sick pay schemes were relatively costly in the food industry com-panies in both inquiries, with about 40 per cent of I.W.S. respondents and 50 per cent of Glasgow respondents spending more than one per cent of payroll on their schemes. Chemical companies in the Glasgow inquiry showed a high proportion of high-cost schemes with 52 per cent costing over one per cent. It is possible that the compara-tively low ratio of wage-costs to total costs in chemicals and food has some influence, since employers in these industries are likely to be much less concerned about the level of labour costs, but the small number of schemes in metal manufacture were relatively inexpensive, despite the capital-intensive nature of the industry. It seems likely that the tradition of the industry is more important: chemicals is a new industry with a progressive outlook, and the food industry has usually been associated with welfare-minded companies. In these industries sick pay schemes are more likely to be introduced than in heavy industry where tradition, if not 'anti-welfare', is at least less conducive to welfare schemes of many kinds; a 'good employer' in iron and steel, for example, will spend very much less on welfare facilities than the good employer in such industries as food, chemicals or light engineering.

3. The Effect of Sick Pay Schemes

Except where sick pay schemes are directly related to earnings, it is rather difficult to estimate how far they go to alleviating any hardship during sickness. We have seen that National Insurance benefit is considerably below average normal work income, but the diversity of industrial sickness benefit plans is such that their success in filling the gap will vary widely. With a wage-related scheme the relationship between earnings and the basic wage is important, since if there is a substantial earnings drift sickness benefit will be much less sufficient to protect the standard of living. For example, in an industry where earnings may regularly be half as much again as the basic wage a sick pay scheme which makes up National Insurance to three-quarters of the basic wage will still give an employee less than half of his normal income. There are of course schemes more generous than this which will provide a greater degree of income-security, but there are probably more which are less favourable. Where a flat-rate sum is added to National Insurance benefit, the effect is equally uncertain since it depends on the size of the employer payment and the relation of total benefit to normal earnings, but if the flat-rate sum is, say, two or three pounds, the result may be to give total benefit nearer to normal income than a wage-related scheme.

In the present situation, however, any addition to sickness benefit must be welcome. The Institute of Community Studies commented in their report that 'the question which is obviously crucial to the men and their families is whether they continue to get paid by their employer while they are ill'.[1] But as we have seen, there are several factors which can diminish the importance of sick pay, quite apart from inadequate benefits. First, benefit periods are usually relatively short so that a man's entitlement under the industrial scheme may cease just when he begins to need more money, as his other resources give out: here again the financial problem of the long-term sick appears.[2] Secondly, where a discretionary sick pay scheme operates it may not be clear to an employee whether he will receive benefit or, if he does, for how long the benefit will be continued. Thirdly, and most important, sick pay schemes are by no means universal throughout industry, and less than half of the total number of wage-earners are covered. It is also paradoxically true that it is among those whose need is likely to be greatest that coverage is least extensive. For staff employees, whose incomes are higher, are very much more likely to be members of a sick pay scheme than manual workers, and many wage-earners' schemes discriminate in favour of the long-service high-wage employee.[3]

If the contribution of sick pay schemes to income-maintenance is difficult to evaluate, there is more evidence on their employment effects. The employer who introduces a sick pay scheme is probably doing so after a rational calculation of the advantages and disadvantages to his firm of such a move. There are several consequences of a decision to pay employees during sickness absence, not all of them definite or foreseeable, quite apart from the cost of the scheme itself. First, there is the effect of a scheme on absence, and

[1] Phyllis & Peter Willmott, 'Off Work through Illness', *New Society*, January 10, 1963.

[2] The Ministry of Pensions estimated in June 1961 that between 19 and 25 per cent of incapacitated men and between 11 and 15 per cent of incapacitated women were actually receiving sick pay. The difference between these figures and the 57 per cent mentioned earlier arises from the limited duration of employers' sick pay and the number of the long-term sick.

[3] The M.P.N.I. survey found that over 60 per cent of men above 45 were covered by sick pay schemes.

here the published data is somewhat contradictory. The survey by the Industrial Welfare Society found that sickness absence had increased in less than a quarter of the firms who introduced sickness payment schemes. In the remainder, sickness absence was unchanged.[1] In another I.W.S. report covering forty-five firms, only eight said that absence had increased.[2] Two more detailed studies of individual undertakings reached a different conclusion. One of these studies[3] described two companies V and Z, the former with a sick pay scheme, the latter without. The initial level of sickness absence in Company V was about twice that in Company Z. The introduction of a scheme into Company Z led to 'an immediate and spectacular increase in absence',[4] which by the following year was at a comparable level to that in Company V. The second study covered 275,000 industrial employees in four Government departments and examined the effect on sickness absence of a scheme introduced in September 1948: here again sickness absence increased dramatically; in fact, 'recorded sickness absence as a whole appeared to have doubled'.[5]

There appear to be good reasons why sickness absence should increase. If employees begin to receive a higher income during sickness, they will be able to convalesce properly or to stay off work when previously they had come to work though not really fit to do so. To some extent then, there might be a better standard of health in the long run, though a larger number of short absences than before.[6] Again, if statistics of all absences have not been carefully kept, sickness absence may appear to increase simply because under a sick pay scheme there is an incentive for employees to have their sickness properly classified, while if there is no payment during sickness, they may not bother registering sick or presenting a medical certificate. Any increase in sickness absence of this kind should be balanced by a reduction in absence for other reasons.

The possibility, or probability, of abuse of a sick pay scheme can-

[1] *Survey of Sickness Absence in relation to Sickness Payment Schemes, Jan.–June* 1950; Industrial Welfare Society, 1950.

[2] W. Durham, *Sick Pay Schemes and Benevolent Schemes Among Hourly Paid Employees*, Industrial Welfare Society, 1957.

[3] R. A. Denerley, 'Some Effects of Paid Sick Leave on Sickness Absence', *British Journal of Industrial Medicine*, 1952, 9, p. 275.

[4] Ibid.

[5] R. B. Buzzard and W. A. Shaw, 'An Analysis of Absence under a Scheme of Paid Sick Leave', *British Journal of Industrial Medicine*, 1952, 9, p. 282.

[6] The Ministry of Pensions survey showed that among men who received sick pay a rather higher proportion had at least one absence from work than was found among those without sick pay; for the sample as a whole, the number of days of absence was no higher, though in social classes III, IV and V (which would include most manual workers) men who did receive sick pay had a larger number of days of absence than men who did not get sick pay. For women, on the other hand, the number of days of incapacity was *less* for those who received sick pay.

not be neglected, but the importance of this in increasing absence depends to a large extent on the mechanism of the scheme. If, for example, sick pay is given for all absences including periods of less than three days for which no medical certificate is required, there is likely to be an increase in short absences, while if there is a waiting period of three to five days the employee has some incentive to prolong his absence so that he can draw sick pay, especially if sick pay for the waiting days is then given. Many schemes do not pay at all during the waiting days, and some try to cut down unnecessary absence by allowing a cumulative entitlement, so that an employee who has not used up his yearly allocation can build up credit as insurance against a long illness.

The problem of fixing the duration and amount of benefit is to provide some protection of income while maintaining the incentive for the employee to get back to work. Indeed, if normal income at work is high enough there is a considerable incentive not to report sick at all. Denerley found that despite the introduction of a sick pay scheme, employees on a very lucrative piece-rate job maintained a low record of sickness absence while that of the rest of the factory increased significantly: but 'when the spur of high earnings was removed the rate of absence immediately climbed to the high level which existed in the rest of the factory'.[1] In the Government departments surveyed by Buzzard and Shaw, flat-rate workers had a markedly higher rate of absence than incentive-paid workers.[2] This may have been a result of the particular scheme under which time-rated workers received full pay while sick, so that there was no financial incentive for them to resume work, whereas the incentive-paid worker could have been receiving in sick pay considerably less than his normal earnings.

There are a number of reasons, then, why absence should increase when a sickness payment scheme is introduced, though the amount of the increase will depend on the response of the work-force and the type of the scheme. But there are other factors which in the longer run may cause a decrease in sickness absence. For one thing, as employees become accustomed to the scheme, malingering or taking advantage of the scheme will decrease. Also one of the reasons for the introduction of a scheme is to improve the health of the work-force, and to the extent that this aim is fulfilled, sickness absence will be reduced. The resultant of these two sets of forces, leading in the short-run to an increase and in the long-run to a decrease, would tend to give a sharp increase in sickness absence on the inception of a scheme, followed by a gradual decline. It seems likely that the level of sickness absence which eventually comes to be accepted as

[1] Denerly, op. cit., p. 377.
[2] Buzzard and Shaw, op. cit., pp. 288-9.

P

normal will be higher than if there had been no sickness payment scheme in operation, but how much higher it is impossible to say without making detailed assumptions as to the mechanics of the scheme and the characteristics of the work-force.

A sickness payment scheme may have some effect on the distribution and mobility of labour, and indeed, if intended to have this effect, must be counted a failure if it does not in some way favourably influence the supply of labour (or, more exactly, of employees) to the firm. One of the reasons why an employer introduces a sick pay scheme is as an inducement to employees to work for him, by offering them a degree of income-security during illness. If he is first in the field with this particular benefit, then he may succeed in attracting labour, but if his immediate competitors in the labour market also have sick pay schemes, this will cancel out most of the effect on the allocation of labour. There may still be some effect if the relative merits of one scheme over all the others can be communicated to the prospective employee and if it makes any impression on him. Of course if one firm does innovate by introducing a sick pay scheme which is an attraction, the natural consequence would be for other firms to take defensive measures by retaliation in kind, and schemes can become a factor in the retention of labour already with the company. It might seem that most companies tacitly admit this by making sick pay more generous for long-service men who are probably valuable to the company; this gives the older employee a vested interest in staying with the company. It is difficult, though, to sort out this kind of influence from the notion that better sickness benefit is a glorified long-service bonus; it is given to employees not because they are especially difficult to replace, but simply because they have been with the company for a long time, irrespective of their value. Whichever of these two views is most often correct— and it is probably the latter which predominates—sickness payment schemes in their present form could have a depressing effect on the mobility of older workers, but since these workers tend to be immobile anyway the effect is not likely to be large. It is doubtful, too, whether the prospect of sick pay is of much importance in acting as an attraction to workers, especially as schemes become more widespread throughout industry, and if sick pay was a potent factor in attracting or retaining employees, one might have expected a very much faster spread of schemes—via the collective bargaining process or because of employer initiative—than has in fact occurred.

IV. THE FUTURE OF PUBLIC POLICY

Sections II and III have suggested that neither public nor private programmes are wholly successful in providing for those who are sick, but they did not make any systematic attempt to justify this assertion. This section sets out criteria of success and failure and measures against them the present provisions against income-loss during sickness. It also considers the relationship between public and private schemes and possible lines along which public policy may develop, and examines the probable future of company sick pay schemes in the wider framework of income-security and social policy. There are, however, two cautions which must be borne in mind. First, it is not possible to judge on completely objective criteria what *should* be done, especially in so emotive a field as social security and social policy. Consequently, the argument depends on individual assumptions and whether one agrees with the general drift of the argument depends on whether these assumptions and the broad point of view are acceptable. Secondly, any study with a predictive element is liable to error, and when it is concerned with a subject on which statistical evidence and past experience may be quite contradicted by political and social considerations, the error may be large. The conclusions should therefore be read as looking forward from one particular point in time, early 1964.

1. *The Criteria*[1]

The problem is to provide security against income-loss during sickness in the most efficient and economic way possible. Fortunately, the provision of sickness benefit infringes rather less on broad issues of economic policy than other types of social security scheme. Old age pensions, for instance, can only be discussed in relation to a large number of economic and social issues such as the present and future age structure of the population, the actuarial requirements of such a scheme, their effect on the distribution of income and many other factors concerned with the accumulation of large amounts of capital as contributions, and the problem of guaranteeing benefits against inflation while retaining some measure of financial integrity. Similarly, State unemployment aid must be determined in the wider and more important context of whether steps are being taken to eradicate the causes of this unemployment. In the short-term, sickness can be treated as a datum. Although over a decade or so expenditure on public health and medical research may yield a lower level of sickness, it is possible and indeed necessary to set out the conditions under which sickness benefit is paid without considering any such improvements, for they are liable to come so slowly as not to affect the current situation.[2]

[1] The criteria set out here are the most important ones discussed and elaborated by Dr Holmans in Chapter 6, Section I.

[2] The statistics of Part I show no significant decrease in either yearly number of claims or days of incapacity between 1952–62. This point will be further discussed later.

Five criteria of efficient protection were outlined in Chapter 6 above. First, sickness benefit should be 'adequate'. It is extremely difficult to define objectively what adequate benefit is. Complete income-security would require no drop in earnings, which in present circumstances is not the case for most manual workers except those who are living on the very edge of poverty and whose normal income is only just sufficient or for those who receive full pay for sickness absence up to some maximum period. But what is adequate differs between individuals and places and varies over time, and one may have a different notion of what is sufficient according to the circumstances of each individual case and to one's own personal opinions, but if the scheme is properly to fulfil its purpose, it should be possible to pay different amounts to beneficiaries in different circumstances. The structural factors affecting the adequacy of benefit will be dealt with later; let us assume for the moment that two-thirds of normal income will enable a family to live without its standard of living suffering unduly in the short-run. We shall make no assumptions at this stage about the source of this income.

A sickness benefit scheme must provide adequate benefit, but must also fulfil four other criteria to prove that it does so efficiently. First and most important of these, it should be comprehensive in its coverage so that as many as possible of those at risk should be eligible for benefit. Secondly, if this is to be the case and if it is impossible immediately to introduce a comprehensive scheme, the speed with which coverage spreads is important. If coverage of eligible people spreads too slowly so that many who wish to be insured are unable to obtain protection, the scheme will be a failure. Thirdly, if sickness benefit is to be efficiently provided, administration of the scheme must be reasonably cheap so that too large a part of contributions is not swallowed up by administrative costs; and fourthly, it must be speedy in operation so that beneficiaries do not have to wait an undue length of time for the benefits owing to them.

2. The Criteria and the Present British Situation

How do present-day British standards measure up to these five criteria, taking first the National Insurance scheme? On the credit side, it is comprehensive in its coverage of the working population; only a relatively small number of people are excluded from the scheme and they are there through choice rather than because they are poor risks or otherwise unacceptable to the scheme. The administration of State sickness benefit is efficient, though speed of benefit payment is sometimes criticized because of the system of waiting days.[1] The scheme might be criticized for giving insufficient opportunity for differentiation to meet individual circumstances,

[1] See New Society, op. cit., January 10, 1963.

since it gives extra payments only in the form of marriage and child allowances. But the most commonly alleged fault of the State sickness benefit is simply that benefit is quite inadequate, as the evidence of Section II, Part 3 shows. Sickness benefit for a single man is now only about one-fifth of average industrial earnings, while that for the standard family is about two-fifths. By any standard of income-maintenance, this is quite insufficient, yet it is possible to argue most convincingly, given certain assumptions on what kind of social security one wants, that the whole system of social insurance *does* provide for differentiation and adequate benefits, for in addition to standard sickness benefits National Assistance supplements are available to augment any which are insufficient for a family's basic needs. Though National Assistance seems, rightly or wrongly, to be less acceptable on social grounds, the point is that it is available to those who need it.

State sickness benefit alone therefore fails the test of adequacy. This criterion cannot be applied directly to company sick pay schemes. In themselves they are obviously not adequate, as they are intended to pay only an amount additional to benefit already being received, but even allowing for this, many private schemes are inadequate since they do not make up benefit to two-thirds of normal income. Private schemes are certainly not comprehensive, as they cover only about half of the working population and a smaller proportion of manual workers, and this greatly reduces their potential effect in making total sickness benefit an adequate amount. In addition, private schemes appear to have spread only slowly in the last few years. Their rate of growth may speed up, but spontaneous introduction of schemes to cover the whole working population would take a very long time. An important advantage of private sick pay schemes is that it is relatively easy to differentiate between various groups of employees or even between individuals, and each firm can tailor its scheme to fit its own experience of sickness absence and labour turnover and to its particular structure. Within a company too, differing provision can be made for high or low wage employees by providing benefit related to wages or earnings. It is interesting and important to note, however, that some schemes do not in fact take this opportunity of differentiation to provide a greater degree of income-security, preferring instead to pay benefit as a flat-rate sum. Thus a considerable theoretical advantage of the private plan turns out to have less practical significance. Clearly, many private schemes would fail to satisfy even this criterion, just as they generally fail to satisfy the others.

3. *The Place of Company Schemes*
Obviously any further discussion on the future of industrial sick pay

schemes can proceed only after we have made some judgement on the most desirable basis of the National Insurance system. There are two broadly opposed views on the place of State social security in providing for income-loss during sickness, and they may be presented in over-simplified terms as follows.[1] The first believes that State benefit should be a flat-rate minimum; people should be encouraged to provide for their own welfare by saving or private insurance, and only those who are in demonstrated need should receive further State benefit.[2] The alternative view is that social security should be available to everyone as a right, that benefits should be related to normal income with a progressive system of income-related contributions.[3]

Whether National Insurance sickness benefit ought to be paid as a right or should go only to those in need is the political decision which is at the root of the whole controversy over the public and private provision of welfare.[4] The benefit-according-to-need hypothesis, with high benefits going only to those who have proved that they are in need, is on the face of it an attractive one. In purely economic terms this would seem to be the most efficient use of resources, since the State could allow those who had a sufficient level of income to provide for themselves, instead of levying taxes to provide social security benefits for all. Public resources could then be concentrated on those whose need was proved to be greatest, the amount redistributed would be considerably smaller, and the State's administrative costs lower than with a comprehensive scheme. But Chapter 6 has shown that while this may result in efficiency and economy to the State, the individuals requiring coverage against sickness may be less well off and the criteria of efficient protection may not be as easily fulfilled. For there are considerable disadvantages in individuals having to make their own arrangements for coverage against income-loss through sickness, either by private insurance or by thrift. For one thing, benefits under private insurance may well be less adequate than under social insurance, partly because of higher administrative costs, though this may matter less since those who are insuring in this way may well be able to afford the higher premiums. For sickness, too, private insurance schemes tend to require fairly severe qualifying standards so that comprehensive coverage may not be achieved of all those who ought, according to their income level, to be insuring privately. Few would deny that comprehensive coverage against loss

[1] Professor Wiseman outlines these two views in more detail in Chapter 7, Section IV, where they are particularly applied to pension provision.

[2] This is roughly the type of proposals advanced by Beveridge in *Report on Social Insurance and Allied Services*, and is akin to the existing structure of National Insurance.

[3] The Labour Party proposals contained in *New Frontiers for Social Security* are of this type.

[4] This issue is discussed at length in Chapter 6.

of income through sickness is a desirable aim, and it is possible, while maintaining this, still to believe that the individual should be allowed freedom of choice on how income-security should be provided. But there will still be people who, through ignorance, lack of foresight or inability, may not be covered, and if one really wishes everyone to be protected, there is a certain inconsistency in rejecting social insurance, the one method which ensures that this can be accomplished. Whether it be a good thing or not, most people do live well up to their incomes and spend in the expectation that this income will continue, so that savings to meet unforeseen contingencies are unlikely to be adequate for any but a short illness, especially if their real value has been reduced by rising prices. For simplicity, then, and because it seems a realistic approach, this discussion will proceed on the assumption that the Welfare State in the shape of a social security system is here to stay, in conception if not in detail.

If the *status quo* is not be radically altered and if some form of compulsory insurance against sickness should continue, we must next examine the nature of employer or company sick pay schemes and where they should fit into the whole network of social security. Why *should* any employer be responsible for providing sickness benefit for his employees? There is, of course, a pseudo-legal concept of responsibility according to which the employer would be liable if the absence was the result of a work accident or of an illness which was a reasonably direct consequence of the type of work. The employer is then under an obligation to help the worker maintain his standard of living by paying sickness benefit. The old Workmen's Compensation regulations were based on this type of legal liability for accident and industrial disease, and present legislation still treats absences from work because of occupational sicknesses as different from sickness arising out of other causes, by establishing a higher rate of benefit for the former type of incapacity.

But this legalistic reasoning does not satisfactorily explain the basis of company sick pay schemes as they operate at present. Quite apart from the incredibly complex problem of defining an occupational disease or an industrial accident there are two main difficulties. First, if a particular trade has a higher-than-average sickness or accident rate, it is likely to be closely regulated by laws laying down safety precautions. Then in occupations recognized by workers as dangerous or undesirable, it is usual and sometimes necessary for higher wages offsetting these disadvantages to be paid in order to attract labour. An employer might thus justifiably claim to have discharged any responsibility to his workers; on the one hand he is trying to keep the sickness rate low by adhering to the safety regulations, while on the other hand the employee is compensated for the higher probability of his being off sick by receiving higher wages from which he can save or insure privately against loss of income during sickness. The second difficulty is that a definition of responsibility which distinguishes between occupational and non-occupational sickness tells us little about why the employer should pay benefit for the latter type of absence which is unconnected with the work environment. Few sick pay schemes do make this distinction, since most give benefit for all kinds of certifiable absence. It is clear that this particular concept of responsibility cannot account for sick pay schemes already in existence, and would not be a satisfactory basis on which to extend industrial schemes by law or negotiation.

Section III has already suggested that one of the stock arguments in favour of sickness benefit schemes is of doubtful validity, namely their effect on the supply and mobility of labour.[1] So too is another proposition, that the standard of health of the work-force will in the long-run be improved. This may be true for the labour force as a whole—though even here the effect may be so long-run as only to lengthen life expectancy[2]—but given some degree of labour mobility a particular company may find the improvement negligible. At the least, an economic calculation of the benefits against the costs might well show a sickness benefit scheme to be unprofitable, especially in view of the increased absence which it is likely to engender. Though on the national scale we may now be more healthy than ever before, there has been little or no reduction since 1948 in the yearly number of new claims for sickness benefit, so that any improvement in health standards must have been counterbalanced by other factors leading to an increase in claims. What is true of the national scheme would probably also apply to an industrial sick pay plan. But merely to give reasons why a company may introduce sick pay does not really answer the question of what employer responsibility, if any, happens to be. Schemes can come into being because of a moral judgment, an economic calculation, trade union pressure, the demonstration effect of what other companies are doing, the desire to have a 'good' name, and so on. We must look in a more general way at sick pay schemes, independent of the reason for their introduction, by recalling how

---

[1] This argument is however valid when applied to staff employees. The rapid spread of pensions and sick pay schemes suggests that for a company not to have them would be a considerable disadvantage in attracting and retaining staff, especially higher management.

[2] The point has been made that further marginal increases in health expenditure are unlikely even to do this, since the death rate is as low as one might expect with the present population structure. This marginal expenditure might then be considered 'uneconomic' in that it will not entail any necessary increase in national income. See D. S. Lees, 'The Economics of Health Services', *Lloyds Bank Review*, April 1960; also Jack Wiseman, 'Cost-Benefit Analysis and Health Service Policy', *Scottish Journal of Political Economy*, February 1963, which discusses the effect of increased investment in health.

they are generally constructed and what they are trying to accomplish.

The constitution of an industrial sick pay scheme is largely conditioned by the existing structure of the State social security system, and the future development of these schemes is entirely dependent on what the Government decide to be the National Insurance sickness benefit. Once the political decision has been taken to provide a certain sum during sickness, industrial schemes may appear as a residue—either because of some deficiency in the income protection provided by the social security system, because of new legal compulsion, or through the workings of the labour market mechanism— or they may cease to be important. In Britain up till now industrial schemes have partly filled the gaps left by the State system. Indeed for staff employees they have given complete income protection, because most staff schemes are compulsory and make up sickness benefit to normal salary. It is one of the strange anomalies of the British wages structure, that those who are best able to take care of themselves—because their income is higher and habits of saving likely to be stronger—and who are most likely to be informed about and acceptable to private insurance, are compulsorily members of such generous company schemes.[1] Manual workers or wage-earners, if they get any sick pay at all, receive an amount which brings sickness income from the State closer to normal income, without completely protecting the standard of living. Since company schemes are in practice so closely connected with the National Insurance system and in view of the Government's apparent willingness to rely for the present on company schemes to supply sickness income additional to National Insurance benefit, there is some logic in regarding them simply as an extension of the social security system. The employer who does introduce a sick pay scheme is taking upon himself something of the function of the State, in providing a certain part of income during sickness. In saying this we do not need to assume that the employer is the sole source of finance of the scheme; he will almost certainly not be paying the full cost out of profits, since employees may be receiving lower wages than otherwise or consumers paying higher prices, so that like State social security the scheme would be financed on a tripartite principle with contributions from employer, employee and consumer (or taxpayer). The difference is that the relative shares are not determined by administrative decision as in National Insurance, but by economic factors such as

---

[1] At the same time we must assume that the cost of staff sick pay schemes is taken into account in salary determination. Thus if staff were in the same position as most manual workers and were not given income protection, salary rates might be correspondingly higher. Nevertheless this favoured treatment of salaried workers is a source of considerable political indignation.

trade union bargaining power, company profitability and the demand conditions for the product.

4. *Three Possible Solutions*

There are three main ways in which company sick pay schemes might evolve in the future, depending on the development of the National Insurance scheme. First, if sickness benefit related to income became available under the State system, company schemes could provide only a small element of further graduation. Most employers would probably feel that it was not worthwhile to keep manual workers' schemes going, though staff would presumably continue to receive complete income protection. Secondly, if sickness benefit as a whole were to be income-related, company schemes could take over completely the responsibility for providing benefit in the short-run, say for the first three weeks.[1] Thirdly, if National Insurance benefit were to remain a flat-rate sum as at present, industrial schemes could develop to provide any graduation of benefit which might seem desirable. The assumption in two of these cases is that industrial schemes ought to be continued, and this view has been challenged: some believe that companies which provide sickness benefit, far from doing a worthwhile job, are infringing upon the rights of the individual by giving him no choice on how to spend part of his income, just as social insurance means compulsion of much the same kind. Instead of being entitled to industrial sickness benefit, the employee should be paid the value of his labour services in cash; if he wishes to insure against sickness, he can do so privately, but neither the State nor his employer ought to decide this for him.[2] The contrary objections to the continuation of company sick pay schemes are that State benefits alone ought to be sufficient to protect the standard of living of the worker without recourse to other income from company schemes: the State ought to close the gap which exists between what under present regulations it does provide and the income it ought to provide as a right. Proponents of this philosophy commonly point out that it is illogical to condemn compulsory social insurance while accepting equally compulsory staff sick pay schemes as a good thing.[3] However for the sake of simplicity we shall assume that these and other objections influence policy decisions only in so far as they are embodied in the three cases listed above.

We must also remember that though the criteria of efficiency are valid in economic terms, they fail to admit that people have pre-

---

[1] A scheme of this type was suggested by the *Economist*, January 10, 1963.

[2] A statement of this view can be found in A. Rubner, *Fringe Benefits: the Golden Chains*, London, Putnam, 1962.

[3] See, for example, B. Abel-Smith, 'Beveridge: Another Viewpoint', *New Society*, February 28, 1963; and *New Frontiers for Social Security*, op. cit.

ferences about how they should provide or be provided for during sickness, and that these preferences may directly contradict one of our criteria of efficiency. Much of what follows is based on personal views on what ought to be done, and will not be accepted by those with different opinions, prejudices or assumptions. But there is also a kind of collective conscience which must be taken into account, an expression of prevailing climate of opinion, often called social justice. This is an amalgam of economic, moral, ethical, sociological and often quite irrational qualities. No matter how economically efficient a scheme may be, if it appears to many not to be acceptable because it in some way infringes the canons of social justice, it will be widely condemned. The present system of National Assistance is a case in point, and it is frequently supposed that any system based primarily on need and a means test is lacking in social justice.

If the State wishes to minimize transfer payments and its own costs of administration, this is most easily done by finding out who is in need, paying benefits to them, and letting those who can provide for themselves. However, the aim of any social security programme is much more complex than simply minimizing State intervention, and if the view is accepted that the most desirable aim of any sick pay is to safeguard the standard of living of those incapacitated, the sickness benefit which they receive should logically be related to their normal income. The three possible future developments suggested above all acknowledge this, but they differ in the allocation of financial responsibility, how much public authorities should pay and how much the employer.

(a) *A National Income-Related Scheme*. The practical application of this type of scheme can cause many problems. First, should benefit be related to wages or earnings? Since the standard of living is ordinarily determined by earnings, sick pay should be related to earnings, but this could give rise to a peculiar situation. For if sick pay were given at the rate of two-thirds of normal earnings, an employee earning 50 per cent above his basic wage would be paid, while sick, exactly the same as a man working a full week for the basic wage. There is nothing in any way unfair or illogical about this nor can an objection be sustained on economic grounds. Indeed it can be convincingly argued that the basic wage is an outdated concept; what with overtime, bonuses and other extra payments, very few workers are paid at the basic wage and for most it has lost its meaning. It may to some people seem anomalous that one man should be paid the same while off sick as another gets while working, but the fault lies in the wages structure rather than in the wage-related sick pay scheme. There is a second complication, however, in the uncertainty of the disincentive effect of too high a level of sickness benefit. The studies discussed earlier show fairly conclusively that sickness benefit—and especially a high rate of benefit—leads to more absenteeism. It is difficult to say exactly when employees begin to prefer leisure at sickness income to work at normal income since this depends not only on the relation between benefit and earnings, but on such things as number of dependents, how many incomes come into the household, and the financial commitments of the worker.[1] Another factor which may strengthen the disincentive to work is the level of benefit compared with the level of income which the employee regards as permanent and continuing. If benefit is related to earnings which include a fairly large element of transitory income, it may approach close to permanent income and so make the employee less inclined to return to work. This in turn raises the question of the time-period of earnings to which reference must be made when benefit is decided. If the period is too long it may fail to take account of rapidly rising wages, yet it ought in some way to appreciate transitory or seasonal components in income. Whatever reference period is chosen, the administrative arrangements for keeping track of weekly earnings would be extremely complex, and also very costly.[2]

There are a number of additional disadvantages of an earnings-related scheme. For example, what benefit rates should apply to those whose incapacity had lasted for some time? In a period of rising prices, a rate based on their earnings at the beginning of incapacity would soon become inadequate; a periodic review of benefits for the long-term sick would clearly have to be undertaken. But there are various criteria on which these benefits could be based—the Labour Party suggest an index of average national earnings[3]—and this point may in practice not be a serious one. A more important one is that any earnings-related scheme would logically not pay benefit according to need but rather to previous income, and this would require a basic reshaping of the present National Insurance system. At the moment standard benefit is supplemented by marriage and child allowances, presumably and quite reasonably because a married man with children has greater economic responsibilities than a single man, but if an income-related scheme operated, those earning the same amount would receive sickness benefit at exactly

[1] At the same time, under a well-regulated system, the employee would have no choice since he would not receive sickness benefit if he was fit to work. The disincentive effect of high rates of benefit is less important than for an unemployment scheme for there is a reasonably objective criterion as to whether a man should receive benefit or not. The fact that the disincentive effect may be important is itself an admission of a faulty administrative structure.

[2] These points have been made both by N.E.D.C., *Conditions Favourable to Faster Growth*, para. 50, and by the T.U.C. in a recent policy statement on social security.

[3] *New Frontiers in Social Security*, op. cit., p. 15.

the same rate irrespective of need or family circumstances. The effect would be even more noticeable if method of calculating benefit were weighted in favour of the low-wage employee, as the Labour Party has suggested, so that 'the proportion received by the lower-paid worker will be rather larger and by the higher-paid rather less'.[1] For young low-wage employees would then receive more proportionately (and perhaps absolutely) than older higher-wage employees with dependants. The Labour Party would here appear to have backed away from the logic of any scheme relating benefits to wages or earnings, as their intention is to increase the allowances for dependent children, instead of opposing 'the payment of dependents' allowances in social security benefits on the grounds that no such recognition of family responsibilities is to be found in the wage system,'[2] but most people would probably agree that a pure wage-related system which did not take account of these factors is socially unjust, however rational economically.

This pinpoints the crucial weakness of any income-related scheme. In theory, the system is undoubtedly the best way of providing income-security. Most of the drawbacks which have been discussed above could be overcome simply by administrative decisions based on probability assumptions: if it became clear that the wrong decision had been taken, it could be easily changed, since there is no basic structural weakness in the scheme. Provided administration was economic and practicable, the criteria of efficiency could be better satisfied by an income-related scheme than by any other. But one cannot expect considerations of social justice to rule in such a system unless these considerations are also paramount in the whole process of wage settlement. To put it more broadly an income-related scheme can only be as satisfactory as the wage structure on which it is based, and, in Britain, the wage structure is so complex and riddled with so many anomalies and vicissitudes that one hesitates to reflect it in the whole system of social security.[3] Indeed the social injustices which so many observers have noted in the wages system might be reinforced or take a new life by their transfer to another sector of the economy. We need not reject a national earnings-related sickness benefit scheme, but if the wages structure of this country is ever to be reformed, it would be well to do this before the whole framework of social security comes to depend on it.

(b) *Short-term Company Schemes and Long-term State Scheme.* Let us now turn to another possible line of development which envisages

---

[1] *New Frontiers in Social Security*, p. 15.
[2] E. M. Burns, *Social Security and Public Policy*, McGraw-Hill, 1956; p. 41.
[3] Though we are dealing only with sickness benefit, one may assume that unemployment benefit would also be income-related.

a different distribution of expenditure on sick pay schemes. This admits the existence of industrial schemes, but allows them a different role from that which they play today. Chapter 6 has already suggested that there might be considerable administrative advantages in relying on private schemes to provide short-term benefits. This would mean the complete integration of these industrial schemes with the social security system, and is perfectly feasible, if one accepts employer-provided sickness benefit schemes as an extension of that system. For example, firms might be 'statutorily required to pay, say, 75 per cent of a man's wages (on presentation of a doctor's certificate) during his first three weeks of sickness in any year, provided the man had been in their employment for more than a certain period'.[1] This kind of plan suffers from the disadvantages enumerated above which are common to any income-related scheme. But there are several additional questions which raise doubts on the desirability of this type of integration.

First, on what basis is State sickness benefit to be calculated? If it is to be flat-rate and pitched at a level lower than 75 per cent of average earnings, the incapacitated worker might suffer a considerable drop in income when after three weeks he transfers from the industrial scheme to the state. If needs during sickness are considered, it may be just at this time that a higher rate of benefit is most necessary. If State benefit is also to be income-related, there would appear to be administrative disadvantage in giving the employer the responsibility of paying the first part of sickness benefit. For employees who were not eligible for the three weeks industrial benefit because of length of incapacity or an insufficient qualifying period of employment would continue to be catered for by the State. The revised National Insurance system would still require detailed records of the earnings of these casual workers, and therefore presumably of all workers since all employees might at some time cease to be entitled to employer-provided benefits. There seems little advantage on administrative grounds for requiring the employer to pay the first few weeks of benefit if the transfer from his scheme to the State scheme might be so troublesome. This would only add another organizational problem to those already extant without any compensating merit.

Although State expenditure would decrease, aggregate expenditure on sickness benefit would almost certainly increase. Sickness benefit given at the rate of 75 per cent of earnings for up to three weeks could be a very substantial cost to the employer, depending on the strength of the various factors affecting sickness absence, particularly the effect of the introduction of such a generous scheme. It is quite probable that over one year sickness absence could cost the employer

[1] *Economist*, January 12, 1963; p. 91.

as much as holidays with pay do at the moment, say 4 per cent of payroll or more, and total administrative costs would tend to be higher than with a national earnings related scheme. All in all, this particular combination of employer and State sickness benefit seems unlikely to provide efficient coverage against income-loss, for the practical difficulties are formidable.

(c) *A Development of the Present Method.* The third possible method of using schemes provided by employers in conjunction with the State system of social security is to allow such schemes to provide the graduated part of sickness benefit over and above a flat-rate State benefit. This has the advantage of being not too radical a departure from the present situation, though it does involve an explicit recognition that the State should do no more than provide a certain proportion of normal income, and that employer schemes should act simply as an extension of this State responsibility. If the graduated portion were to be negotiated rather than legally required, this would also be in the tradition of British employer-employee relations, and there are several reasons why collectively-bargained schemes might be preferable to those laid down by statute. First, legal regulations could probably only establish minimum standards, which might in themselves inhibit further growth: the minimum might tend to become the maximum. Secondly, differentiation of benefit will be simpler the more homogeneous is the work-force, and arrangements are likely to be easier to make for one firm than for the labour force as a whole.[1] Thirdly, many of the points which in a national scheme have to be decided by administrative edict can be settled by employer and union according to their own particular circumstances. For example, the plant wage structure may determine what level of graduated benefit is best or whether it ought to be based upon wages or earnings, and other decisions can be taken in the light of the sickness record and labour force structure.

If however employer schemes are not to be legally required, it is likely to be a long time before comprehensive coverage is achieved. American experience suggests that the spread of welfare schemes through collective bargaining is likely to be slow, with a high proportion of eligible employees remaining outside their scope. British bargaining structure is even less suited to this kind of negotiation, and the relative failure of Government attempts to encourage negotiation of redundancy agreements[2] indicate that the spread of coverage

---

[1] It would probably be necessary to simplify National Insurance benefits by eliminating child allowances, otherwise calculation of graduated benefit could be much more complex.

[2] See *Security and Change*, Ministry of Labour 1962, and Ministry of Labour *Gazette*, February 1963.

would be even slower here. This is the main disadvantage of this type of scheme; though it is essentially a modification of the existing framework, there would have to be considerable re-thinking on the parts of both employers and unions. For one thing, the employer would have to accept that industrial sick pay schemes were complementary to the State scheme, and, more important, be prepared to introduce such a scheme even though on strict economic criteria it might not be worthwhile for his own particular firm. It is possible, though, that this would be less illogical and undesirable when measured against the alternative of terms imposed by State legislation or of a national income-related scheme financed partly by much higher employer contributions.[1]

At the same time, the trade unions would need to recognize their responsibility for bargaining on sick pay as one of the terms and conditions of employment. Until recently trade unions were relatively uninterested in this particular benefit, but recently the Electrical Trades Union negotiated a national sick pay scheme on behalf of its members, and this may prove to be only the first of many such gains. But it does seem more likely that trade union pressure will continue to be political, and oriented towards the national wage-related scheme of the Labour Party type.[2] In any case, the national bargaining structure is not a very satisfactory mechanism for determining sick pay arrangements as the rates of benefit may be held down to the level which the least profitable firm can afford and there may be conflicts of interest between various groups in the same union. Yet detailed plant bargaining in Britain is only in its infancy and in a multi-union firm, differences can easily arise over the relative merits of bargaining claims and the importance which the unions attach to them. Such inter-union disputes are especially likely where low-wage and high-wage employees are in the same plant; the former may wish to demand wage increases while the latter feel that they can afford to take the increase in the form of sick pay. Negotiation of graduated sick pay schemes would obvious require a high degree of union co-operation, as well as an increased sense of social responsibility from both sides. There is little in recent industrial history to suggest that these transformations would be quickly or easily brought about. The changing of attitudes, opinions and prejudices is always hard, and this third method of reforming sick pay might well be more difficult to bring about than either of the first two, for the changes which it would necessitate are not so much administrative or struc-

---

[1] In the terminology of Section III of the introduction, employers would have to recognize that the cost of sick pay schemes was 'social investment' in the labour force, and that returns accrued to society as a whole from their expenditure.

[2] The T.U.C. have already called for this type of social security system.

tural alterations which can be legislated into being as disturbances
of established roles and shifts in ways of thinking.

V. CONCLUSION: THE FUTURE OF COMPANY SCHEMES

Having examined some of the ways in which public and private provision of sickness benefit might be integrated, we may turn finally to
consider what is likely to happen to industrial sick pay schemes in the
next few years. Once more we must first assess what will happen to
the State scheme, and here many uncertainties enter in. If the Labour
Party comes to power, there will be a compulsory income-related
scheme with benefits around half of earnings, with more for low-wage
and less for high-wage employees. Contributions will also be income-
related 'a fixed proportion of earnings, subject to an upper limit', and
'employers will pay more than at present'.[1] The scheme thus becomes
frankly redistributive, with the better-off paying higher contributions
and receiving proportionately lower benefits. This would appear to
be broadly in tune with the prevailing concept of social justice,
though whether the worker with above-average earnings will be
entirely satisfied is another matter.

The Conservative answer to this would at present (early 1964) seem
to be continued reliance on the principle at increasing flat-rate
benefits and using National Assistance to fill any gaps, but this
might prove an electoral handicap on the grounds that it is socially
less acceptable than the rival income-related scheme, if economically
more respectable. There has however been some sign that official
Government thinking is moving towards income-related benefits, at
any rate for unemployment benefit. There is, of course, a more
straightforward way of providing benefit weighted in favour of low-
income groups, simply by raising flat-rate benefits, say, to around
£8 10s. for a married couple. This would have exactly the same effect
as the Labour Party's income-related scheme, by giving low-wage
workers considerably more than half-pay, and high-wage workers
considerably less. The main objection is the extra cost of contributions, since both parties appear to have ruled out the idea of
levying contributions related to income while maintaining flat-rate
benefits. Yet there is no obvious reason why this should not be done;
while both social justice and economic considerations demand that
income-related benefits should be financed by graduated contributions, it is not necessary that flat-rate benefits should be financed by

---

[1] *New Frontiers in Social Security*, p. 14. An estimate in *The Times*, October
4, 1963, was that, while the employer *share* of the total cost of social security
would be the same, total employer contributions would be some 60 per cent
higher. Similarly, the State contribution in absolute terms would be more than
double.

Q

flat-rate contributions; a scheme which levied graduated contributions to pay flat-rate benefits would however be very redistributive,
which would not commend it to many sections of the Conservative
Party, and it seems unlikely to be put into practice.[1]

With these two possible developments of the State scheme in
mind, we can draw up a balance sheet of reasons why industrial sick
pay schemes are likely to decline or to flourish. On the debit side
there are two main reasons why industrial sick pay schemes are
unlikely to grow in coverage and may well contract. First, an income-related scheme may provide the average worker with a
sufficient income during sickness without any employer supplementation, perhaps as much as the total received by most employees in
industrial schemes at the moment. At this stage of income-protection
there must be a good deal of uncertainty about the disincentive effect
of too high a level of sickness benefit on absence from work, and most
employers are likely to feel that any further benefit from an industrial
scheme, even if administratively worthwhile, would be ill-advised.
The second reason is one of cost. We have already seen that more
generous social security benefits are likely to be accompanied by
increased contributions, especially from employers. In this case, the
essential identity of private and public welfare schemes will no doubt
quickly be recognized by employers. Companies will be loath to grant
sick pay schemes and to foot the cost of these schemes when they
are already paying a higher legally-required payment to finance
improved social security benefits. Employers would probably point
out to their workers that the improved public provision costs
industry as much in social charges as the present National Insurance
contribution plus a company scheme, and that it is unreasonable to
expect continuation or introduction of a supplementary scheme.
These two factors, higher State benefits and an increased cost to the
employer, could mean that there is no increase in the numbers of
manual workers covered by sickness benefit schemes, and perhaps an
absolute decline.

On the other hand, there are several institutional influences which
could work in the opposite direction. First, any recasting of National
Insurance whether as an income-related scheme or not will almost
certainly be to the advantage of the low-wage worker at the expense
of those with above-average earnings, either by income-related
benefits weighted in favour of those with low wages or by increasing
flat-rate benefits. The higher level of contributions levied on high-
wage workers will give them a lower take-home pay, and the combination of (relatively) lower benefits and higher contributions could

---

[1] This would however be a logical development if the Government wished to
increase flat-rate benefits while maintaining a fairly low rate of contributions for
low-wage workers.

create a demand for industrial sick pay schemes, thus giving an opportunity for higher coverage of this class of employee. Whether this opportunity will be taken is another matter, and this depends on the interaction of the other factors which might be favourable to sick pay schemes. Trade union policy is one of these. If trade unions made a determined effort to obtain sickness benefit for their members they might well succeed; the E.T.U. has already done so. But the campaign seems largely to be based on the insufficiency of the present National Insurance scheme and the comparatively small employers' contributions,[1] and introduction of a graduated scheme would take the wind out of the unions' sails since it would at once improve the income-protection prospects of the lower-paid and increase the liability of employers. Also, high-wage employees or skilled men are commonly in trade unions catering for most grades of worker, and there could be opposition to differential claims on behalf of one fairly small group within the union. Trade union opinion is now much more reconciled to private sick pay schemes than a few years ago. The General Council of the T.U.C. has 'considered' the subject, and is discussing with the British Employers' Confederation ways of increasing the numbers of sick pay agreements.[2] This is a much more cautious approach than that favoured by some union leaders who are very much in favour of sick pay; the A.E.U. have put forward a claim for a national sick pay scheme, while a recent conference of trade unionists agreed that unions 'should seek to expand the scope and concept of fringe benefits',[3] including sick pay. At the same time, however, a successful motion at the T.U.C. Congress while welcoming the encouragement to negotiate sick pay, warned that 'any successes . . . should not be used by the Government to prejudice existing rights to National Insurance benefits during periods of incapacity or to deflect Congress from its ultimate objective of seeing those National Insurance benefits raised to a proper subsistence level',[4] and it does seem that the trade unions are intent on securing increased industrial *and* National Insurance sickness benefits. But this trade union opinion on industrial sick pay schemes is little more than a broad policy statement which may never have real expression, since the practical difficulties are considerable. Any spread of sick pay schemes is likely to originate, as it has in the past, with the employer, and the reasons for their existence and introduction would also be much the same. The companies making up National Insurance benefit to the full rate of earnings will presumably continue to do so, and those which see a sick pay scheme as a moral obligation

---

[1] A recent A.E.U. claim was founded on these points.
[2] T.U.C. Congress Report 1962, pp. 126–7.
[3] Reported in *The Guardian*, May 27, 1963.
[4] T.U.C. Congress Report 1962, p. 447.

or a useful demonstration of their own welfare-mindedness may be little affected by accounting considerations.

The position of staff sick pay schemes is also likely to be little affected, as a national income-related scheme would presumably have an upper limit on benefit which would leave considerable scope for employer augmentation. There is good reason to suppose that the present practice of allowing sickness absence on full pay will continue and be extended as a staff condition of employment, and this suggests an additional reason for the expansion of sick pay schemes for certain wage-earners. There has recently been a campaign among certain white-collar unions for 'staff conditions' for their members, and this would involve the extension of staff conditions of employment—pensions, holidays, sick pay, dismissal regulations and so on—for white collar wage-earners.[1] It is possible that these union efforts will succeed in getting sick pay schemes, especially if the companies feel that this would give advantages in getting labour. Indeed the labour market implications of sick pay might provide one of the strongest reasons for expansion of wage-earners' schemes in general, for if employers believe that security of income during sickness is becoming more important in the mind of the wage-earner, and if the national scheme does not seem adequately to provide this security for the high-wage employee, there may well be a considerable expansion of sick pay schemes for such employees, in the hope that this might help to attract or retain employees. But it would be rather difficult to devise such a scheme only for high-wage employees, for the obvious solution of a lengthy qualifying period does not really work, since it removes much of the attractive element—a sick pay scheme applying only to those with five years' service will not attract employees to that company—and it also has no effect on the short-service man whom the employer may wish to keep with his company. Under the circumstances, a company scheme may have to cover most or all of the workers, though an income-related national scheme would mean that the cost of benefits for low-wage workers is small.

This last section has not enabled us to say what *will* happen to employer sick pay schemes, but it has brought out their close relationship with the social security system and emphasized that their future development depends on the politicians' decision on the type of National Insurance scheme we should have. Even though so many unknown and changeable factors are involved and even if the abiding impression of this analysis is that institutional, social or even random influences are just as important as economic calculations in deter-

---

[1] The Electricity Council offered 'staff status' to their manual workers, but negotiations have since broken down, partly (according to reports) because of disagreement over the fringe benefits to which such staff/manual workers would be entitled.

mining the form of industrial sick pay schemes, it would seem unduly timid to close this Chapter without some subjective expression of what should happen and some prediction of what will happen.[1] If a national income-related scheme is introduced—and there is no doubt that such a scheme would best meet our five criteria of efficiency, provided that problems of administration can be overcome—then company sick pay schemes for wage-earners will play only a small part in providing income-protection: they will be more important for high-wage workers whose State benefit will be relatively less. If the State scheme follows the present pattern but with an increase in the flat-rate benefit, manual workers' sick pay schemes may increase in numbers, but coverage is likely to be limited (as it is now) and the benefits, and cost, not very high. Sick pay schemes will not figure prominently in the bargaining demands of the large manual workers' trade unions; though they may appear in the first round of claims, interest will continue to be centred on wages and hours. The result of all these forces should be that sick pay schemes for manual workers will spread only slowly and will not become as common a condition of employment as industrial pension schemes are at the moment. The final word must however be one of caution, and a mention of one of the reasons why this conclusion may not be accurate. We must assume that there will be no Government measures to give financial inducements to employers who provide sick pay schemes; it is interesting to contrast the large number of employees covered by industrial pension schemes—presumably because of the financially attractive basis of contracting-out—with the small numbers covered by redundancy schemes, few of which have been negotiated despite Governmental exhortation and encouragement. If the spread of sick pay schemes were to be stimulated by financial means, this would in effect be an explicit recognition by the State of the essential identity of private and public welfare provision.

[1] The prediction is based on reasonably objective facts, and could of course be completely contradicted if employers suddenly became more 'welfare-minded' and introduced sick pay schemes which were economically illogical.

CHAPTER 9

REDUNDANCY

D. J. ROBERTSON

I.

The results presented in Chapter 3 suggest that in 1960 redundancy payments were a relatively small proportion of the total cost of fringe benefits, amounting to less than one per cent of payroll in most of the firms participating in the enquiry. However, payments to meet redundancy may be made on an *ad hoc* basis to meet an immediate situation, and it is unlikely that these were fully recorded by the enquiry. In addition, 1960 was a 'good' year as far as unemployment was concerned, and in 1962–3 expenditure on all types of redundancy payments is likely to have been considerably greater. Despite these qualifications, the judgement that redundancy payments do not constitute a very large charge on the employer still seems entirely valid and justifiable. Nevertheless, the importance of the issues raised by redundancy and redundancy payments must not be underestimated. Many wage-earners spend their lives among continual rumours about the state of employment over the next few months in their own particular type and place of work. Fear of the social and economic hardships associated with unemployment is deeply rooted in the minds of the wage-earning labour force, especially when the cause is said to be 'redundancy', with all the nuances of uselessness which this now implies.

The problem of definition which the term 'redundancy' presents is both important and difficult. One possible popular definition would be to say that redundancy is simply another word for unemployment.[1] but this is not wholly tenable, since it is generally agreed that

---

[1] This is the definition implicit in Chapter 6. Dr Holmans' treatment of the issues raised therefore differs radically from that followed here. Only the third set of circumstances discerned by Dr Holmans—the consequences of technical change—are entirely within the concept as used here. The two discussions offer interesting contrasts in approach.

DOI: 10.4324/9781003184706-9

redundancy is in some way associated with losing a job. Unemployment is compatible with never having had a job, or having lost it so long ago that the dominant circumstance is now the fact of being unable to find work, rather than the loss of the original job. Further, a worker may become unemployed through leaving his job voluntarily for one reason or another: redundancy usually has the connotation of 'the involuntary loss of a job through no fault of the worker concerned'.[1] The problem of redundancy, therefore, is not simply that of the unemployed. It includes the need to alleviate the sense of insecurity of those who feel at risk of losing their jobs and so becoming unemployed. The actual condition of redundancy means having a job to begin with, the job being lost 'through no fault of the worker'. Moreover, redundancy implies more than losing a job which has been held only for a very limited period of time: it would be meaningless to talk of a frequent reiteration of employment followed by unemployment as redundancy since this is better described as casual labour. For redundancy to be a meaningful term, then, it ought properly to be associated with a previous state of employment and with losing a job (which has given the illusion of stability to its holder) in circumstances which did not follow from industrial misconduct, and with at least some inference that the consequence will be unemployment.

This may appear to be rather a laboured discussion trying to make more explicit well-understood conventions about the meaning of a word which is in common use without ambiguity, but it is essential to distinguish between redundancy and unemployment, to make it clear that redundancy payments are connected with the process of losing a job and less directly connected with the possibility of long-continued absence of employment. Secondly, redundancy is by no means necessarily the prior circumstance which has brought unemployment to the bulk of the unemployed. Some have not worked before, others have never had a stable job from which they might become redundant.

This Chapter is mainly about arrangements for redundancy which are made or might be made, with or without Governmental backing, in particular places of employment or by particular firms. From the point of view of the individual worker, however, and indeed for many aspects of social well-being, it matters little whether arrangements designed to alleviate particular misfortunes such as redundancy are partially or wholly provided by the State or by employers so long as the benefit afforded is equally satisfactory. In consequence, this Chapter like several others in this volume cannot be confined to fringe benefits provided by employers and has to make some excursions into the hotly-disputed territory of Governmental policy

[1] 'Redundancy—A Survey of Problems and Practices', The Acton Society Trust.

in relation to unemployment. This intermingling of discussion of private and of social welfare has in any event been quite inevitable because of the evident increase in governmental concern with redundancy during the first years of the nineteen-sixties. At the time of writing (early 1964) it is not clear what will be the final shape of the Government's future policy on redundancy. Changes in policy were hinted in the Queen's Speech in November and are known to be under discussion 'with interested parties'.[1]

Thus this Chapter is concerned primarily with redundancy and with the policies of employers towards redundancy benefits. It also, however, has to say something on possible intervention by the State to sponsor or control private arrangements. Moreover, since these matters are interrelated with unemployment insurance under the National Insurance Acts, some discussion of possible changes in unemployment insurance is also necessary. Since the policies of the State have not at the time of writing been clearly formulated in public, though they have been rumoured or foreshadowed in the Press, this discussion will necessarily be tentative.

II. PRESENT REDUNDANCY AGREEMENTS

It is difficult to discuss current redundancy agreements generally, since there are so many different types. Perhaps the most common form of those currently existing is no more than an informal understanding between official or unofficial workers' representatives and management that in any particular circumstance which results in substantial unemployment for groups of workers, management will take action to minimize the severity of any hardships which might occur. A redundancy policy, as distinct from the somewhat narrower term 'redundancy payment scheme', might, for example, principally consist of a statement that the rule of 'last in—first out' will be adopted should be it necessary to reduce the scale of the labour force. This type of rule, especially if it is understood that it will be applied slowly and so will be assisted by natural wastage, has the immediate consequence of giving considerable stability and sense of security to those who have been 'in' for a long time and therefore are unlikely to be 'out' unless very substantial redundancy occurs.

There can, moreover, be little doubt that in addition to the formalized agreements to pay compensation for redundancy, which cover a minority of wage-earning employees in this country, there exists in the minds of management a large number of assumptions about the

[1] If legislative action is not taken in advance of a General Election—and time is running short—the outcome of the election could alter policy. Recent newspaper hints suggest that changes in unemployment benefit are now more in the Government's mind.

need to pay some kind of compensation to workers who are laid off unexpectedly, other than for their own misconduct. As this type of incident has arisen, managements have shown themselves to be prepared to make some kind of concessionary payments. These have not always been conceded without argument—for example, the motor industry since the War has a history of disputes designed to secure redundancy compensation[1]—and the amount of the payment actually made has frequently been far from large. It is likely, however, that formal redundancy agreements do not cover, either in the minds of management, as an expression of their unspoken intentions and their implicit cost, or in the minds of trade unionists and workers, as an expression of what they would put up with should the circumstances arise, anything like the potential outlay on redundancy payments. Whether redundancy policy is expressed in formal agreements or is merely an indication of good intentions, it is an intrusion of the hypothetical future; whether employers have redundancy schemes or not, they will not normally wish to be paying off regular employees. The amounts paid out under redundancy agreements obviously go to a much smaller group than the number of people who are covered by them and feel their protection, though on the other hand payments which might be made were redundancy to arise could be large and affect larger groups of workers than formal redundancy agreements.[2]

Over 200 actual agreements making provision for redundancy are summarized in the Ministry of Labour's pamphlet 'Security and Change' published in 1961.[3] This source is well known and there is no need to give lengthy details here. We can, however, summarize one or two clear impressions which are of general validity, though subject to exceptions in one case or another.

Redundancy agreements are normally concerned with the period of notice as well as with redundancy payments, and some do not actually involve the employer in making redundancy payments, but simply require a longer period of notice for employees with long service, so that such employees will have time to look for another job. But the employee may still be at work during the period of notice and since he will be anxious to save for a possible period out of work afterwards, he may not be prepared to lose working time. While he

[1] Cf. J. Bescoby and H. A. Turner, 'An Analysis of Post-War Labour Disputes in the British Car-Manufacturing Firms', *Manchester School*, May 1961.

[2] In all fifty-four cases of the closure of a factory or a part of a concern noted by the Ministry of Labour in the three years prior to January 1963, 'the procedure was devised specially to cover the particular circumstances' and in fifty cases severance payments, in all but one as a lump sum, were made. Cf. Ministry of Labour *Gazette*, February 1963.

[3] A further survey on 'Redundancy in Great Britain' appears in the Ministry of Labour *Gazette* for February 1963, and discusses 371 policies—an increase of 60 per cent in the number of policies. The general conclusions are not affected.

will have time for reflection and planning, he may thus be short of the actual time necessary to go and look for another job. Moreover, the men discharged with less service and at shorter notice may have picked up the good jobs.

Secondly, a number of agreements using length of service to determine the period of notice and the scale of redundancy payments also vary these payments according to the age of the person becoming redundant. The Acton Society Trust, in the pamphlet previously cited, specified those in their late forties and early fifties as being most vulnerable:

'1. At this age a man is usually still educating his children.
2. He is usually still paying for his house and possibly for his furniture too.
3. He is not so easily retrained as is a younger person.
4. Apart from the material difficulty, already mentioned, he is not psychologically so ready to tear up his roots and move elsewhere.
5. He is too young to be given an early pension.
6. It is much more difficult for him to get a job elsewhere in competition with younger men.'

Thirdly, while most firms offering redundancy compensation have varied the amount of payments with length of service and also, less frequently, with the age of the recipient, the maximum payments, generally given in the form of lump sums, have reflected a few weeks' rather than a few months' pay.

Fourthly, in addition to specifying longer periods of notice as part of the redundancy conditions for employees with some length of service, most of the agreements examined by the Ministry of Labour commit the management to give as much forewarning as possible on future changes in labour requirements. However, one of the chief difficulties in doing this is that employers run the risk of losing their labour before they are ready to do so.

Finally, recorded agreements show an interesting concern with the definition of redundancy. Most of them have some kind of preamble about the occasions upon which money will be payable. All speak of circumstances outwith the control of the worker, such as technological change, or changes in demand for particular products. Many stress the fact that the manager has to make the final decision upon whether a worker should or should not be employed, but add that the manager can obtain helpful advice from his workers' representatives so long as they are not antagonized by the way in which the redundancy is handled. The main problem is to decide whether unemployment resulting from a general trade recession is a situation in which redundancy payments will be made, or whether it should be confined to those factors that are more immediately related to the particular conduct of the firm in question, such as the introduction of new machinery causing a large displacement of workpeople.

In the nationalized industries, the attitudes upon which redundancy policy is based are similar to those in private industry. Schemes are designed to provide compensation when workers are made redundant as a direct consequence of some technical or trading change which necessitates that the Board in question should terminate their services. The obligation to consult and the obligation on the industry to do its best to minimize the need for dismissals are written into the agreements. In general, however, the level of redundancy compensation offered by the nationalized industries is substantially above that customarily found in private industry. In all cases compensation is based on length of service : at the upper reaches of service the arrangements suggest recognition of early retirement rather than redundancy payments as such, though there is in these schemes, as they presently exist. some risk that the older employee may obtain a very handsome redundancy payment but lose his pension since he has been forced to leave his work before he is due for a pension but too late to find another job. It is in relation to the level of redundancy compensation offered to workers who have a reasonable opportunity of finding another job that the nationalized industries appear generous as against private industry. Thus, for example, the National Coal Board under an agreement concluded in 1962 bases its scheme on a period of twenty-six weeks during which benefit will be payable if the worker has not found another job. The amount of unemployment benefit is assessed at two-thirds of the appropriate wage rate payable to the particular class of worker declared redundant.

III. GOVERNMENTAL ARRANGEMENTS UP TO MID 1963

The Conservative Party have always emphasized the point that security against dismissal without notice (or with a very short period of notice) is an important aspect of security of employment, since a period of notice can be used to look for another job. For example, a statement of policy in 1946 proposed a Workers' Charter which said that 'every worker will be given a statement setting out the terms and conditions of his job. We believe that these statements should provide for a period of notice that takes into account a man's length of service'. This stress on the importance of the period of notice has been reflected in the 1963 Contracts of Employment Act which requires an employer to give a written contract of service and to allow a period of notice of at least a week rising to two weeks after two years' service and four weeks after five years' service. This will bring British practice much more into line with that in Europe. It can hardly be argued, however, that simply possessing a written contract and being allowed a few weeks' notice gives protection against the consequences of unemployment. The Act is important as an indication of the trend of Government thinking, but it is relatively much less important than the issue of redundancy payments to employees. There are circumstances where a period of notice strictly applied can be a positive disadvantage to the worker, and it is often best for a worker who is about to lose his job to move to a new job with the minimum of delay. Morever, some employers have been arguing that the Act can be used to put pressure on the workers to work longer notice while written contracts can be used as a weapon against unofficial strike action.

If a worker loses his job he has to face the issue of the suitability of his past experience for the opportunities available in the market. This raises questions of training and retraining workers who have been set aside by the labour market and find it difficult to obtain alternative employment. The Government has retraining centres which up till recently have been largely devoted to the training of disabled workers. Recent developments, however, indicate the beginning of a marked expansion of retraining facilities. The Government also aid the operation of redundancy policies by making the services of the Ministry of Labour Employment Exchanges fully available to firms who wish to carry out a planned run-down of their labour forces, accompanied by attempts to fit these people into alternative jobs. On such occasions the Exchanges will accept advance notice of those going to lose employment and will work in co-operation with the firm to try to place men in advance of their becoming redundant.

Though these matters are important, and though there are signs of a new policy on redundancy coming from the Government and forming part of the alternative proposals of the Opposition, the State's contribution to the problem of redundancy is still an attempt to give some degree of income-security through the mechanism of the National Insurance Acts and their well-established provisions for paying out unemployment benefit. Anyone who has paid his contributions to National Insurance for at least six months, as the vast majority of contributors have done, is entitled to benefit for a minimum of six months at rates which allow variations according to the number of dependants. The period of payment of benefit may go on for much longer than six months, but in any case the claimant is entitled to National Assistance both during that period and when it finishes, so that the benefit may be supplemented or replaced from a different source. The payments do not, however, vary according to occupation or according to the frequency with which benefit is in fact drawn by any one claimant, nor do the contributions vary with income. Indeed, the present legislation on unemployment insurance benefits is not specifically concerned with redundancy at all in the sense in which redundancy is defined in this Chapter. It is the fact of the man being unemployed that attracts benefit not the circumstances by which he became unemployed or his previous experience and employment. There is no attempt to distinguish between the frequently-unemployed casual labourer and the man who has lost a job which he has had for twenty years without previously having to draw unemployment benefit. Far from paying special attention to redundancy as it has been here defined, the present arrangements ignore the special issues raised by redundancy of the regular employee. Indeed, unless we assume that unemployment is a risk which equally affects us all, the present scheme cannot be regarded as 'insurance' as that term would be defined by a private insurance agency, since an insurance scheme would attempt to minimize and forecast risk by an accurate assessment of its possible occurrence, and so differentiate between the risk of unemployment affecting one type of person in one type of employment and that affecting another. Insurers either adjust their premia or adjust their benefit according to a series of calculations based upon splitting the total group wishing to be insured into significantly different categories which are estimated to have statistically, though not necessarily individually, different experience in relation to the risk against which the insurance is to provide cover. There is clear evidence that the risk of unemployment varies by occupation, by industry, and generally also as between wage-earners and salaried workers. It is therefore quite possible to relate contributions to benefit according to some kind of insurance principle, but the State scheme does not do so.

Since redundancy has meaning only as a term applied to a period of unemployment following upon employment, it implies a subdivision of the population at work which attempts to separate those who are most likely to experience unemployment from those who are least likely. This would be a separation by types of occupation and industry as well as an individual categorization which would single out those who did not in fact have frequent unemployment in their record. It would only be if the State scheme were so varied in the benefits it paid as to give larger or more prolonged benefits to those who were less likely to fall out of work that it would in any way correspond to a redundancy insurance scheme reflecting the nature of the previous employment. A scheme of this type would naturally involve either an increased general premium or contribution, or some form of subsidization out of general taxation, or a reduced benefit to those who are frequently out of work. The last possibility is socially unacceptable and may be dismissed. Indeed, social pressures are likely to be active in raising the minimum level of unemployment benefit rather than reducing it, and the choice appears to lie in principle between an increased premium or a subsidy out of general taxation, though in practice it might not be as stark as this. Unemployment insurance has not been severely strained due to full employment conditions, and since increased benefits to those who are rarely out of work would *ex hypothesi* be rarely paid, such a change might not be costly and the scale of benefits in relation to length of service could be adjusted to hold costs down. The likely outcome would be that the present degree of cross-subsidization of the frequently by the infrequently unemployed would be reduced, the contribution marginally increased, and the risk to the general revenue of a deficit due to unemployment benefits in conditions of heavier general unemployment marginally increased.

The uneven incidence of unemployment is emphasized by available analyses of the unemployed. For example, a survey conducted by the Ministry of Labour in August 1961 and published in the Ministry of Labour *Gazette* for April 1962,[1] indicated that Ministry officials thought that of those claiming benefit, 65 per cent of men and 61 per cent of women were difficult placing propositions. Most of this sample were unskilled, and over 40 per cent had had more than one spell of unemployment within the year. Even in contemporary full employment more than half of the wholly unemployed may have been without work for more than eight weeks. To a marked degree the unemployed, in conditions of general full employment, comprise a group who differ in many respects from the regular labour force and their problems may be treated as separate from those of redundancy facing regular employees.

Table 67 analyses the incidence of unemployment as evidenced by the drawing of unemployment benefit.[2] The Table shows that even after twelve years less than 30 per cent of the male insured population and of the single females had drawn benefit at all. The younger people were specially prone to draw benefit, but they became more stable as they grew older. In all age groups and for both sexes the figures suggest that the risk of unemployment is somewhat less likely for those who have survived two or three years without suffering from it. Figures for married women are not given in Table 67, first because the data are much less adequate since special contribution arrangements allow married women to work without being eligible for benefit, and secondly, because the figures for married women are

[1] Cf. L. C. Hunter, 'Unemployment in a Full Employment Society', *Scottish Journal of Political Economy*, November 1963.

[2] The scope, and therefore the interpretation of the figures, is to some extent limited by their compilation. No worker who was under fifteen on June 30, 1949 (and no immigrant since that date) is included. Those who were of minimum pensionable age by the end of December 1960 (65 for men and 60 for women) were excluded. Those who died or emigrated during the period were also excluded. Nevertheless the results shown cover the majority of working men though a smaller, and probably more variable, proportion of single working women.

TABLE 67. *The Incidence of Unemployment: the Percentage Drawing Unemployment Benefit for the First Time between 1949 and 1961 by Age and Sex*

	YEAR	16–20 YEARS	41–45 YEARS	ALL INSURED PERSONS PERCENTAGE	CUMULATIVE PERCENTAGE
			MALES		
1.	1949–50	6·6	4·9	6·4	6·4
2.	1950–1	3·9	2·6	3·0	9·4
3.	1951–2	4·6	3·9	3·6	13·0
4.	1952–3	5·0	2·5	3·2	16·2
5.	1953–4	3·6	1·3	1·9	18·1
6.	1954–5	2·5	1·2	1·6	19·7
7.	1955–6	1·9	1·1	1·4	21·1
8.	1956–7	3·2	1·6	2·0	23·1
9.	1957–8	2·9	1·8	1·8	24·9
10.	1958–9	2·7	1·8	2·0	26·9
11.	1959–60	1·4	0·9	1·2	28·1
12.	1960–1	1·1	0·6	0·8	28·9
	All years	**39·3**	**24·3**	**28·9**	**28·9**
		FEMALES (SINGLE, WIDOWED AND DIVORCED)			
1.	1949–50	4·6	4·5	4·5	4·5
2.	1950–1	2·7	2·3	2·5	7·0
3.	1951–2	9·1	5·3	6·4	13·4
4.	1952–3	3·7	2·3	3·0	16·4
5.	1953–4	2·2	1·3	1·4	17·8
6.	1954–5	1·3	1·1	1·2	19·0
7.	1955–6	1·2	1·5	1·5	20·5
8.	1956–7	1·6	1·6	1·4	21·9
9.	1957–8	1·6	2·1	1·6	23·5
10.	1958–9	2·2	1·2	1·4	24·9
11.	1959–60	1·8	1·3	1·0	25·9
12.	1960–1	0·6	0·4	0·6	26·5
	All years	**32·9**	**25·2**	**26·4**	**26·5**

The table header reads: AGE GROUP BY AGE AT START OF STUDY : PERCENTAGE DRAWING UNEMPLOYMENT BENEFIT FOR FIRST TIME

Source: Ministry of Pensions and National Insurance.

somewhat higher than for single women and are obviously affected by special causes. The natural corollary to this Table is that unemployment tends to affect a rather limited group in the conditions of general full employment to which we have become accustomed, and it does so repetitively rather than spreads over the population as a whole.

IV. THE POSITION OF THE FIRM AND THE EMPLOYEE

This section will be concerned to set out the problem of redundancy afresh and to attempt to indicate ways of handling it with the aim of improving the lot of the redundant worker without running into seriously adverse economic effects, especially for the companies concerned. It is again assumed that redundancy and redundancy payments relate to the situation in which a worker who has formerly thought his employment to be secure loses that employment through no fault of his own.

The labour force is interested in redundancy payments for the same reason as most people are interested in any form of insurance scheme—because they are aware of the risk, are not entirely sure whether the risk may not befall them, and wish to be prepared. A redundancy payment scheme can be important not merely because it offers security to those who become redundant, but because it gives assurance to a very much larger population who feel themselves to be at some risk, for full employment, on almost any definition, is compatible with some unemployed. In fact, during full employment the unemployed are a rather separate group with different characteristics from the employed, so that few people who are 'employable' are out of work for long in general conditions of full employment.[1] Nevertheless, provisions against redundancy can offer a sense of security to those in employment, in the same way as does any insurance scheme: the effects of an insurance scheme against death by cancer spread much beyond the dependants of those who actually die from this disease to the very many more who take some comfort from having provided against the contingency. The risk is not a certainty: those who benefit from provisions against the risk are more numerous than those who suffer from the calamity which is at risk.

1. The employers' problem

In the absence of State intervention redundancy policy must be formulated by employers. What are the benefits and the demerits of redundancy provision from the point of view of the employer? We may set aside aspects of redundancy arrangements other than that of redundancy payments whether as a lump sum or as an income during some period after the loss of employment. For the most part, such other measures relate to helping workers to find alternative employment or to the period of notice.

A firm contemplating introducing a redundancy payment scheme has two main issues to resolve. First, it will want to limit its obligation to pay redundancy compensation so that this does not occur when it is simply adjusting its labour force in consequence of some normal or periodical fluctuation which has been anticipated. The obligation to pay must be confined to a situation where the change in employment is unusual or unexpected. Secondly, the individual employer, while possibly being prepared to offer redundancy compensation for most circumstances within the limits of the continued

[1] Cf. L. C. Hunter, op. cit.

existence of the firm, will have less latitude for manoeuvre if the redundancy is created from sources external to the firm, such as some form of Government intervention, and will in any event want to protect himself against an obligation to pay workpeople redundancy payments in circumstances in which the firm is going out of existence and cannot honour any of its obligations as it would wish. There is inevitably some point at which the individual firm will wish to resile from its redundancy obligations, passing the burden to the State. It is therefore clear that the State would need to play at least a residual role in providing redundancy payments if a complete coverage of the working population were in any way to be attempted. Moreover, small firms might for a variety of reasons find it impossible to institute a scheme of their own and this would leave room for a State scheme.

Is it possible for a firm to devise a scheme which will not incur an obligation to pay compensation to those who are not long-serving and which will also limit obligation to pay so that it does not occur for normal periodic fluctuations? Whatever the workers may think, the employers will certainly take the view that redundancy payments should only be made where there is agreement that the contract to employ did imply continuity of employment. This depends on the proportion which the total amplitude of fluctuations in employment due to normal or anticipated circumstances bears to the average level of employment, and of the proportion which regular employees form of the total labour force. The term 'regular employees' could be used to signify those who have been employed without a special mention of the temporary character of the work. This is, in most circumstances, likely to be a high proportion, since the present relatively short periods of notice in British industry, even after the Contracts of Employment Act becomes operative, preclude much need for the employer to indicate the temporary character of his employment. In consequence, the best criterion available is not whether the job was described as permanent or temporary, but whether the employee has demonstrated by dint of long service, not only that the employer has in fact offered him continuing employment, but that he has been willing to accept a permanent employment relationship.

The proportion of the total labour force of a factory which is in fact 'long service' is a function of the employment policy of the employer and of the willingness to stay of the worker. Production characteristics greatly influence employment policy. A management will be more interested in having a regular labour force if its factory is engaged in regular production than if production fluctuates due to variations in demand or in the supply of raw materials. Though variations in the demand for labour may be caused by factors which are

R

not directly related to the methods of production, many types of work require a method of production which presupposes regularity of output and hence of employment. The process of mechanization tends to gear the size of a labour force to the size of a designed production unit, with less possibility of variation in output between different parts of a factory, and often a factory must run at a fairly substantial proportion of its capacity if production is in any sense to be economic. However, even with mass production techniques and the necessity for a regular high level of output, there can still be variations in the size of the labour force, though there cannot in the short-run be substantial reductions in manpower. It would be rash to generalize, but many types of manufacturing industry, and also service industries and office and similar types of employment, are designed to run economically with a particular size of labour force. Therefore there will be some proportion of his labour force which an employer can think of as being permanently required so long as his enterprise remains in existence. This proportion will naturally vary according to the labour turnover which is normally to be expected, saving a major recession. We may assume that a minimum proportion of normal average employment is essential if a firm is to continue to exist, and also that a firm will, other things being equal, prefer this minimum proportion to consist of permanent long-service employees. As proof, we need only mention the costs of turnover, the obligation to retrain and the need for a period of service to go by before a new employee develops a sense of loyalty and of belonging to his new firm.

The problem is different and more complex if the firm thinks it is likely that it will go out of existence altogether. In this case the basis of providing for redundancy compensation is entirely different, for the shut-down may require paying off a substantial labour force rather than a smooth and slow run down from full production to zero employment. The income to meet redundancy payments can no longer come from the continuing income of the firm, since the payments do not represent a contract between employees of the firm and a continuing management. Moreover the payment of redundancy compensation is in direct conflict with the claims of a body of shareholders to whom the company has a legal obligation, since they are the owners of the remaining assets, and who wish to disband the company without loss to themselves.[1] It is inevitable that a firm should put rather more severe limitations on the amount of redundancy payments in such circumstances, and in consequence the obligations of the State may be thought to be increased.

[1] This is what happened in the *News Chronicle* case when the directors were prevented from making redundancy payments because of their obligations to shareholders. See *Parke v. Daily News* [1962], Ch. 927, and *Modern Law Review*, 25, 1962; pp. 715–19.

A second factor affecting the stable proportion of a labour force is the employee's willingness and ability to stay. Workers retire or die or leave employment on marriage, and there is always an influx of new workers from entirely obvious causes. In addition, labour turnover among newly recruited workers is generally high: it is not the case that all people joining a particular employment intend to stay in it for a number of years. There is certainly a substantial wastage of employees within the first year of service, which appears to be due both to dissatisfaction with the job in question and a natural tendency to look for alternative opportunities. The proportion of its labour force to which any one firm might decide to promise redundancy compensation would be varied in relation to these known habits of its labour force. Thus, if the decision were made to regard a five-year period of service as a minimum qualifying period, this could be related to whatever is the known tendency of the labour force to remain in employment for that length of time. By manipulating the

TABLE 68. *Labour Turnover by Industry Group* (*Number of Discharges and Other Losses per* 100 *Employed at Beginning of Four-week Period*)

INDUSTRY GROUP	PERIOD ENDING 18/8/62			AVERAGE 1960-2[1]		
	MALES	FEMALES	TOTAL	MALES	FEMALES	TOTAL
Food, Drink and Tobacco	2·8	4·8	3·7	3·0	5·1	3·8
Chemicals and Allied Industries	1·2	2·9	1·7	1·5	3·2	2·0
Metal Manufacture	1·4	2·2	1·5	1·8	2·7	1·9
Engineering and Electrical Goods	1·6	2·8	1·9	2·0	3·5	2·3
Shipbuilding	2·5	2·3	2·4	2·5	2·0	2·4
Vehicles	1·3	2·6	1·5	1·5	2·9	1·7
Metal Goods not elsewhere specified	1·8	1·9	2·2	3·0	3·9	3·4
Textiles	1·9	2·7	2·3	2·6	3·5	3·1
Leather, Leather Goods and Fur	2·9	2·9	2·9	2·6	3·4	2·9
Clothing and Footwear	2·2	3·2	2·9	2·4	3·4	3·1
Bricks, Pottery, Glass and Cement	1·9	2·4	2·1	2·4	3·1	2·6
Timber, Furniture, etc.	2·1	1·9	2·1	2·7	3·4	2·9
Paper, Printing and Publishing	1·3	2·6	1·8	1·5	3·1	2·1
Other Manufacturing Industry	1·9	3·3	2·5	2·4	3·4	3·0
All above	1·7	3·1	2·2	2·1	3·6	2·6

[1] The returns on which the statistics are based are made to the Ministry of Labour at three-monthly intervals: these figures are therefore an average of eight such returns.

Source: Ministry of Labour *Gazette*.

figure of length of service the proportion of the average number of employed to whom compensation is offered could be varied. There is, however, no possibility of being prècise on any kind of general estimation of the proportions of a typical labour force which can be expected to give particular lengths of service. Labour turnover statistics are notoriously unsatisfactory, suffering from many differences in the definitions used by different firms, but the statistics relating to labour turnover which have the widest application are those obtainable from the Ministry of Labour *Gazette*. Some of this material is summarized in Table 68.

The figures in Table 68 are collected on the basis of a comparison between the number of persons who were on the books of a firm at the beginning of a four-week period and were no longer employed at the end of the period with the number employed at the beginning of the period. Such figures will understate the full extent of labour turnover by omitting those who both join and leave the firm within the four-week period, but they do not presuppose a minimum of four weeks' service since an individual who joined the firm the day before that commencing the four-week period and left the day after would be included in the account. On this definition there is a regular 2 or 3 per cent marginal change-over of labour in industry in each four-week period. Unfortunately we cannot proceed from these figures to say how many workers leave with less than a given period of service, nor can we say anything about the pattern of leaving of those of different ages, and the data give no help in defining causes of leaving. A 3 per cent turnover in a four-week period could mean a 40 per cent change-over per year at one extreme, or at the other extreme no more than 4 per cent per year with the margin of new employees changing each four-week period.

There are no further official statistics to guide this discussion, and the extent to which and the manner in which particular firms keep records of labour turnover are so variable as to make any comprehensive assessment quite impossible. Enquiries were made from a number of firms during the investigation which preceded the writing of this Chapter, but the material does not permit systematic presentation. Three generally accepted propositions can be asserted without adequate documentation but also without a very great risk of error. First, turnover is much heavier among newly-recruited workers than for those with a moderate length of service. Therefore figures of turnover in a short period cannot simply be multiplied to give the overall effect on a labour force over a longer period. Secondly, the older worker changes his job less readily than the younger worker, though naturally the number of leavers rises with the advent of retirement. The younger worker has less continuity of service than the older, not only because he is younger but also because he is more likely to have changed his job. Thirdly, dismissals due to redundancy or other means are usually much smaller in number, in contemporary conditions of full employment, than the total volume of those leaving voluntarily for all causes.

It is possible to produce rather more systematic material for the nationalized industries about these matters and this material is summarized in Table 69. It is particularly important to note in the case of the coal industry how large labour turnover on wastage is, in total, relative to loss of employment due to redundancy or dismissal. (This information is not available for other industries.) These figures show that a large enterprise of this type can generally use wastage over a period as a satisfactory substitute for redundancy, though the possibility of geographical reallocation is also important in these industries where jobs are more or less standardized.

TABLE 69. *Wastage of Labour in Nationalized Industries* 1957–61

YEAR			WASTAGE OF LABOUR AS PER CENT OF NUMBER EMPLOYED			WASTAGE DUE TO DISMISSAL AND REDUNDANCY AS PER CENT OF TOTAL WASTAGE
			BRITISH TRANSPORT COMMISSION	GAS COUNCIL	NATIONAL COAL BOARD	NATIONAL COAL BOARD
1957	..	..	18·7	23·3	9·2	6·5
1958	..	..	16·6	18·4	8·9	7·3
1959	..	..	17·5	22·1	11·2	12·9
1960	..	..	18·6	27·2	15·5	4·7
1961	..	..	19·5	25·5	13·0	4·4

Source: Annual Reports.

To summarize the discussion so far: we can anticipate that a proportion of the employees of any firm will not qualify for redundancy payments on any definition which requires a period of service before entitlement, and also that the proportion who do qualify will be substantially less than the average size of the labour force. The numbers of workers dismissed for reasons of redundancy or other causes after long service would seem likely to be rather small in most circumstances. Certainly there is a margin available to the employer who wishes to use it to run down his labour force by taking account of normal wastage. The figures presented are not conclusive, but they certainly suggest that a policy of redundancy compensation which offers compensation only to employees with a certain minimum qualifying length of service, might in normal circumstances be likely to give satisfaction to the longer-service employee without great cost to the employer.

2. Some issues for the employee

No matter what his status or his previous employment, every employee who falls out of work has to face at least two problems, that of finding another job, and that of paying his way in the meantime. These are factors of which any provisions for redundancy have to take account; though the latter is normally the main feature of a redundancy *scheme*, a *policy* for redundancy should be designed to help the redundant employee to minimize this period of unemployment.

The problem of finding another job is partly one of time to look for another job and partly one of help, since the redundant employee may have little information on his local labour market. Firms can help by giving a longer period of notice to a redundant worker, to allow him a longer time to adjust to the need to find new employment; but if a large number have been paid off the long-service worker may find that he has lost opportunities of other jobs to others with shorter service and so a lesser period of notice. From the point of view of the employee, therefore, an arrangement for redundancy which includes a longer period of notice must allow him to take a job at any time within that period of notice and not simply at its termination. An employer could find such an arrangement difficult to operate since he might face a sudden shortage of labour during the period of notice, but a redundancy arrangement designed to assist the worker can hardly be helpful if it prevents him from getting another job. If it is to be an effective contribution to redundancy 'policy, a longer period of notice needs to be obligatory on the employer but optional to the employee, and the employer must count any dislocation as an inevitable cost of redundancy. The most clear-cut aid that an employer can give to a redundant employee, however, is to help him to get another job. The co-operation of the Ministry of Labour can be of considerable value in doing this, but firms may be able to use their influence with others in the neighbourhood or to act as an informed employment agency which knows both the type of work and the men, and so find them other work directly. Further difficulties arise if the demand for a particular type of redundant labour is falling, so that workers cannot be placed in jobs similar to those they have previously held. In this case new employment will mean new training and though a large firm may sometimes be able to retrain redundant labour and re-absorb it in another section of its own organization, the ultimate liability to provide or co-ordinate retraining must rest on the State.[1]

The short-run problem of redundancy, however, is that anyone who loses his job normally loses his primary source of income, and only a very large amount of savings would prevent the average man from finding this worrying. Moreover, savings, though they may help to meet unexpected contingencies such as unemployment, are also

[1] The State is now beginning to take increased responsibility in this field—for example in the Industrial Training Act, 1964.

generally designed to accumulate for use in old age. The prudent employee might reasonably be invoked to carry a reserve of money against falling out of work and other disasters; but the presence of that money will not mean that he suffers no hardship by becoming redundant, since he will be using for unemployment money which he had hoped to save for a further and more inevitable contingency, that of having to retire. In any case most workers are not well equipped with readily available finance which enables them to dispense with their weekly wage.

To some extent a loss of regular income can be met by economies. There are, however, a number of items in any man's expenditure which can only be cut down with difficulty. Local authorities, landlords or building societies do not look with any degree of favour on those who suddenly cannot afford to pay the cost of housing. The local authority will not do without payment of the rates unless with a deal of formality which it is not pleasant for a man to undergo. Hire-purchase companies are willing to forgo their payments only for a limited period. Only a certain portion of the average man's outlays can readily be trimmed when the source of his income is cut back. Indeed, it is arguable that the more secure a man has previously been, the more this problem of reduced income meeting unreduced expenditure is likely to worry him, not only because he will be unaccustomed to coping with such a difficulty, but also because he may with some reason have allowed his previous security to permit more fully-committed expenditure; the casual worker will be much more accustomed to sudden imbalances of income and expenditure. Second only to another job, the worker who is about to become redundant wants help in meeting his bills and as far as possible a continuance of his income during the period in which he may be unemployed. The longer the period of unemployment lasts, the more urgent does this need become, since short-term economies and drawing on savings will begin to be more difficult as time goes by.

Both a promise of help in finding a new job and that of help with income during the interregnum may be sources of comfort to the worker who fears the consequences of redundancy even though it has not actually arisen. A worker will want to be aware of the provisions of a redundancy scheme so that he can have the sense of security which comes from feeling that the risks attendant upon redundancy have in some way been provided for, though, paradoxically, the initial reaction of the work-force to a redundancy scheme may be greater insecurity through suspicion of the management reasoning behind the scheme. However, long service in itself confers a sense of security, both of employment and income: employees who have been with a firm for some time develop a resistance to the thought of moving, and once accustomed to a regular source of income it is less easy for them to move on without worrying about the insecurity that results. In a more intangible way, even the familiarity of a regular place of work gives a sense of security and stability to the working life. Thus the same kind of criterion, length of service, which is likely to be favoured by an employer in considering redundancy compensation, also has great influence on the subjective attitudes of the worker who associates security and stability as a normal and accepted part of his life with a long period of service in one employment.

Some degree of security is valuable and necessary for the operation of the labour market. The 'secure' employee is more likely to identify his interests with those of his firm: the idea of loyalty to a firm, though highly intangible, is attested as important by many managements. Moreover, while the labour market needs mobility between jobs for its operation, it also requires that as many as possible of those who move should be looking for permanent and stable types of employment. Drifters are of no particular value to most employers, and the concept of desirable mobility should not be confused with that of 'unnecessary' turnover, where a worker may move from job to job, simply because there is no particular reason why he should stick in one rather than another. This type of undesirable turnover is reduced in circumstances in which a redundancy scheme puts a premium on continued employment in the one place. Moreover, the worker may be more conscious of the need to find a job in which he proposes to stay and where he will seek security if in that job he will be insured against the cost of redundancy. Thus the attraction of security may encourage workers to seek to find employment in which they may continue for some time and to be reluctant to move simply for the sake of moving. As long as a marginal amount of mobility is retained to balance the labour market, security as a conscious motive in the worker can be a desirable aid to the development of a healthy labour market.

There are two types of security at issue for a worker seeking stable employment, security of employment such that he has a job which gives him a continuing sense of participation in the life of the community and, very importantly, gives him an income and so confers security of income. If he achieves permanent employment the worker will have both forms of security, though the secure portion of his income may be less than his usual earnings if bonus and other variable forms of income are important. A redundancy scheme cannot *ex hypothesi* give security of employment in the one place of employment but it can give security of income for a period of time which may carry the worker over to another job. The payments made by a redundancy scheme may be regarded by an employee as 'compensation' for loss of employment, but will necessarily be used to maintain income if another job is not immediately to be found. A redundancy scheme which offers a lump sum payment to the redundant worker, while it reflects the aspect of compensation for job-loss and is certainly not affected by the interval of unemployment between the redundant job and further employment, has for the worker the disadvantage that he has to budget his lump sum in terms of income for an indefinite period. A scheme which offers a series of payments of income corresponds more adequately to the worker's need for security in income. It then, however, becomes open to the employer to arrange the scheme so that he can stop the flow of income when a further job is found thus saving his funds, but not giving an assured payment in compensation for loss of employment. Payments in the form of income are probably preferable in the interests of the worker. Administratively the simplest way of making income payments is to offer them for a fixed period to the redundant workers, possibly in relation to length of service. There is, however, something to be said for stopping payment earlier if a worker has found another job, provided the saving is reflected in more generous provision for those whose job-hunting takes longer.

The introduction of a redundancy scheme may have in common with other forms of fringe benefits dependent on length of service such as pensions, the effect of making a worker reluctant to change from a job in which he has built up claims to benefit. This feature of all such schemes is a bar to mobility for the individual worker who may be inhibited from moving to a new and better job. On the other hand it increases the stability of the labour force and a redundancy scheme may make it easier for a firm to change the pattern of its employment without causing vigorous resentment among its labour force. The worker who does actually move to new employment of his own free will shares with the worker who takes on a new job, having become redundant in his last, the disadvantage of being without built-up claims to redundancy compensation in the new job, if such claims are based on length of service. Even if most forms of employment gave stability the need to have some mobility for workers in search of better jobs and some redundancy would therefore inevitably leave a number of workers at risk of redundancy and without the prospect of an established position in a firm's redundancy arrangements. This is a major reason why such private schemes could not completely replace the State's unemployment insurance arrangements even for workers in regular employment. In the case of the casual worker unemployment insurance by the State scheme cannot be replaced by arrangements introduced by private firms, and for such workers improvements in the State scheme are of great importance. In any trade which suffers from large fluctuations in demand over short periods of time short periods of employment are likely and help in redundancy depends on the State's unemployment insurance.

V. FUTURE POLICY

This concluding section puts forward some policy proposals for the future. Unfortunately, however, it is at the time of writing well-known that the Government has new ideas on redundancy policy but there has been no announcement as yet on what the final proposals are: some of the remarks here may therefore be out of date before this Chapter appears in print. Redundancy policy can be discussed under four main headings: (1) period of notice and advance warning; (2) re-training; (3) redundancy payment schemes by firms, and (4) Governmental arrangements and proposals. The first two of these headings will be very brief. The discussion under the third heading is rather longer and is essentially a summing-up of the previous section of this Chapter (Section IV) which outlined the position of the firm and the employee. Here we try to pull the strands together and to indicate lines of future policy for redundancy schemes provided by firms. The fourth heading—on redundancy arrangements by Government—discusses changes in the present system of National Insurance. It is freely admitted that such a discussion inevitably makes various assumptions about the wisdom of different types of social policy: a personal bias on the part of the author is inescapable.

1. *Period of notice and advance warning*
The periods of notice which have been customary for manual wage-earners hardly allow a worker time to look around and assess alternative opportunities. An extension of the period of notice both by law and by custom is an obvious recommendation designed to assist the worker in finding new employment. If the extension of the period of notice is construed so as to give the employer the power to hold the worker while the process of notice is being worked out, the worker may lose opportunities to others who, because of having had shorter service, also have a shorter period of notice to run. Thus such extensions must allow the worker to leave should another job offer itself within the period. A more general advance warning of forthcoming reductions of the labour force may sometimes be thoroughly desirable. A reduction in recruiting can avoid holding a surplus of labour when the cuts begin to arrive, while the natural process of labour turnover and wastage may do away with the need for formal redundancies at all. To put the point in its most general terms: a well-thought-out policy for labour may avoid the worst aspect of redundancy—lack of intelligent anticipation. The Contracts of Employment Act will be helpful if it is not misused by employers; but legislation is no substitute for a thoughtful personnel policy on the part of employers.

2. *Provision for retraining and reallocating redundant labour*[1]

There is no automatic balancing mechanism by which workers with one type of skill are transformed into labour of another type. By and large, the movements in demand for very big categories of skill are slow, but they do exist, and can occasionally be severe, as when an industry or occupation experiences a prolonged contraction. In circumstances of this type reallocating labour means retraining as well as simply finding another job. While there have been recent improvements, the present volume of provision for retraining does not ensure the flexibility of the market or constitute an adequate process of adjusting needs to supply, and the volume of retraining should be increased.[2]

3. *Redundancy schemes provided by firms*

Redundancy has been defined earlier in this Chapter as losing a job through no fault of the individual, the job being one which has been held long enough to make the worker a regular and not merely a casual employee. There is a strong case for more redundancy schemes provided by firms to meet the needs of such employees. Redundancy payments are important to the employee to give him time to find a new job while keeping some kind of regular income; without them the worker is forced into sudden cuts in expenditure with disagreeable effects on his standard of living. The introduction of a redundancy scheme increases security of income and may encourage the worker to seek stable employment which has such a scheme. Security as a motive can benefit industrial relations and is not incompatible with the need for adequate mobility. Mobility will benefit the economy if in the process of changing from one job to another the worker is actively seeking to find a job in which he wants to settle down and which offers him continuing employment; this must not be confused with the present high volume of labour turnover which is frequently lacking in directional force and does not necessarily induce a desirable reallocation of labour.

There are difficulties in presenting the case for more private redundancy payments. In some firms there is evidence only of what they did, when on some past occasion, they actually declared redundancy and no background at all of formal agreements. In other cases the agreements have been amplified in the actual event of redundancy. Since the fear of redundancy, and conversely the desire for employ-

[1] There is clearly very much to be said about the problems of training and retraining. We are here no more than stating the general conclusions accepted by most authorities; the means by which they will come about is much more controversial, but too complex to be discussed here.

[2] Cf. D. J. Robertson, 'Shortages of Skilled Workers', *L.C.E.S. Bulletin*, December 1962.

ment security, are to be found not only in those who actually become redundant but in most of the labour force, it is desirable that a redundancy scheme should exist, and be made known to those presently in employment. It may be said that for many people this simply means raising the issue in the mind of a worker who has only the remotest chance of becoming redundant and that it would be better not to worry him. But if the worker will himself think of the possibility that he might become redundant, the promise of compensation will make him feel that the firm has something to lose if it should dismiss him, and he is likely to feel more secure in his mind about the consequences of becoming redundant if redundancy payments give him some degree of income-security. The declaration of a redundancy scheme affecting workers who have little prospect of becoming redundant is an important, and not a costly, policy for a firm to adopt.

The actual drawing-up of an agreement, however, will certainly raise difficult issues. Firms will normally wish to limit their obligations to pay redundancy compensation when the firm itself is going out of business. A limitation which would probably affect more people is that the individual firm is unlikely to be prepared to offer compensation to those who have been in its employment only for a short space of time. Such a limitation simplifies the whole operation of any scheme introduced by a firm since protection in the form of a promise of redundancy payments would then be offered to the part of the average labour force which has already rendered a sufficiency of service as to suggest that it will not readily be paid off. Redundancy hardships are naturally related to the age of a worker since it is well known that an older worker normally finds it more difficult to get alternative employment. On the other hand an older worker would also tend to be a worker with longer present service.

It is, however, difficult to find an exact length of service which ought to be used as a datum for constructing redundancy schemes on this plan. Much would depend upon the characteristic employment structure of the firm and its needs for labour. A firm in an industry where demand for labour fluctuates wildly cannot either expect to have a high proportion of long-service employees or to offer compensation to those whose employment has been relatively short. The maximum of short-term turnover seems to occur within the first few months of employment; thereafter the labour force shows more tendency to settle down in a job and to regard itself as fixed. Redundancy payments starting from perhaps two years' service may therefore reflect the practical circumstances for most cases.

It is again difficult to generalize about the scale of compensation. However, if attention is concentrated on service as a criterion of eligibility for redundancy compensation the problem is much simplified. The longer-service employee is, by that very fact, least likely to be declared redundant, but the older employee with longer service will probably also require longer to fix himself in alternative employment should he lose his job and may therefore require some substantial amount of redundancy compensation. Younger employees are likely to find it easier to get other jobs. If we are to advance from the present situation by which a worker can generally only have a week's period of looking round for alternative employment while he spends his week's 'lying time', then we must obviously be thinking in terms of at least a month as a typical, and perhaps minimal, period during which redundancy compensation would be payable, with longer periods for those with longer service. The present importance of such matters as one week's lying time, accumulations of bonus and accumulations of holiday credits as providing a practical substitute for redundancy compensation should not incidentally be overlooked. The unfortunate thing is that these payments are reflected in due course in losses of opportunities when a new job is obtained. A man no longer has accumulated holiday pay. and he has a week to work before he qualifies for new pay, this week becoming his new 'lying time' in case he loses his new job.

Since the redundant worker is subject to continued demands on his income and has lost his source of income it follows that a redundancy payment scheme based on income payments is more in line with the needs of the situation and is to be preferred to a lump sum benefit. If, however, the lump sum is large the worker may use it as income over a period.

If such redundancy schemes were to be more extensively introduced by firms several groups would be left out of them. The casual or short-term employee would obviously not be included, but a list of exclusions would also have to mention those who, having shifted from a job in which they had long service and a redundancy scheme, then found themselves losing their newer job without being covered for redundancy. Those being made redundant by a firm closing down might also be unprotected. These considerations lead us into discussions of Government policy.

4. State provision for redundancy

At the time of writing, apart from provisions for retraining and for longer periods of notice, the State's contribution to the problem of redundancy payments is unemployment benefit supplemented, if need is proved, by National Assistance. Unemployment insurance, since it is undifferentiated by length of service or in frequency of drawing benefit, is not specifically a redundancy scheme as redundancy has been defined in this Chapter, but rather generalized unemployment insurance.

A government which wishes to make improved provision for any form of social hardship has three broad choices open to it. It may, by legislation and/or persuasion, improve the adequacy of private provision; it may itself take steps to introduce a State scheme to provide aid or benefit; or it may combine private provision with a State scheme. Unofficial reports in the press[1] suggest that the Government is contemplating following the first of these alternatives as its policy for redundancy, by compelling employers to offer severance pay at, according to reports, the rate of one week's pay for each year of service restricted to those with a minimum of five years of service who are over 26 and under 65. Such a scheme is in general agreement with that proposed for private firms above except that it appears to offer a lump-sum benefit rather than an income flow. It could be argued that to legislate on this would have the effect of discouraging private initiative by firms. On the other hand, firms could offer extra benefits, and the benefits proposed as a minimum, according to press reports, whether they are thought to be satisfactory or not—and they seem on the low side to the present writer—are not out of line with what private firms appear to have been prepared to offer up to now. If such legislation were passed the benefits would be gradually improved in future legislation. While such legislation would therefore be welcome it is, however, hardly a contribution by the State itself. Since private schemes exist and redundancy is so much bound up with the experience of particular firms it seems desirable, though this is a matter for personal judgement, that the State, in making its own contribution, should prefer both to improve the private schemes and supplement them with its own arrangements, rather than supplant all private schemes with a State scheme.

National Insurance benefit, provided the applicant has a minimum number of qualifying weeks of contribution, is simply based upon a minimum and flat-rate estimation of his needs as expressed by his family's circumstances. It is not in any way related to the length of his previous spell in employment, to the frequency with which he draws benefits (except in relation to the extreme cases of those who have managed to disqualify themselves for benefit for a period), or to the previous income of the insured person. As we have seen, it is not really an insurance scheme at all since it takes no account of known differences in the risk of given individuals becoming unemployed; for example, the average clerical worker pays the same amount of contribution with less risk, from the point of view of the scheme, of benefit having to be paid to him.

This scheme could be changed into a kind of redundancy com-

---

[1] e.g. The *Financial Times*, November 19, 1963. Cf. 'Chronicle', *British Journal of Industrial Relations*, March 1964, p. 119. Very recent newspaper reports suggest that these plans have been abandoned in the face of resistance from both employers and trade unions.

pensation scheme if it differentiated payment partly to reflect the incidence of unemployment for any given individual, the duration of unemployment, and the previous income of the individual. To answer the question of how generous it might become in offering compensation to those who become unemployed after a long spell of employment we must seek facts on the frequency with which individuals draw benefit. There are no direct statistics on this point. The material given in Table 67 above, however, shows, from 1949 when the scheme became fully effective, the dates upon which people first drew benefit, giving a cumulative proportion of those who have drawn benefit at any time. The inference of the Table is clear; while a substantial portion had come along to draw benefit fairly soon after the scheme started, large numbers went many years before drawing benefit and at least two-thirds of the insured population still have not drawn any at all.

Any examination of the characteristics of those who most frequently draw unemployment benefit and of those who rarely, if ever, do so, leads to the conclusion that it would be feasible, probably without very large costs, to provide for the possibility of larger benefits for unemployment among those with a record of regular employment. The right to such extra benefit for one or more periods of unemployment would be dependent on the number of previous contributions. Since those who are earning high incomes are frequently, though by no means invariably, people who are less frequently unemployed a further small addition to contribution rates might well be sufficient to gear unemployment benefit in some measure at least to previous earnings. Most of those with high earnings are presently contributing to unemployment insurance without expecting to get any benefit which is of significant value to them as against their present incomes. A graduated scale of contributions, beginning with the basic amount as at present but going up to some higher level for those with a certain income or above, could be associated with higher benefits for larger incomes.

There would be problems in marrying such a State scheme to individual firms' redundancy schemes. It may well be, however, that the precedent already followed in the case of graduated pensions, which allows those who are members of a scheme with certain stated characteristics to opt out of the graduated element in the State scheme, could be followed here. There would require to be some provision, whereby, if a firm became unable to pay its redundancy compensation for stated reasons, the employee could revert to a scale of payments in the State scheme related to the frequency with which he had been unemployed and, if possible, his previous income. In general, however, the function of such a State scheme might be to complement rather than to supplant redundancy schemes arranged by particular firms.

The problems of casual workers frequently unemployed would not be solved by such a proposal. The case of the casual worker, the casualness of whose employment is a product not of his own tendency to move or be moved from job to job but of a characteristically fluctuating demand for labour in the industry of which he is part, is different from that of the worker whose employment record is poor without reference to the special circumstances of the industry in which he customarily seeks work. Casual work in industries with fluctuating demand can to some extent be reduced by associating workers with the industry rather than particular firms, on the ground partly that at the industry level demand for labour will be less erratic since the fluctuations of demand by particular firms will be averaged out, and partly that special arrangements to cope with the special circumstances of an industry's labour force can be more readily made at the level of the industry rather than at the level of the firm. The dock industry is the great illustration of such a problem of 'decasualization'. The present policies of that industry indicate the way in which such a problem may be approached: though the National Dock Labour Board scheme is by no means perfect, and will be improved in future, it is a notable advance on previous labour conditions in the docks. A redundancy scheme developed by the State out of present unemployment insurance might well have a special relationship with those industries, such as the docks, where long-run security of employment with any one firm is extremely difficult to achieve.

A redundancy scheme which is based on redundancy following regular employment cannot of itself improve the circumstances of the more general case of the worker with an above-average record of unemployment. An improvement in the unemployment benefit made available to those with more than usual unemployment would require an increase in the basic rate, or flat-rate, of unemployment benefit. The present level of benefit is sustained by a system of cross-subsidization by which contributions from all employed are applied to the relief of the unemployed. Since unemployment is not an equal hazard to all this means that all pay contributions for some to draw benefits. There is no reason why such cross-subsidization should not be associated with a graduated scheme of benefits, nor is there any reason why the flat-rate of benefit should not be increased, if this is thought advisable, alongside a graduated scheme. This is simply a matter of the arithmetic of relating contributions to benefits to ensure a subsidy from the less to the more frequently unemployed.

CHAPTER 10

THE GROWTH OF HOLIDAYS WITH PAY IN BRITAIN

G. C. CAMERON

I

There must be very few employees in Great Britain today who do not receive holidays with pay as a normal condition of employment, and it is rather surprising to realize that most manual workers[1] have only achieved this right within the last forty years and that in many major industries general acceptance of holidays with pay only dates from about the time of the Second World War. At present there is little uniformity in the provision of paid holidays since there is no general legislation laying down basic conditions, and although various governments have sought to influence the general climate of opinion by providing favourable conditions for their own employees, they have not interfered with the voluntary collective holiday agreements made by trade union officials and employers in individual industries. These agreements are still the most common guarantee of paid holidays for manual workers and as such they extend into almost every industry in the country. Almost all of the three and a half million workers in Wages Council industries, however, have their holiday arrangements guaranteed by statutory Orders.

Section II of this Chapter traces the historical growth of holidays with pay for manual workers in relation to three time periods. The first period will cover the position up to the end of the First World War—a period in which extremely few manual workers enjoyed paid holidays. In the second period, from about 1919 to 1945, the principle of holidays with pay was increasingly accepted; here the 1938 Committee of Enquiry will be discussed at length. Finally we shall look briefly at the post-war attempts to consolidate and in some cases to extend the right won in the inter-war years, and Section III con-

[1] This term is used loosely in this Chapter to mean non-staff workers or 'wage-earners'.

S

DOI: 10.4324/9781003184706-10

tinues by documenting the recent campaign for a third week's paid holiday. Section IV takes up three particular problems concerned with the future trend of holidays: first, the cost of extra holidays; secondly, the possibility of additional holidays for special groups of employees; and thirdly, the desirability of legislation establishing paid holidays, with special reference to comparisons between Britain and Europe.

II. THE HISTORY OF PAID HOLIDAYS[1]

1. *1880–1918*

The picture in the late nineteenth century and early twentieth century is reasonably clear. Whilst salaried employees had grown accustomed to one or two weeks' paid holidays each year,[2] paid holidays for the manual wage-earner were exceedingly rare. This did not mean, of course, that the wage-earner did not take any holidays at all, for in the words of Booth:

'comparatively few employments are so constant as not to yield holidays enough, and in some cases when the slack season falls at a convenient time of year advantage is taken by those who can afford it to arrange a week at the seaside.'[3]

Holidays such as Christmas and Easter were, of course, observed, and in some areas of the country summer holidays were taken at particular times and recognized by the employers as 'traditional holidays'. Thus the 'Wakes' in Lancashire, the Boulingtide holidays in the Yorkshire woollen industry, and the 'Fair' holidays in Glasgow, came to be typical examples of regular unpaid summer holidays. More generally, manual workers were also likely to receive a holiday on Bank Holidays,[4] and after the widespread application of the provisions of the 1901 Factory and Workshop Act (which had specifically guaranteed six days holiday per annum, on either public holidays or other days, for young persons and women workers), most manual workers could count on at least one week's holiday. Thus the Board of Trade's 'Earnings and Hours Inquiry' of 1906 showed that the average number of holidays taken was 11 to 12 days a year, varying from $8\frac{1}{2}$ days accorded to workers in chemicals, paper printing, food, drink and tobacco, to 9 days for building workers, 10 for the textile industry and 13 for engineering and steel operatives.[5]

---

[1] This section is based on an earlier draft prepared by Mr M. A. Utton, now of the University of Reading.

[2] See *Report of the Committee on Holidays with Pay*, Cmd. 5724, 1938.

[3] C. Booth, *Life and Labour of the People*, Vol. IX, p. 71.

[4] Bank Holidays were introduced by the Bank Holidays Act of 1871.

[5] In some industries the workers organized holiday funds into which they made weekly contributions in order to provide income during their non-earning holiday periods.

Although the vast majority of workers took unpaid holidays, there were a few paid holidays in single firms, and in some cases for certain grades of worker throughout an industry. Phelps Brown cites an agreement of 1886 in the Gas, Light and Coke Company of London, which accorded one week's holiday with pay and a gratuity of 4s 6d to all workers in the company's carbonizing departments who had twelve months continuous service and fewer than seven days absence (excluding illness).[1] Some company agreements on holidays with pay were even further qualified. For example, the scheme in operation at Cadbury's Bournville works allowed manual workers paid holidays provided they were good 'timekeepers', and in the case of exceptionally punctual employees extra paid holidays were allowed. 'To stimulate *good time* the *gift* (i.e. holidays with pay) was made subject to deductions for late time, but also subject to extension in cases of marked punctuality. . . . The Scheme has been most effective in establishing punctuality throughout the works. . . .'[2] 'Welfare can pay' might be a fair assessment of this 'gift'.

There is some evidence that a few industry-wide collective-agreements giving paid holidays were in operation in the railway service, public utility service and newspaper printing,[3] and many company agreements were in existence in retail distribution. In general, however, before the First World War, extremely few manual workers enjoyed paid holidays.

2. *1919–1945*
By the end of the First World War the attitude to holidays with pay for the manual worker had considerably changed. In some industries there was a genuine desire to understand and remove the causes of labour unrest, and the relief engendered by the end of hostilities meant that in all industries there was a willingness to reward labour for its war efforts. Thus in 1919 manual workers in most industries received considerable wage increases and a substantially shorter standard working week. In a few cases covering approximately one million manual workers holidays with pay agreements were added to these improvements. By 1922, these paid holiday agreements had spread to other industries so that by that date there were 21 general agreements, and 94 local or district agreements, together with an unspecified number of private agreements.[4] The general agreements covered all the manual workers in a given industry, the district agreement was applicable to a particular industry in a given locality, while

[1] E. H. Phelps Brown, *The Growth of British Industrial Relations*, London 1960, p. 86.
[2] E. Cadbury, *Experiments in Industrial Organization*, 1912 (italics added).
[3] See Committee on Holidays with Pay, op. cit., p. 8.
[4] Ministry of Labour *Gazette*, 1922.

the private agreements covered the employees of a single plant, or the manual workers in all of a company's branches. For the most part, these agreements provided for paid holidays varying in length from three to twelve days (exclusive of paid public holidays) and in most cases qualification for this required continuous service of between six and twelve months.[1] In most agreements no other qualification than length of service was required, but a few specifically mentioned that paid holidays were subject to other conditions such as punctuality or no absenteeism. Almost all schemes were non-contributory and financed entirely by the employers, but in a small number of cases the employees and employers made weekly contributions to a holiday fund which was drawn upon at holiday time. The pattern of payment established in these agreements was normally for time workers to receive an amount equal to full weekly rates whereas piece-rate workers were paid according to an 'average week' based on the weekly earnings of some preceding period. For example, in the paint, colour and varnish trades this period was one month, whereas in the printing industry it was six months.

The years from 1919–1922 were extremely important for the growth in numbers covered by paid holidays, since they saw a concentrated application of the principle of paid holidays as expressed in many general, district and private agreements. In this short space of about four years more manual workers came to be covered by new agreements than had been the case in the previous 30 or 40 years, but 1922 effectively marked the end of the first phase of the general extension of paid holidays, for in the following 16 years the total number of manual workers covered by agreements hardly increased at all.[2] It is also important to note that all of these agreements were reached by voluntary negotiations between employers and representatives of the employees, and not by general legislation. Furthermore, nearly all of the general agreements were concluded in industries with Joint Industrial Councils (or with a similar form of employer-employee council known as Interim Industrial Reconstruction Committees) and there seems little doubt that the co-operative spirit which was engendered in these consultative councils found practical expression in the granting of better conditions to labour in general, and of holidays with pay in particular.[3] Significantly most of the general agreements were in non-manufacturing industries such as the public utilities (e.g. gas, water, tramways), the retail side of the

[1] In some agreements employees who left their employment before they had taken a holiday received some additional payment. For example, in the printing industry employees who left after six months' service were entitled to one day's additional payment for each two months' service completed.

[2] It is difficult to be very precise about the numbers covered by all agreements since the Ministry of Labour kept no record of 'private' agreements.

[3] See J. B. Seymour, *The Whitley Council Schemes*, p. 59.

distributive trades and such service industries as boot and shoe repairing, all of which were probably operating under conditions of growing demand.[1] All of the major manufacturing industries, including textiles, engineering, shipbuilding, metal manufacture, and building, agriculture and coal mining, remained without general agreements on holidays. In these industries there were no Joint Industrial Councils[2] and after 1920 came the rapid onset of high unemployment with the consequent fall in wages. Also it would have been difficult to formulate a holiday scheme in some industries in which labour turnover was high. All these factors prevented the employer from granting holidays unilaterally, while trade unions were too busy trying to maintain the *status quo* in wages and hours to consider action on holidays. Whatever the reasons, the failure to establish paid holidays for manual workers in the few years favourable to social change—1919–21—meant that in conditions of falling or depressed trade when all cost increases were vigorously opposed by the employers, there was even less chance of extensions of holidays with pay. During the twenties and early thirties, when the main task of trade unions was not to improve labour conditions but simply to prevent existing wage rates from being depressed even further, it is not surprising that the question of holidays with pay was not raised at the T.U.C. until 1929, or that in 1925 a Private Member's Bill calling for six consecutive days holiday with pay for all employed persons with twelve months continuous service in one company, did not receive a second reading.

In 1929, however, the subject of holidays with pay was actively debated following the decision of the newly-elected Labour Government to give one week's paid holiday (six days) and five paid public holidays to all employees with one year's service in Government industrial departments. Although this was not a completely new departure on the part of the Government,[3] the fact that the great majority of Government employees were now covered by the policy induced the unions to take up the matter, and at both the Trades Union Congress and T.G.W.U. conference of 1929, motions were adopted calling for the statutory enforcement of a fortnight's paid annual holiday for all workers. The scene then shifted to Parliament where in November 1929, a Labour member introduced a Private Member's Bill calling for eight consecutive days of paid holiday for

[1] It is also noticeable that in many of the industries concluding agreements at this time, labour costs as a percentage of total costs were probably relatively low as compared with such industries as mining, engineering and shipbuilding.

[2] See Henry Clay, *The Problems of Industrial Relations.*

[3] Prior to this general enactment 38,000 Government workers in five Departments (The Post Office, Office of Works, Stationery Office, Royal Mint and Ministry of Agriculture) had already been given holidays with pay ranging from six to fourteen days—Information given by Financial Secretary to the Treasury. H.O.C. 26/7/28.

all employees who had been with the same firm for 12 months. The comprehensive debate on this Bill demonstrated that on the whole the House was in favour of the principle of holidays with pay, but many speakers stressed that a measure as important as this must be fully examined with specific reference to the costs which each industry would bear if the Bill became law, and also in relation to the effect of legislation on the traditional (voluntary) negotiating machinery.

The case for legally required holidays with pay was simply expressed. The proposers argued that this was no new principle since three million employees[1] already enjoyed paid holidays, and the Bill would simply add nine million employees to the list. The Government itself had set the pattern for this extension of holidays with pay, and now all other industries should follow suit. Furthermore, if this were done Great Britain would only be emulating what had already been achieved in many European countries. Though increased costs would fall on each industry it was argued that holidays with pay would inevitably improve the health of the working population and consequently improve their labour efficiency, so cancelling out any cost rise in the long run. Payment for holidays would also have an important employment multiplier effect since some trade unionists argued that manual workers would spend their wages in ways which would help the catering industry, the seaside resorts and transport industries.

In putting forward amendments, several Conservative members stressed that they did not disagree with the principle of holidays with pay, but could not accept the Bill as it stood. They argued that a measure as general as this ought to be fully discussed by all interested parties—Government, employers and employees' representatives—with a view to estimating the effects on the traditional machinery of negotiation, and only then should the Government contemplate action. Secondly, it was argued that many industries would be unable to bear the added cost of holidays without passing on the increase to the consumer, and this would ultimately lead to unemployment; in this context, agriculture, shipping, mining and the heavy industries were specifically mentioned.

The attitude of the Government was ambiguous. The Parliamentary Secretary to the Minister of Labour, whilst wholeheartedly accepting the principle of the Bill, felt that it was too simply drafted and did not cover many of the important intricacies, such as the period and type of qualifications, the question of contributory or non-contributory schemes, and the methods and amounts of wage payment during holidays. More important from the point of view of progress of the Bill, he could not give any guarantee that the Government would find time for the further stages of the Bill, and although

[1] This figure covered all employees whether manual or non-manual.

the amendment was defeated and the Bill given a Second Reading and passed to a Standing Committee, it made no further legislative progress. During the Committee stage the Government promised to conduct extensive discussions with the employers and unions on the subject and as late as June 19, 1930, the Minister of Labour told the original proposer of the Bill, Mr E. Winterton, that these discussions were continuing.[1] After this date nothing more was heard of the matter, and even the persistent Mr Winterton remained silent.[2] Later evidence suggests that the discussions were deferred due to the economic depression of 1930–1931.[3]

In 1936 the issue was again vigorously debated in Parliament, mainly because the Government decided to abstain from voting on an I.L.O. Draft Convention which called for annual paid holidays of at least six working days for all persons with one year's continuous service.[4] Labour members pressed the Government to introduce legislation on the question and in November 1936, introduced a Private Member's Bill similar in content to that of 1929. This received an extremely full debate on the Second Reading and was passed to a Standing Committee, but at this stage the Government intervened by calling for a full investigation of the matter, and subsequently in March of 1937 appointed a Committee of Inquiry under Lord Amulree

'to investigate the extent to which holidays with pay are given to employed workpeople and the possibility of extending the provision of such holidays by statutory enactment or otherwise; and to make recommendations.'

The Committee took just over a year to make its report (April 1938) but in the interim there was a great increase in the number of collective agreements granting holidays with pay to manual workers. In July 1937, the employers in the engineering industry reached agreements with the unions over increased wage rates and holidays with pay for all workers.[5] Approximately 600,000 workers were covered by this agreement and other major industries quickly followed this important precedent. In September the first local agreement covering coalminers was negotiated in the Nottinghamshire coalfield, and similar agreements rapidly spread throughout the min-

[1] H.O.C. of that date.

[2] He lost his seat at the General Election of October 1931.

[3] Report of the Committee on Holidays with Pay: op. cit., p. 6.

[4] The Government felt that the whole question of 'intermittent employment' should be examined before International Regulations could be framed, and they favoured the continual discussion of this problem with a view to extending holidays with pay.

[5] For each full week's work performed there was credited to the employee, as an ex gratia allowance in respect of holidays, a sum representing 1/50th of the appropriate daytime rate plus time workers' bonuses. These credits were accumulated in a special holiday fund and paid out at recognized holiday times.

ing industry. The shipbuilding industry followed the pattern early in 1938, as did the production side of the steel industry. With this concentrated period of collective agreements the number of workers enjoying paid holidays almost trebled within two years. From an April 1936 figure of 1½ million—a figure which had remained almost static for more than ten years—the coverage increased to 4 millions.

There can be little doubt that the rapid increase in the number and coverage of new collective agreements, originally initiated by the aftermath of the I.L.O. discussions, and the setting up of the Committee of Enquiry, resulted from the desire of the employers to preserve the principle of voluntary collective bargaining, and in particular to prevent a matter with such important cost implications from becoming the subject of legislation. In addition, it was probably felt that legislation would only apply to those who had no agreements in force, and employers were anxious not to have harsher legal conditions imposed on them than they could secure by collective bargaining. It is also plain that by 1937 many industrialists felt able to sanction expenditure on holidays for manual workers in view of the general improvement in the level of aggregate demand and the fall in unemployment.[1] It is significant that the extension of holidays with pay agreements in 1937 and 1938 coincided with sizeable net increases in wage rates and net decreases in hours of labour, as it had done in 1919. Moreover, by 1937 the average level of wages had for the first time in the thirties climbed back to the level gained in 1924.[2] It was against this background of improved labour conditions and a considerable extension of the number of employees receiving paid holidays, that the Amulree Committee held its meetings.

3. *The Amulree Committee 1937–1938*

The first task of the Committee was to make some assessment of the number of 'employed workpeople' who were receiving holidays with pay and after considering the various possible interpretations of this phrase, the Committee decided . . .

'workpeople coming within the employment field including unemployed who are either manual or non-manual workers in receipt of not more than £250 per annum.'

The total of workpeople covered by this definition was greatly in excess of the number classified as receiving holidays with pay under the Ministry of Labour estimates.[3] Thus the Committee estimated

[1] In the middle of 1936 unemployment fell below the 2 million mark for the first time in five years.

[2] See Ministry of Labour *Gazette*, February 1938, p. 85.

[3] The Ministry figures related only to collective (and not private) agreements and left out 'large numbers of salaried clerks and shop assistants and other salaried employees who were regularly granted holidays with pay'.

that out of a total of 18½ million employed workpeople approximately 7¾ million were in receipt of paid holidays. This total was made up in the following way:

(a) Three million manual wage-earners covered by collective agreements at the beginning of March 1938.

(b) One and three-quarter million clerks, draughtsmen and typists.

(c) One million shop assistants.

(d) Half a million other salaried employees and workers on standing wages.

(e) A quarter of a million manual wage-earners covered by arrangements other than collective agreements.

(f) One million in public administration and defence.

(g) Three-quarters of a million domestic staff and miscellaneous occupations.

The Committee gave several reasons why there were as many as ten and three-quarter million workers not provided with paid holidays. First, many workers were in industries where 'the conditions of employment', or 'the nature of the employment contract', made it difficult to conclude agreements. Here the Committee was clearly referring to seasonal, casual and 'high turnover' work, as in agriculture and building. Secondly, there were industries which were subject to severe foreign competition and consequently only able to absorb any cost increase, such as paid holidays, by passing this on to the consumer and thus causing unemployment. The examples of coal-mining, cotton and wool textiles, and shipping were specifically given. Thirdly, there were many workers in small and miscellaneous industries and in trades where industrial organization was weak who were not covered by paid holidays.

On the basis of these figures and classifications, the Committee then considered the case for extending the principle of holidays with pay by statutory enactment or by other means. Evidence in favour of legislative action was given by the T.U.C. representing four million workpeople, 'certain individual employees, social workers and publicists'. Their main contention was that paid holidays should be enjoyed by everyone for reasons of a broad social character connected with the development of human personality. Paid holidays would also contribute considerably to efficiency and better health by reducing industrial fatigue. Moreover, paid holidays enforced by statute would remove the unjustifiable distinction between manual and 'black-coated' workers, and would cover a large body of unorganized workpeople who seemed unlikely ever to receive the benefits which so many already enjoyed. Although it was recognized that the cost of paid holidays would vary from industry to industry, in no case was the rise in costs likely to be excessive, nor could the industries concerned claim that they could not afford to pay for this benefit to labour, since contemporary data suggested a substantial rise in profits for many industrial companies. In the light of this evidence the T.U.C. called for a statute which would guarantee 12 working days paid holiday exclusive of Bank and public holidays provided the worker had been in continuous employment for twelve months. For those who had not been employed for this length of time it was proposed that for each completed month of service at least one day's paid holiday would be given.[1]

The National Confederation of Employers Organizations, representing employers of over seven million workpeople, rejected this call for legislation, and argued that statutory enforcement on a question intimately related with the whole question of wages would undermine the system of joint negotiation and take away from employers and workers in each industry the freedom to decide what was best for those industries. They further stressed the view that a general statute would be unworkable since conditions between one industry and another varied tremendously. Their opposition was also expressed in disputing the claims made by the T.U.C. that the increased costs of a paid holiday could be borne by all industries. This, they said, was patently untrue, particularly of those export industries where any added cost rise of this kind would simply lead to a fall in revenue and a rise in unemployment and thus defeat the whole object of giving increased leisure. It was also argued that if there was any compulsory advance in labour costs (i.e. through paid holidays), this would have to be taken into account at any subsequent wage negotiation, despite the fact that employers had already made allowances for savings for holidays in previous wage agreements. This evidence seems to indicate that the solid opposition of the employers' organizations was mainly to the idea of the statutory enforcement of paid holidays and not to the principle itself, and this appears to be borne out by the rapid progress made in collective agreements at the time when the Amulree Committee was sitting.

It is quite clear that the Committee was impressed by both sets of arguments, those in favour of paid holidays by statute and those in favour of leaving the matter to traditional negotiating machinery, and in view of the rapid development of collective agreements its Report recommended that an annual holiday with pay statute should not be introduced until the Parliamentary Session 1940–1. It advocated that all industries lacking paid holiday agreements giving at least one week's holiday should make every possible effort to conclude a collective agreement and so avoid being covered by legislation. For those industries where employment was intermittent or with several employers throughout the year, the Report thought that the

[1] There were various other non-statutory proposals made for holidays with pay; but most speakers called for statutory enforcement.

introduction of a card system might be necessary so that various employers could contribute to the yearly holiday payment.

A further recommendation which was immediately accepted was that Trade Boards, Agricultural Wage Committees and any other statutory bodies set up to regulate minimum rates of wages should be empowered to consider and determine whether one week's paid holiday should be granted. This part of the Report was put into effect by the Holidays with Pay Act 1938, which provided for those areas of employment where employee organizations were weakest and where collective agreements providing holidays were least likely to be concluded.[1]

The position at the beginning of the Second World War, therefore, was one in which the long process of establishing the *principle* of paid holidays was almost completed. Voluntary agreements extended over a wide area of industry, and for those remaining without provision for paid holidays, all indications were that the Government, accepting the recommendations of the Amulree Committee, would introduce comprehensive legislation in the session 1940–1. Though the onset of war put paid to this last measure, the growth of negotiated paid holidays was most marked during the period 1940–5. Several influences helped to bring this about. In the first place, the Amulree Report led to renewed efforts for voluntary agreements on paid holidays; allied to this was the general spirit of management—labour co-operation which prevailed during the war and led to the setting up (or re-creation) of many Joint Industrial Councils which subsequently concluded general agreements on holidays with pay. Second, the Control of Employment and National Arbitration Order of 1940 also brought about a spread of collective agreements for it stipulated that conditions recognized by organizations representing a substantial proportion of employers and workers in any industry and district had to be observed by employers generally in that industry or district. Evidence of the growth of employers' acceptance of holidays with pay is found in the war-time holiday agreement covering the building and civil engineering industries which had generally been recognized as a difficult case because of the intermittent employment and frequent change of employer experienced by most employees. This paid holiday scheme was administered and interpreted by a special company known as 'Building and Civil Engineering Holidays Scheme Management Limited' on which were represented both parties to the agreement. The scheme required the employer to pay a weekly credit of 1/6d in the form of holiday stamps affixed to the operative's holiday credit card. Both stamps and cards were to be purchased by employers from the management

[1] By December 1938, ten Trade Boards and twenty-seven Agricultural Wage Committees had met to consider action according to the Act.

company and the operative was not entitled to holiday credit for any week during which he was wholly absent owing to sickness, accident or other cause or for any week during which the holiday was taken. All operatives were to be entitled to an annual holiday of six consecutive working days between April 1st and October 31st and a sum equal to the credits on his cards would be paid to him by his employer when the holiday was taken and the amount later recovered by the employer from the management company. The credit would be handed over by the operative to the employer on entering new employment in the same way as his insurance card.

In consequence of the many new agreements and wider application of existing agreements, extremely few workpeople were without at least one week's paid holiday by the end of the Second World War.

4. The Post-War Period

In the thirties the fight to establish the principle of holidays with pay for manual workers was waged largely on the grounds of equality and the general entitlement to an obvious right to enjoy leisure. Moreover, because of the low level of aggregate demand and the depressed state of some of the basic industries which at that time did not have holiday with pay agreements, those arguing for the general right to 'paid leisure' realized that success was unlikely to be speedy or general if the battle was fought out at a collective bargaining level. The campaign for holidays with pay therefore quickly resolved itself into a struggle over the necessity and practicality of general legislative provisions.

After the Second World War, a high level of aggregate demand and the continuing shortage of skilled and unskilled labour ensured a strong bargaining position for the individual unions, so that improvements in holiday provisions were rapidly obtained at the end of the war. In fact, by December 1946, there were over 1,100 collective agreements of all kinds (including agreements in individual companies) providing for holidays with pay for between eleven and twelve million wage-earners compared with ten million in 1944.[1] There had also been considerable improvements in the length of holidays: by the end of 1946 nearly all workers received six working days leave and six public holidays, but in a few cases these provisions had been extended to give twelve working days holiday with pay. As in 1919–20 these extended provisions were largely concentrated in the consumer goods industries such as boot and shoe manufacture, retail distributive trades and the public utilities such as electricity supply. Extensions of paid holidays had also been made under statutory orders in some Wages Council trades.

There were further additions in 1947, mostly in the food and drink

[1] Ministry of Labour *Gazette* 1946, p. 344.

(manufacturing) industries, and as a result of an arbitration tribunal award workers in the privately owned section of the road passenger transport industry received increased holidays with pay on completion of three years' service. By 1952, most of the major industries previously uncovered by general or district agreements granting two weeks paid holiday had made new agreements to this effect. In May 1952 the Ministry of Labour calculated that of the total number of wage-earners (including shop assistants) covered by agreements or statutory orders, more than two-thirds were entitled to paid holidays of twelve days or two weeks (exclusive of public holidays), but one-quarter to paid holidays of six days or one week, whilst the remaining workers were entitled to periods of intermediate duration. In productive industries, as distinct from service industries, more than two-thirds were entitled to at least twelve days or two weeks paid holiday.

By 1959, when the most recent Ministry of Labour survey was published, manual wage-earners in general were entitled to paid holidays and the improvements recorded since 1952 have taken the form of extensions in the duration of holidays. Since 1952 agreements providing longer holidays had been made principally in certain branches of mining and quarrying, wool textiles, building and civil engineering construction. The conclusion of the survey was that 'in very few industries are wage-earners entitled to only six days (or one week) of paid holidays and again in very few are they entitled to more than two weeks'.[1] This position remained substantially unchanged up to 1963, and by March 1964 it was estimated that 96 per cent of manual workers were entitled to basic holidays of two weeks, though about 15 per cent of this number are in industries where extra holidays may be given to long-service employees.[2]

III. THE THIRD WEEK

Though less than 3 per cent of manual workers are entitled to basic holidays of more than two weeks, there has been since the late 1950s a vocal if somewhat ineffectual campaign for a third week's holiday with pay by many of the larger trade unions. In contrast to the 1930s these union ambitions have been focused at the collective bargaining level rather than through centralized campaigns—Parliamentary debate on the advisability of extending holidays has been extremely infrequent—and such general claims as have appeared have pointed to superior holiday provisions in other countries and appealed for equality of British practice. However, in conditions favourable to union bargaining claims, longer holidays have been only one of the

[1] Example and quotation from Ministry of Labour *Gazette* 1959, p. 89.
[2] *Statistics on Incomes, Prices, Employment and Production, No. 8*, HMSO, March 1964; Section D.8.

many possible objectives of policy, and a less crucial one than such basic employment issues as improvements in wage rates and shorter hours.

It is, therefore, the policies and actions of individual unions which are important in determining the strength of the third week movement. Though the topic has been discussed regularly at T.U.C. level, the General Council has not attempted in recent years to seek legislation, nor even to present to the Government the co-ordinated views on holidays with pay of all affiliated trade unions.[1] The debate at the 1960 Annual Congress on a motion calling upon the General Council 'to use all endeavour to establish three weeks' holiday with pay throughout industry' is most instructive. Mr Harry Douglas argued on behalf of the General Council that each union must decide upon its own priorities when it was seeking benefits for its members since some might want longer holidays with pay, others a shorter working week, and consequently . . .

'if unions themselves accept the fact that the unions in the individual industries must decide the priorities then the General Council will view with more favour, a third week's holiday with pay, and accept and support the motion.'[2]

The policy subsequently adopted by the General Council has been wholly consistent with this attitude. At the 1962 Congress, for example, the General Council announced that they had assisted those unions giving high priority to the need for three weeks' holiday, by supplying them with domestic and foreign information on holidays with pay together with arguments and statistics in favour of their objective,[3] though at the 1963 Congress holidays with pay appeared only as an adjunct to a resolution on shorter hours of work.[4]

In terms of the growth of holidays with pay, then, the actions of individual unions are most important. One of the first unions to aim at the third week's holiday was the Association of Engineering and Shipbuilding Draughtsmen. There is evidence that as early as 1955 several individual companies were conceding this objective to long-service draughtsmen. By 1957, the Clerical and Administrative Workers Union had also been successful in achieving longer paid vacations for clerks, and most of these agreements were also conditioned by service qualifications. By 1959, various groups of em-

---

[1] It is interesting to note that at the Annual T.U.C. Congresses of 1944, 1945, 1946, motions were carried seeking legislation for two consecutive weeks holiday. In 1947, 1948, 1949, the General Council was able to persuade delegates that legislative provisions needed further consideration in view of the need for increased production and the benefits which a shorter week had conferred.

[2] T.U.C. Congress *Annual Report* 1960: p. 345.

[3] T.U.C. Congress *Annual Report* 1962; p. 126.

[4] T.U.C. Congress *Annual Report* 1963; p. 454.

ployees in the public service—including Post Office workers, prison and fire service officers and policemen—had all achieved a third week's holiday. The success of these groups induced many of the major unions to attempt to obtain the third week for manual workers. In April 1960 the electricity supply industry became the first large industry to agree to extra holidays for its manual workers, and the N.U.G.M.W. won a claim before the Industrial Court in March 1961 which awarded all gas industry workers with ten years' service three extra days holiday, with a full week extra for those with fifteen years' service. It is highly significant that the first three week coverage of manual workers should come in the public utility sector, for the gas and electricity industries were amongst the first industries to concede both the first and second weeks' paid holiday to manual workers. In these instances it could be a combination of rising demand for the industries' products, low labour-cost content, and continuous processes which lend themselves to phased holidays, which account for the ability and willingness of the employers to allow these claims. With important precedents behind them, both the E.T.U. and the N.U.G.M.W. can now seek equality of practice for their members in other industries and perhaps reduce the service qualifications for those who have already obtained longer holidays. Other major unions vary their tactics for achieving the third week. For example, the N.F.B.T.O. does not wish to press a claim based on service differentials in an industry in which movement in and out of the trade is high. Instead the union simply presses for three weeks' holiday for all manual workers regardless of their length of service.[1] This would be strenuously opposed by the employers if the union asks for the third week in the summer at a time when the building industry is busiest.

IV. THE FUTURE TREND IN HOLIDAYS WITH PAY

This description of the preliminary skirmishes in the third week battle leaves unanswered the major question on holidays with pay, whether longer holidays, and particularly the third week, will in the near future be granted to many British manual workers. Opinions differ on this. The Ministry of Labour believed in September 1963 that the situation then—with less than 3 per cent of workers having more than two weeks basic holiday—was unlikely to change very much in the near future,[2] and certainly progress had thus far been small, though the six months since then has seen longer holidays granted in a number of cases. So much depends on such factors as

[1] See later discussion.
[2] *Statistics on Incomes, Prices, Employment and Production*, No. 6, HMSO, September 1963; Section D.8.

the bargaining strategy of individual unions, their success in other claims, the profitability of industries, and the reaction of Government, these render very doubtful any prediction as to whether (or when) the third week will become general. One authority offers the tentative opinion that the early 1970s will see three weeks' holiday as a generally accepted condition of employment.[1] Nonetheless, it appears that some *extension* of holidays is likely, even if on a much more gradual basis than the conferring of another week's holiday.

There are three main issues to be discussed here. First, what are the economic costs of extra holidays, and for simplicity we shall here deal mainly with the third week; secondly, is it desirable that extra holidays should be granted only to certain types of employees; and thirdly, should Britain come more into line with Continental practice by providing a legal minimum duration for holidays?

1. *The Cost of Extra Holidays*

The cost of extra holidays will obviously vary from industry to industry and according to the method by which the extra days are allocated. Broadly, there seem to be four main methods of taking an extra week's holiday. First, it can simply form a consecutive addition to an existing summer holiday to give three weeks; secondly, the extra week might be split into two or three shorter periods and added to already existing public holidays, for example at Christmas or Easter, so as to give several breaks of four or five days length; thirdly, some employers allow their work-force to choose the days on which the extra holidays are to be taken. The N.C.B. for example allows some 'rest days' to be selected at a local level, so that the labour force can attend local functions of interest.[2] Finally, it is possible to specify a holiday period during which time the extra leave is taken at the discretion of the individual employee. In the first three examples cited, producing units normally close down altogether, whereas in the fourth, the extra week is not associated with a shutdown.

We shall here consider only the costs of holidays as they affect the individual employer. Clearly the interrelations between holidays in different parts of industry are also very important; if, for example, a supplying firm closes down for holidays, this may lead to shortages of vital components in an assembly firm and consequent loss of output. This has been a continual problem in the motor industry

[1] Hugh Clegg, *Implications for Management of Longer Standard Holidays*, Occupational Papers No. 9; British Institute of Management, 1963.

[2] The N.U.M. and the N.C.B. have agreed to seven extra 'rest days' for miners, instead of the original N.U.M. claim for a shorter working week. The agreement, effective from May 1, 1964, allows miners to take two rest days consecutively (and no more) and stipulates that four rest days are to be taken when the collieries are already closed, e.g. Christmas or Easter. *The Guardian*, January 17, 1964.

and the trade unions in that industry have prepared a common plan under which all motor manufacturing plants will close during the same two week summer period.[1] This type of plan is very necessary for industry, but it cuts right across the hopes of the Government as expressed in the Board of Trade's recent paper on staggered holidays. This suggested that the only way to reduce the present congestion and overloading of holiday and transport facilities would be to induce people to take 'secondary' holidays outside the summer months during which most holidays are at the moment concentrated, since it was unlikely that the number of main holidays taken outside the congested months could be increased. (The motor industry plan will in fact increase the concentration of holidays in June and July.) The conclusion was that 'any solution for the situation revealed must depend mainly on action which only private individuals and bodies can take, [and though] most of the changes would not themselves be matters for direct Government action, it does not seem likely that they would be made except in the context of a concerted national effort'.[2] This might well take the form of discouragement of a third week added to present summer holidays, in favour of one of the other methods described above.

Bearing this in mind, then, we can delineate four potential economic costs to the individual firm of the extra week's holiday—production loss, under-utilization of fixed capital, administrative expense and holiday payments.

(a) *Loss of Output*. When one week's holiday with pay was granted in any industry it was thought by many that over the year there would be no loss of output, since a man's efficiency would so benefit from the rest from work that increased productivity would result in as much being produced in fifty-one weeks as had previously come from the full year. This argument in terms of some increase in efficiency can be applied to the second week of paid holidays, though whether the production loss can be entirely offset by higher productivity is doubtful. Some of those in favour of the third week have concentrated on its psychological revitalising effects, rather than stressing its physical effects. As one speaker at the T.U.C. Annual Congress put it : 'holidays are for the mental peace of the worker, so that he can begin to feel relaxed and give deeper appreciation to the things that are around him, the beauties of nature, and so on.'[3]

[1] *Financial Times*, January 10, 1964. The plan only applies to members of the Engineering Employers' Federation.

[2] 'Staggered Holidays', Ministry of Labour *Gazette*, August 1963; p. 313. A recent debate in Parliament announced changes in school examination dates and a postponement of August Bank Holiday which it is hoped will facilitate staggered holidays. See *The Guardian*, February 13, 1964.

[3] T.U.C. *Annual Report* 1961; p. 416.

T

There are so many imponderables here that it is impossible to forecast what precise effect the third week would have on aggregative output, but it is unlikely that the efficiency of the labour force would be significantly improved and from this standpoint it seems inevitable that the extra week's holiday will simply mean one week's loss of production with a consequent increase in unit costs.

There may, of course, be individual instances in which this loss of output is minimized by especially favourable circumstances, as for example in industries with a demand lowpoint at the time of the extra week, or in trades where output can be built up prior to the holiday break and increased stocks delivered to distributors to cover the lengthened shutdown. Of course this may involve firms in premium rate payments to workers and distributors during the pre-holiday period, and these extra costs must be offset against the minimization of lost output.

This ability to stockpile the product appears to be one of the main considerations permitting the use of the rest days scheme in the N.C.B., and it may even be that the loss of output in this scheme is very low since frequently single-day holidays, taken throughout the year, may have a better effect on 'after holiday output', than the effect of a consecutive week added to the existing summer or public holidays.[1] In those industries where stockpiling is impossible, e.g. electricity supply, or where the nature of the product precludes long shutdowns or frequent short shutdowns, e.g. service or continuous process industries, extra holidays would have to be taken at the individual's discretion within a specified holiday period. Whether this method involves a serious loss of output will depend on such factors as the level of demand during the holiday period, whether labour can be easily redeployed, or whether the loss of one worker seriously affects the output of a particular group.[2]

There may be further net production advantages of the extra holiday and particularly for the third summer week, not in terms of the ability to maintain supplies, but in using the works shutdown for the thorough overhaul of equipment, or for trying out new techniques of production, introducing new lay-outs or tooling up for new lines. To take one of these possibilities, summer servicing of equipment may be extremely useful particularly in industries where winter coincides with peak demand, optimum capital utilization and minimum servicing of equipment: the electricity supply industry provides a good example of this.

[1] The administrative costs of such schemes may however be high: see part (c) of this section.

[2] It is not only the absence of direct productive workers which may effect output: the absence of supervisors may cause a reduction of output, while under-staffing of checking inspectors may mean a reduction in output quality, with a rise in the rate of defective products.

All of these methods of minimizing the effects on output of the third week do not however, contradict the general conclusion of some increase in direct costs, for all the measures mentioned above either involve extra work and cost preparatory to the shutdown, or the presence of some manual workers and some managers during the shutdown at premium rates,[1] or in cases where a shutdown is impossible the continual administrative and supervisory problem of ensuring that an adequate labour force is always on hand.

(b) *Under-Utilization of Fixed Capital.* If the holiday period cannot be used for capital servicing, or plant improvements, then a loss of productive time due to holidays, will probably result in fixed capital assets being under-utilized with a consequent rise in unit costs of production. Of course, if a firm wishes to run its capital equipment at full stretch, it can do so by hiring labour at premium rates; in this case there will be no 'capital' cost, but unit costs of production will be increased because of higher labour costs. Let us assume here, though, that equipment is being used at less than optimum output. With hired machinery or equipment bought with a specific asset life (both in terms of time and utilization) an additional week's holiday simply means that hiring charges or the initial acquisition cost of the equipment must be spread over a smaller volume of output than was considered economic at the time of hiring or acquisition. This obviously is equally true of all fixed operating costs, such as rent and rates, though once again the actual effect of the under-utilization of fixed assets on unit costs will vary from industry to industry. Generally speaking industries with short-life capital assets (e.g. transfer equipment in car plants) attempt to use 'round-the-clock' utilization, and a shutdown for an extra week may mean that the lost productive time cannot be regained before the assets are replaced. Thus, if in those industries with short-life assets, and fixed costs as a high proportion of total costs at a given level of output, an extra week's holiday may result in a noticeable rise in unit costs.

(c) *Administrative Expense.* Little is known of the administrative expenses associated with extended holidays, but logically the incremental time spent by staff employees in arranging holidays, notifying employees, paying holiday pay and the material costs of keeping records of entitlement to extra holidays, should all be included as costs of the extra week. Where the holiday is taken as an extended summer vacation or added to existing public holidays these marginal administrative costs may not be high. Holidays phased over a long

---

[1] Administrative expense may increase since arrangements must be made for these holiday workers to receive days in lieu at a later date. See (c) below.

period or where entitlement to extra days is tied to factors such as service or attendance require detailed records so that deputies can be appointed, and in these cases administrative expense in the form of staff time may be considerable.

(d) *Holiday Pay.* The data in Chapter 3 shows that most companies spent between 4 and 6 per cent of payroll on annual and public holidays so that each week accounted for about 2 per cent of payroll. But the majority of British manual workers do not receive holiday pay based on their earnings. In the enquiry by the University of Glasgow, about 80 per cent of workers got holiday pay related to their basic rate with, in many cases, some percentage addition to that rate, the formula being agreed by collective bargaining. Only 14 per cent of workers were paid according to earnings in some predetermined time period.[1]

These figures raise two issues. First, if most workers are given holiday pay based on earnings, is the rise in payroll costs likely to be more or less than one-fiftieth of total payroll costs? Secondly, if holiday pay is substantially less than normal earnings, is this likely to cause social hardship to workers receiving the third week. The answer to both these questions once again varies from industry to industry and between companies within industries. A detailed survey of holiday payments within twenty-three metal manufacturing companies,[2] for example, showed that 13 per cent of companies made holiday payments at the basic rate, 52 per cent paid the basic rate plus one sixth of that rate, and 35 per cent paid according to earnings, some with a stipulated maximum. An analysis of engineering industry payments[3] for holidays shows even more complicated arrangements, with a great variety of methods of reaching pay assessments, some even including deductions for absenteeism and 'hours lost'. The most common method of payment was basic rate plus one-sixth which was found in companies employing about two-thirds of the industry labour force. Less than 30 per cent of employees were simply paid the basic rate, and 6 per cent of all employees received holiday pay based on their earnings.[4] These figures suggest that in many industries the rise in payroll costs due to the third week would be something less than 2 per cent, though it is clearly possible that in some companies, and at some periods, when little overtime is worked, payment at the standardized basic rate plus one-sixth may be near the average of

---

[1] Most of these workers were in textiles, or in bricks, pottery and glass.

[2] Based on Glasgow University inquiry data.

[3] Both metal manufacture and engineering are normally regarded as 'earnings' industries, industries where average earnings are often far in excess of basic rates.

[4] These figures should be regarded as approximate, since in some cases the exact formula for holiday pay was not clear. It is certain, though, that less than 10 per cent of employees were paid at the full rate of earnings.

employee earnings, and in these instances the rise in payroll costs would be about 2 per cent. Yet this does not alter the conclusion that the widespread existence of basic rate payments, the limitations put on holiday pay based on earnings, and the exclusion in most cases of bonuses, all indicate that the increase in payroll costs due to an extra week's holiday will be less than 2 per cent.

It is sometimes suggested that workers who are paid at the basic rate during holidays may be unwilling to take a third week's holiday if the amount of earnings thereby foregone would have been well above the basic rate. There is no doubt that a substantial number of workers in high-earnings industries do receive a basic holiday pay which is less than normal earnings, and even basic rate plus one-sixth may not approximate to an average of normal earnings. But hardship in these cases is likely to be minimized since, where holiday pay as some function of basic rate is much less than average earnings, earnings themselves are likely to be high, and savings for holidays would therefore be possible. The problem of the basic rate payments remains and although the figures given do not of themselves prove hardship, they suggest that if the third week is taken many workers normally paid on piece-rates, for example, may find they will have to save for this week in order to prevent a reduction in their normal weekly consumption pattern.[1]

(e) *The Aggregate Costs of the Third Week.* The effect of extra holidays on labour costs therefore depends on whether payment is at basic rate or earnings, and in the latter case whether holiday pay is truly representative of normal earnings. But even if we assume for simplicity that a third week would mean an additional 2 per cent of annual wage costs being spent on holidays, the effect on labour costs will vary widely between industries and firms. Table 29 in Chapter 3 showed the wide range of wage costs as a proportion of total costs, with, at the extremes food, drink and tobacco, in which wage costs were only about 6½ per cent of total costs, and shipbuilding, where wage costs accounted for about 31 per cent of total costs. A very approximate indication was given in that table of how a 2 per cent increase in fringe benefit costs—the increase which a third week's holiday would mean—might affect total labour costs in manufacturing industries. The proportion which fringe benefit costs form of total labour costs would increase, on average, from 2·15 per cent to 2·46 per cent: the maximum increase is in shipbuilding, from 2·94 per cent to 3·55 per cent. On this evidence, the effect of the third week would be small, but there will be considerable variation within industries, and it is probable that the third week would cost much

[1] This may be especially true if the third week is taken consecutively in the summer.

more in non-manufacturing and in service industries such as distribution and transport.

This calculation has not been extended to estimate the additional administrative and capital costs of an extra week's holiday, and although the foregoing discussion suggested that in some instances they may be considerable, it is not possible to predict the exact incidence. We have also assumed that there are no future benefits coming from increased productivity, or savings through utilization of the holiday period for maintenance or changing production lay-outs. The net result of all of these factors is probably that even in manufacturing industries holidays are more expensive, because of administrative and capital costs, than the estimates in the previous paragraph, though an extra week would be unlikely to add as much as 1 per cent to total costs in most industries.

2. Paid Holidays for Special Groups

Whatever the actual costs of a third week's holiday, employer reactions to union claims for longer holidays for the whole work-force have generally been unfavourable because of the excessive cost, especially as the holiday claim has normally been tied to a wage demand which unions have been unwilling to drop. Consequently in many of the agreements for longer holidays which have so far been concluded, employers have attempted to minimize the extra costs by granting longer holidays only to particular groups of workers, often those with long service. This approach has the merit of allowing the employer to reward employees for long service, and may also be aimed at reducing turnover, though its efficacy in this respect must be somewhat doubtful since young workers who are most mobile are not affected and the older workers to whom the policy applies tend to be highly immobile in any case.

There are disadvantages for both unions and employers in holidays based on long service. Obviously only a small number of employees will actually receive the longer holiday, especially since redundancy or turnover could mean that few attain the necessary service qualifications. This may not be important in industries with fairly stable employment and a low rate of labour turnover—commonly industries with a high proportion of skilled workers—but in many industries service qualifications would need to be fairly short, as for example, in building and parts of engineering: in these industries trade unions would concentrate on seeking longer holidays for all workers. The most important disadvantage to the employer is the inconvenience of having part of his work-force off on holiday while the majority of employees are still at work. The Board of Trade survey in 1960 showed that three-quarters of manufacturing firms shut down for annual holidays. Such a close-down is impossible where only part of the work-force enjoys extra holidays and since long-service employees tend to be skilled men or those in supervisory positions, their absence on holiday may cause considerable difficulties in re-phasing production or leave the plant undersupervised.

There are other criteria on which to define special groups of employees to whom extra holidays might be given. In Europe, for example, it is common for young workers and those in dangerous occupations to be accorded longer holidays.[1] There has recently been in this country more extensive use of arguments based on improving the status of workers whose tasks are said to be increasingly complex or responsible, or whose jobs are changing and moving into the 'white-collar' bracket,[2] for these workers extra holidays are sought as proof of their 'staff position'. The negotiation of benefits on such intangible grounds as these could, however, lead to continual differential claims from unions representing various groups of employees, each of whom feel themselves to be just as deserving as every other special group. Management might then find itself faced with a leap-frogging situation, in which the variety of holiday provisions would be a constant bone of contention. The administrative inconveniences both of protracted negotiations and in the establishment of criteria for special group status appear to be strong arguments in favour of standard extra holidays for all employees.

However we must not theorize too much on what is essentially a subject for collective bargaining in the individual firm. For both management and unions an agreement according extra holidays to a special group, be they long-service employees or 'staff operatives', may be perfectly satisfactory. Both sides may feel themselves to have scored a victory. Management may consider they have limited the cost increase, while the unions can feel the agreement to be the thin end of the wedge, and that they have secured a position from which further extension of holidays will be possible.

3. *Holidays with Pay and Statutory Considerations*
Since 1945, the development of holidays with pay has depended almost entirely on the action of individual unions and employers in negotiations. At no time has the Government attempted to impose holiday provisions by statute, nor has it even accepted responsibility for bringing international recommendations to the notice of those who make collective agreements. The British Government reply to an I.L.O. proposed recommendation on paid holidays is a model of caution in its adherence to the 'voluntary' approach to

---

[1] See Part 3 of this section.

[2] One large electrical engineering company conceded large holidays to their draughtsmen in order to cut down turnover and in so doing openly accepted the 'staff status' of this group.

industrial bargaining; it concludes that the acceptance of this responsibility by the Government or the suggestion that decisions on holidays should be framed in conformity with the Resolution 'would be contrary to the principles upon which industrial relations in the U.K. are based'.[1] Neither side of industry has been particularly in favour of legislation. The British Employers' Confederation are firm upholders of the voluntary principle, while the T.U.C. has been disinclined to do more than acknowledge holidays as one legitimate goal for which unions may aim. The General Council has recognized the right of unions to choose their own bargaining priorities.[2]

It is difficult, therefore, to pretend that there has been a demand for legislative provision of holidays, from either side of industry. But if we accept the philosophy that paid holidays are a basic right which all workers ought to enjoy on equal terms and to an increasing degree, the case for legislation is stronger. For at present this right is being limited by current methods of bargaining which are not only protracted but inequitable, in the sense that longer holidays are granted to the most powerful and persistent claimants or to those in 'welfare-minded' firms or in certain industries where labour costs are comparatively unimportant. The less fortunate workers in other industries only achieve equality of treatment after many years, and may soon fall behind again as longer holidays are once more granted in the leading industries.

On grounds of equality, then, the solution might be for the Government to stipulate a minimum holiday period which all workers with a given number of years' service would enjoy: for example, a worker might get two weeks after one year, and three weeks after five years' service. This move would, however, be welcomed neither by unions nor by employers. For one thing, employers in all industries would find their labour costs compulsorily increased and refuse to grant other claims which individual unions might regard as much more important. On the other hand, it would allow powerful unions to concentrate on wage claims if they did not have to consider holidays, now legislated, as one possible bargaining issue. A most important related issue is that both sides of industry would lose part of their cherished freedom to settle terms and conditions of employment by collective bargaining. It is a debatable point whether the sacred cow of 'free collective bargaining' should now be tethered, if not done to death. What is certain is that unions and management would resent legal regulation of this kind and would fight strongly to resist it. From the point of view of the national economy too, a legal minimum holiday would be disadvantageous, since it would add to costs in labour-

[1] International Labour Office, *Holidays with Pay*, Geneva, 1954; p. 6.
[2] The 1960 T.U.C. *Annual Report*, p. 345, makes this clear. At the 1963 Conference, longer holidays were mentioned only once in passing during the debates.

intensive industries, with probable price increases as a consequence. Workers in these industries would in the long run get longer holidays through the normal collective bargaining process, but a fairly sudden legal extension of holidays would not allow employers to phase the increases over periods when the effect of the extra cost on prices could be minimized.

For these reasons, then, a legislated holiday period seems unlikely. More to the point, it seems unnecessary since there is effectively a minimum holiday period of two weeks and any firm not providing this would be at a considerable disadvantage in attracting labour. Also, trade unions seem content to let the third week or other extra holidays spread by ordinary bargaining procedures; the speed of extension will undoubtedly be a function of the strength of unions' desire for longer holidays, for the third week might be roughly equivalent in cost terms to the foregoing of about half of one year's wage claim. The only advantage of legislation—and this is not an unmixed blessing—is that it would bring about speedily what the normal collective bargaining process will eventually bring in any case.

TABLE 70. *Annual and Public Holidays in Britain and Europe* 1963

COUNTRY	ANNUAL HOLIDAY		PUBLIC HOLIDAYS	NOTES
	STATUTORY	COLLECTIVE AGREEMENT		
Belgium	12 days	—	10–15 days	—
France	18–24 days	—	1–5 days	Most industries now give 24 days annual holiday.
Germany	15–18 days	Variable	10–13 days	95 per cent of workers get 18 days annual holiday or more; extra days according to age.
Italy	10 days	2–8 days	17 days	Extra days annual holiday for long service.
Netherlands	6 days (minimum)	13-18 days	7 days	Statutory 6 days applies only to those not covered by collective agreement. Extra days may be given for long service.
United Kingdom	—	12–18 days	5–6 days	97 per cent of workers have 12 days annual holiday.

Source: Ministry of Labour *Gazette*, October 1963.

Political circumstances may alter this state of affairs, for if Britain does eventually join the European Economic Community, it may be necessary for the Government to give a strong lead in the improvement of holiday provisions. Table 70 shows British and European practice in 1963.

Clearly, the holiday provisions in Europe were much more favourable, especially since the number of paid public holidays is larger in every country except France, ranging up to seventeen days in Italy. Article 120 of the Treaty of Rome provides that 'member States shall endeavour to maintain the existing equivalence of paid schemes', while further articles, construed together, stipulate that members will promote the improvement of living and working conditions so as to permit 'the equalization of such conditions in an upward direction', and machinery is to be provided to prevent any disparity between legislative provisions and administrative enforcement of working conditions which could distort the process of competition within the Common Market.

If British holiday provisions were to be 'harmonized' with those of the Six, there would have to be a very rapid spread of longer holidays. This would not presuppose legislation, for the Government could simply announce the period within which holidays had to be extended and the minimum provisions which would apply at the end of the period. The *timing* of longer holidays would still be a matter for the processes of collective bargaining, though the employer would be negotiating to some extent under the shadow of impending legislation. Then, of course, trade unions would be anxious to lift holiday provisions as far as possible above the legal minimum. Whatever arrangements were made, the rôle of Government would be very different from its views, expressed in 1954 and quoted above, since it would require to persuade or coerce both sides of industry to fall into line. It is obvious that the extension of longer paid holidays would be a much more rapid and uniform process (as well as a more painful one for some industries) if Britain did join the Common Market.

V. CONCLUSION

This summary of the implications of the extension of paid holidays, and in particular the third week, is inevitably conditioned by numerous uncertainties. Even leaving aside the variety of forms which the third week can take, it is clear that the magnitude and incidence of cost varies from industry to industry, not only because the labour element in total costs is not the same in any two industries, but also as a direct result of the varying administrative complexity of arranging such extended holidays. Morever, our ignorance of the effects of extra holidays upon labour productivity, or of the compensating advantages which the close-down of a plant can bring, means that the net economic costs to the employer or the economy as a whole of giving longer paid holidays cannot accurately be assessed. Finally, the existence in many industries of agreements allocating extra holidays only to long-service employees adds another uncertainty to any aggregative estimate of cost, since this would have to cover such factors as the likely turnover, absenteeism, redundancy and other factors which affect the proportion of the labour force qualifying for longer holidays.

Research into all of these considerations would obviously remove some of the imponderables which at present bedevil any economic argument over the extension of holidays, but it cannot remove what may be the major uncertainty surrounding the method by which longer holidays are to be attained. For a political decision alone can determine whether the U.K. joins the Common Market and accepts the Treaty of Rome; this would inevitably introduce a greater element of regulation and conformity in British paid holiday practice.

If Britain does not join the Common Market then the extension of the third week and longer holidays in general will be a lengthy process, since the evidence suggests that there is no substantial demand, by any of the interested parties, for statutory enforcement of longer holidays. Nor apparently is there likely to be an effective demand for longer holidays through collective bargaining, for recent negotiations indicate that while additional holidays do form part of many unions' priority list, they are not in the last resort thought to be as important as the more traditional aims, such as the shorter working week or the annual wage increase.

While arguments may rage about the method of providing holidays, the rates of payment, and speed of extending longer holidays to all workers, these are in a sense administrative questions. Holidays with pay are already one of the most important conditions of employment, and the predictable improvements in the standard of living and the increased demand for leisure of the average worker will result in the continuing development of longer and better paid holidays.

CHAPTER 11

COMPANY WELFARE BENEFITS

A. G. P. ELLIOT

I

Perhaps more than any other form of fringe benefit, the so-called welfare benefits—subsidized canteens, playing fields, social clubs and the like—are vestigial remains of the attitude of management in a different age. It is probably fair to say that their continued existence is due not merely to an active belief on the part of management that they are necessary for the efficient working of an industrial enterprise, but also in part to resistance to change. For change is clearly in the air. In the last ten years there has been both keener examination of the real costs of such benefits and a reappraisal of the effects which they have, particularly in an industrial society where real wages have been rising steadily and where affluence now extends to the shop-floor.

It would be facile, though possible, to trace the welfare concept back to the Middle Ages when the master stood *in loco parentis* to his apprentices. More plausibly, it might be attributed to the depression which followed the Napoleonic Wars and which resulted in a general movement towards defining minimum conditions for workers, at least partly because of the emergence of trade unionism. This has expression in the limited legislation of 1819 and the Factory Act of 1833 which was the basis of nineteenth-century reform. In 1831, too, the nineteen acts regulating payment in truck were replaced by a general prohibition of payment of wages in goods; the truck system had been extensively used in many trades during the latter half of the eighteenth century, and it had enabled employers to beat down real wages by forcing employees to take part in their remuneration in kind, or spend part of their incomes at company shops.[1] The aboli-

[1] See G. W. Hilton, *The Truck System*, Cambridge, 1960. Hilton (p. 40) quotes estimates that the cost advantage to a company operating a truck shop was generally about 10 per cent on wages, though some goods were over-valued by 35 per cent or more. The loss of annual income to the individual worker was unlikely to be more than 10 per cent.

DOI: 10.4324/9781003184706-11

tion of these particular 'fringe benefits' was mourned by few employees.

The modern growth of company welfare facilities really stems from the last quarter of the nineteenth century. By this time the era of social reform had left its mark on industry in a variety of ways. The recently-established Factory Inspectorate had begun to make an impact generally, with its insistence that employers should consider their workers as human beings. It was at this time that several large firms instituted large-scale welfare undertakings such as the Bourneville Estate and the Port Sunlight scheme. Of course, the idea of company-provided housing for workers was not new. It had been implicit in Owen's New Lanark scheme some 100 years before, and had appeared in many schemes throughout the nineteenth century.[1] Sometimes companies were motivated by social or moral considerations, but often, too, the reason was mainly geographical. In the mining and textile industries, where the workplace might be rather isolated, a company often provided houses for workers to rent. The terms on which they did so—whether they were subsidized or exploited—were largely determined by the attitude of the employer, and 'mining communities were specially susceptible to the good or evil effects of the policy adopted by the employers to the general life of the village'.[2]

By the turn of the century, though, the company attitude to welfare was finding more general expression. By 1909 it was possible for Edward Cadbury to convene a three-day conference of employers on the subject of employee welfare, and three years later a Welfare Exhibition was held at Olympia.[3] Among the topics discussed were athletics and social clubs; these were by now encouraged as a means of promoting the physical well-being of employees, and the annual works outing subsidized wholly or in part by the employer had become a feature of progressive companies. World War I, with its proliferation of munitions factories staffed by women, brought in its train a host of problems, and the Government set up the Health of Munitions Workers Committee in 1915. On the basis of its recommendations,[4] legislation was introduced establishing welfare facilities in all munitions factories employing women. Firms were obliged to provide some fairly rudimentary catering facilities.

There, had of course, been sketchy provision in the Regulations for Dangerous Trades; the Paints and Colours Regulations of 1907,

[1] See W. Ashworth, *The Genesis of Modern British Town Planning*, London, 1954, Chapter V. This gives details of various types of scheme.

[2] Ibid., p. 130.

[3] See M. M. Niven, 'The Beginnings of the Institute', *Journal of the Institute of Personnel Management*, Vol. 29, March 1957, p. 30.

[4] Cmd. 8133.

for example, specified that 'The occupier shall provide . . . a dining room, unless all workers leave the factory during meal hours.' Following the Committee's report, however, the standard clause adopted in Welfare Orders made under Section 7 of the Police, Factories, etc. (Miscellaneous Provisions) Act 1916, was 'The occupier shall provide and maintain for the use of all persons employed in the factory and remaining on the premises during the meal intervals a suitable messroom, which shall be furnished with (a) sufficient tables and chairs or benches with back rests, (b) adequate means of warming food and boiling water, (c) suitable facilities for washing, comprising a sufficient supply of clean towels, soap and warm water. The messroom shall be sufficiently warmed for use during meal intervals. The messroom shall be separate from the cloakroom and shall be placed under the charge of a responsible person, and shall be kept clean.'

Today, the range of employee benefits on which companies may spend money is very wide. Housing is still provided for some manual workers, though with rising incomes, higher standards of public authority housing and better transport facilities this type of benefit is no longer as attractive to the worker as it once was; also the cost of housing has so increased that few companies are willing to undertake the necessary investment, except perhaps to attract or keep a top executive. Discounts on company products are often popular with employees though their cost to the company may be small, while such items as profit-sharing plans, stock purchase schemes and travel subsidies may be important in some companies.[1] However, more important than any of these are the two fringe benefits which are the stock-in-trade of welfare-minded companies and which the inquiry results in Chapter 3 showed to be commonest and most costly. These are the industrial canteen, and sports or social facilities. In the Glasgow inquiry covering the year 1960, over 90 per cent of sample companies had works canteens, at an average cost of just over 1 per cent of payroll; this was much the most expensive type of company welfare scheme.[2] The average cost of sports and social facilities was much less, 0·25 per cent of payroll, but they were present in almost two-thirds of sample companies. We shall therefore concentrate in this Chapter on these two types of benefit.

---

[1] It is interesting to speculate on the future of travel subsidies. As journey-to-work patterns change and the cost of travel rises, firms may become more anxious to grant specific subsidies on travel to individual employees rather than to give an all-round increase in wages to cover the increased cost of living.

[2] A recent Industrial Welfare Society survey of 160 companies showed that the average canteen subsidy per employee was 17s 2d per quarter.

II. INDUSTRIAL CANTEENS

It was in the 1920s that the industrial canteen burgeoned into full flower. The idea that employers should provide cheap, hot meals gained ground rapidly among those companies which considered themselves progressive. The depression of the 1930s and the rationing of the 1940s did nothing to undermine the notion, and it was not until the 1950s that the assumptions on which this type of welfare expenditure is based were seriously questioned.

Today almost every company of any size has a canteen—and, from the accounting point of view, an uneconomic canteen: Durham has stated flatly 'canteen subsidies are normal'.[1] In building a new factory it has been automatic to include a canteen. Only in central city offices has there been any marked deviation from this pattern, and here the alternative of tax-free luncheon vouchers has been widely used in recent years: the subsidy remains, even if the canteen has vanished. It is pertinent to enquire why cost-conscious managements continue to assume so heavy a financial burden on so wide a scale.

In few instances will there be a simple reason. The justification seems often to be compounded of emotion (not infrequently rationalized), acceptance of a social tradition, pressure from employees, and a serious consideration of the true cost of not having a canteen. Surprisingly, in many cases the question has never been examined in detail, and a canteen is regarded as inevitable. Legally this is not so: canteens or messrooms are obligatory only in factories engaged in a prescribed range of hazardous processes—a fact of which many managers appear to be ignorant.

The original welfare argument was based on the nutrition of workers: a canteen ensured that they had a decent meal in reasonable surroundings instead of a perpetual diet of sandwiches eaten in the unhygienic environment of the workshop. Canteens are subject to statutory regulations governing the handling of food and to inspection by public health authorities, and hence a minimum standard of cleanliness can be expected. The man who brings sandwiches and consumes them in the workplace, apart from offending the dietitian, is liable to have unclean hands, imperfectly washed utensils, and his mealtime break may be more difficult to control; in some industries the presence of food or drink may be a potential hazard to the material on which he is working (and vice versa, though it is here that legislation on the provision of canteens becomes operative). There is the possibility that food in the factory may attract vermin into it.

The same basic case often changes its emphasis so far as young

[1] See W. Durham, *The £.S.D. of Welfare in Industry*, Industrial Welfare Society, London 1958, p. 5.

people are concerned. Many companies whose canteen is already subsidized give concessions in the form of cheaper prices to young people, usually those below the age of 18. The thinking behind this appears to be largely concerned with diet: young people, so the argument runs, will, because they earn less than adults, concentrate on the cheap and filling items of food—or do without a meal—and as a result their diet will be deficient at a crucial period in their physical development.

These views, which may be described as essentially humanitarian considerations, probably carry less real weight than formerly. The improved general level of nutrition makes the factory meal less important, and in few industries are adolescent wages so low that young people are unwilling to pay for meals. In passing one is tempted to comment on the doubtful claims which are made for balanced canteen diets: snacks, rather than meals, are growing in popularity with office workers, and among manual workers fish and chips still remains a staple meal in many parts of the country.

A second factor, which is related to but distinct from the welfare justification, is the attitude that canteens are characteristic of good employers—that the company which has a canteen is *ipso facto* a desirable one from the point of view of employees. There appears to be little evidence to support this contention, and although it is rarely made explicitly, it is clear that many managers believe that a canteen is a benefit which is perceived as tangible proof of their firm's solicitude for its employees.

More important is the factor of pressure from employees or potential employees. This falls under two headings: the demand for a canteen, and attempts to influence canteen prices—and hence profit or loss. Generally there appears to have been little interest on the part of trade unions in asking for canteens as a benefit for their members. Nor do firms commonly expect overt demands for them from existing employees, although they do arise in certain circumstances. The small company which expands is one example: where a dozen employees may be content with facilities for making tea, expansion to a hundred may result in a demand for more elaborate provision. In the past there has been pressure to provide special facilities, apart from the main canteen for staff and executives, and many large companies have a hierarchy of dining rooms ranging from a works cafeteria to a lavishly-equipped suite with waitress service for management, which enable the outside observer to deduce an employee's status solely by checking which room he uses; the trend today, however, appears to be towards a reduction in the number of these levels. Younger managers appear to be less concerned with such niceties than were their forebears and do not regard the use of an efficient cafeteria as equivalent to sitting below the salt. Companies employing female labour are more likely to be asked for a canteen than those employing men, especially if the midday break is short: the task of rushing home to prepare a meal and getting back on time is clearly a heavy burden. Where a works is isolated, or employees are drawn from a long distance, there is likely to be more internal pressure.

Often, however, the main pressure comes from potential rather than actual employees. A company which wishes to recruit additional labour—particularly female labour in circumstances requiring a bus journey—may be at a disadvantage if it has no canteen whilst its competitors in the labour market have. Given the existence of a canteen, however, the company's catering policy will often become the focus of intense—and vociferous—employee interest. The fundamental reason for most canteen subsidies is that many companies consider employees will not pay higher prices without unrest. Industrial canteens have to be expensively equipped and staffed to deal with a large volume of diners for an hour or two each day; for the rest of the time the canteen is idle. To load the full overhead into the cost of meals would, even with skilful management, probably raise prices well above the level of those in other catering establishments. In some cases there are legal problems: a company which falls in the category in which provision of catering facilities is mandatory would be open to action if it tried to pass on the overhead cost to employees.[1] Raising canteen prices—particularly the cost of tea—has become invested with a special status in the field of industrial relations. Few employees understand the problem of overheads and fewer sympathise with the company's predicament. Many are convinced that the company is making a profit out of the workers. An investigation by James and Tenen showed that the canteen is frequently used as a scapegoat—workers relieve tension engendered by other matters, e.g. dislike of a foreman, by making complaints about the canteen.[2]

Many managements consider that the easiest solution to their problem is to make the canteen prices cover the cost of wages and foodstuffs only, all other charges being borne by the company. Few canteens, however, have managers trained in financial control, and often the aim of covering these costs is little more than a pious hope; it is, for example, generally regarded as undesirable to change the price of a dish in conformity with seasonal variations in the market price, so there is an inevitable tendency to undercharge when prices are high. Moreover, workers tend to compare prices in the canteen with those prevailing in small cafés, where the labour is often that of

[1] See Industrial Welfare Society, *Legal Problems of Employment*, London 1951, p. 56.
[2] See H. E. O. James and Cora Tenen, 'Grievances and their Displacement', *Occupational Psychology*, Vol. 20, October 1946, pp. 181–7.

U

the proprietor's family on wages below those which the Catering Wages Board lays down for canteens.

Because of the lack of cost control many companies have brought in catering contractors who, using the company's space and equipment, run the canteen on its behalf. The contractors normally provide their own staff and management and sell meals at an agreed price. For these services they are paid a fixed fee. Some are able to provide a better meal at lower cost than could the firm—bulk buying and sound management seem to be the key here—but this is not true of many. The fact that a catering contractor is used does not defend the company from attacks on the quantity and quality of food provided, nor does it allay suspicions that workers are being exploited.

A more recent alternative is the introduction of vending machines, which have been designed to dispense everything from cups of tea to complete meals. At first it was usual for companies to buy machines themselves as a labour-saving device, but there has now emerged a trend for firms to allow contractors to instal machines, service them, and pay a proportion of the income as a fee for the concession. The success of such a venture depends on many factors, not the least of which is the quality of canteen service previously enjoyed. Saving of labour and the economy of bulk buying make it possible for contractors to operate efficiently and it seems probable that the use of vending machines will spread., But even where they are employed many companies will still be subsidizing catering: the return on sales is rarely sufficient to offset the overheads on space devoted to a canteen dining room, however mechanized.

III. SPORTS AND SOCIAL FACILITIES

Beneath the widespread provision of facilities for sports and social activities are two underlying concepts: that such activities help to produce good morale by fostering team spirit,[1] and that sports and 'cultural' activities are good for people. The observer who seeks evidence of the status of team games in the British culture need look no further than his nearest factory.

The range of these activities is extensive. Outdoor games are the most common, with winter football and summer cricket predominating. But industry has kept pace with the changing pattern of recreation in the outside world and newer forms have made their appearance—for example, archery, small-bore rifle shooting, and dinghy sailing. Indoor games are also found—table tennis and billiards are the most usual, but badminton and judo are also widespread. Indoors, however, the accent is less on sporting than on cultural

[1] See, for example, Elizabeth Pepperell, *General Welfare* in Personnel Management Handbook, London 1963, p. 52.

activities: dramatic and operatic societies, film societies and the like.

The essential feature of all these activities is that the company underwrites them to a greater or lesser degree. It is by no means unusual for a firm to lay out a sports field, erect a pavilion, employ groundsmen to look after the field, and provide all the equipment (even including clothing) needed to play. In such a case it is also usual for the company to employ a sports and social secretary, who may be full-time, to look after administration. The overall costs, both capital and running, of such an operation will be far from negligible.

To the dispassionate onlooker this state of affairs may smack of patriarchy, and it is not difficult to trace its origins. Sports and social clubs have their roots in the welfare movement of sixty years ago: this was the era of the cold bath and dumb-bells, of *mens sana in corpore sano*, of the early malnutrition and epidemiological studies. Enlightened employers felt moved to ameliorate the lot of their workers by giving them the opportunity to spend their leisure time in a healthy and improving fashion—though even then they are not without qualms about what they were doing: the 1913 conference organized by Rowntree discussed among other topics 'the danger of sapping the independence and initiative of the employees by too paternal methods of industrial betterment'.[1]

It seems probable that, like many other welfare activities, there was little detailed investigation of costs until recent years. Land and buildings were relatively cheap in pre-war days, and undoubtedly many companies regarded sports clubs as an inexpensive way of earning employee goodwill—it was less costly to hold a good man in employment by affording him the opportunity to play football than to give him an increase in wages. Employees were certainly grateful for the interest which management took in their well-being, and the records of sports and social club meetings of pre-war days are strewn with expressions of thanks to managements for their generosity in providing facilities. As with canteens, an extensive sports and social activity became a hallmark of progressive management.

It was also not without importance in building what is now fashionably termed a public image. Football and cricket clubs entered their teams in local competitions, and, especially in the north of England, special leagues for industrial teams flourished. Some companies became known for the excellence of their teams and managements derived satisfaction from the support which they gave them. The same is true of works' bands: it was not uncommon to find companies advertising 'Second cornet wanted. Tradesmen preferred, but employment as labourer can be furnished.' Instruments and uniforms would be provided, and a professional coach engaged. Other em-

[1] See M. M. Niven, op. cit.

ployees took pride in belonging to a company whose brass band was a household name.

Today the picture has changed considerably. A variety of reasons, part industrial, part social, has led to a lessening of interest both on the part of management and of employees. In many companies sports facilities are used by less than ten per cent of employees, and the proportion shows no signs of growing.

One of the most important factors is the growth of opportunities for recreation generally. Employees can now find outlets for their interests, at little cost, in facilities which are provided by bodies other than their employers. They may prefer to spend their leisure time in their home neighbourhood out of sight of the factory and of the workmates with whom they spend their working lives. In their home club their continued membership is not dependent upon their remaining in the service of one employer: they are members in their own right. Moreover, the quality of other members is not limited by the bounds of the employment policy of one company—a man who is good enough to play for his county, for example, will usually join a good local club rather than a work's club because he stands a better chance of coming before the selectors' eyes. The cinema and more recently television have taken their toll of the onetime band of enthusiastic supporters, and the cars which choke our roadways at weekends bear tribute to the purchasing power of the stratum of society which decades ago was content to spend its spare time on the work's sports ground because it could afford no other outlet.

From the employer's point of view, cost has become a real consideration. Land, buildings, and maintenance are all expensive commodities and many companies feel that they no longer get a return from these assets which justifies continuation of the investment. Morale, it is now perceived, may have more to do with the quality of supervision on the shop floor than with playing fields, and the management may be better advised to spend its money on increasing the wages of foremen than on providing new hockey pitches. There is some support for this view in social science researches which have shown that a generalized regard for a company is uncorrelated with productivity—indeed, in one study in the U.S. it was found that workers who thought well of their employer were less efficient than others.[1]

But apart from the intrinsic cost there are forces at work which cut across the concept of enlightened paternalism which established the playing fields of British industry. As soon as an employer ceases to meet the whole of the cost of social activities and expects employees to make some contribution he is open to a claim for some partici-

---

[1] D. Katz, et al., *Productivity, Supervision and Morale among Railroad Workers*, Michigan, 1951.

pation by employees in controlling them. Many employers do not object to this: they are prepared to allow a sports and social committee to determine the allocation of funds to clubs, for instance, and feel that this delegation is a useful act of joint consultation. Others, however, are reluctant to accede to any request for a share in control, and in some cases fear that the social activities of the company will become a battleground for militant shop stewards.

IV. ASSESSING THE BENEFIT TO THE EMPLOYER

The modern approach to the provision of welfare facilities is essentially a cost-conscious one. A manager asks two questions 'What will be the cost of doing this?' and 'What will be the cost of not doing it?' Twenty years ago, costing in the personnel field was rarely sophisticated enough to give even a reasonable estimate in answer to the second question, but there has been a marked change in this respect in recent years.

An example or two may serve to illustrate the type of thinking which is likely to be encountered today. A company decided to move its development department, manned largely by young, well-paid graduate engineers, away from the factory. Two considerations led to this decision: inadequate space in the factory premises (which were located in a heavily built-up industrial area), and the fact that most of the men concerned lived in a middle-class dormitory area which necessitated a difficult journey to work. The new unit was built in this area. In spite of the fact that they had enjoyed the facilities of a heavily-subsidized canteen in the original location it was decided to provide only vending machines dispensing tea, coffee, sandwiches and confectionary in the new unit. The costs of offering a full canteen service for 100 people were not considered justified by the demand. The possibility now existed for many to go home for a midday meal if they so wished and this, allied to a trend for white-collar workers to be content with a midday snack and to eat their main meal in the evening, reduced the pressure for more elaborate service. The transition was made smoothly, and an unnecessary cost was averted.

In a second case a company with a large clerical staff in the centre of a city needed more office space. A cost investigation showed that to do away with the canteen service and offer luncheon vouchers to all staff would be a cheaper proposition than to rent elsewhere. It was, moreover, welcomed by employees who saw the tax-free voucher as a much more tangible benefit than a canteen subsidy, and who felt that their range of choice of meals was considerably enlarged.

The need for a canteen was thrown up in a third organization when an investigation into labour turnover was carried out. A large proportion of female operatives were leaving after completing an expensive training course; when recruitment, training, and supervisory costs were taken into account the net loss each time a women left was estimated at £150. Interviewing leavers elicited the fact that many of them had to set off for work so early that they tended not to have breakfast, and they felt a need for a hot midday meal. A simple cost comparison showed that it would be cheaper to run a canteen than to continue to lose women for this reason.

Here we have three problems with different solutions, but in each, management has attempted first, to examine the cost of the action to be taken, and secondly, to assess employee attitudes to the present and future situation. The former type of calculation, the answer to the question 'what will it cost?' is relatively easily answered by the combined techniques of the economist and accountant. There will, of course, be several courses of action open to a company and the alternative costs of each must be considered; thus, in our first example, the company chose to introduce a limited vending machine service instead of a full canteen after considering the comparative costs. The second issue is much more difficult. The measurement of employee attitudes must necessarily be imprecise yet it is essential if management is to have a true idea of the demand for each type of scheme, or the cost of not introducing one or the other. If the decision is to be taken on economic grounds, the personnel manager—for he is likely to be the official allocated this unenviable task—may have to attempt some monetary measure of the benefit which a scheme confers on employees, or how they value it. In some cases this may not be necessary. In our second example, there were two clearly defined options, to rent offices elsewhere or to do away with the canteen service, and it was quite clear from the company's point of view that the latter was more advantageous; it so happened that this was also preferred by the employees so no problem arose. Similarly, when two equal cost options exist, the company can allow the employees a free choice as to which one they would like.

On the other hand, considerable difficulties may arise when the option preferred by the company on cost grounds is not one which employees value highly. In its most extreme form this may be when there is no option offered, when a firm simply wishes to withdraw a benefit. What is likely to be the cost of closing down a canteen or ploughing up a sports field, in terms either of increased labour turnover or general employee dissatisfaction? In the third example, it was possible to establish that high turnover was due partly to the lack of a canteen, but where employee discontent manifests itself in a less positive fashion, such as increased wastage, bad timekeeping, or a more strike-prone atmosphere, it may be difficult to estimate the cost, or even to isolate what proportion of the trouble is due to not having a canteen and so be impossible to allocate the cost.

A company's final action on whether to introduce, withdraw or alter a service may therefore consist largely of quantifying as many costs and benefits of various courses of action as is possible, and then choosing the option which economically seems most worthwhile. At the same time, there are social or other considerations which cannot be quantified but which still must be taken into account. The type of non-monetary disadvantages mentioned in the previous paragraph can be itemized and by measuring their likely effect against the cost of the various options, a company can get some idea of how much weight they should be given. It is important, however, that a serious attempt should be made to quantify as many variables as possible and to consider logically all those which are non-quantifiable. This process marks the arrival in the field of welfare of the substitution of estimates for hunches, a cardinal point in much modern writing on management.

However, the discussion in Sections II and III makes it clear that by no means all companies take this 'economic' point of view. Some may still hold paternalistic views and so be prepared to subsidize welfare benefits without question. Others may be aware of the possibility of uneconomic expenditure, but nevertheless prefer to let sleeping dogs lie and to leave methods of subsidy unchanged rather than to risk any employee dissatisfaction, though in so far as any attempt is made to cost these feelings this case would fall under those discussed above. It is probable, though, that for every company vaguely aware of the questionable status of much of their welfare expenditure, there is at least one which has simply not attempted to calculate the costs of canteens and sports or social facilities against the benefits accruing to employees, and the alternative methods of provision. This is partly understandable, because of the comparatively small cost of welfare benefits in most companies, but as firms begin to look with a sharp financial eye at every aspect of their operations—that is, as more and more companies act on estimate rather than hunch—the economic value of these benefits will come to be more accurately estimated.

V. CONCLUSION

Finally, then, what is the likely future of these fringe benefits? It is easier to predict in the case of sports and social facilities. We have already seen in Section III that they have been declining in importance since the inter-war period, and indications are that this process will continue. The geographical dispersion of employees in most companies must hinder any after-work meeting, even if it were desired, and the rise in standards of living means a growing number of other outlets for leisure preferable to company facilities. One suspects that attendances and use by employees of company sports and social facilities is in most cases becoming lower year by year. In some cases, however, where the company is a large employer, its sports and social facilities may be used by many members of the public who have no other connection with the company; the withdrawal of these facilities might involve a considerable loss of general goodwill which would have to be taken into account. On the other hand, the company must consider the cost of continuing to install and service capital equipment, and, more important, the foregone income which may result from owning and using as sports grounds tracts of land whose value may have multiplied many times since they were originally purchased. On balance, it seems that an analysis of the costs and benefits of company sports and social facilities would reveal the wisdom of abandoning them in most cases.

The future of canteens is rather more difficult to predict, since the use of a canteen is usually an integral part of the work-day, and the existence of the canteen seen as an essential condition of employment. There are, however, several trends which are obvious to any caterer. First, the running costs of canteens are likely to rise rapidly: this includes both the cost of food and wages usually covered by prices paid by employees, and heat, light and other overheads which normally form a company subsidy. Secondly, employee tastes are likely to change, perhaps fairly rapidly. This may mean either a different consumption pattern with a demand for more variety and higher quality which will involve a higher standard of catering, or a change in the type of meals provided. Thirdly, the under-utilized capital equipment needed to fit out a canteen is becoming more expensive, especially if rapid changes in tastes do occur which require different techniques.

These trends indicate an increasing company contribution to canteens, and while some firms will no doubt revise the basis of subsidy so as to allow the employee to pay more, it seems probable that there will be a greater tendency to contract out canteen services to specialist companies who can take advantage of economies of scale in bulk buying and management. This will overcome most of the disadvantages mentioned above and apart from removing the company to some extent from the thorny problem of canteen politics and practices, it does give the very important cost control which a company-run canteen may lack, since the subsidy paid as rental to the contracting company will be a determinate sum. Nevertheless, no matter how expenditure is incurred, the canteen subsidy seems likely to continue as much the most expensive welfare benefit provided by most companies.

CHAPTER 12

CONCLUSION

G. L. REID AND D. J. ROBERTSON

I.

Each of the foregoing Chapters has been concerned either to show the quantitative importance of fringe benefits or to demonstrate ways in which they affect our economic life. With the exception of Chapters 2 and 3 which are closely related, each contribution stands more or less apart from every other. With various shades of opinion thus represented there is the advantage, and disadvantage, that the volume as a whole is not dogmatic nor does it seek to take one 'correct' line. Indeed the diversity of political and social assumptions is such that it is possible to detect in the preceding Chapters different conclusions being reached from a substantially similar set of facts. But the doctrine of editorial non-interference can go too far, for the reader might justifiably wish to discover the importance of fringe benefits without reading every Chapter. This Conclusion is our effort to satisfy this demand.

The Conclusion takes the form of a brief discussion under five broad headings of the most notable ways in which fringe benefits may have an effect on the economy or on public policy. To a large extent we are summarizing and bringing together material from previous Chapters and taking up some of the points raised in the Introduction. However, our contributors may not all agree with all of our judgments, so that whilst we have profited greatly from reading their arguments, we must take responsibility for the general tenor of the Conclusion.

II. FRINGE BENEFITS AS LABOUR COSTS

Fringe benefits in the guise of supplementary labour costs are an addition to wage costs which an employer incurs in providing labour. This simple fact is itself of significance, but it is more important

DOI: 10.4324/9781003184706-12

since supplementary labour costs may be subject to a different pattern of fluctuation over time than wages. For example, supplementary labour costs are generally more insensitive to short-period changes in the circumstances of the employer. Some of them are subject to seasonal fluctuations—holiday pay, for example, or sick pay, which will tend to increase during the winter months. Others, such as capital expenditure on welfare projects and some types of pension fund outlays, may continue unchanged though the size of the work-force is reduced, and in the case of many other benefits which apply only to part of the labour force, the cost will remain unchanged if those who leave are non-participants. Then redundancy payments or supplementary unemployment benefits are likely to increase as the economic position of the company becomes adverse, and administrative costs in particular are likely to be inflexible, and fixed in the short-run. In general, the fringe benefits which are very broadly 'welfare' represent an investment in labour resources and though the two most important costs, holiday pay and legally required payments, do vary with the size of the work-force, in some cases there may not be definite knowledge that the burden can be adjusted in proportion as circumstances alter.

The enquiry data set out in Chapter 3 suggests that the average expenditure on fringe benefits in 1960 was about 13–14 per cent of payroll, and unless there has been an unprecedented introduction of new and expensive schemes, this cost did not increase significantly relative to earnings up to the middle of 1963. This average level conceals substantial differences between industries; the average expenditure in food and in chemicals was twice as high as that in shipbuilding, and metal manufacturing was also very low. To the individual firm, too, supplementary labour costs may be quite substantial. About 6 per cent of firms had expenditure of over 25 per cent of payroll, though they were mainly in industries where labour costs are relatively unimportant, so that the effect of fringe benefits on total costs may still have been small. It is impossible to be dogmatic, of course, without making various assumptions on market structure and costs, but our main conclusion must be that the average level of supplementary labour costs, while it may increase in future, is not a very high proportion of total labour costs. A cautionary note, however, should warn against the dismissal of fringe benefits themselves as unimportant. It has been emphasized several times in the preceding Chapters that the cost of fringe benefits cannot be used to measure their value, and the simple fact that they are not particularly expensive should not be allowed to conceal the other finding of Chapter 3, that a large number of firms did have company-financed pension and sick pay schemes and other facilities. Their existence is perhaps of greater importance to employees than their low cost.

III. FRINGE BENEFITS AND INCOMES POLICY

Fringe benefits might possibly be of importance to any national incomes policy either because of the income they provide to employees or because of the costs they impose on the employers. More specifically, is a national incomes policy affected by fringe benefits in such a way either that effective demand is increased to the point at which demand-pull inflation becomes a hazard, or that higher labour costs are in danger of causing compensatory price increases?

First of all, we must ask what the likely effect of a successful incomes policy might be? If the initial position is that expenditure on fringe benefits is constant in relative terms—that it is increasing at the same rate as the increase in earnings, as has possibly been the case in the past few years in Britain—these supplementary labour costs might appear to have little impact on the economy, but there are two reasons why an incomes policy successful in relation to earnings could give them an added importance. First, a moderation in the rate of increase of earnings could lead to demands from employees for deferred wages or indirect improvements in conditions of work in the form of higher employer contributions to pension funds, for longer holidays, more generous sickness benefit, and perhaps for improved welfare facilities. Secondly, if a national incomes policy managed to control local wage agreements employers might try to use these non-wage incentives to increase real remuneration surreptitiously, and to try to influence the supply of labour to their own firms. From both employees and employers, then, there will be pressures making for an increase in money expenditure on fringe benefits.

As extra income accruing to employees, most increases in fringe benefit expenditure are unlikely to be critical for national incomes policy. Those benefits which do provide additional income do not generally add significantly to present aggregate demand, except by maintaining purchasing power during unemployment or sickness. The exception would be an increase in holiday pay, which might add immediately to effective demand, depending on when it was conceded. Despite this, and the effect of longer holidays in reducing the supply of goods and services without a corresponding change in demand, the general conclusion can be that a rise in expenditure on fringe benefits will almost certainly be less inflationary from the demand side than an equivalent increase in wages. From this point of view, a national incomes policy might accommodate an increase in the absolute level of supplementary labour costs.

The effect of such an increase on labour costs could be more significant, and as well as this absolute increase there would also be a relative rise in the cost of more inflexible supplementary labour costs, including perhaps holiday pay and National Insurance contributions within a certain range, because of the slowing down of the rise in earnings. Supplementary labour costs will thus become a larger proportion of labour costs and even if employers find wage costs stabilized, total labour costs may still increase at a faster rate than is desirable. What effect this will have on total costs it is impossible to say without generalizing unduly about the average labour cost-total cost ratio. Of more importance, of course, is the effect on unit costs, and here the problem is to know the relative effects on labour productivity of increases in wages and supplementary labour costs; this will be considered in Section IV. The evidence of the previous section suggests that total costs at least will be little affected by a substantial increase in supplementary labour costs, but it is possible that pressure on slim profit margins would induce price increases which themselves may be sufficient to trigger off compensatory wage demands.

It would be foolish to claim that an incomes policy which does not account for fringe benefits is doomed to failure, yet it is important to recognize that a policy which achieves success in controlling the rise of earnings does not mean that labour costs are likewise stabilized. This point has been obscured by the common and mistaken identification of wage costs and labour costs. Ideally, an attempt to control costs should include supplementary labour costs and fringe benefits should be submitted to any wages policy, but there are obviously considerable problems, for example, even in establishing a common denominator on which to express supplementary labour cost increases. For precision and ease of understanding, they are best expressed in terms of equivalent wage increases, and though this is simple for some explicit items such as holiday pay, it is extremely difficult for others which are indeterminate at the time the agreement is made, or which themselves depend on earnings. Even if this could be done, though, the practical problems of any national policy for fringe benefit costs are obviously very great.[1] It is to be hoped, however, that current enquiries, notably that of the Ministry of Labour into labour costs, may lead to a greater consciousness of supplementary labour costs and their potential importance.

IV. FRINGE BENEFITS AND COLLECTIVE BARGAINING

As several contributors have pointed out, collective bargaining has not generally been the medium through which fringe benefits have

---

[1] Some of the difficulties of submitting fringe benefits to a wages policy are outlined in two articles in the symposium 'Wage Policies of the Wage Stabilization Board', *Industrial and Labor Relations Review*, 7, 2; January 1954, pp. 221–45. These deal with the U.S. efforts to control wages and fringe benefits during the Korean War period.

been introduced. Pension schemes, sickness benefit, company-subsidized facilities, even in some cases longer holidays, have until the very recent past been introduced unilaterally by the employer. Trade unions' reactions ranged from mild interest or indifference to hostility if there was a suggestion that the employer was attempting to wean allegiance from the union to the firm. In the past two years, however, we have seen a sudden change, not so much because trade unions are now for the first time aware of the existence of fringe benefits—for many unions have supported schemes at local level—as because there is a new willingness to demand fringe benefits at the bargaining table, and to pursue these demands through to the point of employer concessions. If trade union interest grows, then what is likely to be the impact on the collective bargaining structure?

If we assume that there are no sweeping changes in the form of British collective bargaining, this does provide a framework within which future progress must be made, either for schemes demanded by the employees or those provided 'voluntarily' by the company. It is self-evident that extensive union demands for fringe benefits will increase the scope and complexity of bargaining since a larger number of subjects will be raised, but it will do rather more than this. For union demands are almost certain to encroach on territory previously considered by employers to be, if not sacrosanct, at least privileged. Imagine, for example, a situation in which a trade union pressed for larger benefits from a welfare scheme which a company had introduced many years previously and since run without interference. The natural reaction of the company might be that this was not a fit subject for collective bargaining, yet if we admit that unions have the right to initiate schemes, they surely also have an equal right to press for improvements in existing conditions. One result of increased union pressure to achieve fringe benefits by collective bargaining might therefore be to introduce to the bargaining table a range of topics which employers now think of as matters for unilateral adjustment.

But we must not imagine that fringe benefits can become an important part of trade union bargaining policy overnight, for there are important structural problems to be solved before this can happen to its fullest extent. For one thing, the security benefits—and these are the ones thought to be important in the near future—are much more successful when operated on a company basis than on an industrial basis. It is true that the Electrical Trades Union has negotiated a sick pay scheme, but the great majority of industrial non-contributory schemes are confined to one company, and it is at this level that fringe benefits can be most successfully negotiated to take advantage of company profitability and local conditions. This will obviously demand a high degree of union co-operation, not only to decide what kind of scheme is most suitable, but also to establish what priority it should have over other bargaining claims; the high-wage union may well be willing to give up more in terms of a wage increase than a union representing low-wage workers.

This raises the important general point—whether the trade unions have really accepted that increases in fringe benefits expenditure by employers can be expected only if less is spent on giving wage increases. During the late 1950s, claims for longer holidays were frequently early casualties as negotiations proceeded; would the same perhaps happen in joint union bargaining for fringe benefits as it became clear that they were substitutes for wage increases rather than additional to them? Here, of course, we once more enter the field of conjecture; the critic of trade unions who sees them as traditionalist and not easily adaptable would claim that they are unlikely to be sufficiently flexible to alter their bargaining techniques to allow this kind of negotiation, and even if they were, the conflict of interests would mean an early breakdown. But even those who take a more sanguine view of trade union leaders and their susceptibility to rational argument must have some doubts on whether plant negotiation of fringe benefits can succeed. The main problem appears to be whether it is possible to justify to the average union member a more moderate level of wage increases; that is, will more orthodox claims succeed in raising the general level of real earnings to such a point that demands for fringe benefits can be accepted as a viable alternative? If, as seems probable, the answer is in the negative, the trade unions have two choices; they can either fragment bargaining even further and enter a different set of demands for high and low-wage workers, or they can bargain on an industry or district-wide basis for such terms as they can get.

So far we have ignored the reaction of the employer to a possible enlargement of plant collective bargaining to include fringe benefits. If he accepts the principle of joint decision in this field, the final collective agreement might approach towards the U.S. model and become something nearer a contract of service specifying many details of the employer-employee relationship, though this would not necessarily be a legally enforceable document. Then the actual process of bargaining itself would change if trade unions recognized the interdependence of their various claims, with the spread of the 'package deal' technique under which employers offer unions a different distribution of an increase in total labour costs between higher wages, shorter hours and more expensive fringe benefits. In its most sophisticated form, this type of collective bargaining would proceed in two stages, the first determining the total amount which the employer is willing to concede, the second deciding how this should be allocated. Superficially it might seem that the employer's main interest is in the first phase, since the form of any increase in labour costs is much less important to him than the amount, but this is too simple a view which is tenable only if we assume that all employees react in the same way to all kinds of remuneration. Obviously at the conclusion of negotiations a company would wish to have agreed on the labour cost increase which would do most to improve productivity. A study mentioned in the next section shows that different types of employees have different preferences for wages or fringe benefits, so that it is improbable that a company could know precisely what the effect of a given increase would be. Yet it may have some guidance from past experience, and what will determine its attitude at the bargaining table is how it thinks employees will react. It is important to note too that the union may have little more idea of what employees really want, and even then bargaining claims must either be some kind of collective average or the opinions of the union leaders.

In any case, the package deal technique which might result if fringe benefits came to be accepted subjects for collective bargaining would lead to a much more complex procedure than present wage negotiations. But, to summarize, there are several reasons why one might not expect rapid growth of fringe benefits through collective bargaining at the local level. First, it is doubtful whether wage levels are high enough for unions generally to persuade their members of the increased desirability of fringe benefits or, alternatively, to accept them as substitutes for wage increases. Secondly, the necessary degree of inter-union co-operation seems at this date in time too difficult to achieve. Thirdly, there is a prospect of increased benefits from State social security; this is something which trade union leaders have constantly urged, and industrial schemes have generally been demanded only on the understanding that they will not be regarded as a substitute for higher State benefits. However, an income-related national scheme is bound to weaken the union's case for more company security benefits, and the higher employer contributions which would result from the recasting of the financial arrangements are likely to check the growth of voluntary schemes (see Section VI below).

V. FRINGE BENEFITS, LABOUR MOBILITY AND PRODUCTIVITY

Full employment may increase the importance of non-wage incentives, but are fringe benefits in their effects on labour mobility and productivity economically worthwhile in the sense that their cost is outweighed by the return to the employer? The argument normally used as economic justification for fringe benefit expenditure may be split into its two parts: first, fringe benefits help to attract 'better' employees to the firm, so increasing productivity by changes in the structure of the labour force; and secondly, the quality of the existing labour force and its efficiency are improved if certain fringe benefits are offered, without the firm attracting any additional employees.[1]

According to the first leg of this theory, the employer who first introduces a particular benefit within his local labour market area stands to gain because of the attraction which this benefit will have. It will induce employees to seek work in his firm, the result being a more productive labour force than existed previously, and the expectation of the employer is that the extra labour cost will be offset by the increase in productivity of his changed labour force. The advantage of the innovator, here as elsewhere, is likely to be considerable, and the result to be an increase in desirable labour mobility with workers moving to the innovating firm from other firms in the labour market. But this argument is in practice somewhat unrealistic since it assumes no reaction or retaliation on the part of the firm's competitors in the labour market. If the demand for labour is high other firms will feel compelled to take defensive measures by introducing some other inducement as a countervailing attraction to the advantages offered by their labour-market competitor. This reaction may take the form of a wage increase, but if, as we are assuming, the process originated with a particular fringe benefit, the other firms may feel that the best defence is a similar benefit, perhaps slightly more advantageous to the employee. In this way, all interested firms in the labour market will have been forced to increase fringe benefit expenditure. There are several points to note about this process. First, the firms which follow the innovator are spending more on labour only as a defensive measure in an attempt to keep the labour force at its present standard. They may in fact be minimising their losses, since their belief is that the alternative of leaving remuneration or fringe benefits unchanged would have led to a deterioration in the quality of the labour force through withdrawals. Secondly, the effect on the mobility of labour is uncertain. While one firm may originally have to set out to poach labour from other companies, the end of the process sees all firms trying to keep their own labour, and the overall effect of the introduction of attractions and counter-attractions is quite likely to be a reduction in labour mobility. Thirdly, the whole cycle depends largely on employer expectations; if one firm has innovated with, say, a sick pay scheme, what determines its competitors' reactions is whether they *think* employees will be attracted by this and in a period of high labour demand they may have to act on their most pessimistic assumptions about what is going to happen,

---

[1] We must again emphasize that the following argument refers broadly to wage-earners. The effect of fringe benefits on mobility of salaried staff may be much more pronounced, in that supplementary benefits of various kinds add much more to income at the executive level.

that is, that their employees will be induced to leave.[1] These firms not only have to decide on their response, but what form it should take, and here again they are forced to estimate what type of remuneration will have the greatest effect on employees. However, it is still possible that the firm which does nothing, either through ignorance or design, will come through unscathed, and that employees are induced to move or stay by factors other than those at work in our hypothetical situation.

The process of attraction and counter-attraction which this theory postulates would explain to some extent the impression that the spread of certain fringe benefits follows a fashion. This has been particularly noticeable in relation to holidays with pay. The concession of two weeks' holiday came with something of a rush in most industries just after the end of the Second World War,[2] and there are signs that the campaign for three weeks is becoming more successful so that it might conceivably be the normal period within a comparatively short time. This tendency for fringe benefits to become 'fashionable' does not stem only from the employees' labour market expectations since, as we have seen, there are other reasons why fringe benefits may be introduced, and in particular trade union pressure will be important in determining the speed with which three weeks' holiday with pay spreads. But the important thing to the employer is that he may feel that he has no choice but to introduce these benefits which to the worker are no longer reckoned as a positive gain, but rather as a background advantage which can be assumed to be present in all decent jobs. The problem facing the employer is therefore the possibility that his additional expenditure will be lost to sight because benefits are so quickly accepted as being normally available.

This pinpoints the main difficulty in estimating the effect of fringe benefits on labour mobility and the reason why the whole discussion must be conducted in qualified terms: this is the impossibility of knowing the reaction of 'the employees', which is also the key problem in assessing the second contention mentioned earlier, that the quality of the existing labour force would be improved and productivity increased if certain fringe benefits were introduced. How *do* employees value fringe benefits and what effect do they have?

In answering these questions we must rely on our previous speculations and a certain amount of information from American experience. There are three facts which would probably be accepted as true of Britain today. First, wage-earners still think of fringe

[1] Some fringe benefits are explicitly intended to retain labour; occupational pensions are most important of these. See Chapter 7, Section IV (2).

[2] There were, however, many other social and economic reasons why the two weeks' holiday swiftly became universal. See Chapter 10.

benefits as additional to normal wages instead of as alternatives for them. Secondly, they would almost certainly underestimate the cost of fringe benefits, partly because many of the benefits are available only to some of the work-force or in special circumstances, partly because other benefits represent *deferred* wages, and partly because companies make little or no effort to inform employees how much fringe benefits cost, if indeed the companies themselves know.[1] Thirdly, it follows that employees would generally prefer a wage increase to a similar increase in fringe benefits, given a choice. If company welfare schemes such as canteens and sports facilities are dismissed as unlikely to have much effect in influencing the distribution of labour, there are two other types of benefit which may be important, additional holidays with pay, and the security benefits, sick pay and pensions.[2] The choice between either of these two types and a wage increase is determined simply by the relative preference of the employee for present income, leisure or income-security, i.e. future income during sickness or old age. Those who think that security benefits are now playing some part in influencing the distribution of labour would assert that the desire for income-security had increased relative to the desire for present income, with the possible spread of fringe benefits by emulation as described earlier.

The important point about the effect of fringe benefits on the distribution of labour is whether aggregate labour productivity is increased, or whether labour productivity for the economy as a whole will be unchanged with labour costs at a higher level than before, even though individual firms may find their labour productivity improved. It is difficult to say which of these two views is most likely. If the firms which are first in the field with fringe benefits are high-productivity companies, and if the reaction of their labour market rivals is insufficient or too late to prevent a change in the distribution of labour, then the shift of employees from low-productivity companies will have a beneficial effect on the economy; the same would be true of inter-industry changes in the distribution of employment, though it is unlikely that fringe benefits alone have much influence here.

Although it is probably true that the most 'welfare-minded' companies with the best fringe benefits do have a higher than average level of labour productivity, the impression remains that fringe benefits have played a comparatively small part in attracting labour to particular companies. Indeed in the period of excess demand for labour which has existed since the war, some benefits are introduced

---

[1] See 'Fringe Benefits', *Personnel Policies Survey No. 55*, Bureau of National Affairs, Washington, 1960.
[2] The contribution of a redundancy scheme to attraction or retention is uncertain: see Chapter 8, Section IV, 2, for one view.

only for their effect in *retaining* labour;[1] if they can simply do this, then they are counted worthwhile. If this were true for all firms, then there would be no improvement in aggregate labour productivity because of fringe benefits, though labour costs would be higher.

The degree to which such changes in the distribution of labour influence aggregate labour productivity depends on what employees think of fringe benefits,[2] and an important contribution in this respect has recently come from an American psychologist.[3] He presented employees with various options of pay or various types of benefit and found that sick leave was most preferred. Longer vacations also came higher than a pay rise in most employees' judgments. Many interesting issues arise from this study, but only two will be mentioned here. First, the benefits most valued by employees were not necessarily those which cost the employer most; this confirms doubts on the validity of the assumption that employer cost equals employee benefit.[4] Secondly, the most important finding of the enquiry was that preferences were significantly affected by demographic and attitudinal variables; these variables included sex, income, number of dependent children, type of job, and 'attitude tone'. It is therefore extremely hard to estimate *a priori* the attractiveness of various fringe benefits to a work-force without taking all these factors into account. It must be impossible to generalize these American findings to Britain, especially in view of the differences in the social security systems and standards of living of the two countries, so that our previous general conclusion, that employees in this country would prefer wage increases, can therefore stand, but it can in no way be regarded as definite. The results of this study are important since they show how difficult it is to say what 'the employees' want, and reinforce the possibility that company, union and individuals will all have different ideas on how an increase in labour costs should be distributed.

The same point can be made in answer to our second query, the effect of fringe benefits on the productivity of the existing labour force, though the relationship between the two would appear to be somewhat distant and the direct effect small. For example, the cost of extra holidays with pay is unlikely to be offset by increased produc-

---

[1] The best example is the occupational pension scheme without provision for vesting, though other benefits can give an employee an increasing interest over time in retaining his employment with one company.

[2] It also depends on which employees are influenced by fringe benefits. It may be that those who are attracted are not 'high productivity' individuals no matter where they work.

[3] S. M. Nealey, 'Pay and Benefit Preference', *Industrial Relations*, October 1963, pp. 17–28.

[4] See Introduction, Section III.

tivity.[1] Similarly, the security benefits will in the short-run simply be a charge on the employer with little corresponding return. Any gain must rest more with the effects of security upon a man's outlook to his work than on any immediate direct willingness to increase output. Nonetheless the effect of fringe benefits on individual output may be profound, for if co-operative work depends upon a feeling of security of income, the fringe benefit expenditure which is designed to meet part of this need may be a more important factor in obtaining a continuing steady performance from the labour force than an immediately higher output. Here again, though, we must conclude that the productivity of different employees will be affected to different degrees by various types of benefit; this perhaps only emphasizes that any improvements in productivity are cumulative and in no sense sudden or dramatic.

Since fringe benefits, security and mobility are intertwined as topics of discussion, it is difficult to be definite. We have put forward a hypothesis of a way in which fringe benefits could influence mobility and hence productivity. Whether or not this is realistic is another matter. Apart from the problem of assessing the importance of security to the employee and the role of fringe benefits in conferring this security, the whole process cannot be divorced from the normal labour market considerations which probably have more effect in determining employer and worker attitudes and reactions. In particular, we must always analyse increases in fringe benefits comparatively, against the result of the alternative increase in wages; in most cases, one suspects, both employer and employee, at any rate in the short-run, might be better satisfied with the latter.[2]

VI. FRINGE BENEFITS AND SOCIAL SECURITY

The relationship between State social security and certain fringe benefit schemes has been the subject of three of the preceding Chapters, and we can only summarize briefly how the security benefits—pensions, redundancy, and sickness benefit—can be directly or indirectly affected by State action.

The first most obvious point is that the prevailing climate of political opinion is all-important. If society believes that the State should play an unimportant role in the economy and that a free enterprise economy is desirable, then it is likely that the State will play a

---

[1] See Chapter 10.

[2] There are, however, some cases where fringe benefits might have a more powerful effect on the labour market than wages. For example, to increase the participation rate of married women with young children, it may be more effective to provide facilities for looking after children at work than simply to increase earnings.

relatively minor role in redistributing income from the employed to those who are unemployed, sick, or retired. In these circumstances private provision against income-loss may be expected and this may appear in collectively bargained industrial schemes. Even if there is an acceptance of some State responsibility for welfare, there may still be an opportunity for security benefits to arise, depending on whether this responsibility is thought to involve the payment only of minimum benefits or whether those provided by the State should be in every way adequate. In the former case there will still be scope for industrial pension and sick pay plans as well as redundancy compensation, assisted perhaps by State encouragement. However where State social security aims at protecting the standard of living, there is unlikely to be much room for industrial security benefits. Employees who are assured a fairly high degree of income-protection during old age sickness or unemployment may not demand industrial schemes, while it is normally considered both by employers and the public authorities that benefits for the employee should be some little way below wages or work-income.

The form of benefit is therefore important and generally there will be a direct correspondence between the governmental concept of social security and the formula according to which benefit is paid; if the State believes that income-protection during incapacity should be provided by the State and financed by redistribution of income, either over time or between persons, income-related benefits leaving less scope for collectively bargained schemes become much more likely. Where, as in Britain up till mid 1964, there have been minimum flat-rate benefits for sickness, unemployment and pensions, the State accepts the responsibility for providing only part of income during incapacity, and industrial schemes can make up State benefits to a reasonable degree of income-protection.

Apart from simply tolerating and accepting the existence of such private provision, the State may treat it as part of social security, and encourage its spread for two main reasons. First, it may feel that company schemes are better able to provide an element of adjustment to individual circumstances. This is true to some extent, but one must be clear what kind of flexibility is desired. Graduation of benefits is normally thought of as involving benefits varying with income, and for pensions, where benefit rates are based on contributions which are in turn related to normal work-income, occupational schemes provided by companies can be useful supplements to a State scheme. Private sickness and unemployment benefit schemes may also provide this type of income-graduation though the number of redundancy schemes which actually ensures a continuing source of income to the employee is very small. But private schemes may well fail to provide continuity of benefit over the long period, and will certainly lack the uniformity which a national scheme can provide. For example, one might realistically wish to pay a high level of unemployment benefit gradually diminishing over time, to encourage desirable labour mobility without stultifying completely the incentive to find work. This type of graduation would be extremely difficult to operate under a complex of private schemes. Then for sickness benefit, graduation over time might desirably operate in the other direction, so that the long-term sick who had exhausted most of their private resources could draw a higher rate of benefit. As it is, most industrial schemes only give sick pay for up to a stipulated maximum period, often six months, so that private benefit tends to run out just when it would be most desirable to increase the rate. In so far as they may provide extra income additional to State benefit, industrial sickness and redundancy schemes for manual workers are valuable, but their success in giving a realistic degree of graduation is questionable. It is also very possible that the aggregate cost of so doing would be greater than if graduated benefit were provided under the State schemes, and there would inevitably be gaps in coverage, differences in the speed with which industrial schemes spread, and variations in levels of benefit according to the willingness or ability of companies to spend money on such benefits.

The second important reason why the State may choose to encourage industrial schemes is simply to reduce the proportion of income redistributed through social security. How much should be spent on social security generally and how this amount should be divided up between schemes are questions for political decision, and the former in particular raises wide issues of public finance with which this volume has not attempted to deal. But if the State, for political reasons or because it wishes to reduce its own administrative costs, decides that it should play a less important role, it may stimulate industrial schemes to provide additional benefits in place of future increases in national rates.

The method of finance adopted for State schemes of social security is, however, in practice likely to be the most important factor determining the distribution of reponsibility for income-security between employer and the State. Social security schemes may be financed either mainly from general taxation or from contributions levied on employer and insured person. If the State moves more towards finance from contributions and decides to levy these contributions on the employer rather than the employee, the payments legally required from the employer will rise, and within aggregate contribution income there will be a shift from the insured person to the employer unless at the same time general taxation moves in favour of the employer. This shift of the burden towards the employer has been developing recently in Britain to a small extent: the graduated pension scheme has reduced the State share and increased the proportion of National Insurance revenue covered by contributions from 74 per cent in 1959 to 79 per cent in 1962, while total employer contributions are now slightly higher than those of employees. Published programmes for the future of social security suggest also that this trend is likely to continue and that the employer share in social security revenue will rise even further, and to the extent that this rise is greater than the corresponding increase in earnings, this element of fringe benefit costs as a percentage of payroll will increase. This of course may mean that employers are reluctant to concede any additional voluntary fringe benefits so that their aggregate cost may be reasonably stable.

In the last resort, however, it is impossible to predict the effect of social security policy on fringe benefits without forecasting the political decisions of the future. There are many influences too which are not predictable, from the social and political framework and the attitude of government and its interpretation of public opinion, to such factors as the general economic background, the desirable size of the public sector, and methods of financing State expenditure. The most we can do is to point out some general principles which may show how events could move.

INDEX

For Product Safety Concerns and Information please contact our EU
representative GPSR@taylorandfrancis.com Taylor & Francis Verlag GmbH,
Kaufingerstraße 24, 80331 München, Germany

Printed and bound by CPI Group (UK) Ltd, Croydon, CR0 4YY

01/05/2025

01858389-0006